The Instructor's Guide for the third edition of *Human Resources Management in Public and Nonprofit Organizations* includes several model syllabi for courses of differing lengths, as well as additional class references. The Instructor's Guide is available free online. If you would like to download and print out a copy of the Guide, please visit:

www.wiley.com/college/pynes

EDUCATIONAL RESOURCES FOR NONPROFIT AND PUBLIC MANAGEMENT

Bryson, *Strategic Planning for Public and Nonprofit Organizations, 3e*

Cohen, *The Effective Public Manager, 4e*

Condrey, *Handbook of Human Resources Management in Government, 2e*

Cooper, *The Responsible Administrator, 5e*

Dove, *Conducting a Successful Capital Campaign, Revised and Expanded*

Feinglass, *The Public Relations Handbook for Nonprofits*

Gastil and Levine, *The Deliberative Democracy Handbook*

Herman, *The Jossey-Bass Handbook of Nonprofit Leadership and Management, 2e*

Keehley and Abercrombie, *Benchmarking in the Public and Nonprofit Sectors, 2e*

Kotler et al., *Museum Marketing and Strategy, 2e*

Lewis, *The Ethics Challenge in Public Service, 2e*

Linden, *Working Across Boundaries*

Oster, *Generating and Sustaining Nonprofit Earned Income*

Pawlak, *Designing and Planning Programs for Nonprofit and Government Organizations*

Poister, *Measuring Performance in Public and Nonprofit Organizations*

Rea and Parker, *Designing and Conducting Survey Research, 3e*

Rainey, *Understanding and Managing Public Organizations, 3e*

Snow and Phillips, *Making Critical Decisions*

Tempel, *Hank Rosso's Achieving Excellence in Fundraising, 2e*

Wholey et al., *Handbook of Practical Program Evaluation, 2e*

HUMAN RESOURCES MANAGEMENT FOR PUBLIC AND NONPROFIT ORGANIZATIONS

A Strategic Approach

Third Edition

Joan E. Pynes

JOSSEY-BASS
A Wiley Imprint
www.josseybass.com

Copyright © 2009 by John Wiley & Sons, Inc. All rights reserved.

Published by Jossey-Bass
A Wiley Imprint
989 Market Street, San Francisco, CA 94103-1741—www.josseybass.com

No part of this publication may be reproduced, stored in a retrieval system, or transmitted in any form or by any means, electronic, mechanical, photocopying, recording, scanning, or otherwise, except as permitted under Section 107 or 108 of the 1976 United States Copyright Act, without either the prior written permission of the publisher, or authorization through payment of the appropriate per-copy fee to the Copyright Clearance Center, Inc., 222 Rosewood Drive, Danvers, MA 01923, 978-750-8400, fax 978-646-8600, or on the Web at www.copyright.com. Requests to the publisher for permission should be addressed to the Permissions Department, John Wiley & Sons, Inc., 111 River Street, Hoboken, NJ 07030, 201-748-6011, fax 201-748-6008, or online at www.wiley.com/go/permissions.

Readers should be aware that Internet Web sites offered as citations and/or sources for further information may have changed or disappeared between the time this was written and when it is read.

Limit of Liability/Disclaimer of Warranty: While the publisher and author have used their best efforts in preparing this book, they make no representations or warranties with respect to the accuracy or completeness of the contents of this book and specifically disclaim any implied warranties of merchantability or fitness for a particular purpose. No warranty may be created or extended by sales representatives or written sales materials. The advice and strategies contained herein may not be suitable for your situation. You should consult with a professional where appropriate. Neither the publisher nor author shall be liable for any loss of profit or any other commercial damages, including but not limited to special, incidental, consequential, or other damages.

Jossey-Bass books and products are available through most bookstores. To contact Jossey-Bass directly, call our Customer Care Department within the U.S. at 800-956-7739, outside the U.S. at 317-572-3986, or fax 317-572-4002.

Jossey-Bass also publishes its books in a variety of electronic formats. Some content that appears in print may not be available in electronic books.

Library of Congress Cataloging-in-Publication Data

Pynes, Joan.
Human resources management for public and nonprofit organizations : a strategic approach / Joan E. Pynes.—3rd ed.
p. cm.
Includes bibliographical references and index.
ISBN 978-0-470-33185-9 (cloth/website)
1. Nonprofit organizations—United States—Personnel management. 2. Public administration—United States—Personnel management. I. Title.
HF5549.2.U5P96 2009
658.3—dc22

2008032854

Printed in the United States of America
THIRD EDITION
HB Printing 10 9 8 7 6 5

CONTENTS

FIGURES, TABLES, AND EXHIBITS

Figures

Tables

Exhibits

EXERCISES

PREFACE

Strategic human resources management (SHRM) is the integration of human resources management (HRM) with the strategic mission of the organization. It adapts human resources policies and practices to meet the challenges that agencies face today, as well as those they will face in the future. What was written in the previous editions of this book is just as important today. Human resources management departments must take a proactive role in guiding and supporting agency efforts to meet the changing demands of their external and internal environments.

Government and nonprofit organizations are facing many challenges: the tight budgets brought about by declines in tax revenues, declines in consumer spending, increases in unemployment, and federal government obligations in Iraq have reduced the federal dollars flowing to programs in state and local government programs. President Bush has proposed reducing Community Development Block Grants, Child Care Development Block Grants, Social Services Block Grants, the Low-Income Home Energy Assistance Program, and other programs. Also proposed are cuts to Medicare and Medicaid, as well as a reduction in funding for the Corporation for Public Broadcasting and the National Endowment for the Arts (Jensen & Perry, 2008). Reductions in public dollars and private donations have required public and nonprofit organizations to lay off staff, even as demands for many services continue to increase. These changes have occurred simultaneously with increasing demands for efficient and effective services.

The new public service has become more diverse. Changing demographics have resulted in an increase in the number of employees who are women, members of ethnic and racial minorities, persons with disabilities, and employees from different generations with different knowledge, skills, abilities, and other characteristics (KSAOCs). Graduates of schools of public policy and administration are likely to take jobs in the nonprofit sector and show a greater interest in seeking employment opportunities in the private sector. Today's graduates are moving across the three sectors, looking for challenging work and the opportunity to learn new skills. Master of business administration graduates are also looking for challenging work. This presents an opportunity and challenge for public and nonprofit organizations to design an HRM system that will recruit individuals wanting a challenge, keep them motivated, and enable them to make a difference through their work.

Changes in information technology and automation have led to the restructuring of many public and nonprofit agencies. Advances in technology have enabled employees to work from their homes, provided opportunities for more flexible work hours, and increased the employment options for disabled individuals. Computer networks, videoconferencing, and streaming video have changed communication patterns. Information technology is increasingly being used not only to automate routine tasks, but also to restructure and integrate service delivery procedures and programs.

Organizations must do more than just adapt to internal changes. They must also seek better ways to meet the expectations of citizens, clients, funding sources, foundations, elected officials, boards of directors, interest groups, and the media.

The public sector is becoming less involved in direct service delivery. Government at all levels is increasingly relying on nonprofit and private sector organizations to provide services. Government work is being implemented through a network of contracting, intergovernmental grants, vouchers, tax credits, regulations, and other indirect administrative approaches. While the federal government in particular is reducing the number of individuals it directly employs, it continues to need a sizable "shadow" to accomplish its mission (Light, 1999). These employees are part of the shadow that is created when public goods and services are provided through private, nonprofit, or state and local entities. According to Light, many of the nation's most challenging public service jobs are now found outside the federal government, not inside it. Kettl (2002, p. 120) notes the following:

> Government has come to rely heavily on for-profit and nonprofit organizations for delivering goods and services ranging from antimissile systems to welfare reform. These changes have scarcely obliterated the role of Congress, the president and the courts. State and local governments have become even livelier. Rather, these changes have layered new challenges on top of the old ones, under which the system already mightily struggles. New process-based problems have emerged as well: How can hierarchical bureaucracies, created with the presumption that they directly deliver services, cope with services increasingly delivered through multiple (often nongovernmental) partners? Budgetary control processes that work well for traditional bureaucracies often prove less effective in gathering information from nongovernmental partners or in shaping their incentives. Personnel systems designed to insulate government from political interference have proven less adaptive to these new challenges, especially in creating a cohort of executives skilled in managing indirect government.

Declining revenues combined with demographic changes, changes in employees' values, and the need to retain effective workers are some of the forces that have compelled public and nonprofit organizations to become concerned with their very survival. These changes require a more flexible and skilled workforce. To survive, organizations need employees with new skills. *Hard Truths/Tough Choices* (National Commission on the State and Local Public Service, 1993) identified five skill areas that the public manager needs: competency in team building, competency in communication, competency in involving employees, commitment to cultural awareness, and commitment to quality. These skills have HRM implications for employee recruitment, selection, and training. Public and nonprofit sector jobs are increasingly professional in nature, requiring higher levels of education. At the same time, there is a decrease in jobs that are physically demanding. Employees in public and nonprofit agencies often deal with a variety of people, many of whom have a stake in the agency. Taxpayers, clients, customers, elected officials, donors, contractors, board members, and special interest groups are just some of the stakeholders concerned about agency performance. Employers must ask themselves how to meet the public's objectives and satisfy the organization's stakeholders.

More recently there has been an emphasis on human capital: a recognition that employees are an agency's most important organizational asset. Workers define its character, affect its capacity to perform, and represent the knowledge base of the organization. Despite this acknowledgment, it has been noted that there is little strategic human capital management being executed in federal agencies. Reports indicate that the following activities are lacking: (1) leadership, continuity, and succession planning; (2) strategic human capital planning and organizational alignment; (3) acquiring and developing staffs whose size, skills, and use meet agency needs; and (4) creating results-oriented organizational cultures. All have been identified as challenges facing the federal government (General Accounting Office 2001a, 2001b, 2002a). State and local governments and nonprofit and for-profit organizations are facing these same human capital challenges (Adams, 2006; Kunreuther, 2005; Cornelius, Corvington, & Ruesga, 2008; Hall, 2006a; Halpern, 2006; Light, 1998, 2000a, 2000b; Partnerships for Public Service, 2005; Brockbank, Johnson, & Ulrich, 2008).

To be strategic partners, HRM departments must possess high levels of professional and business knowledge. HRM must establish links to enhancing organizational performance and be able to demonstrate on a continuing basis how its activities contribute to the organization's success and effectiveness.

Public and nonprofit agencies must be flexible and attuned to the needs of society. They must seek to improve the quality of their services by engaging in SHRM. Recruitment and selection strategies must be innovative, career development opportunities must be provided, work assignments must be flexible, and policies must reward superior performers and hold marginal employees accountable. These policies must be developed and administered according to the principles of equity, efficiency, and effectiveness. Performance standards must be designed to promote the goals and values of organizations.

Historically, HRM has been seen as Cinderella—on the periphery, not integrated into the core of agency functions. Fitz-enz (1996, p. 3) notes that historically personnel departments were either dumping grounds for "organizational casualties"—likable employees who were not proficient in other tasks—or staffed with employees from line functions, neither of whom had any formal education in personnel administration. He also attributes the peripheral relationship of HRM departments to other functional departments to the fact that for years, it was believed that organizations could not measure or quantify what the HRM department accomplished or contributed to the organization's bottom line. HRM departments did not speak in financial terms, the common denominator of business language, and were not very good at communicating the relationship between successful HRM programs and organizational success. As a result, most HRM departments were denied access to the organization's strategic planning processes and forced into reactive activities instead of being allowed to collaborate with the other management teams to formulate policies and determine future objectives. This approach has been a mistake. Research in the private sector has found that returns on wise HRM policies can surpass returns from other resources (Cascio, 2000; Cascio & Boudreau, 2008; Fitz-enz, 1996, 2002). In the public and nonprofit sectors, where 60 to 80 percent of expenditures are for personnel, SHRM is even more important than in the private sector.

Purpose and Audience

This book addresses SHRM issues in nonprofit and public agencies. Although many textbooks address public personnel or HRM, only a few are dedicated to the nonprofit sector, thus omitting a significant partner that provides services beneficial to society. Topics such as recruiting and managing volunteers and working with a board of directors have not been addressed. There are other omissions as well, such as a discussion of nonprofit labor relations. For example, nonprofit labor relations are governed by the amended National Labor Relations Act (the Labor-Management Relations Act), while most federal employees fall under the Federal Service Labor-Management Relations Statute (Title VII of the Civil Service Reform Act of 1978), and state and local government employees are guided by their respective public employee relations statutes. In the public sector, an applicant's or employee's religion is irrelevant, and discrimination because of religion is prohibited. However, religiously affiliated nonprofits that provide services of a religious nature may, in special circumstances, discriminate against applicants or employees on the basis of their religion.

Because service provider nonprofits are typically the recipients of government contracts and grants, a new intergovernmental environment has emerged as nongovernmental organizations have increasingly been used to implement public policy. Kramer and Grossman (1987) and Salamon (1995, 1999) refer to this new interorganizational environment as the "new political economy," the "contract state," or "nonprofit federalism," while Light (1999) refers to it as "shadow government."

The emphasis in this book is on nonprofits that are closely associated with providing a public benefit or service or with solving a problem on behalf of the public interest. It focuses on nonprofits that are responsible for delivering health care, social services, education, arts, advocacy, and research. The objectives of these nonprofits often parallel those of many government agencies in terms of the individual and community services they provide.

Public organizations and nonprofits are similar in that they define themselves according to their missions or the services they offer. These services are often intangible and difficult to measure. The clients receiving public or nonprofit services and the professionals delivering them make very different judgments about the quality of those services. Both sectors are responsible to multiple constituencies: nonprofits are responsible to supporters, sponsors, clients, and government sources that provide funding and impose regulations; and public agencies to their respective legislative and judicial branches and to taxpayers, cognate agencies, political appointees, clients, the media, and other levels of government (Kanter & Summers, 1987; Starling, 1986). Lipsky and Smith (1989–1990) comment that public and private service organizations share many characteristics: the need to process clients through systems of eligibility and treatment, the need to maintain a competent staff to be effective, and the need to account for financial expenditures. These organizations are also expected to be fair (equitable), accommodate likely and unanticipated complexities (responsive), protect the interests of sponsors in minimizing costs (efficient), be true to their mandated purposes (accountable), and be honest (fiscally honorable).

The conceptual foundation of this book is strategic human resources management. SHRM is the integration of human resources management with the strategic mission of the organization. It adapts human resources policies and practices to meet the challenges agencies face today, as well as those they will face in the future. Human resources departments must take a proactive role in guiding and supporting agency efforts to meet the changing demands of their environments. The information provided in this book is to be used to improve the effectiveness of HRM activities.

In many organizations, HRM policies and practices develop as needed, with little integration of the organization's future needs. Often policies are developed to solve an immediate problem, with no thought to their long-term implications. Such policies and practices lock the agency into inflexible modes of operation, leaving them unable to see that other strategies might be more appropriate.

This book emphasizes the importance of HRM functions, revealing them as major contributors to the accomplishment of the agency's mission in the present and as the agency changes. The purpose of the book is to provide practitioners, policymakers (such as elected officials), and board members of local, state, federal, and nonprofit organizations with an understanding of the importance of SHRM in managing change. It provides the guidance necessary to implement effective HRM strategies.

The book was also written to be a textbook for use in public administration and nonprofit management graduate programs that offer courses in personnel administration, HRM, strategic planning, and nonprofit management. While the literature on nonprofit management has increased in recent years, little information exists that addresses nonprofit HRM concerns. This book should help fill that void. As more public administration programs offer a specialization in nonprofit management, it is important that resources be available to target the challenges that both the public and nonprofit sectors face.

Overview of the Contents

Part One introduces the context and environment of human resources management. Chapter One discusses human resources management and explains what public and nonprofit organizations are, how society and workplaces have changed, and the HRM implications of those changes. Chapter Two explains how SHRM and human resources planning are imperative if agencies are going to remain competitive and be able to accomplish their missions; it also discusses how the role of human resource specialists has to change as well. Chapter Three presents the legal environment of human resources management, and Chapter Four discusses the importance of managing diversity if organizations expect to prosper. The importance of managing volunteers and how SHRM practices can assist in making the volunteer experience productive for the agency and satisfying to the volunteers and board members is the topic of Chapter Five.

Part Two presents the techniques and functional areas of HRM. Examples are provided in each chapter. Chapter Six explains the importance of job analysis before executing HRM policies or developing job descriptions, performance appraisal instruments, training and development programs, and recruitment and selection criteria. A variety of job analysis techniques are discussed. In Chapter Seven, recruitment and selection techniques are explained. Drug testing, physical ability tests, psychological examinations, and other selection techniques used in the public and nonprofit sectors are summarized. At the end of the chapter, important psychometric concepts are explained. There is also information on practical intelligence, emotional intelligence, adaptability, multiple intelligences, and organizational citizen performance behaviors. Performance management and evaluating employees' performance is the focus of Chapter Eight. Different performance appraisal techniques are explained and their strengths and weaknesses identified. The importance of rater training and documentation is noted. Ethical issues in performance appraisal are discussed, as are merit pay and 360-degree evaluations. Chapter Nine identifies the internal and external factors that influence compensation policies and practices. The techniques used to develop pay systems are discussed. Examples of job evaluation systems are provided, and nontraditional pay systems are explained. In Chapter Ten, employer-provided benefits and pensions are discussed.

The focus of Chapter Eleven is training and development activities. Changes in technology and demographics and the development of new responsibilities and expectations have made training and career development more important than ever before. Identifying training needs, developing training objectives and the curriculum, and evaluating training are explored. Different training formats are summarized. The chapter concludes with examples of management training and career development programs. Chapter Twelve discusses collective bargaining in the public and nonprofit sectors. The legal environment of labor-management relations for nonprofit, federal, state, and local employees is explored. Definitions and explanations are provided for concepts such as unit determination, union security, unfair labor practices, management rights, impasse resolution, and grievance arbitration. The reasons that unions exist in the public and nonprofit sectors are examined. Chapter Thirteen discusses strategic human resource management and information technology. The last chapter provides an overall conclusion. It summarizes the key lessons presented in the book, which I hope will convince public and nonprofit administrators of the importance of strategic HRM.

Tampa, Florida
November 2008

Joan E. Pynes

ACKNOWLEDGMENTS

A number of people have made valuable contributions to this book. I thank Allison Brunner, Rebecca Heider, and Kathleen Dolan Davies from Jossey-Bass, as well as the four anonymous reviewers for their helpful comments and suggestions, which I have made whenever possible.

As in the first edition, friends, colleagues, and students provided assistance by contributing workplace examples, reviewing chapters, or both. Specifically, I thank Anne Goldyche Dailey, Patricia Goldstein, and Patricia Murray for their observations of working in and with public and nonprofit agencies. Thanks are also extended to Mike Durham, general counsel for the Highlands County Sheriff's Office, who provided me with updated information for the content under constitutional rights in Chapter Three.

Special acknowledgment goes to my husband, Mike McNaughton, for his sense of humor, editorial assistance, and encouragement. I express my appreciation to my sister Robyn for her encouragement as well. Like the first and second editions, this book is in honor of my mother, who always inspired me to do my best.

In memory and honor of my parents

THE AUTHOR

Joan E. Pynes is a professor of public administration at the University of South Florida. She received her B.A. degree (1979) in public justice from the State University of New York at Oswego and her M.P.A. degree (1983) and Ph.D. degree (1988) in public administration from Florida Atlantic University. She is the author of articles and chapters on public and nonprofit human resources management.

PART ONE

HUMAN RESOURCES MANAGEMENT IN CONTEXT

Public and nonprofit organizations are confronting a variety of economic, technological, legal, and cultural changes with which they must cope effectively if they are to remain viable. The key to viability is well-trained and flexible employees. To be responsive to the constantly changing environment, agencies must integrate their human resources management (HRM) needs with their long-term strategic plans. The five chapters in Part One explain how society and workplaces have changed and what the strategic human resources management (SHRM) implications of these changes are for organizations.

Chapter One discusses some of the differences between public sector agencies and nonprofit organizations. It reviews some of the external factors that affect the internal operations of an organization, such as changes in economic conditions and the fiscal uncertainty that such changes can bring to an agency, and the social and cultural changes affecting the demographic composition of the workforce. Most organizations today have a more diverse group of employees than ever before, bringing different experiences and new expectations into the organization. The legal environment must always be monitored for change. Equal employment opportunity, labor relations, and compensation and benefits are all regulated by law.

There is also an increased emphasis on accountability and performance management in public and nonprofit organizations. Staff need critical knowledge skills, abilities, and other characteristics (KSAOCs) to perform their jobs, but they also need to be flexible and willing to deal with rapid and unstructured change. Knowledge-specific skills and general competencies are important. To make this possible, HRM needs to be more closely integrated with the organization's objectives and mission.

Chapter Two addresses the strategic side of HRM and the importance of strategic human resources and human resources planning. It explains why SHRM and human resources planning are critical if agencies are going to accomplish their missions. SHRM believes that realistic planning is not possible unless strategic planning takes into consideration information on current and potential human resources. Human resources planning requires the assessment of past trends, an evaluation of the existing situation, and the projection of future events. The external and internal environments must be scanned, and changes that might affect an organization's human resources must be anticipated and planned for if organizations wish to remain viable.

Chapter Three focuses on the legal environment and federal laws governing equal employment opportunity. Equal employment opportunity requires that employers not discriminate in the administration and execution of all HRM practices, such as recruitment, selection, promotion, training, compensation, career development, discipline, and labor-management relations. To understand the legal environment of equal employment opportunity, public and nonprofit administrators must be familiar with the laws and regulations that govern its implementation.

Chapter Four is devoted to exploring the issues of managing a diverse workforce. As already noted, the composition of public and nonprofit workforces has changed. Women, racial and ethnic minorities, and older, disabled, homosexual, and transgendered workers are more visible in today's workplace than in the past and may not always be accepted by other employees and managers. Other types of diversity issues exist in agencies as well. Diversity must be understood if organizations want to deal effectively with employees regardless of their personal characteristics. When diversity is well managed, all employees are supported, valued, and included. A supportive work environment enables employees to achieve their fullest potential.

Chapter Five discusses the use of volunteers in the public and nonprofit sectors. These volunteers provide a range of services. Some serve as board members for nonprofit organizations or on local government commissions or boards. Others provide assistance in cultural, recreational, social service, health care, and educational agencies. Still others supplement paid staff in professional roles.

CHAPTER ONE

INTRODUCTION TO HUMAN RESOURCES MANAGEMENT IN THE PUBLIC AND NONPROFIT SECTORS

After reading this chapter, you should be able to:

- Understand the responsibilities and roles of human resources management
- Understand what constitutes public organizations
- Explain why civil service systems or merit systems exist in the public sector
- Understand what constitutes nonprofit organizations
- Identify the challenges facing human resources management today

Human resources management (HRM) is the design of formal systems in an organization to ensure the effective use of employees' knowledge, skills, abilities, and other characteristics (KSAOCs) to accomplish organizational goals. HRM concerns the recruitment, selection, training and development, compensation and benefits, retention, evaluation, and promotion of employees, and labor-management relations within an organization. In public and nonprofit agencies, the greatest expenses and the greatest assets are employees. Unlike many for-profit organizations, which can use technology to automate the production of their products and reduce staff, public and nonprofit organizations typically provide some type of service. Thus, they rely on the professionalism and competence of their employees.

Machines cannot be substituted for most public and nonprofit employees. As a result, public and nonprofit agencies are labor intensive; employee costs are typically between 50 and 80 percent of their budgets (Cascio & Boudreau, 2008; Fitz-enz, 2000). Employees are also the greatest assets of public and nonprofit organizations. Whether referring to top leadership, department directors or managers, or first-level employees, the quality and competencies of the workforce differentiate successful agencies or departments from others. Why is one police department more effective than another when dealing with similar problems and situated in local governments with similar incomes and demographics and with similar responsibilities? Why is one substance abuse treatment center more effective than another if they are using similar clinical protocols and techniques and have clients with similar problems? The answer is likely to be related to the professionalism and competencies of their employees. The study of HRM has existed for a long time, despite having different names. Frederick Taylor's scientific management addressed the principle of breaking job positions down into their simplest tasks. Scientific management was concerned with production efficiencies through making the best employee and job match. It also addressed employee motivation by developing incentive pay systems.

Additional psychological aspects of HRM were developed to select individuals for military positions. Intelligence, aptitude, and psychological tests were developed to screen and place employees in various positions. The field of industrial-organizational psychology has played and continues to play a critical role in the development of HRM activities. Human resources management has evolved to encompass systems for the effective recruitment, selection, evaluation, and training and development of employees. Compensation studies to pay employees fair salaries and provide them with benefits that are important to them are also important components of HRM systems. Fair compensation serves to retain and motivate employees.

Human resources management responsibilities change as society changes. Today, public and nonprofit organizations are facing serious economic challenges, changes in the legal environment, and social, cultural, generational, and educational changes. A strategic human resources management system identifies these changes and challenges and develops effective human resources strategies to address them.

The Public Sector

The public sector is composed of a variety of government organizations. Government agencies are owned and controlled by the people. Government is used to maintain a system of law, justice, and social organization. It protects individual rights and freedoms, provides security and stability, and provides direction for the nation. Government provides public goods, regulates certain industries and activities, and corrects problems that the markets create or are unable to address (Rainey, 2003).

In the United States, we have a variety of federal, state, and local government agencies.

Federal employees work directly for federal agencies and receive their compensation and benefits from the federal government. Federal Bureau of Investigation agents are federal employees, as are doctors working for the National Institutes of Health and the Centers for Disease Control. Other federal employees may work for the Federal Aviation Authority, the Securities and Exchange Commission, and the Food and Drug Administration. (To see the scope of federal departments and agencies, go to http://www.whitehouse.gov/government/independent-agencies.html.) In 2006, 2.7 million employees were employed directly by the federal government (U.S. Census Bureau, 2006).

State employees work directly for state agencies and receive their compensation and benefits from state governments. Each state has a different number of state agencies. The compensation and benefits given to state employees vary across the states. In 2006, 5.1 million employees were employed directly by state governments (U.S. Bureau of the Census, 2006).

There are more than eighty-eight thousand units of local government: counties, cities, villages and townships, and special districts such as school districts, fire districts, park districts, hospital districts, museum and zoo districts, and parks and recreation districts. Local government employees work directly for local units and receive their compensation and benefits from the local governments and taxing districts. The number of local units varies across the states, as do compensation and benefits given to local government employees. Even within the same county, county employees may be paid different salaries from employees working for city governments located in the county. Also, special district employees receive different salaries and benefits. There is often little consistency across local government units. In 2006, the number of local government employees was 11.9 million. Most public employees work for local units (U.S. Bureau of the Census Annual Survey of Government Employment, 2006. http://www.census.gov/govs/www/apes.html.)

Individuals working directly for federal, state, or local units are considered to be government employees. In a democracy, government is owned by all of its citizens, and most of the revenues that support government agencies typically come from taxes. Government's objectives are political in nature. Public agencies are influenced by certain values found in the private sector such as efficiency, effectiveness, timeliness, and reliability. But they are also influenced by values not necessarily found in the private sector and often in conflict with one another, such as accountability to the public at large and elected officials, being responsive to rule of law and governmental authorities, being responsive to public demands, being open to external scrutiny and criticism, adhering to strict ethical standards, and conducting pubic affairs with the goals of fairness, equal treatment, social equity, and impartiality (Rainey, 2003).

Civil Service and Merit Systems

Many public agencies are required to comply with civil service or merit systems to facilitate these values and objective employment practices in public agencies:

◆ ◆ ◆

- *Federal government.* The Pendleton Act, passed in 1883, set up an independent, bipartisan civil service commission to make objective, merit-based selections for federal jobs. Those individuals best qualified would receive a job or promotion based on their KSAOCs. The terms *civil service system* and *merit system* are often used interchangeably. This is because merit provides the foundation for civil service systems. The ability to perform tasks is dependent not on political affiliation but on individual skills and abilities (that is, merit considerations). The intent of the merit system was to remove the negative effects of patronage in appointing individuals to federal positions. Public employees were expected to perform their work in a politically neutral manner. In 1978, the Civil Service Reform Act made changes to federal personnel policies. The Civil Service Commission was eliminated, and the Office of Personnel Management and the Merit Systems Protection Board took its place.

However, being politically neutral, along with experience, education, and expertise are still important criteria for selecting federal employees.

- *State governments.* The federal government encouraged state and local governments to develop civil service or merit systems as a condition of receiving federal grants (Aronson, 1974). The federal government has a vested interest in seeing that state and local programs supported by its funds are administered in an efficient and professional manner. The recipients of federal monies were to ensure the proper administration of grant programs. Standards were initially issued in the 1930s and continued through the 1970s when the Intergovernmental Personnel Act of 1970 was passed, which gave grants to state and local governments to improve their personnel practices. The authority for state merit systems is typically outlined in state statutes, which direct a specified agency to issue the necessary rules and regulations that have the effect of law and the necessary administrative procedures to carry out its provisions. Most civil service systems have independent civil service commissions that are patterned after the first Civil Service Commission. They are bipartisan in composition and usually have three to five members who serve staggered terms. They are typically appointed by the governor. They are usually responsible for overseeing hiring and promotions, but they may also be involved in adjudicating grievance or discharge hearing and developing or approving job classification schedules.
- *Local governments.* The administrative structure and the authority granted to local governments are typically found in their charters. This provision for chartering local governments is found in state constitutions and state statutes. For example, the Illinois state statute permits seven varieties of local government structure: aldermanic-city, trustee-village, commission, manager, special charter, strong mayor, and administrator. Each form has its own rules for the selection and type of officers, their powers and responsibilities, and their general operations. Any municipality may adopt the civil service provisions of the Illinois Municipal Code. However, they are not required to do so. Should they adopt civil service provisions, they must adhere to them. All relevant officers and employees must be appointed, promoted, and removed according to civil service rules.

◆ ◆ ◆

In jurisdictions with civil service systems in place, applicants are typically appointed after they have passed a standardized selection procedure. The selection procedure could consist of written examinations, a combination of prior experience and education, or oral interviews. Where competition exists for positions, candidates are ranked by their scores, with the agency appointing one of the top-ranking candidates.

Different rules apply to different civil service systems. Some systems allow managers to select one of the top three ranked candidates to be selected, others allow one of the top five ranked candidates to be selected, and others allow a larger range of acceptable candidates. Some public employees are exempt from civil service requirements. The exemptions permit chief executives to select people who are in agreement with their priorities for policymaking and politically sensitive posts. In most state and local governments, department directors are appointed by the chief executive. Many public sector HRM regulations and responsibilities are codified in statutes, which means that any changes need the respective legislative body to make the change. Chief executives and managers often have limited administrative and managerial discretion. Increases in compensation and benefits are often dependent on legislative approval.

The federal and state governments grant hiring preference to veterans of the U.S. armed services. Additional points may be added to the scores of eligible veterans applying for public sector positions.

Economic Challenges

Seventy-one percent of low-income families work. More than half of these families are headed by married couples. One in five workers is employed in occupations where the median wage is less than $8.84 an hour. According to *Working Hard, Falling Short: America's Working Families and the Pursuit of Economic Security* (Waldron, Roberts, Reamer, Rab, & Ressler 2004), compensation for one-fourth of wage earners in the United States is so low they are barely able to financially survive. Not only do these families suffer from low incomes, but they usually lack medical insurance, often spend more than a third of their income on a place to live, and do not receive paid parental leave from their employers to deal with family issues and emergencies.

This report is consistent with U.S. Census data indicating that the number of Americans living in poverty and without health insurance is significant. In 2007, 37.3 million people were in poverty. The poverty rate for blacks is 24.3 percent, Hispanics 21.5 percent, non-Hispanic whites 8.2 percent, and Asians 10.3 percent. For children under eighteen years old, the poverty rate is 18.0 percent, and the number in poverty is 13.3 million (DeNavas-Walt, Proctor, & Smith, 2008). When times are tough, the demand for public services grows. Low-income residents are dependent on a variety of services, such as housing assistance, assistance for medical care, food, unemployment benefits, transportation, and utility bills.

Middle-income Americans are increasingly concerned about jobs, health insurance, pensions, housing, and income security as well. Wage and salary increases have not kept up with increases in the cost of housing, gasoline, food, education, and insurance. Residents concerned about their living expenses tend to keep a closer eye on government spending and want tax relief. At the same time, state and local governments are facing budget deficits and have to make budget cuts. Problems with the housing markets and foreclosures, leading to reduced property taxes, reductions in sales taxes due to declines in consumer spending, and increasing unemployment rates have led to reductions in spending, so state and local revenues are falling (Prah, 2008).

As a result of difficult economic times, federal, state, and local governments are looking to reduce expenses. Strategies to save money include not hiring employees with benefits. Examples include hiring supplemental direct-hire employees who work irregular hours; they receive a paycheck from the agency for time worked, but do not receive health insurance, retirement pensions, vacation or sick leave, and other benefits. In some organizations, they are referred to *as other personnel services workers*.

Governments are also using more contract workers. These workers work for public agencies, but they are procured through a staffing agency or other third party. These work arrangements, as well as seasonal, part-time, on-call, and temporary agency work, are referred to as *nonstandard work arrangements* (Thompson & Mastracci, 2005). Privatization and contracting-out services are also being used increasingly by public sector agencies.

Privatization and Contracting-Out Services

Privatization and contracting out occur when public sector agencies contract with private nonprofit, private for-profit, or other public agencies to provide specific services. A typical privatization agreement specifies that a private or nonprofit entity is responsible for producing particular services. The public employer chooses the service level and pays the amount specified in the contract, but leaves decisions about production methods to the contracted firm. From an administrative perspective, privatization is often viewed as a way to save tax dollars, reduce the public payrolls, minimize government spending, and boost productivity.

Supporters claim that contracting out government programs will lead to greater efficiency and more effective operations. They maintain that competition and fewer restrictions allow the contractors to be more cost-efficient and responsive and that cost savings can be achieved through the economies of scale used by one vendor to provide services to many communities and organizations. It is believed that nonprofit and private firms, not hampered by bureaucratic rules and regulations, can be more innovative than public sector ones (Osbourne & Gaebler, 1993; Savas, 2000, 2002). However, research on the cost savings of privatization is inconclusive. There are examples of sweetheart deals with contractors, cost overruns, inefficiencies, and less-qualified staff providing important services. Furthermore, transparency, accountability, and concern for the public interest are often lacking (Feeney & Kingsley, 2008; Greenblatt, 2004; Light, 2008; Lee, 2008; Moe, 1987; Sclar, 2001; Starr, 1987).

Technological Innovations

Economic challenges have brought about an increase in accountability and demands for greater productivity. Innovations in technology are changing the way public sector organizations are structured and how work is organized and managed. *E-government* has been defined as "the use of information technology to support government operations, engage citizens, and provide government services" (Cook, LaVigne, Pagano, Dawes, & Pardo, 2002, p. 3). Within that definition are four dimensions that reflect the functions of government itself:

Economic challenges have brought about an increase in accountability and demands for greater productivity.

- *E-services*—the electronic delivery of government information, programs, and services often over the Internet
- *E-management*—the use of information technology to improve the management of government, from streamlining business processes to improving the flow of information within government offices
- *E-democracy*—the use of electronic communication vehicles, such as e-mail and the Internet, to increase citizen participation in the public decision-making process
- *E-commerce*—the exchange of money for goods and services over the Internet, such as citizens paying taxes and utility bills, renewing vehicle registrations, and paying for recreation programs, or government buying office supplies and auctioning surplus equipment

Organizations need to recruit and hire people with a new set of skills and orientation to fit the new culture. Key SHRM challenges facing organizations will be the ability to attract and hire qualified applicants and to provide training for incumbent employees so that the benefits of technology can be realized.

The Nonprofit Sector

Nonprofit sector is the collective name used to describe organizations that are not government or private for-profit organizations. They have also been called the *voluntary sector*, the *third sector*, and the *philanthropic sector*. Nonprofit organizations are chartered by each state and are conferred special tax-exempt status by the states and the Internal Revenue Service (IRS). The IRS exempts nonprofits from paying federal corporate income taxes, and state and local governments may grant nonprofits exemptions from property and sales taxes.

To be recognized as a nonprofit, an organization must possess the following general characteristics: (1) it is specifically designated as a nonprofit when organized; (2) profits or assets may not be divided among corporate members, officers, or directors in the manner of corporate dividends; and (3) it may lawfully pursue only such purposes as are permitted for such organizations by statute (Oleck, 1988). Internal Revenue Code 501(c) lists the types of associations, corporations, and trusts that can qualify for federal tax exemption (Table 1.1).

The largest nonprofit classification is 501(c)(3) nonprofits, referred to as *public charities*. The IRS defines a public charity as an organization that normally receives a substantial portion of its total income directly or indirectly from the general public or government. This is different from 501(c)(5) (labor and agricultural organizations) and 501(c)(6) (business leagues) classifications, which derive most of their money from members and are organized to primarily serve the interests of their members.

Individuals and corporations who give money to 501(c)(3) organizations can deduct the value of the gift from their taxable income. Of the 1.4 million nonprofit organizations registered with the IRS in 2004, nearly half a million collected more than twenty-five thousand dollars in gross receipts and are therefore required to file a Form 990 annually. Public charities with less than twenty-five thousand dollars in gross receipts are not required to file a Form 990. Therefore, the number of 501(c)(3) organizations is higher than what is reported to the IRS (Boris, 2006). Human

TABLE 1.1. IRS ORGANIZATION REFERENCE CHART

Section of 1986 Code	Description of Organization	General Nature of Activities	Application Form Number	Annual Return Required to Be Filed	Contributions Allowable
501(c)(1)	Corporations organized under act of Congress (including federal credit unions)	Instrumentalities of the United States	No form	None	Yes, if made for exclusively public purposes
501(c)(2)	Title holding corporation for exempt organization	Holding title to property of an exempt organization	1024	990 or 990-EZ	No
501(c)(3)	Religious, educational, charitable, scientific, literary, testing for public safety, to foster national or international amateur sports competition, or prevention of cruelty to children or animals organizations	Activities of nature implied by description of class of organization	1023	990 or 990-EZ, or 990-PF	Yes, generally
501(c)(4)	Civic leagues, social welfare organizations, and local associations of employees	Promotion of community welfare; charitable, educational, or recreational	1024	990 or 990-EZ	No, generally
501(c)(5)	Labor, agricultural, and horticultural organizations	Educational or instructive, the purpose being to improve conditions of work and to improve products of efficiency	1024	990 or 990-EZ	No
501(c)(6)	Business leagues, chambers of commerce, real estate boards, etc.	Improvement of business conditions of one or more lines of business	1024	990 or 990-EZ	No
501(c)(7)	Social and recreational clubs	Pleasure, recreation, social activities	1024	990 or 990-EZ	No
501(c)(8)	Fraternal beneficiary societies and associations	Lodge providing for payment of life, sickness, accident, or other benefits to members	1024	990 or 990-EZ	Yes, if for certain Sec. 501(c)(3) purposes

501(c)(9)	Voluntary employees beneficiary associations	Providing for payment of life, sickness, accident, or other benefits to members	1024	990 or 990-EZ	No
501(c)(10)	Domestic fraternal societies and associations	Lodge devoting its net earnings to charitable, fraternal, and other specified purposes. No life, sickness, or accident benefits to members	1024	990 or 990-EZ	Yes, if for certain Sec. 501(c)(3) purposes
501(c)(11)	Teachers' retirement fund associations	Teachers' association for payment of retirement benefits	No form	990 or 990-EZ	No
501(c)(12)	Benevolent life insurance associations, mutual ditch or irrigation companies, mutual or cooperative telephone companies, etc.	Activities of a mutually beneficial nature similar to those implied by the description of class of organization	1024	990 or 990-EZ	No
501(c)(13)	Cemetery companies	Burials and incidental activities	1024	990 or 990-EZ	Yes, generally
501(c)(14)	State-chartered credit unions, mutual reserve funds	Loans to members	No form	990 or 990-EZ	No
501(c)(15)	Mutual insurance companies or associations	Providing insurance to members substantially at cost	1024	990 or 990-EZ	No
501(c)(16)	Cooperative organizations to finance crop operations	Financing crop operations in conjunction with activities of a marketing or purchasing association	No form	990 or 990-EZ	No
501(c)(17)	Supplemental unemployment benefit trusts	Provides for payment of supplemental unemployment compensation benefits	1024	990 or 990-EZ	No

(Continued)

TABLE 1.1. IRS ORGANIZATION REFERENCE CHART (*continued*)

Section of 1986 Code	Description of Organization	General Nature of Activities	Application Form Number	Annual Return Required to Be Filed	Contributions Allowable
501(c)(18)	Employee funded pension trust (created before June 25, 1959)	Payment of benefits under a pension plan funded by employees	No form	990 or 990-EZ	No
501(c)(19)	Post or organization of past or present members of the Armed Forces	Activities implied by nature of organization	1024	990 or 990-EZ	No, generally
501(c)(21)	Black Lung benefit trusts	Funded by coal mine operators to satisfy their liability for disability or death due to black lung diseases	No form	990-BL	No
501(c)(22)	Withdrawal liability payment fund	To provide funds to meet the liability of employers withdrawing from a multiemployer pension fund	No form	990 or 990-EZ	No
501(c)(23)	Veterans organization (created before 1880)	To provide insurance and other benefits to veterans	No form	990 or 990-EZ	No, generally
501(c)(25)	Title holding corporations or trusts with multiple parents	Holding title and paying income from property to 35 or fewer parents or beneficiaries	1024	990 or 990-EZ	No
501(c)(26)	State-sponsored organization providing health coverage for high-risk individuals	Provides health care coverage to high-risk individuals	No form	990 or 990-EZ	No
501(c)(27)	State-sponsored workers' compensation reinsurance organization	Reimburses members for losses under workers' compensation acts	No form	990 or 990-EZ	No
501(c)(28)	National Railroad Retirement Investment Trust	Manages and invests the assets of the Railroad Retirement Account	No form	Not yet determined	No

501(d)	Religious and apostolic associations	Regular business activities. Communal religious community	No Form	10659	No
501(e)	Cooperative hospital service organizations	Performs cooperative services for hospitals	1023	990 or 990-EZ	Yes
501(f)	Cooperative service organizations of operating educational organizations	Performs collective investment services for educational organizations	1023	990 or 990-EZ	Yes
501(k)	Child care organizations	Provides cares for children	1023	990 or 990-EZ	Yes
501(n)	Charitable risk pools	Pools certain insurance risks of 501(c)(3)	1023	990 or 990-EZ	Yes
501(q)	Credit counseling organizations	Credit counseling services	1023	1023	No
521(a)	Farmers' cooperative associations	Cooperative marketing and purchasing for agricultural procedures	1028	990-C	No
527	Political organizations	A party, committee, fund, association, etc., that directly or indirectly accepts contributions or makes expenditures for political campaigns	8871	1120-POL 990 or 990-EZ	No

Source: Adapted from Internal Revenue Service. (Rev. June 2008). *Publication 557 Tax-Exempt Status for Your Organization.* www.irs.gov/pub/irs-pdf/p.557.pdf_(pp. 65–66).

service organizations are the most common type of public charity nonprofits (35 percent), followed by education nonprofits (18 percent), health care nonprofits (13 percent), public and societal benefit nonprofits (12 percent), and arts, culture, and humanities nonprofits (11 percent) (Table 1.2).

The National Taxonomy of Exempt Entities, developed by the National Center for Charitable Statistics, provides this classification system for public charity nonprofit organizations:

A. Arts, Culture, and Humanities
B. Education
C. Environmental Quality, Protection, and Beautification
D. Animal-Related
E. Health
F. Mental Health, Crisis Intervention
G. Diseases, Disorders, Medical Disciplines
H. Medical Research
I. Crime, Legal-Related
J. Employment, Job-Related
K. Food, Agriculture, and Nutrition
L. Housing and Shelter
M. Public Safety, Disaster Preparedness, and Relief
N. Recreation and Sports
O. Youth Development
P. Human Services
Q. International, Foreign Affairs, and National Security
R. Civil Rights, Social Action, and Advocacy
S. Community Improvement and Capacity Building
T. Philanthropy, Voluntarism, and Grantmaking Foundations
U. Science and Technology
V. Social Science
W. Public and Societal Benefit
X. Religion-Related
Y. Mutual and Membership Benefit
Z. Unknown

There are nine major groups, twenty-six categories, and over four hundred subcategories (Table 1.3).

There are approximately 9.4 million 501(c)(3) nonprofit employees and approximately 4.7 million full-time equivalent volunteers. Combined, the workforce is more than 14 million workers (Salamon & Sokolowski, 2006).

TABLE 1.2. NUMBER OF NONPROFIT ORGANIZATIONS IN THE UNITED STATES, 1996–2006

	1996		2006		
	Number of Organizations	Percentage of All Organizations	Number of Organizations	Percentage of All Organizations	Percentage Change
All nonprofit organizations	1,084,939	100.0%	1,478,194	100.0%	36.2%
501(c)(3) public charities	535,930	49.4	904,313	61.2	68.7
501(c)(3) private foundations	58,774	5.4	109,852	7.4	86.9
Other 501(c) nonprofit organizations	490,235	45.2	464,029	31.4	–5.3
Small community groups and partnerships	Unknown	NA	Unknown	NA	NA
501(c)(3) public charities	535,930	49.4	904,313	61.2	68.7
501(c)(3) public charities registered with the IRS (including registered congregations)	535,930	49.4	904,313	61.2	68.7
Reporting public charities	224,316	20.7	347,414	23.5	54.9
Operating public charities	192,927	17.8	295,355	20.0	53.1
Supporting public charities	31,389	2.9	52,059	3.5	65.9
Nonreporting, or with less than $25,000 in gross receipts	311,614	28.7	556,899	37.7	78.7
Congregations (about half are registered with IRS)[a]	—	0.0	385,874	26.1	NA

(Continued)

TABLE 1.2. NUMBER OF NONPROFIT ORGANIZATIONS IN THE UNITED STATES, 1996–2006 (*continued*)

	1996		2006		
	Number of Organizations	Percentage of All Organizations	Number of Organizations	Percentage of All Organizations	Percentage Change
501(c)(3) private foundations	58,774	5.4	109,852	7.4	86.9
Private grant-making (nonoperating) foundations	56,377	5.2	105,187	7.1	86.6
Private operating foundations	2,397	0.2	4,665	0.3	94.6
Other 501(c) nonprofit organizations	490,235	45.2	464,029	31.4	−5.3
Civic leagues, social welfare organizations	127,567	11.8	116,539	7.9	−8.6
Fraternal beneficiary societies	102,592	9.5	84,049	5.7	−18.1
Business leagues, chambers of commerce	68,575	6.3	72,549	4.9	5.8
Labor, agricultural, horticultural organizations	61,729	5.7	56,460	3.8	−8.5
Social and recreational clubs	57,090	5.3	56,778	3.8	−0.5
Post or organization of war veterans	30,578	2.8	35,164	2.4	15.0
All other nonprofit organizations	42,104	3.9	42,490	2.9	0.9

Note: Excludes out-of-scope organizations.

Sources: IRS Business Master File 01/2007 (with modifications by the National Center for Charitable Statistics at the Urban Institute to exclude foreign and governmental organizations). Reprinted with the permission of the Urban Institute. NCCS Web site, Number of Nonprofit Organizations in the United States, 1996–2006. http://nccsdataweb.urban.org/PubAppa/profile.1.pho?state=US.

[a]The number of congregations is from the Web site of American Church Lists (http://list.infousa.com/acl.htm), 2004. These numbers are excluded from the totals for the state, since approximately half of the congregations are included under registered public charities.

TABLE 1.3. NATIONAL TAXONOMY OF EXEMPT ENTITIES: BROAD CATEGORIES

Major Group	Categories
Arts, culture, and humanities	A
Education	B
Environment and animals	C, D
Health	E, F, G, H
Human services	I, J, K, L, M, N, O, P
International, foreign affairs	Q
Public, societal benefit	R,S, T, U, V, W
Religion related	X
Mutual/membership benefit	Y
Unknown, unclassified	Z

501(c)(3) Nonprofits

Charitable nonprofits are private organizations that serve a public purpose. Because they operate under a nondistribution component, this prohibits the distribution of profits or residual earnings to individuals who control the entity. As such it is believed that they possess a greater moral authority and concern for the public interest than private for-profit organizations. Nonprofits often perform public tasks that have been delegated to them by the state or perform tasks for which there is a demand that neither government nor for-profit organizations offer. They provide myriad services, such as helping the disadvantaged, providing medical services, supporting museums and cultural activities, preserving the environment, and funding medical research.

Nonprofits are thought to be more flexible than government agencies. They can experiment with new programs, responding more quickly to new social needs. Instead of government getting involved in new or controversial programs, it often gives money to nonprofit agencies to do this work instead. Nonprofits get financial support, and clients receive services. Government, through the conditions it places on agencies that receive public funds, still has some influence but can quickly disassociate itself from programs when things go wrong. There are often certain societal needs that may be too expensive to be provided on a private for-profit basis. Therefore, in the United States, both government and the nonprofit sector provide certain services whose costs exceed their market value (Douglas, 1983; O'Neil, 1989; Salamon, 1999; Weisbrod, 1997).

Public administration practitioners and scholars have increased their attention to nonprofit organizations as governments have more frequently used such agencies to provide health and human services. Among the examples are organizations established to prevent child abuse, domestic violence, or homelessness; assist the disabled, the elderly, or the mentally ill; or provide day care, counseling, vocational training and rehabilitation, or community and neighborhood centers (Kramer & Grossman, 1987; Lipsky & Smith 1989–1990; Salamon, 1999).

Public assistance reaches nonprofit organizations indirectly through federal, state, and local governments that contract with nonprofit agencies to provide public services. Many people do not realize that "rather than depending mostly on private charity and volunteers, most nonprofit service organizations depend on government for over half of their revenues; for many small agencies, government support comprises their entire budget in contrast to the traditional relationship of two independent sectors; the new relationship between government and nonprofits amounts to one of mutual dependencies that is financial as well as technical. The lines between public and private are blurred" (Lipsky and Smith, 1989–1990, p. 625).

This blurring is especially vivid in health and human services. Government, nonprofit, and for-profit organizations are subject to similar regulations, dependent on the same revenue sources, hire the same types of professional staff, and perform similar functions. However, public organizations and nonprofits are similar in that they define themselves around their missions or the services they offer. These services are often intangible and difficult to measure. Both sectors are accountable to multiple constituencies. Nonprofits must be responsive to supporters, sponsors, clients, and government sources who provide funding and impose regulations. Public agencies must be responsive to their respective legislative and judicial branches, taxpayers, cognate agencies, political appointees, clients, the media, and other levels of government.

501(c)(4) Nonprofits

Social welfare organizations are often referred to as *advocacy organizations*. The American Civil Liberties Union, the National Rifle Association, and the Sierra Club are examples. They cannot receive tax-deductible gifts, they engage in more lobbying activities, and they can advocate for specific issues. They, along with 501(c)(3) nonprofits, constitute what is referred to as the *independent sector* and are public serving (Wetizman, Jalandoni, Lampkin, & Pollak, 2002). Many 501(c)(4) nonprofits have affiliated 501(c)(3) nonprofits to assist with fundraising, and they often establish foundations since donations to them are not tax deductible. And many 501(c)(3) nonprofits have affiliated 501(c)(4) organizations to engage in lobbying and advocacy activities. This is because 501(c)(3)nonprofits have more restrictive limits on their lobbying and political advocacy activities than 501(c)(4) nonprofits.

The Alliance for Justice provides live as well as online workshops and publishes booklets and fact sheets on the permissible advocacy activities for 501(c)(3) and 501(c)(4) organizations. Nonprofits organized under Section 527 are permitted to be active in political campaigns, although they cannot communicate with candidates or members of their staffs and advocacy activities.

Nonprofit Administrative Structures

A nonprofit's administrative structure is governed by its bylaws, internal documents that typically define most operational and management policies. Bylaws regulate the organization's procedures and internal practices, as well as define the duties, powers, and limitations of the directors, officers, and other agents. Like all other important documents, bylaws should be reviewed periodically and updated.

Nonprofit organizations possess legal power. Directors are elected or appointed to the board and are authorized to manage and direct the affairs of the organization. They act on behalf of the organization but do not have ownership powers within it; their control is managerial and proprietary. They are free only to change policies and short-range purposes unless the charter or bylaws permit the directors to change the fundamental purpose or policies. Many states permit the delegation of direct authority to committees to study and make recommendations about some matter or to manage routine affairs.

The human resources committee, responsible for developing personnel policies, may recommend employee and executive director salary ranges and benefit packages to the board, as well as evaluate the executive director. It may also handle employee grievances. Although the board may delegate its authority to committees, it has not delegated its responsibility; it must still supervise and hold accountable the activities of the committees.

The nonprofit sector is often referred to as the *voluntary sector* because nonprofit agencies are often dependent on the use of volunteers to assist in executing their missions. Additional information on volunteers and governing boards is provided in later chapters.

Nonprofit Economic Challenges

Nonprofits are facing severe economic challenges. Declines in public revenues mean less support for many of these organizations. Uncertain financial times place additional stresses on them. Increased unemployment often requires the expansion of food assistance, medical aid, and job training, rent assistance, or retraining services. These services are typically provided by nonprofit agencies, which must absorb an increase in demand for services without increasing their staffs and possibly facing layoffs themselves.

Nonprofit agencies are affected by economic uncertainty in other ways. Individuals who have been or might be laid off are less inclined to spend money on cultural activities than more securely employed people. Nonprofits that rely on gifts between one hundred and three hundred dollars are very vulnerable because these are often the donors most affected by hard economic times. Civil rights groups and community improvement organizations tend to experience gains when the economy is strong and harder crashes during bad times (Hall & Kean, 2008). Nonprofits that rely on government aid are also facing hard times. The housing crisis of 2008 is resulting in lower property tax revenues, which are forcing state and local governments to reduce their budgets.

There is a greater emphasis on social enterprise and social entrepreneurship activities as well. Nonprofits are expected to diversify their revenue streams and eliminate their reliance on public monies or foundation grants. The leadership of nonprofit organizations must understand, supervise, and implement finance strategies and social marketing. Tough financial times also provoke a greater scrutiny on performance outcomes and indicators of effectiveness.

The New Public Service

Recent graduates of schools of public policy and administration are twice as likely as members of earlier classes to take first jobs in the nonprofit sector and have shown an interest in working for the private sector as well. The nonprofit sector is attractive to graduates because they are motivated and believe they will find more challenging work and a greater opportunity to acquire new skills than in government service (Light, 2003). As a result, government trails the private and nonprofit sectors in competing for new graduates. Once working outside government, these new graduates are likely to remain there because government offers few opportunities to enter at the middle and senior levels (Light, 2003).

Public charity 501(c)(3) and social welfare 501(c)(4) nonprofits share a common purpose of serving the public. They also share the community-oriented values of public administration, such as being responsive, being open to external scrutiny and criticism, conducting public affairs with the goals of fairness and social equity, addressing what they perceive to be community or societal problems, and defending individual rights, commitment to democratic ideals, and citizen and community participation and involvement. They are mission driven, and although operating in the black is a goal, profit is not the reason for their existence. Public and nonprofit administrators must behave responsively and ethically at all times, acting in the public interest.

Recent graduates of schools of public policy and administration are twice as likely as members of earlier classes to take first jobs in the nonprofit sector and have shown an interest in working for the private sector as well.

Today's Context for Human Resources Management

Human resources management is critical if organizations are to be effective. Public and nonprofit organizations are labor-intensive enterprises depending on the knowledge, skills, abilities, and other characteristics of their employees. To be successful, organizations need to develop progressive HRM practices. Understanding the legal environment that impacts HRM, the social and cultural changes affecting society and organizations, the generational changes taking place in today's work environments, and changes in the educational opportunities available to incumbent employees and future employees is important.

The Legal Environment

Public and nonprofit agencies must comply with federal, state, and local laws; with executive orders and the rules and regulations promulgated by administrative agencies such as the Equal Employment Opportunity

Commission and the Department of Labor; and federal and state court decisions. Equal employment opportunity, labor relations, and employer contributions to benefits such as retirement plans and pensions, workers' compensation, and unemployment are regulated by law. These topics and employment at will are discussed in greater detail in later chapters.

Social and Cultural Changes

The demographic composition of American society is changing. Hispanics (who can be of any race) are now the largest minority in the United States, at approximately 44.3 million, 15 percent of the nation's population. As of 2006, the black or African American population, including those of more than one race, surpassed, 40.2 million (U.S. Census Bureau, 2007d), the Asian population was 19.9 million, American Indian and Alaskan Native 4.5 million, and Native Hawaiian and other Pacific Islander 1 million. The number of Americans who declared themselves as two or more races is greater than 6 million. The population of non-Hispanic whites who indicated no other race totaled 198.7 million.

The minority population in the United States is now at 100.7 million. Approximately one in three U.S. residents is a minority. Foreign-born workers make up approximately 15.3 of the civilian labor force sixteen years of age or older (U.S. Census Bureau, Hispanic Americans by the Number 12/19/07; 2006 American Community Survey).

Nontraditional families are now prevalent. Divorce, death, domestic partners, and different generations of the same family living together have become commonplace. More than 2.5 million grandparents are raising their grandchildren (U.S. Census Bureau, 2007c). Nationally, 43 percent of unmarried couples living together are raising children, nearly matching the 46 percent figure for married couples. According to the 2000 Census, one-third of lesbian couples and one-fifth of male couples have children at home (Cohn, 2003; U.S. Census Bureau, 2003). Same-sex couples accounted for one in nine of the total unmarried live-in households; however, this number may be understated because of fear of prejudice or confusion over the unmarried partner category (Marquis, 2003). In 2005, 51 percent of women said they were living without a spouse, up from 35 percent in 1950 and 49 percent in 2000 (Finding Family, 2007; Roberts, 2007).

Because of the increase in single-parent families, families in which both parents work, employees taking care of elderly parents and young children, and children living with caregivers other than their parents, organizations need to provide employees with more flexibility and options in choosing work schedules and benefits. Issues such as day care, elder care, assistance with family problems, and spousal involvement in career planning have become important workplace issues.

Employers face new issues arising from the diverse workforce. They must offer more flexible work schedules to accommodate training, education, and family demands. They must also provide greater opportunities for work-based learning to prepare future workers and upgrade the skills of current workers. The increased diversity of the workforce poses new challenges for the systems that educate and train workers. These systems must accommodate ethnic and cultural differences, provide for the needs of working families and individuals with disabilities, and address gaps in literacy and job skills among some immigrant populations. This will require increased investments in adult literacy and English as a Second Language programs, more opportunities for continuous learning to stay competitive, and expanded access to work supports to sustain labor force participation. Employers need to manage a diverse workforce. They will need to ensure that agency rewards such as promotional opportunities and compensation are determined by job performance, initiative, or special skills, not by racism or sexism.

There has been a shift in the attitudes and values of employees. Employees are now seeking a balance between their personal and work lives and demanding more leisure time to spend with their families. Attitudes toward work have also changed: a greater number of employees want challenging jobs and the opportunity to exercise discretion in the performance of their tasks. Improving the quality of work life has become important. Empowerment, teamwork, quality improvement, job design, labor-management cooperation, and participative management are expected. Organizational culture will need to be changed if organizations wish to attract, motivate, and retain a competent workforce.

Generational Challenges

Many workforces today are composed of four generations of workers: the traditionalists or matures, born between 1925 and 1945; the baby boomers, born between 1946 and 1964; Generation Xers, born between 1965 and 1980; and the millennials, born between 1981 and 2002. Baby boomers are the largest segment (at least for now) followed by Gen-Xers, millennials, and traditionalists.

Each generation is characterized as having its own work-related behaviors. Traditionalists and baby boomers have typically remained with one organization throughout their working lives. They accept organizational policies and procedures more readily than the other generations and have lower expectations of work and life balance. Some of the keys to motivate them include recognizing their experience and contributions and providing them with opportunities to share their knowledge with less-experienced employees. Gen Xers tend to be results oriented, they are less comfortable with established procedures that may no longer be effective, and they expect the employer to be supportive of a balance between work and life. Some of them may have expected to spend their career with the same organization. They may be motivated by working in a flexible environment and being provided with learning and development opportunities. Millennials tend to be comfortable with technology, which they have grown up with. As a result, their attention spans are believed to be shorter and more focused on visual and auditory prompts. They are socially minded and goal oriented; drawing the connection between their work and how it contributes to organization goals and public service is likely to motivate them. They are likely to prefer working in a collaborative, flexible environment and being provided with learning and development opportunities. However, the learning and development opportunities need to be delivered in an experiential manner.

Agencies need to prepare for the impending retirements of traditionalists and baby boomers. They need to engage in workforce and succession planning and develop strategies for sharing knowledge and experience. Many retired employees want to continue working, although in another capacity than in their former jobs. Many retirees from the private, for-profit sector are looking for new opportunities in public service. Public and nonprofit organizations should be able to accommodate them with flexible work schedules, flexible benefits, and flexible compensation plans (Decker, 2008; Yang & Guy, 2006).

Educational Challenges

At a time when workforces require greater skills, fewer low-income students are attending college, and those who have enrolled have acquired a greater amount of federal student loan debt. At the same time the changing demographics of American society have called attention to inequities in postsecondary education. Black and Hispanic students earn bachelor's degrees at a substantially lower rate than white students.

Future college-age cohorts will look different from previous generations of college-age students. It is estimated that 80 percent will be nonwhite and almost 50 percent will be Hispanic (Advisory Committee on Student Financial Assistance, 2001).

Today's knowledge-based economy makes college more important than ever before. Nearly 60 percent of jobs today require at least some college. The new economy is making a baccalaureate degree the equivalent of a high school diploma in the old economy. It is estimated that shortages of workers with postsecondary-level skills could grow to 14 million by 2020. In order for the nation as a whole to maintain a competitive economic edge, the workforce must have education and training beyond high school. Six out of ten jobs now require at least some postsecondary education and training (Carnevale & Desrochers, 2003).

Conclusion

Public and nonprofit agencies must change. Nonprofits, dependent on government for a significant share of their revenue, must compete with other nonprofits, government agencies, and for-profits for shrinking dollars. Faced with the same changes that are confronting public organizations, nonprofits must demonstrate they are capable of providing cost-effective professional services. The nature of work has changed, and like public agencies, nonprofit organizations require their employees to have more professional and technical skills. In both sectors, there is a greater reliance on technology. Advances in technology call for advanced education, continuous training, and the addition of new benefits, such as educational leaves or tuition reimbursement. Jobs may have to be redesigned in order to take advantage of employee skills and to enhance job satisfaction. Job rotation, job enlargement, and job enrichment have become SHRM components.

Public and nonprofit administration must meet the challenge of changing social needs and priorities, new directions in public policy, demands for greater citizen involvement in the decision-making process, and pressures for increased accountability and productivity.

An uncertain external environment, coupled with changing needs for organizational skills, has facilitated a shift in the importance of HRM functions. Organizations need individuals with the right technical knowledge, skills, abilities, and other characteristics, but they also need people who are flexible and willing to deal with rapid and unstructured changes. Public and nonprofit jobs are increasingly more professional in nature, requiring higher levels of education. At the same time, the number of jobs requiring manual labor is decreasing. Employees in public and nonprofit agencies need to be able to deal with a variety of people, many with a stake in the agency. Taxpayers, clients, customers, elected officials, foundations, donors, contractors, board members, and special interest groups are just some of the stakeholders concerned about agency performance. Studies have indicated that relationships exist among an agency's strategy, its human resources planning and HRM practices, and its performance.

Exercise 1.1: Art Museums Are Looking for Leaders

Today, a museum director needs both an advanced degree in art history and curatorial experience, as well as the financial acumen and managerial skills of a chief executive. "The demands placed on directors are broader than twenty years ago. Then there was greater public support, so you didn't have to raise so much money. Nobody thought about earned income revenue from restaurants, shops, or partnering with Wolfgang Puck" (Finkle, 2007).

Now, most museum directors have to think about generating revenue streams and charitable donations, as well as tending to the permanent collection and acquisitions. Although they may have a chief financial officer and development team, directors generally serve as the museum's public face of fundraising. They are also ultimately responsible for covering the costs of acquisitions and operations.

Questions

1. Given the economic climate in the United States, if you are a member of a search committee looking to recruit an executive director for a museum, what knowledge, skills, abilities, and other characteristics would you emphasize?
2. What about a different type of nonprofit organization? Do you believe that financial and management skills are as important as the knowledge an executive director has in the substantive area of the nonprofit: for example, an educator leading a school, a social worker leading a social service agency, or an athlete leading a sports and recreation program? Explain your reasoning.

Chapter Questions

1. In a small group, each member should select three HRM challenges discussed in the chapter and describe how they are evident in a current or past employer. If you are unemployed at present, discuss how the HRM challenges might be affecting your university.
2. In your opinion, discuss why it is important for HRM to evolve from an administrative and operational role to a strategic one.

Online Activities

1. Visit the U.S. Department of Labor, Bureau of Labor Statistics Web page and review *Occupation Outlooks and Demographics Data.* What additional workforce changes do you believe might take place in the next five to ten years? What strategies will public and nonprofit agencies need to implement to be prepared for the future?
2. Visit the *Monthly Labor Review Online.* Review the two most recent editions, and select two articles from each edition. What topics are discussed, and why do the authors think they are important? Explain your answer.

CHAPTER TWO

STRATEGIC HUMAN RESOURCES MANAGEMENT AND PLANNING

After you have read this chapter, you should be able to:

- Describe the changing role of human resources management
- Define human resources planning and identify steps in the planning process
- Identify factors to consider in forecasting the supply and demand for strategic human resources management (SHRM)
- Explain why SHRM is critical for public and nonprofit organizations

Strategic human resources management (SHRM) is based on the belief that to be effective and able to adapt to changes quickly, agencies need realistic information on the capabilities and talents of their current staff—in essence, their human resources.

SHRM refers to the implementation of human resources activities, policies, and practices to make the necessary ongoing changes to support or improve the agency's operational and strategic objectives. Agency leaders need to understand how their workplaces will be affected by impending changes and prepare for those changes. Agency objectives should be formulated after relevant data on the quantity and potential of available human resources have been reviewed. Are human resources available for short- and long-term objectives? To be competitive, organizations must be able to anticipate, influence, and manage the forces that have an impact on their ability to remain effective. In the service sector, this means they must be able to manage their human resources capabilities. All too often, agencies have relied on short-term service requirements to direct their HRM practices without giving much thought to long-term implications. By invoking SHRM, agencies are better able to match their human resources requirements with the demands of the external environment and the needs of the organization. The human resources focus is not just an individual employee issue; it also encompasses integrating human resources into the organization's strategy and becomes part of the visionary process. Strategic planning, budgeting, and human resources planning are linked in SHRM, the integrative framework that matches HRM activities with strategic organizational needs.

The nonprofit and public sectors are facing significant numbers of impending retirements from the traditionalists and baby boomers in their workforces. Research funded in part by the Annie E. Casey Foundation and reported in *Nonprofit Executive Leadership and Transitions Survey* (Teegarden, 2004) found that 65 percent of the survey respondents anticipate executive transitions in their agencies by 2010. Follow-up studies addressing the wave of retirements in the nonprofit sector—*Up Next: Generation Change and the Leadership of Nonprofit Organizations* (Kunreuther, 2005) and *Staying Engaged, Stepping Up: Succession Planning and Executive Transition Management for Nonprofit Boards of Directors* (Adams, 2006)—predict that the first wave of retirements will occur in 2010 and the second wave in 2020. According to *Ready to Lead: Next Generation Leaders Speak Out*, a national study produced in partnership by CompassPoint Nonprofit Services, the Annie E. Casey Foundation, the Meyer Foundation, and Idealist.org, despite the many disincentives to becoming a nonprofit executive director, a significant number of younger people are willing, but not necessarily ready, to lead at this time (Cornelius, Corvington, & Ruesga, 2008). Hall (2006a) and Halpern (2006) also note the need to address strategic human resources planning in the nonprofit sector.

The nonprofit and public sectors are facing significant numbers of impending retirements from the traditionalists and baby boomers in their workforces.

Between 2008 and 2013, nearly half of federal workers will be eligible to retire, including nearly 70 percent of senior managers. By 2018, about 60 percent of the federal government's white-collar employees and 90 percent of the Senior Executive Service will be eligible to retire. The Senior Executive Service (SES), established by the Civil Service Reform Act of 1978 and effective in July 1979, is designed to improve the executive management of the government and to select and develop a cadre of highly competent senior executives with leadership and managerial expertise. Approximately 60 percent of federal jobs are in professional and administrative occupations, which implement the predominantly knowledge-based work of the government (Nelson, 2007; Partnership for Public Service, 2005). Montgomery County, Virginia, estimates that 50 percent of its senior managers will be eligible for retirement in 2010 (Ibarra, 2006; Turque, 2006).

Across the United States, there is a concern that city manager positions will go unfilled as increasing numbers of city and county managers retire. As far back as 2002, 43 percent of city and county managers were between the ages of fifty-one and sixty (Blumenthal, 2007). A survey of New York businesses found that six in ten surveyed reported it is likely that their organizations will face a shortage of qualified workers in the next five years (Bridges & Cicero, 2007).

Impending retirements are not the only reason for public organizations to implement SHRM. SHRM is also important for public and nonprofit agencies facing layoffs and job cuts. State and local governments across the country are facing severe revenue shortfalls and are planning to eliminate funding for many programs and services. The strategies they are using to balance their budgets are to reduce or eliminate services, lay off employees, and increase and institute user fees for many of the services that will remain. Individuals remaining after the layoffs need to possess the requisite knowledge, skills, abilities, and other characteristics (KSAOCs) to keep the programs and services operating effectively.

This chapter discusses SHRM, the changing role of HRM, and human resources planning and illustrates the importance of all these concerns to organizational vitality and success.

The Changing Role of Human Resources Management

Public, nonprofit, and for-profit organizations are facing some daunting challenges. For HRM departments to play a strategic role, they must focus on the long-term implications of HRM issues. For example, how will changing workforce demographics and workforce shortages affect the organization, and what strategies will be used to address them?

The downsizing and reorganization of public and nonprofit agencies, along with a strong focus on results, are forcing agencies to validate their business processes, reassess the role of the HR function, and evaluate the adequacy of the work performed by HR employees.

To be strategic partners, HRM departments must possess high levels of professional and business knowledge. HRM must establish links to enhance organizational performance and be able to demonstrate on a continuing basis how HRM activities contribute to the success and effectiveness of the organization.

Unfortunately, many HRM departments have spent their time ensuring compliance with rules and regulations, so they lack the skills and competencies to act as a strategic partner. For organizations to be successful in implementing SHRM, they need the collaborative effort of agency leaders and human resources (HR) professionals, who themselves need the knowledge and skills to undertake a more proactive role. In "Why We Hate HR," Hammonds (2005) notes, "The human resources trade long ago provided itself, at best, a necessary evil—at worst, a dark bureaucratic force that blindly enforces nonsensical rules, resists creativity, and impedes constructive change. . . . They are competent at the administrivia of pay, benefits, and retirement, but companies are increasingly farming those functions out to contractors who can handle such routines at lower expenses" (p. 40).

To identify the skills that high-performing HR professionals need, Dave Ulrich and Wayne Brockbank, professors at the University of Michigan and other partners, conducted the 2007 Human Resource Competency Study. Over the course of the research, they identified six core competencies: credible activist, cultural steward, manager/organizational designer, strategy architect, business ally, and operational executor (Brockbank, Johnson, & Ulrich, 2008; Grossman, 2007):

- The *credible activist* is respected, admired, and listened to and offers a point of view, takes a position, and challenges assumptions by:
  - Delivering results with integrity
  - Sharing information
  - Building relationships of trust
  - Doing HR with an attitude (taking appropriate risks, providing candid observations, influencing others)
- The *cultural steward* recognizes, articulates, and helps shape an organization's culture by:
  - Facilitating change
  - Crafting culture

    - Valuing culture
    - Personalizing culture (helping employees find meaning in their work, managing work/life balance, encouraging innovation)
- The *talent manager/organizational designer* masters theory, research, and practice in talent management and organizational design by:
    - Ensuring today's and tomorrow's talent
    - Developing talent
    - Shaping the organization
    - Fostering communication
    - Designing reward systems
- The *strategy architect* knows how to make the right change happen by:
    - Sustaining strategic agility
    - Engaging customers
- The *business ally* contributes to the success of the organization by:
    - Serving the value chain
    - Interpreting social context
    - Articulating propositions
    - Leveraging business technology
- The *operational executor* administers the day-to-day work of managing people inside an organization by:
    - Implementing workplace policies
    - Advanced HR technology

The Office of Personnel Management (1999a, 1999b, 2000a) conducted a special study, "HR: An Occupation in Transition," and as a result of its research, developed HR competency roles drawn from the work of the National Academy of Public Administration, the International Personnel Management Association for Human Resources, and the Office of Personnel Management's Personnel Resources and Development Center. These are the HR competency roles:

- *Strategic partner.* Serves as a partner with management, sharing accountability with line management for organizational results. The HR professional works with management to analyze and devise solutions to organizational problems and is involved in strategic planning and aligning HR with the organization's mission and strategic goals.
- *Leader.* Ensures that merit-system principles are adhered to, along with other issues of ethics and integrity, while serving as a champion

for diversity. In addition, balances the need for employee satisfaction with organizational goals.

- *Employee champion.* Serves as a voice for employee concerns and deals with employee problems. Ensures fair and equitable treatment for employees and represents employee concerns and issues to management.
- *Technical expert.* Possesses a high level of HR knowledge and the ability to strengthen HR programs to better meet organizational goals.
- *Change consultant.* Serves as a catalyst for change in the organization by helping the organization see the need for change, providing training, installing new information systems, and adjusting compensation strategies to meet changing job requirements.

Human Resources Outsourcing

Another change in human resources management is the increasing use of human resources outsourcing (HRO, 2007; Coggburn, 2007; U.S. Government Accountability Office, 2004a; Rainey, 2005). Federal agencies, state and local governments, and many nonprofits often find it advantageous to outsource some or all of their HRM responsibilities. Many smaller organizations outsource services such as payroll and benefits, and in fact, a variety of HRM activities can be outsourced. The journal *HRO Today* provides a resource guide with almost fifteen hundred providers in a number of service categories. HRM services that can be outsourced include these:

- *Benefits consulting services:* Benefits program design, cost containment, enrollment, actuarial analysis, and full-service administration. Other areas are health care strategy and plans, retirement plan design, life insurance, long-term and disability selection of plan providers and administrators, and assessment of employee behavior and benchmarking.
- *Payroll software and services:* Payroll processing, withholding, and benefits accrual services.
- *Health benefits services:* The administration and management of health care plans that may include consumer-driven health care plans, health maintenance organization plans, preferred provider organization plans, point-of-service plans, health savings accounts, fee-for-service plans, and wellness programs.

- *Recruiting, staffing, and search services:* The provision of online, recruitment technology, search, temporary staffing, and full-service recruitment process outsourcing.
- *Relocation services for employees moving from one community to another:* Relocation firms typically make their money though commissions from home sales and moves.
- *Screening and workplace security services:* Drug testing, background screening for applicants and existing employees, academic verification, resident work eligibility, employment history, and workplace security functions.
- *Human resources information systems and Web-based services:* The provision of HR services through human resources information systems and Web-based services.
- *Incentive services:* Developing employee recognition programs, measuring return on investment of such programs, providing technology support for incentive programs, and purchasing gift certificates and gift baskets for employees.
- *Information technology services:* Application development, architecture consulting, business intelligence, content management, data security and warehousing, enterprise resource planning, e-procurement, system integration, technology infrastructure, and Web hosting and development services.
- *Professional employer organizations (PEOs) and administrative services organizations (ASOs):* Coemployment service, where employees are paid under the PEO's federal employer identification number and placed on the PEO's benefits program and workers' compensation policy. ASOs offer many of the same services as a PEO but under a non-coemployer relationship.
- *Enterprise HRO services:* Comprehensive HR functions such as benefits consulting and administration, employee recognition and incentives, human resources information systems and human resources information technology, payroll, recruiting and staffing, relocation, screening, training and development.

The public sector has been reluctant to pursue human resources outsourcing aggressively as unions do not approve of outsourcing when it means the termination of staff. Also, many HRO services are provided by employees working in other countries, meaning that jobs are transferred out of the United States and local communities.

Strategic Human Resources Management

Strategic planning is the process that enables public organizations to guide their future activities and the use of their available resources. It assists elected officials, funders, foundations, citizens, business partners, and public administrators in determining organizational purposes and objectives. The strategic planning process permits the external forces that affect the organization and the people in it to be identified. These forces may include workforce patterns, economic conditions, competition, regulation, social values, and technological developments. After the external factors are assessed, the internal strengths and weaknesses of the organization's incumbents must be identified. Factors to include in an internal assessment are current workforce skills, retirement patterns, demographic profiles, and employee capabilities.

The agency's vision, mission, and measurable goals and objectives drive the identification of future functional requirements, which in turn drive the analysis and elements of the workforce plan. The question to ask is, "What key functions need to be performed to move in the direction set out in the strategic plan?" This may include many current functions, in addition to forecasting important future functions and activities. This information can be used to forecast the organization's capabilities to confront its future opportunities and threats. The ultimate feasibility of strategic planning depends on the people who make it operational.

Agency leaders need to understand how their workplaces will be affected by impending changes and prepare accordingly. A number of reports alert public managers to the need to become proactive and develop a strategic HR plan:

- *The Case for Transforming Public-Sector Human Resources Management* (National Academy of Public Administration, 2000)
- *Federal Employee Retirements: Expected Increase Over the Next Five Years Illustrates Need for Workforce Planning* (U.S. General Accounting Office, 2001a)
- *Workforce Planning Resource Guide for Public Sector Human Resource Professionals* (International Personnel Management Association for Human Resources, 2002)
- *Human Capital: A Guide for Assessing Strategic Training and Development Efforts in the Federal Government* (U.S. General Accounting Office, 2004b)
- *Human Capital: Federal Workforce Challenges in the 21st Century* (U.S. General Accounting Office, 2007b)

I have already noted in this chapter a number of reports addressing the need for nonprofits to become proactive as well (Teegarden, 2004; Kunreuther, 2005; Adams, 2006; Hall, 2006a, 2006b; Halpern, 2006).

Human Resources Planning

Human resources planning, a critical component of strategic planning and SHRM, is the process of analyzing and identifying the need for and availability of human resources to meet the organization's objectives. In an effort to be proactive, the U.S. Office of Personnel Management (2005) developed a five-step workforce planning model:

> *Step 1: Strategic direction.* This involves linking the workforce planning process with the agency's strategic plan, annual performance and business plan, and work activities required to carry out long- and short-term goals and objectives.
>
> *Step 2: Analyze the workforce, identify skills gaps, and conduct workforce analysis.* This involves determining what the current workforce resources are and how they will evolve through turnover; developing specifications for the kinds, numbers, and locations of workers and managers needed to accomplish the agency's strategic requirements; and determining what gaps exist between the current and projected workforce needs.
>
> *Step 3: Develop an action plan.* This involves the identification of strategies to close gaps, plans to implement the strategies, and measures for assessing strategic progress. These strategies could include recruiting, training and retraining, restructuring organizations, contracting out, succession planning, and technological upgrades.
>
> *Step 4: Implement the action plan.* This involves ensuring that human and fiscal resources are in place; roles are understood; and the necessary communication, marketing, and coordination are occurring to execute the plan and achieve the strategic objectives.
>
> *Step 5: Monitor, evaluate, and revise.* This involves monitoring progress against milestones, assessing for continuous improvements, and adjusting the plan to make course corrections and address new issues.

Anticipating Future Needs

Forecasting is used to assess past trends, evaluate the existing situation, and project future events. Forecasting and planning are complementary in that forecasts identify expectations, while plans establish concrete goals and objectives. Forecasting has become increasingly important as a large segment of the public workforce is inching toward retirement. Agencies must consider how to allocate people to jobs over long periods and try to anticipate expansions or reductions in programs or other changes that may affect the organization. Based on these analyses, plans can be made for the recruitment and selection of new employees, the shifting of employees to different programs or units, or the retraining of incumbent employees.

A demand forecast anticipates the workforce that will be needed to accomplish future functional requirements and carry out the mission of the organization. In this step, a visionary staffing assessment against future functional requirements is conducted. The result is a forecast of the type of competencies, numbers, and locations of employees needed in the future. An important part of the demand forecast is examining not only what work the agency will do in the future, but how that work will be performed. Some things to consider include the following:

- How will jobs and workload change as a result of technological advancements and economic, social, and political conditions?
- What are the consequences or results of these changes?
- What will the reporting relationships be?
- How will divisions, work units, and jobs be designed?
- How will work flow into each part of the organization?

Once these questions have been answered, the next step is to identify the competencies employees will need to carry out that work. The set of competencies provides management and staff with a common understanding of the skills and behaviors that are important to the agency. Competencies play a key role in decisions on recruiting, employee development, personal development, and performance management.

Forecasting HR requirements involves determining the number and types of employees needed by skill level. First, agencies need to audit the skills of incumbent employees and determine their capabilities and weaknesses. Positions must also be audited. In most organizations, there are likely to be jobs that are vulnerable because technology or reengineering is ready to replace them. Job analyses must be conducted to provide information on existing jobs. The basic requirements of a job should be defined and converted to job specifications that specify the minimum KSAOCs necessary for effective performance. The skill requirements of positions do change, so any changes that occur must be monitored and reflected in the job specifications.

It is not enough to monitor changes in positions; organizations must also keep abreast of the skills that their employees possess. Human resources planning uses data inventories to integrate the planning and utilization functions of SHRM. Data inventories compile summary information, such as the characteristics of employees, the distribution of employees by position, and employees' performance and career objectives. Specific data that are typically catalogued are age, education, career path, current work skills, work experience, aspirations, performance evaluations, years with the organization, and jobs for which one is qualified. Expected vacancies due to retirement, promotion, transfer, sick leave, relocation, or termination are also tracked. Using a computerized human resource information system (HRIS) to compile these data makes the retrieval of information readily available for forecasting workforce needs.

Information technology enables organizations to maintain and retrieve information and records with greater accuracy and ease than older methods. An HRIS provides current and accurate data for decision making and broader applications, such as producing reports, forecasting HR needs, strategic planning, career and promotion planning, and evaluating HR policies and practices. Having accessible data enables HR planning and managerial decision making to be based to a greater degree on information rather than perceptions. Common applications of HRISs include maintaining employee records, overseeing payroll and benefits activities, handling absence and vacation records, and administering recruitment and training programs, employee communications, and affirmative action tracking.

Many agencies use networks as part of their HRIS. Many agencies allow employees to read current job openings and apply for positions online. They also provide information on employee benefits, training opportunities, and occupational safety and health information.

Developing an HRIS can be expensive; therefore, it is important that department managers and users, HRM professionals, and technology experts jointly develop it and plan for its implementation. Some factors that should be considered when developing an HRIS are the anticipated initial costs and annual maintenance costs, the ability to upgrade the system, the availability of relevant software packages for users, compatibility with current information technology systems in place, the availability of technical support to maintain the system, the ability to customize the system for different information, the time required to implement the system, and the amount of training required for users to become proficient.

When forecasting the availability of human resources, agencies need to consider both the internal and external supply of qualified candidates. The internal supply of candidates is influenced by training and development and by transfer, promotion, and retirement policies. Assessing incumbent staff competencies is crucial. An assessment of employees' competency levels will provide information for determining the number of those available for and capable of fulfilling future functional requirements. It will also provide salient information as to what recruitment, training, and other strategies need to be deployed to address workforce gaps and surpluses.

A succession analysis should be prepared that forecasts the supply of people for certain positions. Succession plans should be used to identify potential personnel changes, select backup candidates, and keep track of attrition. The external supply of candidates is also influenced by a variety of factors, including developments in technology, the actions of competing employers, geographical location, and government regulations.

SHRM attempts to match the available supply of labor with the forecast demand in the light of the organization's strategic plan. A gap analysis is the process of comparing the workforce demand forecast with the workforce supply projection. The expected result is the identification of gaps and surpluses in staffing levels and competencies needed to carry out future functional requirements. A gap occurs when the projected supply is less than the forecast demand. It indicates a future shortage of needed employees. Strategies such as recruitment, training, and succession planning will need to be developed and implemented.

The Community Association for Rehabilitation, a Palo Alto, California, charity that helps people with disabilities, spent one year developing a plan that includes how to manage operations in an emergency, as well as policies on how to search for a new leader when its executive director retires (Hall, 2006a, 2006b). Another nonprofit, Bethel New Life, a religious group that provides low-cost housing and other services in Chicago, developed a two-year succession plan that addressed practices that the agency needed to revise. It also surveyed staff and board members to determine what skills and attributes their new leader should have, hired a consultant to help the search, and appointed a committee of board members to work with the new executive director for the first six months on the job (Hall, 2006b).

When Santa Fe, New Mexico, looked for police officers to fill existing vacancies, it advertised across the United States. The city embarked on a nationwide advertising campaign and offered a ten thousand dollar bonus to experienced officers who transferred to Santa Fe's police force (Auslander, 2007).

A surplus occurs when the projected supply is greater than forecast demand. This indicates future excess in some categories of employees that may also require taking action. The surplus data may represent occupations or skill sets that will not be needed in the future or at least not to the same degree. Retraining, transfers, or separation incentives may need to be implemented to address surplus situations.

If necessary skills do not exist in the workforce, employees need to be trained in the new skills, or external recruitment must be used to bring those skills to the organization. The employer must identify where employees with those skills are likely to be found and develop recruitment strategies.

In the mid-1990s, the Commonwealth of Pennsylvania studied the age patterns among its employees to see what skills the state would lose over the next five to ten years. It then began targeting recruitment toward acquiring those skills. It conducted direct recruiting campaigns to hire employees with accounting, budgeting, personnel administration, and computer technology skills. Those candidates were placed in special state-run classes designed to develop their expertise. Six percent of the state workforce (six thousand people, actually 6,712) retired in 2007—among them, social workers, troopers, secretaries, liquor store clerks, park rangers, correction officers, and attorneys. By 2012, another 41 percent of salaried employees under the governor's jurisdiction will be eligible to retire as well. The plan was for vacancies caused by retirements to be filled through promotions and lower-level vacancies to be filled mostly by external applicants. There were opportunities for recent college graduates and entry-level people interested in working for the state (Helton & Jackson, 2007; Mauriello, 2007).

Organizations facing a worker shortage may be able to postpone the retirement of or recruit older workers. In an effort to retain the knowledge base of an agency or to better serve its clients, some organizations have developed creative ways to encourage retirement-eligible employees to remain on the job. They have improved training opportunities and technology to impart different skills, divided full-time positions into part-time work, and offered telecommuting as an option. Some organizations have phased retirement plans that permit employees to reduce their hours or responsibilities in order to ease into retirement. This provides an opportunity

In an effort to retain the knowledge base of an agency or to better serve its clients, some organizations have developed creative ways to encourage retirement-eligible employees to remain on the job.

for experienced workers to mentor younger employees and transfer institutional knowledge. In this way, organizations continue to gain benefits from soon-to-be-retiring workers' skills and expertise. Unless an organization has a mechanism in place to preserve worker knowledge, its loss can have a negative effect on the organization. Experienced workers often possess valuable knowledge and understand the cultural nuances of organizations. SHRM should follow these trends and anticipate how they may affect their agencies.

An example of poor SHRM took place in 2007 in Atlanta, Georgia, at Grady Memorial Hospital, Georgia's largest public hospital. In an attempt to halt its declining revenue and increased expenses, it offered early retirement to 562 employees: 422 employees took it, twice as many as anticipated. One-third of the departing employees were nurses, nursing assistants, clerks, and other workers in patient care. Another 13 percent came from laboratories and radiology. "The impact of the buyout goes beyond the number of jobs involved," said Curtis Lewis, chief of Grady's medical staff. "In a cash-strapped hospital with aging equipment and a largely indigent patient population, people learn to make things work and maximize resources. . . . In addition, the senior staff developed long-term relationships. Those are the things you lose" (White, 2007, p. D11).

Strategies that can be implemented to halt the retirement of productive employees are offering part-time work with or without benefits (depending on the employee's need), training employees to develop new skills, transferring employees to different jobs with reduced pay and responsibilities, and addressing any age-bias issues that may exist in the agency. Organizations that cannot halt the retirement of productive employees need to set up a system for transferring knowledge to younger employees.

Implementing Strategic Human Resources Management

HRM departments seeking to implement an SHRM system must expand their scope of activities beyond their traditional tasks and functions and enter partnerships with managers and employees. Working together provides managers and employees with a better understanding of HRM issues, and

HRM staff become better informed about the needs of the employees and departments.

SHRM is a process that must be implemented throughout the organization in such a way that it becomes the template for organizational change and innovation. The Partnership for Public Service (2006) has developed a process overview for federal executives, but its prescriptions apply to managers in all organizations:

◆ ◆ ◆

- *Build a planning project team.* When assembling a planning team, include HR professionals as well as agency leaders. Agency leaders provide sponsorship for the planning process and strategic directions for the plan, while HR professionals bring other expertise. The process must be collaborative, and those charged with responsibility for the plan must be given the necessary time and resources. The planning project team should identify the approach taken, the tasks associated with implementing those tasks, and time frames in which to complete them. Accountability among team members is important.
- *Review relevant inputs.* Once the planning team is in place, collect and analyze information about the workforce and review relevant documents. The team should also review agency and department strategic plans; existing human capital plans; retirement, attrition, and hiring projections; staffing and recruitment plans; external stakeholder issues and concerns; employee views; and other successful models of SHRM.
- *Engage managers.* Senior managers should be engaged while developing the plan. There should be a cross-section of senior managers representing the full range of major functions. Managers typically are most aware of the challenges to a unit's mission and its workforce.
- *Assess challenges and devise solutions.* The planning team should collaborate to identify challenges and develop solutions. Quantitative data about the workforce should be reviewed, including information about retirement, attrition, and hiring projections; staffing plans; and employee feedback. Qualitative information that should be considered includes information about strategic goals and priorities, the workforce needed to achieve those goals, and potential challenges to building or maintaining the workforce.
- *Draft the plan.* Before writing the plan, prepare a comprehensive outline and solicit feedback from agency leaders and managers, employees, and external stakeholders. The plan should also set out a time line for action,

the tactics to be used, the tasks associated with each change initiative, time frames for completion, those responsible for each item, and the metrics for assessing success.

Evaluating the Effectiveness of Strategic Human Resources Management

To evaluate the effectiveness of SHRM, SHRM audits and HR benchmarking and return on investment analysis can be used.

SHRM Audit

One method used to assess SHRM effectiveness is an HRM audit, an in-depth analysis that evaluates the current state of SHRM in an organization. The audit identifies areas of strengths and weaknesses and where improvements are needed. During the audit, current practices, policies, and procedures are reviewed. Many audits also include benchmarking against organizations of similar size or industry. A number of areas are typically included in an audit:

- Legal compliance (Equal Employment Opportunity Act, Occupational Safety and Health Act, Fair Labor Standards Act, Employment Retirement Income Security Act, Family and Medical Leave Act, privacy)
- Current job descriptions and specifications
- Valid recruiting and selection procedures
- Compensation and pay equity and benefits
- Employee relations
- Absenteeism and turnover control measures
- Training and development activities
- Performance management systems
- Policies and procedures/employee handbook
- Terminations
- Health, safety, and security issues

HR Benchmarking and Return on Investment

Human resource management departments, like other units, are being asked to demonstrate their value to public and nonprofit organizations.

Human resource audits and HRIS are being used with greater frequency to obtain information on HR performance. Once information on performance has been gathered, it must be compared to a standard. One method of assessing HR effectiveness is comparing specific measures of performance against data on those measures in other organizations known for their best practices.

Employee costs in public and nonprofit organizations can be anywhere from 50 to 80 percent of expenses; therefore, measuring the return on investment (ROI) in human capital is necessary to show the impact and value of SHRM. According to Fitz-enz (2000, p. 3), "Management needs a system of metrics that describe and predict the cost and productivity curves of its workforce." Quantitative measures focus on cost, capacity, and time, whereas qualitative measures focus on more intangible values such as human reactions. ROI calculations are used to show the value of expenditures for HR activities. Human resource activities and programs that have been subject to measurement include training programs, diversity programs, wellness and fitness initiatives, safety and health programs, skill-based and knowledge-based compensation, performance improvement programs, education programs, organizational development initiatives, change initiatives, career development programs, recruiting systems, and technology implementation (Phillips & Phillips, 2002).

Despite the belief that only for-profit organizations can evaluate ROI programs, public and nonprofit agencies can use measures of performance such as productivity, quality, time improvements, and cost savings through efficiency enhancements as well as qualitative measures.

Problems and Implications of Strategic Human Resources Management

Research demonstrates the importance of SHRM. Why then is HRM often considered a secondary support function rather than a driver of an organization's future? A number of reasons may exist. There are also financial costs associated with SHRM. Some public organizations may be reluctant to spend additional resources on employees, fearing a backlash from its elected officials and citizens. In some instances, leaders may want a greater integration of the HRM function with organizational strategy but often do not understand just what that means. Human resources management professionals may not have the flexibility to initiate new programs or suggest new organizational structures. This is especially true when organizational change issues may challenge existing rules and regulations as well as embedded standard operating procedures.

The Colorado Municipal League surveyed its members on succession planning and found that the respondents believed it was a critical issue and also a challenge (Reester & Braaten, 2006). When asked how well their organization was handling succession planning for executive levels of leadership, 66 percent responded poor or fair. Six primary factors were identified in the inability to establish a quality succession planning program:

- Bigger priorities on the horizon every day.
- Easier to deal with today than build your team for tomorrow.
- Lack of money to support a program.
- Lack of knowledge of the issue among career professionals and elected officials.
- Organizational streamlining has created a time-constrained atmosphere where there is little time to invest in professional development.
- Compensation and benefits are lagging and likely successors will seek the nonprofit or private sector [p. 3].

Based on these few examples, it appears that local governments understand the need for succession planning, but not all have the time, resources, or support to implement it. The Government Accountability Office identified the following reasons that SHRM planning often fails:

- Lack of on-going support and interest from leadership
- Succession planning is not seen as a priority
- Funding is not sufficient
- Recruitment and retention, particularly in critical management areas, is perceived to be sufficient to meet organizational needs
- Resistance from middle managers who already feel overburdened with other "initiatives" not central to their job responsibilities
- Employee suspicion toward unsure program goals, poor communication and organization is too small to sustain a full-scale program [Flynn, 2006, p. 6].

Another reason that SHRM is neglected is that often HRM professionals lack the capabilities and skills necessary to move HRM to a more proactive role. To be strategic partners, HRM departments must possess high levels of professional and business knowledge. They need to establish links to others in the organization who are working to improve performance and be able to demonstrate on a continuing basis how HRM activities contribute to the success and effectiveness of the organization. Unfortunately, many HRM departments have spent their time ensuring compliance with rules and regulations, so they lack the skills and competencies to act as a strategic partner.

Organizational change also requires higher levels of coordination across functions and departments, and employees and management must be committed to continuous improvement. There must be greater interdepartmental cooperation. Trust and open communication across the organization will have to be developed. Organizations must encourage creativity and recognize such creativity through their reward systems. Change requires fairness, openness, and empowerment, but these may be contrary to an organization's existing culture and may require several incremental steps to achieve.

Some employees may be reluctant to change. Over the years, they may have acquired proficiency in the performance of their jobs. Changing their routines and standards of performance, requiring them to learn new skills, or obliging them to work with unfamiliar persons may be unsettling. Employees unwilling or unable to make the transition may choose to resign; some may even attempt to sabotage new initiatives.

Sometimes the political realities of public organizations undermine change. Often elected officials and appointed officials have a short-term perspective regarding how they want agencies to operate. Changes in policies and procedures take time to implement and are often not immediately apparent. Elected officials may also be predisposed to favor short-term budget considerations over long-term planning. In the public sector, support for top administrators may change quickly and often capriciously, and in the nonprofit sector, the board of directors may be reluctant to embrace change. To transform an organization requires chief executive and top administrative support, managerial accountability, fundamental changes in HRM practices, employee involvement, and changes in agency culture.

Conclusion

The future viability of an organization and its HR capabilities are interrelated and must be considered together. Human resources management must be vertically integrated with strategic planning and horizontally integrated with other HR functions such as training and development, compensation and benefits, recruitment and selection, labor relations, and the evaluation of the HR planning process to allow adjustments to be made to confront rapidly changing environmental conditions. Strategic human resources management guides management in identifying and implementing the appropriate HR learning activities for resolving organizational problems or adapting to meet new opportunities.

Strategic human resources management determines the HR needs of the agency and ensures that qualified personnel are recruited and developed to meet organizational needs. Should there be a shift in demand for services, agencies must know whether there are potential employees with the requisite skills available to provide these services and whether the agency's finances can afford the costs associated with additional compensation and benefits. Forecasting an agency's HR supply reveals the characteristics of its internal supply of labor; it also helps to assess the productivity of incumbent employees, implement succession planning and salary planning, and identify areas where external recruitment or training and development are necessary.

Training and development are essential to the effective use of an organization's human resources and an integral part of its planning. Training is used to remedy immediate needs, while development is concerned with long-term objectives and the ability to cope with change. Training and development should be viewed as a continuous process. There will always be new employees, new positions, new problems, changes in technology, and changes in the external and internal environments that require a planned approach to training and development and its integration with other HRM functions. Training and development influence recruitment, selection, career planning, and the compatibility between agency goals and employee aspirations. Training and development programs must be integrated to complement the organization's mission and operations. Organizations should use employees wisely with respect to the strategic needs of the organization.

Turnover, including retirements, must be anticipated and planned for. Human resources management departments must track the skills of incumbent employees and keep skill inventories. Recruitment and training must be tied to the organization's mission. The availability and stability of financial support; the advancement of technological changes, legal regulations, and social and cultural changes; and the evolution of HR requirements must be considered when developing strategic plans.

At one time, organizations hired employees to fit the characteristics of a particular job. Now it is important for organizations to select employees who fit the characteristics not only of the position but also of the organization. Human resources management professionals must serve as internal consultants, working with managers to assess HR needs. Together they must project the demand for services, develop new resources, and determine the appropriate reallocation of services. The SHRM process, once established, can be used to anticipate and prepare for major changes affecting the workplace.

Effective strategic human capital management approaches serve as the foundation of any serious HRM initiative. They must be at the center of efforts to transform the cultures of agencies so that they become results oriented and externally focused. To facilitate these changes, HRM personnel and department managers must acquire new competencies to be able to deliver HRM services and shift toward a more consultative role for HR staff.

Like service industries and new economy companies, public and nonprofit organizations are driven by the knowledge and skills their employees possess. It is shortsighted for elected officials, board members, funders, executives, and other agency leaders to dismiss the importance of SHRM. As important, organizations must reinforce the importance of human capital and the contribution that knowledge management makes to the effective delivery of services. Human resource management departments must have the knowledge, skills, and authority to identify and facilitate changes.

Exercise 2.1: Nature Conservancy's Leader Abruptly Steps Down

One morning in October 2007, Steven J. McCormick, the president of the Nature Conservancy, sent an e-mail to its thirty-five hundred workers notifying them that he had resigned from the agency and his leave would begin immediately. McCormick had worked for the organization for thirty years and had been the president since 2001. In 2006, he earned $375,000. The Nature Conservancy is the largest environmental-conservation charity in the United States and ranked twentieth on the *Chronicle of Philanthropy*'s most recent list of the charities that raise the most money from private sources.

Stephanie Meeks, the chief operating officer, will work as interim president while the organization searches for a permanent successor. McCormick agreed to work with the organization for the next year as a paid adviser to help it through the transition.

Questions

1. What steps can agencies take to make sure they have a succession plan in place?
2. Do you think it is in the best interest of the Nature Conservancy to have McCormick stay on as a paid adviser to help the agency through the transition? Explain your reasoning.

Source: Panepento (2007b).

Exercise 2.2: Travis County, Texas, Facing a Brain Drain

A quarter of Texas's Travis County's four thousand employees are eligible to retire within five years. Many of the county's department heads and managers can retire with full benefits next year. Christian Smith, the county's chief budget and planning officer, informed the *Austin American-Statesman* that most county departments lack succession plans and management mentoring programs.

Travis County had no successor when Mike Trimble, head of the Criminal Justice Planning Department, retired two years ago. The county is still looking for his replacement while discussions of a new courthouse and possible jail expansion continue.

Questions

1. Where do the responsibilities fall in addressing the impending retirements?
2. What steps should Travis County implement to be better prepared for the retirement of department heads and managers, and the four thousand employees eligible to retire within five years?

Source: Toohey (2008).

Chapter Questions

1. Assume the role of the director of human resources management for a public or nonprofit agency you are familiar with. Prepare a written outline about why HRM planning must be a process flowing from the organization's strategic plan. Be prepared to present your outline to the class.
2. In a small group, compare and contrast similarities and differences in how employees are treated among the organizations you work for or have worked for in the past. What factors appear to influence how an organization perceives the value of its employees?
3. Assume that as a result of HRM planning, you discover a shortage of direct service workers but a surplus of administrative workers. Discuss possible actions to address the imbalance, and explain why they must be approached carefully.

Online Activity

1. Go to the U.S. Government Accountability Office (Web site) and review two different reports on human capital. Develop a written proposal for strategies that should be implemented by the agency you work for, or one you have worked for in the past.

CHAPTER THREE

THE LEGAL ENVIRONMENT OF HUMAN RESOURCES MANAGEMENT

After you have read this chapter, you should be able to:

- Understand the federal laws related to equal employment opportunity and their implications for strategic human resources management
- Understand the difference between equal employment opportunity and affirmative action
- Understand the religious exemption from Title VII protections provided to some nonprofit organizations
- Understand the differences between disparate treatment and disparate impact theories of employment discrimination
- Understand the constitutional protections provided to public employees
- Understand the concept of employment at will

The legal environment has a significant influence on public and nonprofit human resources management (HRM). All organizations—public, nonprofit, and private for-profit—must comply with equal employment opportunity laws. Equal employment opportunity has implications for all aspects of strategic human resources management (SHRM): human resources (HR) planning, recruitment and selection, training and career development, compensation and benefits, and performance evaluation to labor-management relations. Public employees enjoy constitutional protections that are not available to nonprofit or private for-profit employees.

This chapter explains the federal legal environment that governs equal employment opportunity, the constitutional rights relevant to public sector employees, and employment at will. Administrators must understand the laws that are important to HRM. These laws are designed to eradicate discrimination in the workplace for non-job-related or non-performance-related reasons. However, many employers do not understand the laws, misapply them, or choose to ignore them. Employers must consider these laws when developing employment policies and practices.

Federal Equal Employment Opportunity Laws

This section explains the federal laws governing equal employment opportunity. It is recommended, however, that you check with your state and local governments' fair employment practice agencies for additional laws and regulations that may have an impact on the equal employment opportunity practices of your agency.

Civil Rights Acts of 1866 and 1871

The Civil Rights Act of 1866, based on the Thirteenth Amendment to the U.S. Constitution, prohibits racial discrimination in the making and enforcement of contracts, which includes hiring and promotion decisions. Nonprofit and private employers, unions, and employment agencies fall under its coverage.

The Civil Rights Act of 1871 covers state and local governments. Based on the Fourteenth Amendment, it prohibits the deprivation of equal employment rights under state laws. It does not apply to private businesses or federal agencies unless there is state involvement in the employment practices in question.

Title VII of the Civil Rights Act of 1964

The Civil Rights Act of 1964, signed by President Lyndon Johnson, covers all employers with fifteen or more employees except private clubs, religious organizations, and places of employment connected to an Indian reservation.

Title VII of the act deals specifically with discrimination in employment: it prohibits discrimination based on race, color, religion, sex, or national origin. The passage of this law was not without controversy. Many politicians (mostly in the South) thought that a federal law forbidding discrimination would usurp states' rights. Congressman Howard Smith of Virginia tried to defeat the bill by including sex as one of the protected classifications. He hoped that the insertion of sex would render the bill foolish and lead to its defeat. The act passed with the inclusion of sex, and today litigation concerning sex discrimination is common.

The Civil Rights Act of 1964 created the U.S. Equal Employment Opportunity Commission (EEOC) to investigate complaints and try to resolve disputes through conciliation. The act was amended in 1972 by the Equal Employment Opportunity Act, which extended its coverage to state and local governments and to educational institutions. At this time, the EEOC was granted enforcement powers to bring action against organizations in the courts if necessary to force compliance with Title VII.

The EEOC requires that most organizations submit annual EEO forms, identifying the demographic breakdown of their employees. Data from these forms are used to identify possible patterns of discrimination in particular organizations or segments of the workforce. The EEOC may then take legal action against an organization on the basis of these data.

Title VII does not prohibit discrimination based on seniority systems, veterans' preference rights, national security reasons, or job qualifications based on test scores, background, or experience, even when the use of such practices may correlate with discrimination based on race, sex, color, religion, or national origin. Section 703(e)(1) of Title VII permits an employer to discriminate on religion, sex, or national origin in instances where religion, sex, or national origin is a bona-fide occupational qualification (BFOQ) reasonably necessary to the normal operation of that particular business or enterprise. For example, a BFOQ that excludes one group (for example, males or females) from an employment opportunity is permissible if the employer can argue that the essence of the business requires the exclusion, that is, when business would be significantly affected by not employing members of one group exclusively. One case that dealt with this issue was *United Automobile Workers* v. *Johnson Controls* (1991). Johnson Controls is a car battery manufacturer that excluded fertile women from jobs where there was high exposure to lead. Fertile men were not automatically excluded and were given a choice as to whether they wanted to risk their reproductive health. The company argued that this policy falls within the BFOQ exception to Title VII. In its 1991 decision, the U.S. Supreme Court disagreed. The Court found that the policy was discriminatory since only women employees were affected by the policy:

> Respondent's fetal protection policy explicitly discriminates against women on the basis of their sex. The policy excludes women with childbearing capacity from lead-exposed jobs and so creates a facial classification based on gender. . . . Despite evidence in the record about the debilitating effect of lead exposure on the male reproductive system, Johnson Controls is concerned only with the harms that may befall the unborn offspring of its female employees.

The Court stated that women as capable of doing their jobs as their male counterparts may not be forced to choose between having a child and having a job.

In general, the position of the courts regarding BFOQs clearly favors judgments about the performance, abilities, or potential of specific individuals rather than discrimination by class or categories. The Supreme Court has said that the BFOQ exception to Title VII is a narrow one, limited to policies that are directly related to a worker's ability to do the job. The burden of proof is on the employer to justify any BFOQ claim.

For most public sector jobs, it is very difficult to substantiate the necessity of gender, race, religion, national origin, age, or disability as a BFOQ. Nevertheless, there are some instances where a BFOQ case can be made. In *Dothard* v. *Rawlinson* (1977), the state of Alabama was permitted to exclude females from being guards in an all-male maximum-security prison where 20 percent of the prisoners were sex offenders. In 1996, the U.S. Court of Appeals at Philadelphia ruled in *Healey* v. *Southwood Psychiatric Hospital* (1996) that gender can be considered a BFOQ for the purposes of staffing a psychiatrist hospital unit that treats emotionally disturbed and sexually abused children. A female child care worker was assigned to work the night shift because the hospital needed a balance of men and women to provide therapeutic care to female and male patients who might want to talk with a staff member of their own sex. The court held that Title VII excuses discrimination that is justified as a BFOQ when it is reasonably necessary to the normal operation of business. The essence of the hospital's business requires consideration of gender in staffing decisions because if there are not members

For most public sector jobs, it is very difficult to substantiate the necessity of gender, race, religion, national origin, age, or disability as a bona-fide occupational qualification.

of both sexes on a shift, the hospital's ability to provide care to its patients is impeded.

The question of whether race, religion, national origin, color, and sex constitute BFOQs arises often in the nonprofit sector. Is gender a legitimate BFOQ for an executive director position at a rape and sexual abuse center? Can a qualified male perform the administrative and leadership tasks, or does the executive director need to be a female? Would race be a BFOQ for a leadership position in a community-based nonprofit that provides services to racial minorities? If a BFOQ is challenged, the burden is on the employer to justify any claim.

Laws That Address Religious Discrimination

Under Section 701(j) of Title VII, employers are obligated to accommodate their employees' or prospective employees' religious practices. Failure to make accommodation is unlawful unless an employer can demonstrate that it cannot reasonably accommodate the employee because of undue hardship in the conduct of its business. In *Trans World Airlines, Inc.* v. *Hardison* (1977), the Supreme Court ruled that the employer and union need not violate a seniority provision of a valid collective bargaining agreement, the employer has no obligation to impose undesirable shifts on nonreligious employees, and the employer has no obligation to call in substitute workers if such accommodation would require more than de minimis cost.

Nonprofit organizations that provide secular services but are affiliated with and governed by religious institutions are exempt from the law under Section 702 of the Civil Rights Act of 1964, which states: "This title shall not apply to an employer with respect to the employment of aliens outside any State, or to a religious corporation, association, educational institution, or society with respect to the employment of individuals of a particular religion to perform work connected with the carrying on by such corporation, association, educational institution, or society of its activities."

Educational institutions such as universities, schools, or other institutions of learning are also exempt from the law. Section 703(e)(2) of the Civil Rights Act of 1964 states:

> It shall not be an unlawful employment practice for a school, college, university, or other educational institution or institution of learning to hire and employ employees of a particular religion if such school, college, university, or other educational institution or institution of learning is, in whole or in substantial part, owned, supported,

> controlled, or managed by a particular religion or by a particular religious corporation, association, or society, or if the curriculum of such school, college, university, or other educational institution of learning is directed toward the propagation of a particular religion.

In *Corporation of the Bishop of the Church of Jesus Christ of Latter Day Saints* v. *Amos* (1987), the Supreme Court upheld the right of the Mormon Church to terminate a building engineer who had worked at its nonprofit gymnasium for sixteen years because he failed to maintain his qualification for church membership. The Court claimed that the decision to terminate was based on religion by the religious organization and thus exempted from the Title VII prohibition against religious discrimination. The Section 703(e)(2) exemption is broad and is not limited to the religious activities of the institution.

Another change with an impact on how one manages religious diversity is the introduction of faith-based initiatives. President George W. Bush signed Executive Orders 13198 and 13199 in January 2001 and Executive Orders 13279 and 13280 in December 2002 requiring executive branch agencies to identify and remove internal bureaucratic barriers that have impeded greater participation in federal programs by faith-based organizations. The executive orders permit religious or faith-based organizations to receive federal funds for use in providing social services. Under the executive orders, these organizations have a right to use religious criteria in the selection, termination, and discipline of employees. Faith-based service providers are permitted to require applicants to be a member of a particular denomination in hiring personnel, though they are still prohibited from discriminating on the basis of race, gender, disability, or national origin.

Pregnancy Discrimination Act of 1978

The Pregnancy Discrimination Act prohibits employment practices that discriminate on the basis of pregnancy, childbirth, or related medical conditions. A woman is protected from being fired or refused a job or promotion because she is pregnant. She also cannot be forced to take a leave of absence as long as she is able to work.

Under the law, employers are obligated to treat pregnancy like any other disability. For example, if other employees on disability leave are entitled to return to their jobs when they are able to work again, so should women who have been unable to work due to pregnancy.

The Pregnancy Discrimination Act requires that employers provide full benefits coverage for pregnancy. A woman unable to work for pregnancy-related reasons is entitled to disability benefits or sick leave on the same basis as other employees unable to work for other medical reasons.

States may pass their own laws requiring additional benefits for pregnant employees beyond the scope of the federal law. The Supreme Court upheld a California law that required employers to provide up to four months' unpaid pregnancy disability leave with guaranteed reinstatement, even though disabled males were not entitled to the same benefit (*California Federal Savings & Loan Association* v. *Guerra*, 1987).

Age Discrimination in Employment Act of 1967

The Age Discrimination in Employment Act (ADEA) was enacted by Congress in 1967 to prohibit discrimination in employment because of age in matters pertaining to selection, job retention, compensation, and other terms and conditions of employment. Congress intended to promote the employment of older persons based on their ability rather than age and to prohibit arbitrary age discrimination in employment. In 1974, the ADEA was amended to extend coverage to state and local government employees, as well as most federal employees.

The ADEA at that time protected workers between the ages of forty and sixty-five. Employers were granted four exemptions to the act: (1) where age is a BFOQ reasonably necessary to normal operation of a particular business; (2) where differentiation is based on reasonable factors other than age; (3) to observe the terms of a bona-fide seniority system or a bona-fide insurance plan, with the qualification that no seniority system or benefit plan may require or permit the involuntary retirement of who is covered by ADEA; and (4) where an employee is discharged or disciplined for good cause.

The ADEA was amended in 1978 by raising the upper limit to seventy years of age; that limit was removed in 1987, meaning that compulsory retirement for most jobs is now illegal. The ADEA applies to employers with twenty or more employees, unions of twenty-five or more members, employment agencies, and federal, state, and local governments.

On April 1, 1996 the Supreme Court ruled in *O'Connor* v. *Consolidated Coin Caters Corporation* (1996) that an individual claiming age discrimination must show a logical connection between his or her age and his or her discharge, but there is no requirement to show that the replacement was under forty years old. Justice Antonin Scalia wrote that "the fact that one person in the protected class lost out to another person in the protected class is thus irrelevant, so long as he has lost out because of age."

In 2000, the Supreme Court ruled in *Kimmel* v. *Florida Board of Regents* that the Eleventh Amendment to the U.S. Constitution bars state employees from suing a state employer in federal court for violation of the ADEA. This ruling does not apply to local government employees or employees working for nonprofit agencies.

The U.S. Supreme Court decision *Smith* v. *City of Jackson* (2005) held that evidence of an employment practice that is neutral on its face but has a disparate impact on older workers could be used in establishing a prima facie case of age discrimination. Defense of an ADEA claim involves showing that factors other than age were determining considerations.

On June 19, 2008, the U.S. Supreme Court ruled in *Meacham* v. *Knolls Atomic Power Laboratory* (2008) the employer has the burden of proof in proving that a layoff or other action that adversely impacts older workers more than others was from "reasonable factors other than age."

American with Disabilities Act of 1990

In 1990, Congress passed the Americans with Disabilities Act (ADA). Title I of the ADA provides that qualified individuals with disabilities may not be discriminated against on the basis of disability in all aspects of the employment relationship, from the application stage through retirement. The law took effect on July 26, 1992, for organizations of twenty-five or more employees and on July 26, 1994, for organizations with fifteen to twenty-four employees. Employment practices covered by ADA include job application procedures, hiring, firing, advancement, compensation, training, and other terms and conditions and privileges of employment.

The ADA recognized the following categories of disabilities:

- Individuals with a physical or mental impairment that substantially limits one or more major life activities, for example, walking, seeing, hearing, or speaking. Examples of other physical and or mental impairments that might be considered disabilities are speech impediments, learning disabilities, AIDS, mental retardation, chronic mental illness, and epilepsy. To qualify as disabled and be protected by the ADA, a person must have substantial limitations on abilities that are "central to daily life," and not only to life in the workplace (*Toyota Motor Manufacturing Inc.* v. *Williams*, 2002).

- Having a record of such an impairment. This could include people who have recovered from a heart attack, cancer, back injuries, or mental illness.
- Being regarded as having an impairment. This would include individuals who are perceived as having a disability, such as individuals suspected of having the HIV virus.

Under the ADA, to be considered qualified, an individual must be able to perform the "essential functions of the position," meaning that the individual must satisfy the prerequisites for the position and be able to perform the essential functions of the job with or without reasonable accommodation.

Employers must provide the disabled with "reasonable accommodations" that do not place an undue hardship on the organization. *Undue hardship* is defined as an adjustment related to an employer's operation, financial resources, and facilities that requires significant difficulty or expense. Undue hardship and reasonable accommodation are to be determined on a case-by-case basis, taking into account such matters as the size of the employer, the number of employees responsible for a particular job or tasks, and the employer's ability to afford the accommodation. Accommodations may include interventions such as reassignment, part-time work, and flexible schedules, as well as modifications in equipment and the work environment, such as acquiring a special telephone headset or larger computer screen or moving a training workshop to a location accessible to wheelchairs.

In 2001, the U.S. Supreme Court, using the reasoning to that in *Kimmel*, ruled that the Eleventh Amendment to the U.S. Constitution bars state employees from suing their state employer for alleged violations of the ADA (*Board of Trustees of the University of Alabama* v. *Garrett*, 2001). This case, like the *Kimmel* decision, limits state employer liability and also limits congressional authority to implement antidiscrimination regulations in state government.

Immigration Reform and Control Act of 1986, as Revised in 1990

Under the Immigration Reform and Control Act, it is unlawful for a person or other entity to hire or continue to employ an alien knowing that the alien is unauthorized to work in the United States. It is not an unfair employment practice to prefer to select or recruit an individual who is a citizen of the United States instead of a noncitizen if the two individuals are equally qualified. Complaints of discrimination are processed in the Justice Department by the Office of Special Counsel for Unfair Immigration-Related Employment Practice.

Civil Rights Act of 1991

The Civil Rights Act of 1991 (CRA) was passed by Congress on November 7, 1991, and signed into law by President George H. W. Bush on November 21, 1991. The CRA provides additional remedies to protect against and deter unlawful discrimination and harassment in employment and to restore the strength of federal antidiscrimination laws that many felt had been weakened by several Supreme Court decisions.

The CRA amends five civil rights statutes: Title VII of the Civil Rights Act of 1964, the Americans with Disabilities Act of 1990, the Age Discrimination Act of 1967, the Civil Rights Act of 1866, and the Civil Rights Attorney's Fee Awards Act of 1976. In addition, three new laws were created: Section 1981A of Title 42 of the U.S. Code, the Glass Ceiling Act of 1991, and the Government Employee Rights Act of 1991. Compensatory and punitive damages were made available to the victims of private and nonprofit employers. Public employees are now entitled to only compensatory damages. There is a cap on damages permitted under the law that is determined by the number of workers employed by an organization.

The CRA extended the application of Title VII and the ADA to U.S. citizens working abroad for U.S.-based employers. It extended the application of Title VII, the ADA, and the ADEA to previously unprotected Senate employees, allowing them to redress employment discrimination claims through internal procedures and a limited right of appeal in federal court.

Family and Medical Leave Act of 1993

The Family and Medical Leave Act (FMLA) was signed by President Bill Clinton shortly after his inauguration in January 1993 and took effect on August 5 of that year. The FMLA applies to all public agencies, including state, local, and federal employers; educational institutions; business entities engaged in commerce or in an industry affecting commerce; and private sector employers who employ fifty or more employees in twenty or more work weeks in the current or preceding calendar year, including joint employers and successors of covered employers.

Family and medical leave is available as the result of the birth or adoption of a child or the placement of a child for foster care; to care for a spouse, child, or parent with a serious health condition; or to accommodate the disabling illness of the employee. To be eligible for the leave, an employee must have worked for at least twelve months and for at least 1,250 hours during the year preceding the start of the leave.

The law requires employers to maintain coverage under any group health plan under the condition that coverage would have been provided if no leave was taken. When the leave ends, employees are entitled to return to the same jobs they held before going on leave or to equivalent positions. An equivalent position is defined as a position having the same pay, benefits, and working conditions and involves the same or substantially similar duties and responsibilities. Employees must be restored to the same or a geographically proximate work site.

Not all employees are eligible for leave under FMLA. An employee who qualifies as a key employee may be denied restoration to employment. A key employee is salaried and is among the highest-paid 10 percent of the employees at the work site. Employees must be notified by the employer of their status as a key employee if there is any possibility that the employer may deny reinstatement. Employees are required to give thirty days' advance notice of the need to take family and medical leave when it is foreseeable for the birth of a child or the placement of a child for adoption or foster care or for planned medical treatment. When it is not possible to provide such notice, employees must give notice within one or two business days of when the employee learns of the need for leave.

Employers can require a medical certification from a health care provider to support leave requests. Employees who are denied leave or reinstatement at the end of leave in violation of the law may file a complaint with the Department of Labor. Employees may also file a private lawsuit against the employer to obtain damages and other relief.

The FMLA does not supersede any state or local law that provides greater family or medical leave rights. Employers covered by both federal and state laws must comply with both. In *Nevada Department of Human Resources* v. *Hibbs* (2003), the Supreme Court upheld the right of state employees to sue their employers (state governments) in federal court for alleged violations of the FMLA.

On January 28, 2008, President George W. Bush signed into law the National Defense Authorization Act of 2008, which expands FMLA for military families. An employee may take up to twelve weeks of unpaid FMLA leave for any qualifying exigency related to a spouse, son, daughter, or parent's active duty or notification of an impending call or order to active duty in the U.S. armed forces in support of a contingency operation. Also, an employee who is the spouse, son, daughter, parent, or next of kin of a covered service member is entitled to twenty-six workweeks of leave during a twelve-month period to care for the service member. The leave is available during a single twelve-month period. On February 11, 2008, the Department of Labor released proposed changes to the FMLA regulations. Employers are well advised to see if and what changes may have been made at http://www.dol.gov/esa/whd/fmla/.

Proving Employment Discrimination

Cases of alleged discrimination in violation of federal or state statutes can be made under one of two theories: disparate impact and disparate treatment.

Disparate Treatment

Disparate treatment occurs when an employer treats an employee of a protected class differently from a nonprotected class employee in a similar situation. For example, deliberately using different criteria for selection depending on the candidate's sex or race would constitute disparate treatment, as when an employer asks female applicants but not male applicants questions about their marital status or child care arrangements or requires African American applicants to take preemployment tests that other applicants applying for the same positions are not required to take.

The following test, set forth in *McDonnell Douglas* v. *Green* (1973), permits plaintiffs to establish that an employer treats one or more members of a protected group differently from members of another group:

1. The applicant or employee is a member of a class protected by the statute alleged to be violated (sex, race, age, national origin).
2. The applicant or employee applied for the vacancy and is qualified to perform the job.
3. Although qualified, the applicant or employee was rejected.
4. After rejection, the vacancy remained, and the employer continued to seek applications from persons of equal qualification.

The Supreme Court established that in disparate treatment cases, the burden is on the plaintiff to prove that the employer intended to discriminate because of race, sex, color, religion, or national origin. In *St. Mary's Honor Center* v. *Hicks* (1993), the Court ruled that in addition to showing that all of the employer's legal reasons are false, an employee must prove that the employer was motivated by bias and show direct evidence of discrimination.

Disparate Impact

Disparate impact occurs when an employer's policy or practice, neutral on its face and in its application, has a negative effect on the employment opportunities of protected-class individuals. *Neutral* means that the employer requires all applicants or employees to take the same examination or possess the same qualifications for the positions. Unlike the examples provided under disparate treatment, in which the employer deliberately treated males and females or black and white applicants and employees differently, under disparate impact all applicants and employees are treated the same, but protected-class members are not hired or promoted. Such impact is illegal if the employment practice is not job related or is unrelated to the employment in question. For example, if an agency hired fifty whites and no Hispanics from one hundred white and one hundred Hispanic applicants, disparate impact has occurred. Whether the employer had good intentions or did not mean to discriminate is irrelevant to the courts in this type of lawsuit. After the plaintiff shows evidence of disparate impact, the employer must carry the burden of producing evidence of business necessity or job relatedness for the employment practice. Finally, the burden shifts back to the plaintiff, who must show that an alternative procedure is available that is equal to or better than the employer's practice and has a less discriminatory effect.

The Uniform Guidelines on Employee Selection Procedures were jointly adopted in 1978 by the EEOC, the U.S. Civil Service Commission, the Department of Labor, and the Department of Justice. Although they are not administrative regulations, they are granted deference by the courts. Their purpose is to provide a framework for determining the proper use of tests and other selection procedures. They are applicable to all employers: federal, state, local, nonprofit, and private.

The Uniform Guidelines and many courts have adopted the four-fifths rule as a yardstick for determining disparate impact: a selection rate, determined by the number of applicants selected divided by the number who applied, for a protected group should not be less than four-fifths, or 80 percent, of the rate for the group with the highest selection rate.

Disparate impact theory has been used in many cases involving neutral employment practices such as tests, entrance requirements, and physical requirements. In 1988, the Supreme Court extended use of the disparate impact theory in cases involving subjective employment practices such as interviews, performance appraisals, and job recommendations (*Watson* v. *Fort Worth Bank and Trust*, 1988). Statistical data based on the four-fifths rule can be used in a disparate impact case to establish prima facie evidence of discrimination when decisions are based on subjective employment practices.

Affirmative Action: Executive Orders and Other Federal Laws

This section explains affirmative action and the requirements imposed on employers through Executive Orders 11246 and 11375, the Rehabilitation Act of 1973, and the Vietnam Veterans Readjustment Act of 1974. Chapter Four briefly discusses equal employment opportunity and the executive orders and federal laws that require employers to engage in affirmative action.

Executive Orders 11246 and 11375

In 1965, President Johnson signed Executive Order 11246, which prohibited discrimination in federal employment or by federal contractors on the basis of race, creed, color, or national origin. In 1967, it was amended by Executive Order 11375 to change the word *creed* to *religion* and to add sex discrimination to the other prohibited items. The executive order applies to all federal agencies, contractors, and subcontractors, including all the facilities of the agency holding the contract. Contractors and subcontractors with more than fifty thousand dollars in government business and fifty or more employees are not only prohibited from discriminating, but must also take affirmative action to ensure that applicants and employees are not treated differently as a function of their sex, religion, race, color, or national origin. The order authorizes the cancellation of federal contracts for failure to meet the order's guidelines. It requires a contractor to post notices of equal employment opportunity and to document its compliance to the Department of Labor.

Executive Order 11246 is enforced by the Department of Labor through the Office of Federal Contract Compliance Programs (OFCCP), a branch of the Department of Labor's Employment Standards Administration. It promulgates guidelines and conducts audits of federal contractors to ensure compliance with the executive orders. The OFCCP is charged with processing complaints as well as compliance review. It reviews complaints and can visit an employer's work site and review the affirmative action plans for compliance with the law. Minority availability is measured by the portion of qualified applicants (actual or potential) who are minorities. OFCCP defines "underutilization" as fewer minorities or women in a particular job group than would reasonably be expected by their availability. When a job group is identified as underused, the contractor must set goals to correct the underutilization. The goals for each underutilized group, together with the utilization analysis, become part of the written affirmative action plan. A federal contractor must monitor information about the status of employees when creating and using an affirmative action plan. The employer must demonstrate that its employment practices comply with Executive Order 11246 and the OFCCP's guidelines by documenting employment decisions on hiring, termination, promotion, demotion, and transfer.

If noncompliance is found, the OFCCP generally first tries to reach a conciliation agreement with the employer. Special hiring or recruitment programs, seniority credit, or back pay may be some of the provisions included in the agreement. If an agreement cannot be reached, the employer is scheduled for a hearing with a judge. If an agreement is still not reached during this time, employers may lose their government contracts or have their payments withheld. They may also lose the right to bid on future government contracts or be debarred from all subsequent contract work.

While equal employment opportunity is a legal duty, affirmative action can be voluntary or involuntary. Although Executive Order 11246 applies only to organizations receiving federal funds, many public and nonprofit organizations have decided to implement voluntary affirmative action programs to redress previous discriminatory employment practices or make their workforce more representative. Involuntary affirmative action is permitted under the Civil Rights Act of 1964, Section 706(g), which states that if a court finds that an employer has intentionally engaged in an unlawful employment practice, it may order appropriate affirmative action. Affirmative action is not required unless the employer has adopted the plan as a remedy for past discrimination or must comply with an executive order required by a federal or state agency requiring affirmative action as a condition of doing business with the government. Employers who are not the recipients of government contracts may be forced to develop affirmative action plans if an investigation by a state or federal compliance agency finds that an employer's personnel practices discriminate against protected-class members.

There are three types of involuntarily affirmative action plans, presented here in order from least restrictive to most restrictive:

- *Conciliation agreement.* After an investigation by a compliance agency, the employer may acknowledge there is merit to the allegation of discriminatory employment practices and agree to change its practices to comply with the recommendations of the compliance agency.
- *Consent decree.* A consent decree is an agreement between an employer and a compliance agency negotiated with the approval of a court and is subject to court enforcement.
- *Court order.* Court orders result if a compliance agency must take an employer to court because neither a conciliation agreement nor a consent decree can be agreed on. If the court finds the employer guilty of discrimination, the judge may impose court-ordered remedies. These can include hiring or promotion quotas, changes in personnel practices, and financial compensation for the victims of discrimination.

The Rehabilitation Act of 1973

The Rehabilitation Act prohibits discrimination on the basis of physical or mental disability. A disabled person is defined as one who has an impairment that affects a major life activity, has a history of such an impairment, or is considered as having one. Major life activities refer to functions such as seeing, speaking, walking, and caring for oneself. Disabled individuals also include those with mental disabilities and may include those with illnesses making them unfit for employment, such as contagious diseases or other conditions (tuberculosis, heart disease, cancer, diabetes, drug dependency, or alcoholism, for example). The Supreme Court ruled in *Arline* v. *School Board of Nassau County* (1987) that individuals with contagious diseases who are able to perform their jobs are protected by the Rehabilitation Act of 1973. It stated that the assessment of risks cannot be based on "society's accumulated myths and fears about disability and disease." Most states have similar laws protecting disabled workers from discrimination.

Section 501 of the Rehabilitation Act requires the federal government, as an employer, to develop and implement affirmative action plans on behalf of disabled employees. Congress enacted this provision with the expectation that the federal government would serve as a model for other employers.

Section 503 requires all federal contractors or subcontractors receiving funds over twenty-five hundred dollars to take affirmative action for the employment of qualified disabled persons. Enforcement is carried out by the Department of Labor's Employment Standards Administration. Under the Rehabilitation Act, as under the ADA of 1990, a disabled person is considered qualified for a job if an individual analysis determines that he or she can, with reasonable accommodation, perform the essential functions of the job. Employers must make such accommodations unless it can be shown that the accommodation would pose an undue hardship on the firm.

Section 504 prohibits federally funded programs and government agencies from excluding from employment an "otherwise qualified handicapped individual . . . solely by reason of handicap." The enforcement of Section 504 rests with each federal agency providing financial assistance. The U.S. Attorney General is responsible for coordinating the enforcement efforts of the agencies.

In 1993, the U.S. Court of Appeals for the First Circuit ruled that an individual who suffered from morbid obesity was denied a job in violation of Section 504 of the Rehabilitation Act of 1973 (*Cook* v. *State of Rhode Island, Department of Mental Health, Retardation, and Hospitals*, 1993).

The Vietnam Era Veterans' Readjustment Act of 1974

The Vietnam Era Veterans' Readjustment Act of 1974, as amended, applies to employers with government contracts of twenty-five thousand dollars or more. Contractors are required to take affirmative action to employ and advance disabled veterans and qualified veterans of the Vietnam era. Enforcement of the act is by compliance to the Veterans' Employment Service of the Department of Labor.

Affirmative Action

Many statutes, executive orders, court decisions, and administrative regulations exist that prohibit employment discrimination due to race, color, sex, national origin, religion, or disability. Employment decisions are to be based on merit and job-related qualifications, not on membership in a certain classification. Equal employment opportunity requires employers not to discriminate in the administration and execution of all HRM practices such as recruitment, selection, promotions, training, compensation, career development, discipline, and labor-management relations. In passing the laws, Congress assumed that outlawing deliberate discrimination and punishing employers found guilty of unfair practices would eradicate the vestiges of years of discrimination.

Although passage of these laws meant that overt discrimination was no longer tolerated, women and minorities were still underrepresented in the workforce. A more assertive strategy was needed to correct for past and existing discrimination. That strategy was affirmative action. Executive Order 11246 states, "An affirmative action program is a set of specific and results-oriented procedures to which the contractor commits itself to apply in a good faith effort." The objective of those procedures plus such efforts is equal employment opportunity.

In 1965, President Johnson signed Executive Order 11246, which prohibits discrimination in federal employment on the basis of race, creed, color, or national origin. In 1968, this order was amended by Executive Order 11375, in which the word *creed* was changed to *religion* and sex discrimination was added to the list of prohibited types. The executive order applied to all federal agencies, contractors, and subcontractors, including all of the facilities of the agency holding the contract, regardless of the location at which the work is conducted. Contractors and subcontractors with more than fifty thousand dollars in government business and fifty or more employees are not only prohibited from discriminating, but must also take affirmative action to ensure that applicants and employees are not treated differently because of their sex, religion, race, color, and national origin. Executive Order 11478 states that the policy of the U.S. government is "to provide equal opportunity in federal employment for all persons, to prohibit discrimination because of race, color, religion, sex, national origin, handicap, or age, and to promote the full realization of equal employment opportunity through a continuing affirmative program in each executive department and agency."

Two executive orders were issued in 2000. Executive Order 13116 requires federal agencies to examine services and prepare a plan to "improve access to federally conducted and federally assisted programs and activities for persons who, as a result of national origin, are limited in their English proficiency." Executive Order 13171 requires the head of each executive department and agency to establish and maintain a program for the recruitment and career development of Hispanics in federal employment. The Rehabilitation Act of 1973 and the Vietnam Veterans Readjustment Act of 1974 also require federal contractors or subcontractors to take affirmative action for the employment and advancement of qualified disabled persons and veterans, and qualified veterans of the Vietnam era.

Affirmative action has often been interpreted and criticized as requiring the implementation of quotas regardless of individuals' qualifications and ability to perform a job. In reality, affirmative action may refer to several strategies, including active recruitment of groups underrepresented in an organization, eliminating irrelevant employment practices that bar protected groups from employment, and, the most controversial one, granting preferential status to protected groups. The effectiveness of affirmative action is represented by the extent to which employers make an effort through their SHRM practices to attract, retain, and upgrade members of protected classes as a condition of doing business with the government.

Critics of affirmative action claim it results in reverse discrimination and that the costs of complying with its guidelines are too expensive. Claims of reverse discrimination suggest that special advantages or preferential treatment given to women and minorities promote unfair treatment against white males and are thus still discrimination. A second argument against affirmative action is that the costs associated with complying with the regulations are high and that compliance results in lower productivity because of a less-qualified workforce. However, there is little evidence to validate these arguments (Kellough, 2006; Pincus, 2003).

Although the executive orders, the Rehabilitation Act of 1973, and the Vietnam Veterans Readjustment Act apply only to the recipients of federal funds, many organizations have decided to implement voluntary affirmative action programs to redress previous discriminatory employment practices or to make their workforce more representative of the constituents or clients they serve.

Constitutional Rights

Public employees have a broad array of constitutional protections that differentiate public employment from employment in the nonprofit and for-profit sectors. Public sector employees' rights and privileges to work are to some extent protected by a broad umbrella of laws that either prohibit a government activity or create an individual right. Many of the constitutional protections afforded to public sector employees were originally enacted to protect free citizens from arbitrary government action in the areas of privacy, expression, association, contracts, and property. Since public sector

Public employees have a broad array of constitutional protections that differentiate public employment from employment in the nonprofit and for-profit sectors.

employees work for the government, the protections are extended to them by operation of the employment relationship.

Many of the rights under the U.S. Constitution are limitations on Congress and the states to exercise certain actions against the citizens and employees. However, these constitutional limitations are not self-executing and therefore must be enforced through the Civil Rights Act of 1871, which was enacted by Congress as part of reconstruction legislation after the Civil War. In the public sector employment arena, it is important to note that 42 USC 1983 is the enforcement vehicle of the other constitutional rights and allows damages only against persons who act "under the color of law," that is, the government, where the government actor subjects any person to a deprivation of any rights, privileges, or immunities secured by the U.S. Constitution or the laws of the United States. Therefore, where a public sector employer is "acting under the color" within the employment relationship or otherwise deprives employees of certain constitutional rights, a cause of action against the employer or other employees may be available to protect the "rights" afforded. However, the employer may be held liable only where it has a policy, practice, or custom that deprives the employee of the right.

Today it is unlikely that employers have written policies that on their face would be a violation of the Constitution. However, many employment actions arise through incorrect policy implementation or in violation of the Constitution through supervisory personnel who deprive employees of their constitutional rights, which gives rise to individual or, in some cases, employer liability. The legal concept of *respondeat superior* ("let the master answer") is generally not available under constitutional claims to hold the employer liable for nonsanctioned official actions of its employees.

Expressive Rights

The First Amendment to the U.S. Constitution protects public employees against unwarranted employer interference with their freedom of speech, expression, association, and religion. It also protects the right of public employees to join a labor union or advocate the joining of associations, the right to speak out on matters of public concern, the right of access to a public employer's property, and freedom from religious discrimination.

Prior to 2006, the prevailing legal theory under the First Amendment was that the interests of public employees in free speech were balanced against the interests of the state, as employer, in promoting the efficiency of the public services it performs through its employees. There needs to be a balance between the interest of a public sector employee, as a citizen, in commenting on issues of public concern and the interests of the state, as an employer, in promoting the efficiency of its public services via its employees. If the disciplined employee did engage in speech protected by the First Amendment through the balancing of interests, the discipline could still be upheld if the employer could show that the employee would have been disciplined for other, legitimate reasons (*Pickering* v. *Board of Education*, 1968; *Connick* v. *Myers*, 1983; *McPherson* v. *Rankin*, 1987; *Mount Healthy*, 1977).

In 2006, the U.S. Supreme Court, in *Garcetti* v. *Ceballos*, pronounced a holding that many feel has reduced the First Amendment constitutional protections afforded to public sector employees in speech cases (Hudson, 2008). The *Garcetti* decision created an additional hurdle for public employees by requiring them to show they were speaking as citizens on a matter of public concern and not simply doing their jobs when they expressed themselves. According to the Court, public sector employees who speak as a result of the required duties of their job do so as employees rather than as citizens and will not be afforded First Amendment protections from subsequent disciplinary action by their employers as a direct result of the speech (Garry, 2007).

Ceballos was a deputy district attorney in the Los Angeles County District Office, who was demoted after filing a deposition memorandum outlining alleged false statements by police contained in an affidavit used to obtain a search warrant and informing defense counsel of those false statements. After being demoted, Ceballos filed a suit alleging that his demotion was a result of his speech protected by the First Amendment. The U.S. Supreme Court held that the First Amendment did not apply because the deputy district attorney spoke as an employee and not as a citizen when he wrote his memorandum (Garry, 2007). The issue presented was not whether the speech was a matter of public concern, but whether it was made by a government employee in implementing his official duties. Ceballos spoke as a public employee and not as a citizen, so the Court held that his supervisors had every right to criticize his performance and take disciplinary action.

Freedom of Association

Public employees are generally free to join organizations as long as their membership does not create a conflict of interest with their jobs or appears to invite impropriety. Public employees also have broad protections against being forced to join organizations. With limited exceptions, such as in executive policymaking positions, the decisions to hire, terminate, train, transfer, promote, or discipline employees for partisan political reasons are not permissible. The Supreme Court reasoned that the contributions that patronage makes to the government's interests in loyalty, accountability, and party competition are outweighed by its infringement on public employees' freedom of association and belief (*Elrod* v. *Burns*, 1976; *Branti* v. *Finkel*, 1980; *Rutan* v. *Republic Party of Illinois*, 1990). Moreover, public employees cannot be required to join labor unions as dues-paying members, but may be included as bargaining unit members for the purposes of voting and contract application. Generally, dues-paying members are assessed fees to contribute to their fair share of contract negotiations, contract administration, and other privileges afforded under the contract, but bargaining unit members may not be.

Limits on Political Participation

Public employees can be restricted from participating in partisan political activities. The 1939 Political Activities Act, more commonly referred to as the Hatch Act, prohibits federal employees covered by it from taking an active part in political campaigns. The act prohibits federal employees from engaging in political activity while on duty, wearing campaign buttons in the office, and putting campaign bumper stickers on government vehicles. It also bans soliciting and accepting or receiving political contributions, and it prohibits employees from using their official positions to influence or interfere with an election. In addition, the Office of Special Counsel (OSC), an independent agency that investigates and prosecutes allegations of improper political activities by government employees, has rendered opinions that limit persons from running for a partisan office where the individual is directly or indirectly responsible for funds arising from federal grants. In those cases, the individual may need to resign from public employment to run for a local office. Violators can be prosecuted under federal law and even lose their jobs.

An interesting issue has risen as a result of the Internet. Today political messages, campaign solicitations, and cartoons come to individuals' e-mail in-boxes. The OSC notes that receiving an e-mail may not be under an individual's control; however, public employees should not forward an e-mail that urges a vote for a specific candidate or seeks to raise campaign money. Blogging about politics from work is not permissible, and blogging from home may also get a federal employee in trouble (Barr, 2008).

The political activities of most state and local government employees are also restricted by state or local governments' "little Hatch Acts." What is permitted and what is proscribed vary by state. Many of the state laws are less restrictive than the federal Hatch Act and permit state and local employees to engage in more political activity then federal counterparts are allowed. It is important for public employees to review current federal and state laws, along with local ordinances, resolutions, and regulations, to determine permitted political activity.

Privacy Rights

The Fourth Amendment to the U.S. Constitution bars unreasonable searches and seizures and essentially provides zones of privacy. However, not every intrusion on a privacy interest is a search, and employers can and do limit the zones of privacy in the workplace.

Public employees do not lose their Fourth Amendment Rights against unreasonable searches or seizures because they work for the government instead of a private employer (*National Treasury Employees Union* v. *Von Raab*, 1989). Where employees have a "reasonable expectation of privacy" under employment circumstances, the Fourth Amendment provides protection unless a search warrant is issued by a detached magistrate based on probable cause.

Due Process Rights

This area of the law is in constant development as societal values and ideologies ebb and flow. There are two concepts of recognized due process: procedural and substantive. Procedural due process is a concept adopting fundamental fairness as the rule of law to effect decisions that affect individual rights. Due process in this context is not necessarily a tangible right; rather, it relates to the preprocesses afforded to individuals before tangible rights are affected by government. Essentially procedural due process requires the government to provide reasonable notice and an opportunity to be heard within a fair forum under just conditions before a person's rights are negatively affected. Fairness is an objective standard and naturally depends on a multitude of considerations. Procedural due process is a check on arbitrary, capricious, or discriminatory decisions by government officials in individual cases. When invoked in the public employment context, it protects public employees from arbitrary discharge. If nothing else, procedural due process procedures create the opportunity for individuals to protect rights and interests through the discovery of arbitrary or capricious government action. In order to comport with procedural due process, a public sector employer must give the affected employee notice, a meaningful opportunity for the employee to respond to charges and to present evidence, and the right to an impartial decision maker.

Not all substantive due process rights are codified in the Constitution. The Fifth and Fourteenth Amendments' substantive due process provisions allow the courts to recognize tangible interests dependent on the concepts of liberty. The Fifth Amendment applies to federal government action and the Fourteenth Amendment to actions of the respective states. In limited circumstances, these amendments provide substantive due process rights to protect individuals against the deprivation of life, liberty, or property without the procedural due process of law. The concepts of life, liberty, and property are ever evolving, and therefore substantive due process rights are recognized on a case-by-case basis. In addition, at minimum, these amendments to the Constitution require a rational basis supporting government actions. In the context of equal protection not affecting a protected class of individuals, the government is not required to treat everyone the same, but it does mandate that it treat similarly situated groups in a like manner unless it can establish a legitimate reason that is rationally related to the employment decision. Where a protected class of individuals is at issue, for example, gender or race, the judicial scrutiny increases and therefore affords greater protection to these classes.

Additional Protections for Employees

Public and nonprofit employees may also have additional workplace protections that prohibit arbitrary and unfair treatment from employers through local, state, or federal statutes.

Whistle-Blower Protection

A whistle-blower is an employee, former employee, or contractor of an agency who reports agency misconduct. Generally the misconduct is a violation of law, rule, or regulation or a direct threat to public interest, such as fraud, health and safety violations, or corruption. Whistle-blower laws and policies are designed to protect employees who report wrongdoing, illegal conduct, internal fraud, and discrimination from retaliation (Harshbarger & Crafts, 2007). The federal government and many state and local governments have some sort of statutory or common law whistle-blower or antiretaliation laws. Many nonprofits have developed their own internal whistle-blower policies, as well. Harshbarger and Craft (2007) note that internal whistle-blower policies can be used to identify problems in the workplace. With whistle-blower protections in place, intervention and prevention methods can strengthen and support a workplace culture of integrity, openness, transparency, and two-way communication. Even without internal policies, nonprofits have been advised to adhere to the whistle-blowing provisions of the Public Accounting Reform and Investor Protection Act of 2002, more commonly known as the Sarbanes-Oxley Act. The act was passed as a reaction to the Enron, Tyco, Adelphia, and WorldCom corporate scandals that cost investors billions of dollars and lead to diminished confidence in the securities markets.

Public and nonprofit employers need to be aware of the Whistle Blower Protection Act of 1989 and the state and local laws in jurisdictions in which they are located, and they must comply with any internal policies in regard to whistle-blowers. Public, nonprofit, and for-profit employees are typically covered by whistle-blower or antiretaliation laws. Like the federal whistle-blower laws, state and local governments have recognized with laws a public policy exception to the doctrine of employment at will.

Employment at Will

The doctrine of employment at will provides that an employer may discharge an employee for any reason, not prohibited by law, or for no reason. However, there are some exceptions:

◆ ◆ ◆

- *Public policy exception.* Under the public policy exception, an employer may not fire an employee if it would violate the state's public policy or a state or federal statute.
- *Implied contract exception.* Under the implied contract exception, an employer may not fire an employee when an implied contract is formed

between an employer and employee, even though no express, written instrument regarding the employment relationship exists.

Proving the terms of an implied contract is often difficult, and the burden of proof is on the employee who has been fired. Implied employment contracts are most often found when an employer's personnel policies or handbooks indicate that an employee will not be fired except for good cause or specify a process for firing. If the employer fires the employee in violation of an implied employment contract, the employer may be found liable for breach of contract.

- *Good faith and fair dealing exception.* The exception for good faith and fair dealing represents the most significant departure from the traditional employment-at-will doctrine. Rather than narrowly prohibiting terminations based on public policy or an implied contract, this exception inserts a covenant of good faith and fair dealing into every employment relationship. It has been interpreted by some courts to mean either that employer personnel decisions are subject to a "just cause" standard or that terminations made in bad faith or motivated by malice are prohibited.

◆ ◆ ◆

Employers may not fire at-will employees for refusing to commit illegal acts, and if the employment handbook or agency policy outlines procedures that must be followed before an employee can be terminated, those procedures must be followed. If the employer fires an employee without following established procedures, the employee may have a claim for wrongful termination. Employers in all sectors must be aware of exceptions to the employment-at-will doctrine. Essentially these concepts are developed under the rubric of procedural and substantive due process as discussed above. In addition, the courts have found that public employees have liberty interests (quasi-property rights) in their reputation as it relates to public employment. The liberty interest does not necessarily protect the job, but it allows the employee to invoke a liberty-interest hearing after termination. The hearing allows the employee to have the last word within the public personnel file.

Conclusion

Equal employment opportunity has continued to evolve, and it now prohibits not only race discrimination but discrimination against sex, religion, color, national origin, disability, and age. The equal employment opportunity and affirmative action laws create legal responsibilities for employers and affect all aspects of the employment relationship. Recruitment, selection, training, compensation and benefits, promotions, and terminations must all be conducted in a nondiscriminatory manner.

Whereas equal employment opportunity is a policy of nondiscrimination, affirmative action requires employers to analyze their workforces and develop plans of action to recruit, select, train, and promote members of protected classes and develop plans of action to correct areas in which past discrimination may have occurred. Affirmative action in the United States is jointly determined by the Constitution, legislative acts, executive orders, and court decisions. The Office of Federal Contract Compliance Programs is responsible for developing and enforcing most affirmative action plans, although the Equal Employment Opportunity Commission enforces affirmative action plans in the federal sector.

Affirmative action is used by the federal government to promote a more diverse workforce. Recipients of federal funds are required to develop affirmative action plans that encourage the recruitment, selection, training, and promotion of qualified disabled individuals, Vietnam War veterans, and individuals who may have been discriminated against because of their race, sex, color, and national origin. Affirmative action plans can be involuntary or voluntary. Involuntary action plans have increasingly come under intense scrutiny, and affirmative action itself is being challenged. On April 1, 2003, the Supreme Court heard arguments challenging the use of race in the admissions policies at the University of Michigan and its law school (*Gratz* v. *Bollinger*, 2003, and *Grutter* v. *Bollinger*, 2003, respectively).

Major corporations, including Microsoft, Bank One, General Motors, Shell, and American Express, and the Army, Navy and Air Force academies filed briefs supporting the University of Michigan's race-conscious admissions policies. Supporters of using race as one of many factors in the admissions process believe that diversity creates stronger organizations. On June 23, 2003, the Supreme Court upheld the affirmative action plan of the law school. Justice Sandra Day O'Connor, writing for the majority, which included Justices Stephen G. Breyer, John Paul Stevens, Ruth Bader Ginsburg, and David H. Souter, stated:

> The hallmark of the law school's policy is its focus on academic ability coupled with a flexible assessment of applicant's talents, experiences and potential "to contribute to the learning of those

> around them." . . . The policy aspires to "achieve that diversity which has the potential to enrich everyone's education and thus make a law school class stronger than the sum of its parts." . . . We have held that all racial classifications imposed by the government "must be analyzed by a reviewing court under strict scrutiny." This means that such classifications are constitutional only if they are narrowly tailored to further compelling governmental interests. . . . To be narrowly tailored, a race-conscious admissions program cannot use a quota system. . . . Instead a university may consider race or ethnicity more flexibly as a "plus" factor in the context of individualized consideration of each and every applicant. . . . The Law School engages in a highly individualized, holistic review of each applicant's file, giving serious consideration to all the ways an applicant might contribute to a diverse educational environment . . . In order to cultivate a set of leaders with legitimacy in the eyes of the citizenry, it is necessary that the path to leadership be visibly open to talented and qualified individuals of every race and ethnicity.

In *Gratz* v. *Bollinger*, however, the Court found the University of Michigan's undergraduate affirmative action admission program unconstitutional. Chief Justice William Rehnquist, writing for the majority, stated, "The university's policy which automatically distributes 20 points, or one-fifth of the points needed to guarantee admission, to every single underrepresented minority applicant solely because of race, is not narrowly tailored to achieve the interest in the educational diversity." In essence, the Court ruled that race and ethnicity may be taken into account as a "plus factor" when making admission decisions, but limited how much a factor race can play in the selection of students.

Several other federal court decisions concerning affirmative action have been especially important. One case addressed affirmative action and the granting of federal contracts, and the second case dealt with affirmative action and law school admission policies. In *Adarand Constructors* v. *Pena* (1995), the Supreme Court ruled that federal programs that use race or ethnicity as a basis for decision making must be strictly scrutinized to ensure that they promote compelling government interest and they are narrowly tailored to serve those interests. Federal affirmative action programs giving preferences to minorities are subject to the same strict scrutiny applied to state and local programs.

In *Hopwood et al.* v. *State of Texas et al.* (1996), the Fifth Circuit Court of Appeals struck down the University of Texas Law School affirmative action program, which viewed minority and white applicants for admission separately, resulting in an unconstitutional quota system. The court ruled that racial diversity can never be a compelling government interest and that racial diversity "may promote improper racial stereotypes, thus fueling racial hostility."

At this time, the Supreme Court has upheld the use of court-ordered affirmative action programs designed to eliminate egregious past discrimination (*United States* v. *Paradise*, 1986) and voluntary affirmative action plans designed to increase the representation of women and minorities in nontraditional jobs or in traditionally segregated positions (*Johnson* v. *Santa Clara Transportation Agency*, 1987; *United Steelworkers of America* v. *Weber*, 1979). Voluntary affirmative action plans are permitted as long as they meet four conditions: (1) the affirmative action plan is temporary, (2) it is undertaken to eliminate manifest racial imbalance, (3) it is for nontraditional jobs or traditionally segregated job categories, and (4) the plan does not require the discharge of white workers or create an absolute bar to their advancement.

The Supreme Court has not upheld the use of racial quotas when race serves as the only criterion for admission to universities and advanced graduate programs (*Regents of the University of California* v. *Bakke*, 1978) or when race is used to abrogate seniority systems in layoffs. Hiring and promotional preferences may be permissible to redress past discrimination but not layoffs (*Firefighters Local 1784* v. *Stotts*, 1984; *Wygant* v. *Jackson Board of Education*, 1986).

The focus on equal employment opportunity and affirmative action programs has increased the importance of strategic HRM and planning. Compliance with equal employment opportunity laws and affirmative action regulations is essential to human resources planning and the effective utilization of all employees. One day affirmative action programs may be eliminated, and many of the paperwork requirements for compliance audits will no longer be necessary. However, organizations will still need to develop and implement progressive HRM strategies if they wish to successfully manage a diverse workforce.

Employers must be aware of the legal environment under which SHRM is implemented. Not only do employers need to be aware of the laws governing equal employment opportunity, but they must also be aware of other laws protecting employee rights. Public employers must be careful not to violate the constitutional rights of their employees. Employers in both sectors must be aware of whistle-blower protections acts and employment-at-will exceptions.

Exercise 3.1: A Muslim Woman's Right to Wear a Head Scarf at Work

In 2003, Kimberlie Webb, a practicing Muslim and police officer since 1995, requested permission from her employer, the Philadelphia Police Department, to wear a *khimar*, a form of head scarf extending to the waist, along with her uniform. The police department denied her request as a violation of the department's uniform regulation. Philadelphia Department Directive 78 bars police officers in uniform from wearing religious dress or symbols under all circumstances and makes no medical or secular exceptions.

Webb filed a complaint for religious discrimination with the EEOC. After she filed her complaint, she appeared at work wearing a *khimar* on three separate occasions and was sent home each time. As a result, the commissioner, himself a Muslim, suspended her for thirteen days. Webb then amended her charge in 2004, in which she added an allegation of retaliation. After receiving her right-to-sue letter, Webb filed her complaint in October 2005 against the City.

The city admitted it did not offer Webb a reasonable accommodation, arguing that it would suffer an undue hardship if it were required to accommodate her. In June 2007, U.S. District Judge Harvey Bartle III agreed with the city. He ruled that the "City of Philadelphia has established compelling non-discriminatory reasons for Directive 78 and has demonstrated as a matter of law it would suffer an undue hardship if required to accommodate the wearing [of] a *khimar* by Ms. Webb while on duty as a police officer." The court held that the directive standards were designed to maintain religious neutrality and promoted the need for uniformity, but also contributed to cohesiveness, cooperation, and the esprit de corps of the police force.

Questions

1. Do you agree with the city's and the judge's position? State your reasons.
2. If Webb was not a sworn police officer, do you think there would be a problem accommodating her wearing of the *khimar*?
3. Should organizations have policies in place in regard to the wearing of religious dress or symbols? If so, what should they be?

Source: Webb v. *City of Philadelphia* (2007).

Exercise 3.2: State and Local Laws on Human Resources Management

New York

According to New York State's Labor Law, section 206-c, all employers, regardless of size, are required to provide breast-feeding employees with reasonable unpaid break time or permit them to use paid break time or mealtime each day to express breast milk for their nursing child, for up to three years following the child's birth. The law also requires employers to make reasonable efforts to provide a room or other location "in close proximity" to the work areas where breast-feeding employees can express breast milk in privacy. The law prohibits discrimination "in any way" against employees who choose to express breast milk in the workplace.

New York joins California, Connecticut, Georgia, Hawaii, Illinois, Minnesota, Mississippi, New Mexico, Oklahoma, Oregon, Rhode Island, Tennessee, and Virginia in having passed laws protecting a nursing mother's right to express breast milk in the workplace.

California

California law requires public and private employers who employ over twenty-five employees to provide up to ten days of unpaid leave for a "qualified" employee if the employee's military spouse is on a leave period from deployment in a combat zone with the active duty, reserve military, or National Guard during a period of military conflict. To be eligible, an employee must be the spouse of a qualified member of the military. The term *spouse* includes registered domestic partners. However, requests for family leave from a same-sex registered domestic partner will be uncommon, as service members are still forbidden under military regulations from registering as same-sex domestic partners. A qualified employee is one who works an average of twenty or more hours per week but does not include independent contractors. The law also makes it unlawful for an employer to retaliate against a qualified employee for requesting or taking leave permitted by the new law.

Ohio

The Ohio Civil Rights Commission proposed an expansion of benefits for pregnant workers that requires employers to offer maternity leaves exceeding those mandated by the federal Family and Medical Leave Act. The commission has proposed that businesses with four or more employees offer twelve weeks of unpaid maternity leave to pregnant employees regardless of how long they have worked for the employer. To see if the law was adopted go to http://www.crc.ohio.gov/ocrc_news.htm.

New Jersey

Beginning January 1, 2009, New Jersey workers taking family leave to look after spouses, children, or parents will receive two-thirds of their wages up to $524 a week for as many as six weeks per year. The benefits will be funded by employee payroll deductions dispersed from a state-administered account. The legislature estimated that the plan, which will cost workers $33 a year, will be used by thirty-eight thousand employees, or 1 percent of the state's workforce.

Questions

1. Do you support the laws outlined here? Provide an explanation. Are there any changes you would make? If so, what are they?
2. What are some other state laws or commission rulings that you are familiar with that go beyond the federal laws discussed in this chapter?

Chapter Questions

1. If an employer asked you to review an adverse employment decision to determine if discrimination had occurred, what factors would you consider, and how would you evaluate them?
2. In small groups, discuss the policies and training programs in your organizations that address equal employment opportunity. What recommendations would you make to improve the least successful training program?

Online Activities

1. Visit the U.S. Equal Employment Opportunity Commission (EEOC) Web site, and look under Enforcement Statistics. Compare and contrast the number of allegations received for fiscal year 2007 by age, race, sex, and disability. Which type of discrimination had the highest number of discrimination allegations. Why do you think this is so? Please explain your answer.
2. Does the EEOC Web site provide comprehensive information on the types of discrimination that fall under its jurisdiction? If so, is the information written in a way that would be clear to individuals who are unfamiliar with the topic? What recommendations would you make to clarify the content?
3. Locate your state's fair employment law Web site. Are there other kinds of employment discrimination that are unlawful in your state that are not covered under the federal laws?

CHAPTER FOUR

MANAGING A DIVERSE WORKFORCE

After you have read this chapter, you should be able to:

- Discuss why managing diversity is important to strategic human resources management
- Understand the less obvious types of differences that employees bring to the workplace
- Understand the types of sexual harassment
- Understand why diversity efforts often fail

As the demographics of American society change, so too has the composition of the workforce. Women, persons of color, persons of different ethnic and religious backgrounds, persons with physical and mental disabilities, homosexuals, and transgendered individuals are more visible in the workplace than in the past. To be successful, employers need to manage a diverse workforce and ensure that promotional opportunities and compensation are determined by job performance, initiative, or special skills.

Diversity refers to differences in underlying attributes or nonobservable differences, such as working styles, values, and personality types, as well as differences in culture, socioeconomic background, educational background, spirituality, occupational background or professional orientation, industry experience, organizational membership, group tenure, and spirituality (Denhardt & Leland, 2003; Milliken & Martins, 1996). Loden (1996) defines diversity as the important human characteristics that affect individuals' values, opportunities, and perceptions of self and others at work. She identifies age, ethnicity, gender, mental and physical abilities and characteristics, race, and sexual orientation as core dimensions of diversity. Secondary dimensions of diversity include communication style, education, family status, military experience, organizational role and level, religion, first language, geographical location, income, work experience, and work style.

Page (2007) believes that two people possess diversity perspectives if they mentally represent the "set of the possible" differently (p. 7). He provides an example how one person might organize a collection of books by the author's last name, and another might do so by color of book binding and size. Because of the different perspectives, two people will test different potential improvements and increase the probability of innovation, believing that individuals with diverse perspectives are good for organizations.

Konrad, Prasad, and Pringle (2006) advocate a definition of diversity that emphasizes intergroup interaction and is inclusive of power differences rather than focusing on individual differences. This means explicitly acknowledging the role played by past discrimination and oppression in producing socially marginal groups today. Related to the belief in systemic discrimination, Roberson and Kulik (2007) discuss how understanding stereotype threat, defined as the fear of being judged according to a negative stereotype, can help managers create positive environments for diverse employees. Pitts (2006), in acknowledging three distinct areas of research commonly found in the diversity literature—*integration and inclusion*, *management programs*, and *diversity efforts*—notes a void in the research as to whether diversity efforts lead to improved organization outcomes.

Employers must understand diversity and capitalize on each member's contributions to the organization's effectiveness. Fairness in recruitment, selection, promotion, performance evaluation, training and development, and compensation and benefits are just some of the challenges that strategic human resources management (HRM) faces. The focus of this chapter is on understanding some of the management challenges that diversity brings into the workplace. As an example of the extent of diversity, the 2006 class of New York City police cadets consisted of 284 immigrants. New York City has police officers from Afghanistan, Albania, Argentina, Australia, Azerbaijan, Bangladesh, Barbados, Belarus, Bosnia, Cambodia, Canada, Chile, China, Columbia, Dominican Republic,

Ecuador, El Salvador, France, Ghana, Grenada, Guatemala, Guyana, Haiti, Honduras, India, Indonesia, Israel, Italy, Jamaica, Kazakhstan, Kuwait, Malaysia, Mexico, Moldova, Montenegro, Myanmar, Nigeria, Peru, Philippines, Poland, Romania, Russia, Serbia, South Africa, South Korea, St. Kitts and Nevis, St. Croix, St. Lucia, St. Vincent and the Grenadines, Taiwan, Tobago, Trinidad, Turkey, Ukraine, United Kingdom, Venezuela, Vietnam, and the former Yugoslavia. About 28 percent of the new officers are Hispanic, 17 percent are black, and 8 percent Asian. Approximately 18 percent are women (Newman, 2006).

Some of the examples of diversity in workplaces that follow show proactive attempts in managing a diverse workforce; others demonstrate that improvements can be made in managing diversity:

- Michael E. Guest resigned after twenty-six years in the U.S. Foreign Service in order to protest rules and regulations he believed were unfair to same-sex partners of Foreign Service officers. Although gay men and lesbians are accepted in the State Department, Guest claims the culture has not kept pace with the regulations, especially as Foreign Service officers are being posted in dangerous countries. For example, same-sex partners or unmarried heterosexual partners are refused antiterrorism security training or foreign language training and are not evacuated when eligible family members are ordered to leave. Unlike spouses, they do not receive diplomatic passports, visas, or even use of the State Department mail system. They must pay their own way overseas and get their own medical care, and they are left to fend for themselves if their partner is sent to a dangerous post. Many of the rules could be changed with the Secretary of State's signature. Aaron W. Jensen, president of Gays and Lesbians in Foreign Affairs Agencies, said the leadership met with Secretary of State Condoleezza Rice in 2005 to argue for a change in policies (Kessler, 2007).
- Mark R. Dybul was sworn in as the new AIDS coordinator by Secretary of State Condoleezza Rice in 2007. His partner, Jason Claire, held the Bible as Dybul took the oath. The State Department acknowledges its gay employees, allows their partners to live in official residences overseas, helps them obtain foreign residence visas, and has sent out a cable encouraging U.S. ambassadors to include diplomats' partners in social and official functions (Wright, 2007).
- An African American firefighter in St. Louis, Missouri, found a stuffed monkey hanging by its neck in his firehouse. The city's black firefighters say it was meant to evoke a lynching. The white firefighters say

the monkey was simply hung up to dry after being found at a fire scene (Gay, 2008).

• There are only 110 Hispanic city managers in the United States. Fifty of them are located in Texas. Out of 581 managers in Texas, only 6.8 percent are Hispanic and 91 percent of them are male (Benavides, 2006). More than 35 percent of Texas's population is Hispanic (U.S. Census Bureau, 2006b).

◆ ◆ ◆

For organizations to be successful and minimize conflicts among employees in today's multicultural workplaces, they must comply with the laws governing equal employment opportunity and understand the role that individual differences can play in an organization.

Glass Ceilings

The term *glass ceiling* refers to the artificial barriers that block the advancement of women and minorities to upper-level managerial and executive positions within organizations. Such obstacles must be eliminated.

Studies have shown that African Americans, Asian Americans, Hispanics, and women are underrepresented in upper-level supervisory, management, and senior executive positions of federal employment (Cornwell & Kellough, 1994; U.S. General Accounting Office, 2003; Guy, 1993; Hsieh & Winslow, 2006; Kim, 1993; Kim & Lewis, 1994; Lewis, 1988, 1994; Naff & Kellough, 2002, 2004; Page, 1994, Riccucci, 2002; Sisneros, 1992; Swift, 1992–1993; U.S. Merit Systems Protection Board, 1992). A recent study found that the diversity of the Senior Executive Service (SES) is not going to change much over the next few years unless agencies step up their efforts to recruit and promote minorities in the service. There will be a change in the number of white women, who will essentially replace white men leaving the government (U.S. General Accounting Office, 2003). In 2007, legislation was introduced by Representative Danny K. Davis (D-Illinois) and Senator Daniel K. Akaka (D-Hawaii) to promote greater diversity in the SES. Of the 6,349 career SES members, the General Accounting Office counted 325 African American men, 221 African American women, 164 Hispanic men, 65 Hispanic women,

90 Asian/Pacific Islander men, 56 Asian/Pacific Islander women, 59 American Indian/Alaskan native men, and 27 American Indian/Alaskan Native women. The majority of SES members are white: 3,900 men and 1,436 women (Barr, 2007). Other studies confirm the existence of a glass ceiling at the state and local levels (Bullard & Wright, 1993; Guy, 1993; McCabe & Stream, 2000; Rangarajan & Black, 2007; Rehfuss, 1986; Slack, 1987). Steinberg and Jacobs (1994), and Odendahl and O'Neill (1994) suggest that the nonprofit sector is in reality controlled by an elite male power structure and that within the sector, occupations are distributed according to gender. Women may constitute the majority of the nonprofit workforce, but they are typically prevented from reaching top executive and policymaking positions.

The commitment of women and minorities to their jobs is typically questioned because of their family responsibilities, perceived inability to relocate, or doubts about their leadership styles. The assumption that they are less committed often results in their being bypassed for important assignments and developmental opportunities. However, research indicates that the personal multiple life roles that women play provide them with opportunities to practice multitasking and enrich their interpersonal skills and leadership effectiveness. In other words, they increase their effectiveness in management positions in this way (Ruderman, Ohlott, Panzer, & King, 2002).

Regardless of the employment sector, subtle assumptions, attitudes, and stereotypes exist in the workplace, manifest as organizational cultures that affect the mobility patterns of women and minorities.

The rest of this chapter discusses why managing a diverse workforce is important, the difference between equal employment opportunity and affirmative action, and the implications for managing a diverse workforce. Strategies that employers can implement to accommodate multicultural differences are reviewed as well.

Why Diversity Is Important

Evidence is growing that managing diversity leads to greater service effectiveness, efficiency, and productivity. Diversity can lead to more creative alternatives and higher-quality ideas, primarily from the introduction of different and opposing ideas and viewpoints. Employers who respect their employees are better able to use their talents; diversity helps to increase an understanding of the community and the marketplace and also increase

Evidence is growing that managing diversity leads to greater service effectiveness, efficiency, and productivity.

the quality of team problem solving (Cox, 2001; Naff & Kellough, 2002; Page, 2007).

San Francisco's Asian & Pacific Islander Wellness Center learned that Burmese refugees were starting to move to Oakland, California, and many of them had HIV/AIDS. The charity, which serves Bay Area Asians and Pacific Islanders who have HIV/AIDS or are at risk for the diseases, had staff members and volunteers who were fluent in Samoan, Visayan, Tagalog, Nepali, and many other languages, but not Burmese. The Wellness Center knew little about the Burmese—only that they had fled a military dictatorship and were being resettled by church groups and the United Nations High Commissioner for Refugees. The agency reached out to the new arrivals and discovered it needed someone with expertise in dealing the HIV/AIDS patients. It recruited a Burmese woman and trained her as a case manager. She was able to offer direct assistance to Burmese refugees, providing them with health and safety information, accompanying them to medical appointments, and giving other types of aid (Berkshire, 2007).

When the Wellness Center sought to hire more Burmese case managers, it found many qualified applicants. According to Lance Tome, the executive director, acquiring what he refers to as "cultural competency" required an innovative approach to hiring: "There are a limited number of people who have the knowledge and experience to fill these positions. . . . What we've learned to do is train from the ground up" (Berkshire, 2007, p. D13).

Another example of a nonprofit that is making a conscious effort to become more diverse is the Jewish Board of Family and Children's Services in New York City. The agency first offered services to poor Jewish families and immigrants one hundred years ago and now provides services to more than seventy thousand clients annually, from all racial, ethnic, economic, and religious backgrounds. Many clients today are people of color, and large numbers speak Spanish, Russian, Mandarin, Hebrew, Creole, Yiddish, and other languages. The staff of more than two thousand employees is also racially and culturally diverse and represents a range of professional and paraprofessional disciplines (Greene, 2007).

Because of its original sectarian mission to serve the Jewish community, its name, and the way it was perceived in the local community, the organization saw that it needed to address diversity and multiculturalism in order to improve its competence in serving a culturally diverse population. The executive staff and managers were required to attend a racism training workshop for two-and-a-half days in order to create a common language and lay the foundation for the agency's antiracism organizational plan. At the workshop, the participants learned that structural racism refers to practices, policies, procedures, and the social culture of institutions.

The agency addressed structural racism, with workshops carried out by outside trainers. Its goals were to attract a multicultural staff and better serve its broad array of multicultural clients, but the demographically diverse workforce brought fresh new perspectives as well. They were able to pursue and maintain cases that the all-white staff had not been able to, such as outreach to the community's natural support systems that the white staff might not have thought relevant or because their link to clinical treatment was not obvious to them. They learned that leaders, managers, and supervisors need training to become adept at identifying, analyzing, and nurturing culturally based skills, beliefs, and practices to learn from them and make others aware. The goal was to integrate those skills into the core of the organization's culture to implement systemic and institutional change to affect the agency's practice.

In Florida, the city of Clearwater, the YWCA of Tampa Bay, the U.S. Attorney's Office for the Middle District of Florida, the Bureau of Justice Assistance, the U.S. Department of Justice Executive Office for Weed and Seed, the Regional Community Policing Institute at St. Petersburg Junior College, the Regional Community Policing Institute, the Allegany Franciscan Foundation, the Pinellas County Schools Adult Education Center, the local community and the Mexican government, have collaborated to manage diversity in the community and in its public and nonprofit agencies. In the late 1990s, the non–English-speaking Hispanic community in Clearwater grew to about 15 percent of the city's population, but there were only 5 bilingual police officers on its 250-officer force. The city discovered that young, mostly Hispanic males seemed to fear the police. They would not cooperate with investigations, and other crime problems were not being reported within the Mexican community.

In 1999, the city created the Hispanic Task Force made up of representatives from city departments that deal directly with the public. In 2000, a police officer was appointed to the new position of Hispanic outreach officer to act as a liaison among the police department, the community, and the city government. Members of the task force traveled to Hidalgo, Mexico, to study the cultural differences between the two places. The city then held public forums and asked the Hispanic community to tell them how the city and its respective departments and the police department could improve their service and communicate with the Hispanic community. As a result, a new program, Joining Hands: Operation Apoyo Hispano, was developed. The program consists of ten parts:

1. *Communicators.* Fifteen bilingual interpreters were trained by the police department and the YWCA to assist police officers. The communicators are trained in police procedures and how to translate verbatim, take notes in court, and notify the officers if anything was said to put the officers at risk.
2. *Victim advocacy.* The YWCA program has two full-time bilingual victim advocates to help victims of crime by explaining the criminal justice system and even accompanying crime victims to court.
3. *Mobile outreach program.* To overcome residents' fear of the police and reluctance to come to the police, the police go to the community. Using a mobile command post vehicle, the police department goes where the Hispanic community gathers, from soccer fields to church, and presents information about government services and cultural programs.
4. *Officer recruitment.* The police department is recruiting bilingual officers and offering bilingual incentive pay for new officers.
5. *Television and radio.* The program uses Spanish radio and television stations to reach the community. "Blueline CPD" is a local, live interactive television show in which Clearwater officers answer questions called in by the viewers.
6. *Community education and crime prevention.* The police department and the YWCA conduct programs in both English and Spanish. Topics include immigration, landlord-tenant issues, employment, child abuse, domestic violence, and education.
7. *English for Speakers of Other Languages.* English classes are held to help residents become familiar with English and, in the long run, make them more employable and eligible for higher-paying positions; general educational development (GED) instruction and job training is also offered.
8. *Basic Spanish for officers.* Clearwater police officers and other employees are taught Spanish by the local school board so they will not have to rely on YWCA interpreters. Because there are no bilingual employees in the 911 Communications Center, the center uses an AT&T language line to connect employees with a bilingual interpreter who translates in a three-way call. Having staff who can speak Spanish is important; under the

existing system, time is lost in an emergency, and the cost of the service is expensive.

9. *Training.* Job skills training is offered at the police facility.
10. *Partnership with the regional community policing institute.* As a result of this partnership, a video and printed material to assist other law enforcement agencies has been developed (Clearwater Police Hispanic Outreach) (www.clearwaterpolice.org/hispanic/index.asp)

In the examples cited, the demographics of the community, as well as the clients of public and nonprofit agencies, have changed from the past. San Francisco's Asian & Pacific Islander Wellness Center, the Jewish Board of Family and Children's Services, and the City of Clearwater recognized the changing demographics and needs in their communities and made changes to become more effective in the delivery of their services.

Nevertheless, not everyone is convinced that diversity makes good business sense. Moreover, explaining, demonstrating, and achieving the benefits of diversity is multifaceted, complex, and difficult (Bell & Berry, 2007; Kalev, Dobbin, & Kelly, 2006; Klein & Harrison, 2007; Wise & Tschirhart, 2000).

Sexual Harassment

The daily routines of employees must be free from intimidation and the distraction brought about by sexual harassment. Employers have become more sensitive to the growing need for policies and procedures to eliminate sexual harassment in the workplace. Today, most organizations have sexual harassment policies in place and are demanding that managers and supervisors enforce them.

Sexual harassment is considered to be a form of sex discrimination, falling within the protections of the Civil Rights Act of 1964, Title VII. The Supreme Court ruled in *Meritor Savings Bank* v. *Vinson* (1986) that sexual harassment is a form of sexual discrimination and therefore illegal under Title VII of the Civil Rights Act of 1964. Any workplace conduct that is "sufficiently severe or pervasive to alter the conditions of employment and create an abusive working environment" constitutes illegal sexual harassment. Sexual harassment constitutes discrimination with respect to a person's conditions of employment.

The Equal Employment Opportunity Commission (1989) has defined *sexual harassment* as unwelcome sexual advances, requests for sexual favors, and other verbal or physical conduct of a sexual nature when (1) submission to such conduct is made either explicitly or implicitly a term or condition of an individual's employment, (2) submission to or rejection of such conduct by an individual is used as the basis for employment decisions affecting an individual, or (3) such conduct has the purpose or effect of unreasonably interfering with an individual's work performance or creating an intimidating, hostile, or offensive working environment.

There are two forms of sexual harassment: quid pro quo harassment and hostile environment harassment. *Quid pro quo harassment* exists when the employer places sexual demands on the employee as a condition of that person's receiving employment benefits—for example, when a supervisor requires that a subordinate go out on a date as a condition of receiving a promotion or pay increase. The reverse is also considered quid pro quo harassment. For example, because a subordinate will not date a supervisor, the supervisor retaliates by assigning work of a less desirable nature to the employee or lowers the employee's performance evaluation rating.

Hostile environment harassment does not require the loss of a tangible employment benefit. Instead, the focus is on unwelcome contact that is sufficiently severe or pervasive to alter the conditions of the employee's employment and create an abusive working environment. In *Ellison* v. *Brady* (1991), the Ninth Circuit Court of Appeals created a "reasonable woman" standard that it applied to the issue of whether sexually oriented conduct constituted a hostile or offensive environment. The court believed that it was important to examine the behavior from the perspective of a "reasonable woman" since "a sex-blind reasonable person standard tends to be male-biased and tends to systematically ignore the experiences of women." Since research demonstrates that women and men differ in their responses to sexually oriented behavior, the court believed that it was inappropriate to use the viewpoint of a man (or men in general) to determine whether a reasonable woman would have found the conduct to be unwelcome, a requirement that the woman must meet in order to prevail. The standard moved from the "reasonable person" perspective to the "reasonable victim" perspective.

In *Harris* v. *Forklift Systems* (1993), the U.S. Supreme Court ruled that victims need not show they suffered serious psychological injury as a result of the harassment in order to prevail in court.

In 1998, the U.S. Supreme Court heard three cases dealing with sexual harassment: *Oncale* v. *Sundowner Offshore Services*, *Faragher* v. *Boca Raton*, and *Burlington Industries* v. *Ellerth*.

The *Oncale* case addressed sexual harassment involving persons of the same sex. Joseph Oncale worked aboard an oil platform in the Gulf of Mexico. According to Oncale, his male supervisors and coworkers sexually abused him, pushing a bar of soap into his anus and threatening homosexual rape. Although he complained to his employer, the company did not respond, so he quit.

The U.S. Supreme Court held that "nothing in Title VII necessarily bars a claim of discrimination . . . merely because the plaintiff and the defendants . . . are of the same sex." Title VII of the 1964 Civil Rights Act prohibits sexual harassment between members of the same sex, and the legal standards governing same-sex claims are the same as those applied to claims of sexual harassment by a member of the opposite sex. The Court's ruling resolved a conflict among the federal appeals courts, which had disagreed on whether alleged sexual harassment by a person of the same gender could be considered discrimination in violation of Title VII.

In *Faragher*, the Court held that public employers can be held liable for harassment under Title VII even if the employee has not explicitly alerted the employer about the sexual harassment. Employers may defend against a suit by showing they took reasonable steps to prevent and correct the harassment and the employee failed to take advantage of the employer's procedures.

In *Burlington Industries* v. *Ellerth*, the Supreme Court held that an employer may be held liable in situations where a supervisor causes a hostile work environment, even when the employee suffers no tangible job consequence, and the employer was unaware of the offensive conduct.

As a result of the *Faragher* and *Burlington Industries* rulings, employers will be held presumptively liable for sexually hostile environments created by their supervisors. If an employee is sexually harassed by a supervisor and loses his or her job, is demoted, or is given an undesirable reassignment, the employer will be held legally responsible for the harassment even if company officials did not know about it or had strong antiharassment policies. If the employee is sexually harassed by a supervisor but suffers no tangible job loss, the employer will be held legally responsible for the harassment unless the employer can prove it used reasonable care to prevent harassment through effective policies and complaint procedures, and that the employee "unreasonably failed" to make use of the complaint procedures, and that the behavior would have been stopped had the employee made the harassment known.

Employer Liability

Employers are generally held liable for the acts of their supervisors and managers, regardless of whether the employer is aware of these people's acts. If an employer knew or should have known about a supervisor's or manager's harassment of a coworker and did nothing to stop it, the employer will be liable. The employer may also be liable for behaviors committed in the workplace by nonemployees, clients, or outside contractors if the employer knew or should have known about the harassment and did not take appropriate action. The courts have made it clear that an organization is liable for sexual harassment when management is aware of the activity, yet does not take immediate and appropriate corrective action.

An employer is likely to minimize its sexual harassment liability under the following circumstances if (1) it has issued a specific policy against sexual harassment; (2) it established a sexual harassment complaint procedure with multiple avenues for redress (employees who are harassed by a supervisor must be able to go elsewhere in the organization to file a complaint and not only to their supervisor); (3) the employer educates supervisors and employees as to the actions and behaviors that constitute sexual harassment and alerts the supervisors and employees that the organization will not tolerate such behavior; (4) charges of sexual harassment are investigated promptly and thoroughly; and (5) the employer takes immediate and appropriate corrective action.

The Civil Rights Act of 1991 provides for compensatory damages in addition to back pay for intentional discrimination and unlawful harassment. Private and nonprofit employers may also be liable for punitive damages.

Sexual Orientation

No federal laws prohibit discrimination of the basis of sexual orientation. On November 7, 2007, the Employer Non-Discrimination Act (ENDA) was approved by the U.S. House of Representatives. The vote, 235 to 184, marks the first time that either chamber of Congress has passed employment protections based on sexual orientation, which it defines as "lesbian, gay, bisexual, or heterosexual orientation, real or perceived, as manifested by identity, acts, statements, or association." At the time of this writing, it has not been voted on by the U.S. Senate or signed into law by the president.

ENDA seeks to extend federal employment discrimination protections currently provided based on race, religion, sex, national origin, age, and disability to sexual orientation. If the act were to be passed, it would apply to private employers with fifteen or more employees, employment agencies, labor organizations, and civilian federal employees. It would prohibit public and private employers, employment agencies, and labor unions from using an individual's sexual orientation as the basis for employment decisions, such as hiring, firing, promotion, or compensation. It would also provide for the same procedures, and similar, but somewhat more limited, remedies as are permitted under Title VII and the Americans with Disabilities Act. And it would apply to employees of state and local governments.

Exemptions to ENDA would include businesses with fewer than fifteen employees, it would not apply to the uniformed members of the armed forces, and it would exempt veterans' preferences. The act would exempt tax-exempt private membership clubs and all religious organizations, which is defined to include religious educational institutions. It would not permit quotas or preferential treatment based on sexual orientation or allow a disparate impact claim similar to the one available under Title VII of the Civil Rights Act of 1964. Therefore, an employer would not be required to justify a neutral practice that might have a statistically disparate impact on individuals because of their sexual orientation. It also would not permit the imposition of affirmative action for a violation of ENDA or allow the Equal Employment Opportunity Commission to collect statistics on sexual orientation or compel employers to collect such statistics, and it could not be applied retroactively. Finally, the law, if passed, would not require employers to provide domestic partnership benefits.

Originally ENDA included a provision that would also prohibit discrimination on the basis of gender identity or gender expression, often referred to as *transgendered*, but its elimination was necessary to obtain the support of many of those who voted to support the bill.

Although no federal protection currently exists, many state and local governments have enacted their own laws that prohibit discrimination against gays and lesbians. Some states have amended their human rights acts specifically to prohibit discrimination in employment on the basis of actual or perceived sexual orientation. In other states, governors have issued executive orders. Approximately two hundred counties and municipalities prohibit such discrimination.

There are a number of support groups for public employees across the federal, state, and local governments. In California, the Golden State

Peace Officers Association has a support group call PRIDE Behind the Badge. Other support groups include FireFLAG/EMS in New York City, GOAL-DC: Gay Officers Action League, and the Gay Officers Actions Leagues of New York and New England. There are groups for state employees such as Pride in Wisconsin Government; StatePride: Gay, Lesbian, Bisexual, Transgendered and Allied Employees of the State of Texas; and State Pride for Connecticut pubic employees.

Federal employees are protected by the Civil Service Reform Act of 1978, which prohibits job discrimination for any non-job-related issue. In 1980, the Carter administration issued a policy statement specifically including sexual orientation bias. The statute covered executive branch offices and the Government Printing Office, but not the General Accounting Office or intelligence agencies.

On August 4, 1995, President Clinton issued Executive Order 12968, which forbade federal agencies from using sexual orientation as a reason for denying security clearances to lesbians and gays. The executive order extended coverage to private citizens working for defense contractors, engineering firms, and high-tech industries involved with the government. This order created the first uniform standard for U.S. agencies in granting security clearances and required federal agencies to recognize one another's security clearances. The Defense, Energy, and State Departments, the Office of Personnel Management, the U.S. Information Agency, the Federal Bureau of Investigation, the Secret Service, and the U.S. Customs Service had already stopped using homosexuality as a reason for denying security clearances for civilian workers. In 1998, President Clinton signed an executive order, Further Amendment to Executive Order 11478, Equal Employment Opportunity in the Federal Government, which ensured that all federal agencies would ban employment discrimination based on sexual orientation.

A general support group for gay, lesbian, or bisexual employees working for the federal government exists, called Federal GLOBE. Other federal departments such as the Federal Aviation Association, U.S. Department of Energy, U.S. Department of Labor, and the National Institute of Standards of Technology have their own GLOBE groups for their employees.

What Does It Mean to Be Transgendered?

Transgendered people are individuals of any age or sex whose appearance, personal characteristics, or behaviors differ from stereotypes about how men and women are "supposed to be" (Green, 2000, p. 1). Social scientists use the term *sex* to refer to a person's biological or anatomical identity as male or female and *gender* for the collection of characteristics that are culturally associated with maleness or femaleness. *Gender identity* refers to a person's internal, deeply felt sense of being either male or female, or something other or in between. Because gender identity is internal and personally defined, it is not visible to others. In contrast, a person's gender expression is externally and socially perceived. Gender expression refers to all of the external characteristics and behaviors that are socially defined as masculine or feminine, such as dress, mannerisms, speech patterns, and social interactions.

Gender identity disorder and *gender dysphoria* are terms by which the American Psychiatric Association characterizes the illness of those who are transgendered (American Psychiatric Association, 2000). It is important to note that although transgenderism remains classified as a medical disorder and homosexuality is no longer classified as such, the principal legal tool for protecting people with physical or mental impairments, the Americans with Disabilities Act, specifically excludes use of the act to protect their rights. However, some state laws prohibiting disability discrimination, like those of New Jersey, have found that transgendered people are covered (Gossett, 2006). Over the past few years, many gay and bisexual organizations have broadened the scope of their work to include the issues and concerns of transgendered people. A number of states and local governments, as well as private organizations, offer employee protection to transgendered individuals (Colvin, 2007, 2008).

Changes in the Nonprofit Landscape

Many nonprofit and private employers were at the forefront of prohibiting discrimination against gays and lesbians. They willingly promulgated their own personnel policies that protected the rights of gay and lesbian employees. Not fearing reprisals, many gay, lesbian, and bisexual support groups were founded in those organizations. In addition to nondiscrimination policies, many nonprofit and private employers initiated the extension of domestic partnership benefits to homosexual couples.

The complex environment in which nonprofit administrators operate became even more complicated when the U.S. Supreme Court, in a five-to-four decision, held that the application of New Jersey's public accommodation law to the Boy Scouts of America (BSA) violated the organization's First Amendment right of expressive association (*Boy Scouts of America and Monmouth Council et al.* v. *James Dale*, 2000). The Boy Scouts argued successfully that as a private organization, it has the right to determine criteria for membership. The Supreme Court heard this case on appeal from the BSA in response to the New Jersey Supreme Court's decision against its position.

The New Jersey Supreme Court had held that the Boy Scouts of America is a place of "public accommodation" that "emphasizes open membership" and therefore must follow New Jersey's antidiscrimination law. The court further held that the state's law did not infringe on the group's freedom of expressive association (*Dale* v. *Boy Scouts of America and Monmouth Council Boy Scouts*, 1998, 1999). It thus reasoned that the New Jersey legislature, when it enacted the antidiscrimination law, declared that discrimination is a matter of concern to the government and that infringements on that right may be justified by regulations adopted to serve compelling state interests.

The New Jersey Supreme Court noted the BSA's historic partnership with various public entities and public service organizations. Local BSA units are chartered by public schools, parent-teacher associations, firehouses, local civic associations, and the U.S. Army, Navy, Air Force, and National Guard. Its "Learning for Life" program has been installed in many public school classrooms throughout the country, and many troops meet in public facilities. The BSA in turn provides essential services through its scouts to public and quasi-public organizations.

This close relationship thus underscores the BSA's fundamental public character. Nonprofit administrators must stay current with changing and sometimes contradictory community norms and legal requirements across a diverse set of local communities and reconcile them with mandates from the national or parent organization. This is especially true for sexual orientation discrimination. When confronted with this form of discrimination, nonprofit managers find themselves in a complex legal environment. No federal legislation has been passed defining a national standard; thus, they face a patchwork of state and local laws, executive orders, and judicial and commission decisions barring such discrimination.

The organizations that have withdrawn their support from the Boy Scouts have clearly stated that they cannot fund or support organizations that have policies that conflict with their own antidiscrimination policies. Despite the U.S. Supreme Court's ruling supporting the Boy Scouts of America's exclusionary policy, the stand of the Boy Scouts' National Council to refuse local councils in determining local policy has jeopardized their funding and support from their local communities.

The New Jersey Supreme Court's analysis of the public nature of the Boy Scouts is shared by many. The BSA decision to exclude homosexuals has become controversial. The State of Connecticut, for example, dropped the Boy Scouts from the list of charities that receive donations through a state employer payroll deduction plan. When the Boy Scouts sued the state, saying that the ban was unconstitutional, it lost in two federal court decisions, and the U.S. Supreme Court declined to hear the case, letting the lower court rulings stand (*Boy Scouts of America* v. *Wyman*, 2003; *Boy Scouts of America* v. *Wyman*, 2004). Connecticut has banned the Scouts from using public campgrounds or buildings. Fifty-three local United Way offices have revoked their funding of the Boy Scouts until the BSA rescinds its policy of discrimination against gays and atheists. Many school districts across the country also restricted access to their schools for meetings and events, prompting the passage in 2003 of The Boy Scouts of America Equal Access Act. The legislation prevents public schools and local educational agencies that receive federal funds from denying equal access and fair opportunity to meet, or from discriminating against groups officially affiliated with the Boy Scouts of America or any other youth group listed in Title 36 of the U.S. Code as a patriotic society for reasons based on the membership or leadership criteria or oath of allegiance to God and country.

Although the act no longer permits school districts to have the right to restrict access by the Boy Scouts to their facilities (without jeopardizing federal funds), private corporations such as Levi Strauss and Company, J. P. Morgan, American Airlines, Wells Fargo of Portland Oregon, Hewlett Packard, the *Providence Journal*, IBM, Textron, and CVS Pharmacy have withdrawn hundreds of thousands of dollars in support to the Boy Scouts (Zernike, 2000).

On November 15, 2004, the Defense Department agreed to end its direct sponsorship of Boy Scout troops in response to a religious discrimination lawsuit brought by the ACLU. The ACLU of Illinois charged that the BSA required troops and pack leaders and, in this case, government employees, to compel youth to swear an oath of duty to God. The ACLU charged that this policy violates the religious liberty of youth who wish to participate but do not wish to swear a religious oath and that direct government sponsorship of such a program is religious discrimination. The settlement does not prohibit off-duty public employees from sponsoring Boy Scout troops on their own time, and the Boy Scouts will still have access to any military facilities that are currently made available to other nongovernmental organizations (American Civil Liberties Union [ACLU], 2004).

The City of Philadelphia is now requiring the Cradle of Liberty Council chapter of the Boy Scouts of America to either publicly renounce its membership against people who are openly homosexual or atheists if the organization wishes to remain in its headquarters on city-owned land. If the Cradle of Liberty Council does not, it would need to begin paying two hundred thousand dollars a year in fair-market rent instead of the yearly lease of $1. The city told the BSA it was impossible to reconcile the group's discrimination against homosexuals and atheists with the city's antidiscrimination fair-practices law. The local council maintains it has used a "don't ask, don't tell" practice, but cannot change the policies without violating its charter from the national organization (Slobododzian, 2007; Urbina, 2007). In May 2008, the Cradle of Liberty Council filed a suit and is suing the city to stay in the city-owned space. The federal suit accuses the city of censorship for targeting the Scouts but maintaining free or nominal leases with other groups that limit membership such as the Baptist and Roman Catholic Church groups and the Colonial Dames of America (Dale, 2008; Hinkelman, 2008; Slobodzian, 2008). Although the U.S. Supreme Court upheld the right of voluntary associations to discriminate in regard to their employees and volunteers, the most appropriate policy is for national nonprofit organizations to permit local chapters, sensitive to their community norms, to formulate their own nondiscriminatory policies. Big Brothers Big Sisters of America told its affiliates to give openly gay and lesbian volunteers an equal chance to serve as mentors, and the Girl Scouts of America have deferred to the norms of each local community and let each troop decide how to handle this potentially divisive issue.

The Difference Between Compliance with Laws and Managing Diversity

Equal employment opportunity and affirmative action are legal requirements designed to bring women and minorities into the workforce. Managing diversity requires more than just compliance with laws. The management of diversity consists of "management processes to create a supportive work environment for employees already on board, and to develop and fully include all of them in order to make the organization more productive" (U.S. Merit Systems Protections Board, 1993, p. xiii).

Managing diversity requires more than just compliance with laws.

To manage diversity, employers must first understand and then manage their organizational cultures. The organizational culture is defined as the values, beliefs, assumptions, expectations, attitudes, and norms shared by a majority of the organization's members. Wilson (1989) believes that "every organization has a culture that is a persistent, patterned way of thinking about the central tasks of and human relationships within an organization. Culture is to an organization what personality is to an individual. Like human culture generally, it is passed from one generation to the next. It changes slowly, if at all" (p. 91).

Not only do organizations possess a dominant culture, but subcultures can emerge as well. Subcultures often develop to reflect common problems, situations, or experiences that employees face. Wilson (1989) notes that in the U.S. Navy, different subcultures exist for personnel assigned to submarines, aircraft carriers, or battleships.

Organizational culture is perceived to be valuable when it helps to orient new employees to expected job-related behaviors and performance levels. A strong culture can minimize the need for formal rules and regulations because values, traditions, rituals, heroes and heroines, and the informal communication network that provides information and interprets messages sent through the organization serve to reduce ambiguity (Deal & Kennedy, 1982). Employers must be aware that an entrenched organizational culture can be a liability when the shared culture will not react to change or change to strengthen the organization's effectiveness.

As an example, the FBI is having difficulty recruiting female agents. The FBI has 2,373 female agents among 12,617 agents, or approximately 19 percent of the total number; only 153, or about 1 percent, are black women. Special agent James J. Knight, in charge of recruiting new agents, believes that women often do not consider the FBI because of its history: women were not permitted to become agents until 1972. However, the FBI recognizes that diversity is important: "We're not just working white male cases. . . . There are a lot of communities who don't trust the FBI. If they had somebody from their own community interviewing them, they might be willing to talk more. . . . The FBI needs more than door kickers and encourages women to apply because they often have the cognitive skills needed. Women agents are often adept at finding links among victims in homicide cases who have similar jobs, ages, physical characteristics, residences, friends and acquaintances. Women's verbal skills and the ability to work on teams are strengths. Women are often better able to calm a situation" (Johnson, 2007).

The increase of women, minorities, and persons with disabilities in the workforce is going to continue. The attitudes, beliefs, values, and customs of people in society are an integral part of their culture and affect their behavior on the job. Research has found that men, women, and minorities do not have a common culture or organizational life; rather, each group identifies, defines, and organizes its experience in the organization in unique ways that influence group members' reactions to work assignments, leadership styles, and reward systems (Fine, Johnson, & Ryan, 1990). These differences create the potential for communication problems, which can lead to increased organizational conflict.

Management must balance two conflicting goals: get employees to accept the dominant values and encourage acceptance of differences. Robbins (1991) calls this the "paradox of diversity" (p. 259). It is important for new employees to accept the organization's culture; otherwise, they are not likely to be accepted. But at the same time, management must acknowledge and demonstrate support for the differences that these employees bring to the workplace. Valuing diversity means recognizing and appreciating that individuals are different, that diversity can be an advantage if it is well managed, and that diversity should be encouraged. Accepting diverse ideas encourages employees to be more creative, which leads to greater flexibility and problem-solving capabilities (Fine et al., 1990; Ospina & O'Sullivan, 2003; Page, 2007).

Strategic Human Resources Management Implications for Managing Diversity

Employers must understand that compliance with equal employment opportunity and affirmative action does not necessarily mean that incumbent employees will respect or accept new entrants. Employers need to value the different knowledge and experiences diversity brings to the workplace. Diversity is often addressed in terms of visible differences, such as race, gender, age, or disability. But an employee's sexual orientation, religion, inconspicuous disability, education, work style, lifestyle, and culture are not as readily visible, and various combinations of differences can exist in one person. Even differences of parenthood or responsibility for elderly relatives are components of diversity that need accommodation through parental leaves, flexible work schedules, or child care or elder care assistance. Employers and employees must understand the many dimensions of diversity.

Training management and employees to accept diversity is essential but not enough. Gilbert and Ivancevich (2000) note that even when organizations have implemented policy or training initiatives to focus on diversity, the initiatives often do not translate into changes in the quality of work life for employees. Simply responding to laws, executive orders, or guidelines does not automatically result in greater inclusion. If blatant discrimination does not occur, often more subtle forms of discrimination, such as exclusion from informal work groups, conversations, and social gatherings outside work, happen. These exclusionary tactics lead to reduced opportunities and isolation for minorities and a loss of valuable human capital for the organization.

Cox (2001) suggests that employers conduct cultural and systems audits to arrive at comprehensive analyses of the agency's organizational culture and HRM systems, such as recruitment, performance appraisals, career patterns, and compensation. The objective of the audits is to uncover whether there are sources of potential bias that may inadvertently put some employees at a disadvantage. If changes are made in the system, they should be monitored and evaluated. Continued training and modifications in rewards and sanctions may need to be institutionalized.

Cox (2001) provides three reasons that diversity efforts often fail. Often the problem is misdiagnosed, the wrong solution is implemented or the agency failed to use a systematic approach, or there is a failure to understand the shape of the learning curve for leveraging diversity work. Cox's change model on diversity, presented in Figure 4.1, comprises leadership, research and measurement, education, the alignment of management systems, and follow-up:

- *Leadership* establishes a direction or goal for change (vision), facilitates the motivations of others, and cultivates necessary conditions for achieving the vision. To manage diversity as an approach to achieve its mission and goals, organizations need to establish a clear vision of how a more diverse workforce contributes to the bottom line. Leaders must believe that to integrate a diverse workforce, the company must go beyond what is required by regulation. There must be a business imperative and moral obligation. Mission statements can be modified to incorporate diversity-related goals (Cox, 2001; Gilbert & Ivancevich, 2000).
- *Research and measurement* are important because successful organizational change work must be informed by relevant data, with results systematically measured at pertinent intervals during the process.

FIGURE 4.1. CHANGE MODEL FOR WORK ON DIVERSITY

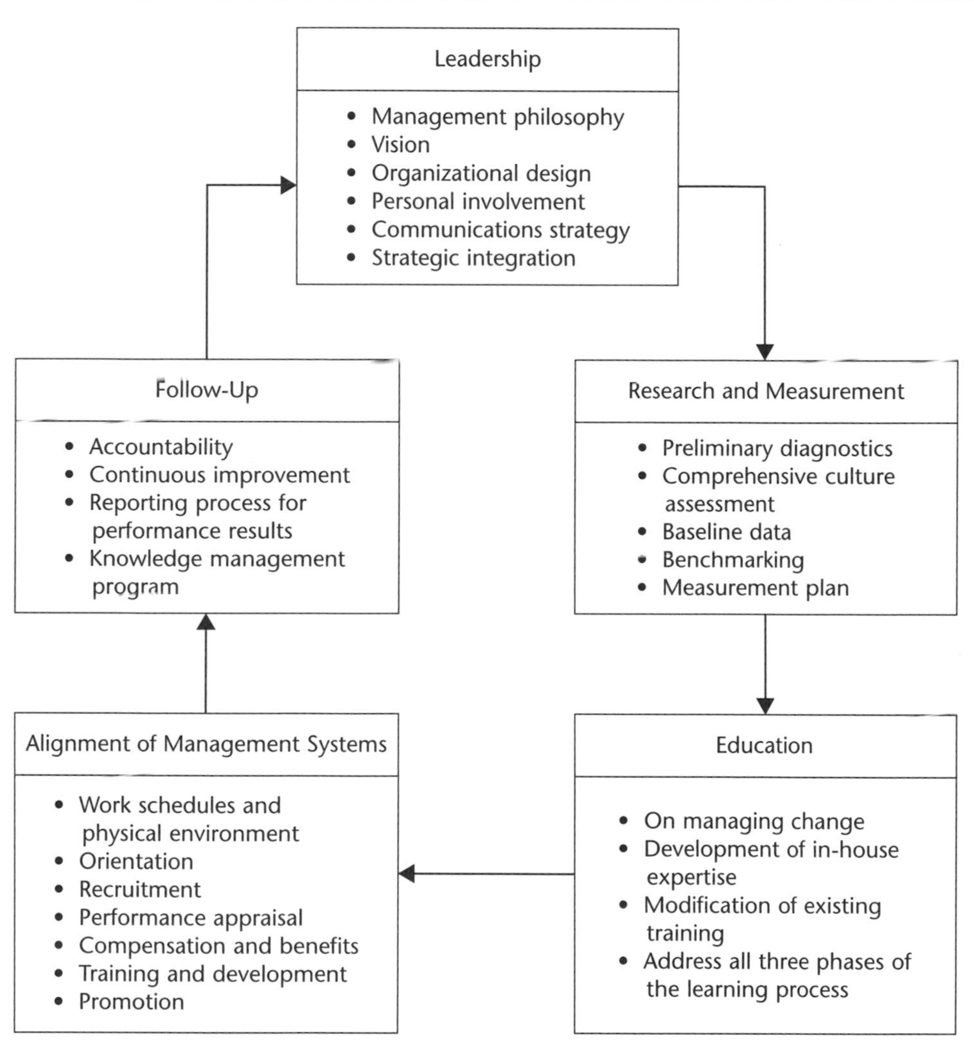

Source: Cox (2001, p. 19). Used by permission.

- *Education* imparts new information and skills that can be used to facilitate change.
- *Alignment of management systems* broadly includes any organizational policy, practice, rule, or procedure. This covers the major HRM activities like recruitment, promotion, performance appraisals,

training and development, compensation, work schedules, employment security, benefits, and the design of the physical environment.
- *Follow-up* involves implementing action, establishing managerial and employee accountability, fundamental changes in HRM practices, employee involvement and buy-in, overreaching corporate philosophy regarding diversity, ongoing monitoring and improvement of the diversity climate, and using multiple measures to evaluate success.

Cox's model is supported by a review of diversity data extending over thirty-one years. Kalev et al. (2006) found that efforts to establish responsibility for diversity see better effects from diversity training and evaluation, networking, and mentoring than diversity programs aimed only to avoid liability in discrimination lawsuits.

Conclusion

Changes in society and the workplace have resulted in diversity becoming an important issue for SHRM. Current personnel systems must be reviewed to recruit and retain a diverse workforce. The organization's culture must be evaluated. This can be done through the review of formal documents, HRM policies and procedures, rewards systems, recruitment and selection procedures, and succession planning. These components should all be interrelated, and attention should be paid to the provision of flexible benefits and alternative work schedules or flextime as they relate to work and family life.

Many agencies, such as those noted in this chapter as well as the Government Accountability Office (2007a), realize that when diversity is well managed, all workers are valued and included. As a result, productivity is improved because the work environment is supportive and nurturing, and contributions are appreciated. The successful management of diversity leads to better interpersonal communication among employees, responsiveness to social and demographic changes, a reduction in equal employment litigation, and a climate of fairness and equity. Diverse groups offer a wider range of ideas because different individuals are likely to perceive problems in a different light and thus develop alternative solutions.

Employers who are mistreated tend to be less productive. Energy is spent feeling anxious, angry, frustrated, or fearful instead of concentrating on job-related tasks. Mistreated employees tend to have greater rates of absenteeism and are more likely to seek other employment opportunities.

Organizations also suffer when their work environments are hostile. Higher turnover rates result in increased recruitment and selection expenses, as well as an us-versus-them atmosphere, which manifests as decreased cooperation and teamwork and increased distrust among employees. Organizations that promote diversity will be able to attract and retain the best employees. Workforces that are representative of the constituents they serve will also be more successful in expanding their constituent and customer base and will be poised to capture new markets.

A supportive environment in which employees can contribute and achieve their fullest potential is necessary. All mangers and supervisors should be held accountable for making the workplace supportive. Diversity programs will not be successful unless top managers provide leadership and exemplify the commitment to diversity. Agency and department mission statements should acknowledge respect for individuals and appreciation for the contributions each can make; they should state that diversity is accepted and valued and there will be equal opportunities for each employee to achieve his or her potential.

At a time when public and nonprofit workforces are facing significant retirements, it is important that they do not lose quality employees and potential employees due to discrimination. As it is, they often have trouble competing with private for-profit employers. Qualified individuals are likely to seek out progressive organizations for employment opportunities.

Exercise 4.1: Susan-Steve Stanton

Steve Stanton served for fourteen years as the city manager of Largo, Florida. In fall 2007, commissioners raised his salary nearly 9 percent to $140,234 a year. But after he publicly stated that he planned to have gender-reassignment surgery and change his name to Susan, the city commission terminated him. His intentions were known to his wife, his medical team, and the city's mayor, fire, and police chiefs. As an at-will employee, Stanton could be terminated at any time, "with or without cause," according to his contract.

City commissioners stated that they heard from dissatisfied employees in regard to the city manager's management style. Employees referred to him as abrupt and condescending, and he required that work be completed his way. Despite this, Stanton had been the city manager for fourteen years, his management style was well known, he had received positive job performance evaluations over the past fourteen years, and his recent performance evaluation provided him with a 9 percent pay increase. City managers typically have contracts noting that they serve at will and can be terminated by a majority vote of council members.

Questions

1. Why do you think Susan-Steve Stanton was fired? Do you believe it was his attitude or his impending sex-change surgery?
2. Should gender identity be protected under local, state, or federal nondiscrimination laws?

Sources: Helfand (2007a, 2007b).

Exercise 4.2: Tattoos and Piercing: Are They Acceptable in Public Safety Positions?

The Texas Department of Public Safety requires its uniformed troopers to cover their tattoos and branding with long-sleeved shirts or skin-toned patches while on duty. The Austin Police Department allows tattoos except on an officer's face and head, and requires that offensive tattoos be covered by the officer's uniform or patches. In 2002, a federal court ruled that the Fort Worth Police Department could require a heavily tattooed officer to cover his body art while on duty.

In Hillsborough County, Florida, the policy for the Sheriff's Office states that patrol deputies, detention deputies, and community service officers cannot get new tattoos that would be visible when they wear their uniforms. Those who already have tattoos must cover them with long-sleeved shirts and pants, even in summer, if supervisors deem the tattoos racist, sexist, offensive, obscene, or excessive. Tattoos that promote or support gang activity or that cover more than half of an extremity also must be covered. Tattoos on the face, head, or neck are banned. Uniformed personnel with acceptable tattoos in visible locations such as the forearm or hand will be grandfathered in. Applicants to the department who have tattoos that cannot be easily covered up will not be hired. The department's appearance policy also forbids male deputies from wearing earrings or visible body piercing. Female deputies can have earrings in only the lower lobes, not the upper cartilage, and not on the lip or in the nose.

The Pinellas County Sheriff's Office and the City of Tampa's Police Department also have policies on visible tattoos. Two other local law enforcement agencies, the City of St. Petersburg Police Department and the Pasco County Sheriff's Office do not have a policy on tattoos.

Questions

1. Is the refusal to hire an applicant with visible tattoos a type of employment discrimination?
2. Does a public safety employer have a right to institute personnel policies in regard to standards for appearance? Should the standards for law enforcement be different from other occupations? Explain your answer.
3. What are some issues that employers should consider when developing general standards for appearance?

Sources: Colavecchio-Van Sickler (2005); Susswein (2006, March 23).

Chapter Questions

1. In small groups, identify and discuss the significant trends related to diversity that have affected your agencies. What SHRM initiatives have been established in your agencies to meet these challenges? Which agency has the most comprehensive initiatives?
2. Can you think of an example when you might have possessed negative assumptions, attitudes, or stereotypes of coworkers or fellow students because they appeared to be different from you? Do you still feel that way today? If not, what changed?

Online Activities

1. Visit the U.S. Census Bureau Web site. Find a state profile with Quickfacts, and identify the demographic trends in that state. What do the trends indicate? How should employers prepare for the future?
2. In small groups, have each individual take on the role of spokesperson for a specific interest group, such as senior citizens, working women, or gays and lesbians, and present the concerns of that group to an employer. Use the Web sites of organizations like the American Association of Retired Persons (AARP), 9 to 5 National Association of Working Women, or the Department of Justice Pride to research your positions. After each group's concerns have been presented, discuss where the interests overlap or are in contradiction. How would an organization address those concerns, and are there any concerns they would not realistically be able to address?

CHAPTER FIVE

VOLUNTEERS IN THE PUBLIC AND NONPROFIT SECTORS

After you have read this chapter, you should be able to:

- Understand the importance of volunteers to strategic human resources management
- Discuss how volunteers assist public and nonprofit organizations
- Explain the variety of methods used to recruit volunteers
- Understand volunteer motivations
- Understand the roles of governing boards in nonprofit organizations

The tradition of volunteerism in the United States began with religious-affiliated organizations and local government councils. Today nonprofit and public sector organizations provide volunteer opportunities ranging from serving as board members of nonprofit organizations to serving on local government boards and commissions. Parents volunteer as coaches for nonprofit and municipality-sponsored sports and recreation activities, and volunteers provide myriad services in public and nonprofit cultural, educational, social service, and health care agencies.

Volunteers assist employees in meeting their agency's mission, and thus become an important part of strategic human resources management

(SHRM) and planning. When one thinks of volunteers and civic participation, nonprofit agencies typically come to mind. However, the public sector has also come to rely on volunteers for an assortment of purposes and in a variety of environments.

While the use of volunteers in the public sector has grown, dependence on volunteer use tends to be more pervasive in the nonprofit sector. The increase in volunteer activities has necessitated the increasing professionalism of volunteer administration. Organizations such as the National Center for Voluntary Action, the Volunteer Center National Network, Minnesota Association for Volunteer Administration, North Carolina Association for Volunteer Administration, New York Association for Volunteer Administration, and South Carolina Association for Volunteer Administration are examples of statewide associations of volunteer administration. There are also regional and citywide associations. The Association for Volunteer Administration has a certificate program for managers of volunteers. Other services include the provision of books, pamphlets, training materials, and videos targeting the recruitment and management of volunteers. These agencies also provide training related to the recruitment and use of volunteers (Brudney, 2001). The National Association of Volunteer Programs in Local Governments is an affiliate of the National Association of Counties. Members have access to a mentoring program, where a coordinator for new volunteers can find resources or seek help from an experienced manager for consultation or support. Other services include training and educational workshops at the national Points of Light conference, as well as state and regional levels. The association provides a quarterly newsletter with program updates, news, and best practices.

In both public and nonprofit agencies, attention should be paid to the recruitment, selection, training, evaluation, and management of volunteers. While volunteers can be tremendous assets to any organization, they also present new human resources management challenges. Administrative responsibilities are increased because agencies must keep records and extend their liability insurance and workers' compensation policies to volunteers.

Managing volunteer programs requires the development of human resources management (HRM) policies and procedures to assist with the integration of volunteers into the everyday operations of the agency. Paid staff, unions, and board members need to support the use of volunteers, oversight needs to be provided so that volunteers are properly used, and strategies need to be developed to motivate and retain volunteers.

This chapter addresses these issues. At the end of the chapter, special attention is given to volunteers who serve on governing boards.

Use of Volunteers

As funding has tightened, government agencies have come to rely on volunteers as a way to deliver services and foster community involvement (National Association of Counties, 2003; Rehnborg, 2005; Sanecki, 2000; Scott, 2003). Volunteers are an attractive resource for agencies because they cost little, can give detailed attention to people for whom paid employees do not always have the time, often provide specialized skills, provide an expansion of staff in emergencies and peak load periods, enable agencies to expand levels of service despite budgetary limitations, and are good for public relations. Public agencies use volunteers to serve on task forces, oversee and instruct in recreation programs, staff libraries, and serve as advocates for community causes. They work as firefighters, as police auxiliary officers, as senior citizens center assistants, as park maintenance workers, as file clerks and office workers, in fingerprinting the public, as hospital and nursing home attendants, in removing litter from highways and community clean-up campaigns, as teaching assistants in school and correctional facilities, as activity assistants for the developmentally and physically disabled, in reviewing grants, in monitoring wetlands, and as museum guides. Volunteers also participate in community programs such as public safety, services for the homeless, AIDS prevention, and in programs addressing the health and well-being of children (Brudney, 1999, Lane, 1995; National Association of Counties, 2003; Rehnborg, 2005; Sanecki, 2000). At least 60 percent of state parks use volunteers, and at least 39 percent of state agencies use volunteers to assist in delivering services (Brudney & Kellough, 2000). In Alaska, volunteer opportunities exist for archaeological assistants, backcountry rangers, museum assistants, park caretakers, and natural history interpreters. Governor Arnold Schwarzenegger of California created a cabinet-level office for volunteer management, whose secretary will play a role in disaster-related planning and response efforts and coordinating volunteers at disaster sites. This office will also manage donations that flow into the state for disaster relief (Steinhauer, 2008). In fiscal year 2005, the U.S. National Park Service's Volunteers-In-Parks program (VIP) used 137,000 volunteers who contributed 5.2 million hours of service. The dollar value of their services was $91.2 million (National Park Service, 2008). Examples of other federal agencies that use volunteers are the Cooperative Extension Service of the U.S. Department of Agriculture, Head Start programs, the Department of Health and Human Services' Older Americans Programs, the Department of Veterans Affairs, the U.S. Forest Service, the Bureau of Prisons, the Department of the Interior, the U.S. Geological Survey, and the Bureau of Indian Affairs (Brudney, 1999).

The Medical Reserve Corps (MRC), sponsored by the U.S. Surgeon General, is composed of organized medical and public health professionals who serve as volunteers to respond to natural disasters and emergencies. These volunteers assist communities nationwide during emergencies and in ongoing efforts for public health. In the past, many medical and public health professionals sought volunteer opportunities to support emergency relief efforts, but there was only a limited organized approach to channel their efforts. The MRC program now provides the structure necessary to deploy medical and public health personnel in response to an emergency: it identifies specific, trained, credentialed personnel available and ready to respond. Volunteers include practicing, retired, or otherwise employed medical professionals, such as doctors, nurses, emergency medical technicians, pharmacists, nurses' assistants, and public health professionals. Community members without medical training are welcome as well; they assist with administrative and other essential support functions. Noncitizen, legal U.S. residents also are welcome to volunteer and contribute their time, knowledge, and skills.

Promising though the use of volunteers may be, agencies must be aware that there are costs associated with volunteer programs. Ellis (1995, p. 3) notes that "because volunteers are agents of the organizations, their work poses potential risk management questions and insurance needs. Anyone acting on behalf of an organization can put others at risk or can be at risk. Volunteers are not inherently more or less likely to have accidents or make mistakes. However, the board should make sure that the organization has taken all the necessary steps to protect the client, the volunteer and the paid staff." This means that volunteers need to be screened for possessing the appropriate qualifications, and they need to be trained. For example, volunteers who would not be hired as police officers because of antisocial or aberrant personalities should not be selected as police auxiliary volunteers. Individuals who exhibit short tempers or low frustration levels should not work with children, senior citizens, or the disabled in capacities that require patience or in situations that despite planning, often become unstructured. To minimize the frequency and severity of mistakes, volunteers need to receive general training concerning the agency's mission, policies, and regulations, as well as training that is tailored to the specialized tasks or responsibilities they will perform.

Promising though the use of volunteers may be, agencies must be aware that there are costs associated with volunteer programs.

Agencies must anticipate the reactions of paid staff and unions if they plan to use volunteers as replacements for paid employees. If volunteer programs are going to be effective, agencies must work with employees to establish the parameters of volunteer programs. Volunteers with the Massachusetts Commission Against Discrimination were helpful in reducing the workload of the paid staff, but in other situations, such as in Michigan, where layoffs had occurred, staff employees resented volunteers who replaced paid staff. In most instances, volunteers are used to enhance the effectiveness of paid staff, not to eliminate paid positions or compensate for deliberately understaffed programs. According to Brudney (1993, p. 130), "The literature leaves no question, however, that volunteer scholars and managers endorse labor's stance that the substitution of nonpaid workers for paid is unethical. No evidence exists that volunteers feel any differently. Hence, if agency administration intended to use volunteers to reallocate funds away from designated positions, they can anticipate resistance from not only employees but also from volunteers."

Volunteer Motivation

Why do individuals volunteer? When surveyed, volunteers expressed a variety of reasons. It appears that both intrinsic and extrinsic rewards motivate volunteers. *Intrinsic rewards* are such things as satisfaction, a sense of accomplishment, and being challenged, which result from the work itself. *Extrinsic rewards* are benefits granted to the volunteers by the organization.

Many individuals use volunteering as a means for career exploration and development. For example, individuals who volunteer at a community nonprofit for developmentally disabled adults can experience what it is like to work with that population. Individuals who volunteer as a reserve police officer can receive enough exposure to determine whether law enforcement is a correct career choice for them. Some people volunteer to develop skills that might enhance their paid positions. For example, volunteering to make presentations in front of large groups, write grants, or prepare budgets develops essential skills that employers need.

Some people volunteer because of the opportunity to meet new people. Some volunteer as a way to contribute or give back to the community in which they live. Some professionals, such as nurses and social workers who are raising small children, keep active professionally through volunteer work. Others volunteer as a way to interact with community leaders or because they value the goals of the agency. Still others volunteer because they are concerned about people or desire personal growth or external recognition (Cnaan & Goldberg-Glenn, 1991; Dailey, 1986; Fisher & Cole, 1993; Pearce, 1993).

There is no one reason that individuals volunteer. What motivates one volunteer may not motivate others. Therefore, the volunteer experience should attempt to provide both intrinsic and extrinsic rewards by promoting satisfying and interesting opportunities and some form of external recognition.

Barriers to Volunteer Recruitment

Research on volunteering has found these barriers: lack of resources such as time, money, information, or skills; lack of opportunities; lack of personal interest; lack of transportation; not knowing how to become involved; no one asked; inadequate volunteer management; not understanding how volunteering can help them personally; lack of child care; low self-esteem or confidence in skills; and cultural or language barriers (Points of Light Foundation, 2000; Sundeen, Raskoff, & Garcia, 2007). Other barriers are having a disability; possessing a criminal record; the exclusion of lesbians, gays, and bisexuals; ethnic minority status; refugee status; and age (Gosport Volunteer Centre, 2004).

Other studies address the role of social anxiety in volunteering, noting that individuals with a fear of new social situations are more likely to make a donation than volunteer their time. When they do volunteer, they are more comfortable engaging in volunteer activities as part of a group such as a church, school, workplace, or family (Handy & Cnaan, 2007).

Recruitment

Volunteers are individuals who donate their time, efforts, and experience to an organization without receiving money or in-kind payment (Brudney, 1990). Consequently, there is a lot of competition among public and nonprofit agencies for these people. Unlike paid staff, who typically initiate the employment process themselves, volunteers need to be recruited. Communication is the key to finding volunteers. People need to know that the agency is looking for and receptive to volunteers. Word-of-mouth referrals from other volunteers or paid staff, newspaper articles and advertisements, radio and television spots, presentations before community or professional groups, and tapping the relatives and friends of clients have proven to be successful methods for recruiting volunteers. Virtual recruitment and volunteering is also becoming more common.

Recruiting volunteers can be difficult. Brudney (1993) found an increase in competition among public and nonprofit agencies for volunteer talent. Contributing to the difficulty in recruiting volunteers is the nature of society today. The United States ranks among the highest on a global scale in the percentage of employees working fifty hours per week or more. Many workers are finding it difficult to balance job and family demands without adding volunteer work. Many Americans believe that the time pressures on working families are getting more severe (Taniguchi, 2006). The increased pressure on working adults with families has forced many nonprofits such as the Girl Scouts of America to target new audiences for recruiting volunteers. One poster to recruit Girl Scout troop leaders developed by the Girl Scout Council of Atlanta shows a girl with green hair and fingernails, and another poster shows a girl sporting a tattoo of the Girl Scout trefoil on her back. The message is, "Sure we wear green. But a lot else has changed." The posters are designed to attract young, single volunteers in their twenties and thirties, not the stay-at-home moms who have anchored the volunteer corps since its inception (Wyatt, 2000). As a result of the many economic and demographic changes affecting communities, some Girl Scout Councils wanting to provide services in rural and urban communities and unable to recruit volunteers have begun to pay "program specialists." The Girl Scouts of West Central Florida developed the job of program specialists. They must meet the standard Girl Scout leader qualifications and go through the same training as a volunteer leader. They can work up to nineteen hours a week, the starting pay is $14.86 an hour, and they are paid for mileage, but do not receive fringe benefits. Without their paid leaders, many girls would never become Scouts.

Other nonprofits are rethinking the assignments they give to volunteers in terms of time, location, and length of commitment. Many communities have established volunteer banks where volunteers can be assigned to projects that do not require a long-term commitment to the agency or require volunteers to work scheduled hours each week.

Virtual volunteering has become more common. *Virtual volunteering* is the use of information and communication technology to permit some part of the volunteering process to be carried out at a distance from the organization (Murray & Harrison, 2005). Murray and Harrison describe four types of volunteering:

1. The volunteer manager uses information and communication technology to recruit volunteers, and the volunteers perform the work virtually.
2. The volunteer manager and the volunteer are matched through traditional methods, but the work is performed virtually.
3. The volunteer manager and the volunteer are matched through virtual methods, but the work is performed in a traditional manner.
4. Recruiting volunteers, seeking volunteer opportunities, and performing volunteer work do not use information and communication technologies.

Internet volunteering is a way to fit volunteering into busy and sometimes unpredictable schedules. Virtual volunteering has been used to conduct research on the Web, track relevant legislation, give specialist advice, design a Web site or newsletter, create databases, provide translation, and provide telephone or e-mail mentoring.

iMentor is a nonprofit organization that encourages volunteers to exchange e-mail with New York high school students. Volunteers and students exchange e-mail messages several times a week on topics such as career development and college applications. Best Buddies, a Miami nonprofit, matches online volunteers with people with mental retardation. Volunteers make a one-year commitment to exchange e-mail messages at least once a week with their e-Buddies. The exchanges encourage participants to develop computer skills and help to ease some of the social isolation they might be experiencing (Wallace, 2001).

The Prerecruitment Process

Before recruitment begins, it is important to identify the types of volunteers needed or the specific skills required. Some agencies might need volunteers to perform clerical or receptionist duties, which require generic skills, while others may need volunteers capable of coaching an athletic team or writing grant proposals, which require specific skills. Some agencies may need a combination of specialized volunteers and volunteers who can be trained to provide support services to paid staff. Still others want volunteers who are qualified to serve by specific education or experience, such as city planning commissions that want to use volunteers to develop and administer zoning laws. Some agencies need volunteers for a finite amount of time to focus on one project or program, while others need volunteer support on a continuing basis, such as for a general educational development or tutoring program.

During the prerecruitment process, it is also important to note whether certain days of the week or set hours are required or whether volunteers may select the days and hours that are most convenient for them. This is important because of decreasing numbers of people who are available to work daytime hours because they are in the paid labor force. Moreover, individuals who hold full-time jobs may be reluctant to volunteer on an ongoing basis. Agencies may need to identify or develop projects that do not require long-term commitments. This is referred to as an episodic volunteer (Macduff, 2005). Many local communities and United Way agencies sponsor "paint your heart out" days or "Christmas in July," which allow a team of volunteers to paint houses or nonprofit buildings, perform landscaping, build fences, patch roofs, and so forth. These projects typically last one day or are completed in a weekend.

There are three types of episodic volunteers:

- *Temporary*. The volunteer provides service for a short duration, perhaps for a few hours or days.
- *Interim*. The volunteer provides service at regular intervals for, say, six months, making a commitment to work on a special project or provide a service for a limited amount of time.
- *Occasional*. The volunteer provides service for regular intervals for short periods of time. This could be someone who volunteers for the same event year after year, say, for an annual fundraising event (Macduff, 2005).

Agencies need to understand how episodic volunteers differ from traditional long-term volunteers and develop opportunities for them. Agencies should try to create positions where the volunteer does not have to be in the office for long periods or can work independently at home, as in Internet volunteer programs.

The Lions Clubs International, Rotary International, and Kiwanis International are reducing their requirements for meeting attendance. They are creating cyberclubs that conduct business on the Internet and family clubs to involve parents and children (El Nasser, 2007). For programs that require consistent hours and long-term commitments, agencies may target retired citizens or students, who are likely to be more flexible than working adults. Research on older adults found that there are now more than 10 million healthy adults with no caregiving responsibilities who are looking for paid and volunteer work (Zedlewski & Butrica, 2007). Another study found that the majority of adults who volunteer while working continue to volunteer after retirement, and a significant share of older adults not involved in formal volunteering activities while working begin volunteering after they retire. The postretirement volunteer groups include 1.3 million new volunteers and 1.9 million experienced volunteers (Zedlewski, 2007).

Agencies must be able to communicate what a volunteer position requires, both verbally and with written job descriptions. Each position should have a description that outlines the job's duties and responsibilities, as well as the knowledge, skills, abilities, and other characteristics (KSAOCs) required to perform it. For example, a volunteer bus or van driver might need a chauffeur's license or be required to take a driving test. Volunteers who want to work with children will be subject to a background investigation. Work hours should also be specified in the description. Prospective volunteers need to be told whether the working hours for a position are flexible or will require a commitment to meet a specific number of hours per week or specific days. In this way, they are clear about what is expected of them (Alexander, 1991; Anderson & Baroody, 1992).

Volunteers should be asked to complete applications identifying their interests, special skills, and preferred working days and hours. This information enables the organization to match the interest and skills of the volunteers with the positions available. For example, someone who volunteers for social interaction would be unhappy working in isolation. Exhibit 5.1 presents the application form used by a local government. Notice the variety of skills the boards and commissions are seeking. Included are the term lengths and how often meetings are held.

The key for motivating and retaining volunteers is finding the best employee-position match. Dailey (1986) noted that job satisfaction plays a critical role in understanding the commitment to volunteer. It is necessary to design volunteer tasks so they are enriching. Dailey found that work autonomy, job involvement, and feedback from the work itself were strong predictors of organizational commitment. Jamison (2003) found that volunteer turnover is reduced when volunteers receive preservice and in-service training and are assigned challenging tasks.

An organization that wants to make itself more attractive to potential volunteers might consider reimbursing clients for out-of-pocket expenses such as meals and transportation, provide flexibility in scheduling volunteer hours, increase position responsibilities, and work with private sector agencies that encourage employee volunteerism. To be competitive in

Exhibit 5.1. Information Sheet on Prospective Appointee for Citizen Board or Commission

Name in full____

Address____

(Number) (Street) (Ward)

Phone ______________(Home); _____________________(Business)

Occupation________________ How long? ____________________

Business address____

(Number) (Street) (City)

How many years have you lived in this city? ______________________

Are you a registered voter in this city? __________(Yes) __________ (No)

Have you ever served on a city board or commission? If so, state name of board or commission______________________ (Years) ________________

Comment on your professional background, specialties, training, or abilities:

____

____

____

List civic, social, and professional organizations to which you belong:

____

____

____

Are you interested in appointment to any particular board or commission?

____

____

(Signature)____________________

(Date)________________________

Please return to: City Clerk

attracting volunteers, agencies must be creative. For certain positions in the State of Alaska state park system, volunteers are provided with housing and an expense allotment (Brudney, 1990, 2001; Mergenbagen, 1991; Watts & Edwards, 1984; State of Alaska, 2008).

Managing Volunteers

Within organizations that use volunteers, there are two or even three hierarchies: volunteers, paid staff, and professionals (Anderson & Baroody, 1992; Fisher & Cole, 1993; Selby, 1978). Volunteers must understand their roles relative to the paid and professional staff. Farr (1983, p. 18) states, "There are two aspects of the staffing issue—who will oversee and coordinate the volunteer effort and how other staff will be involved in working with volunteers." The effectiveness of volunteers depends on how they are integrated into the organization.

Fisher and Cole (1993) recommend that volunteer programs and positions be developed that directly relate to the organization's mission, and the organization's mission should reflect a commitment to volunteers. They provide the following example of a program mission statement (p. 28):

> The agency's volunteer program promotes quality involvement in the delivery of agency services to families based on the following beliefs:
>
> 1. Volunteers bring unique contributions to the delivery of services to families; areas such as prevention, education, and support are best served by their involvement.
> 2. Volunteers allow the agency to expand its resources and reach more families than it could with paid staff alone.
> 3. Volunteers bring a useful community perspective to program planning, implementation, and evaluation.
> 4. Volunteers are strong representatives of the agency throughout the community.

Employee relationships with volunteers are critical. Often there is tension between employees and volunteers. To eliminate this, the plans for volunteer staffing should be developed in two distinct phases. First, the organization should examine the tasks that might best be performed by volunteer staff in the light of the organization's mission, structure, and personnel policies. Second, specific volunteer positions and position guides need to be developed. This step should involve the participation of board members, union leaders, paid staff, direct service volunteers, and clients. It serves to encourage broad support for the volunteer program, as well as to ensure that the creation of volunteer jobs balances the needs of clients, paid staff, and volunteers (Fisher & Cole, 1993).

The following questions should be considered in the development of volunteer positions and position guides (Fisher & Cole, 1993, pp. 30–31):

- What are the characteristics, strengths, and needs of the target population?
- What qualifications will volunteers need in order to serve this population effectively through the program?
- What are the preferences of the target population regarding service delivery by paid staff or volunteers?
- How do the possible volunteer positions relate to the overall mission of the agency?

Ellis (1995) recommends that boards play key roles in supporting volunteer programs. She suggests that they should expect reports on volunteer involvement and schedule time to discuss volunteers; moreover, board members should refer volunteer candidates to the agency and carry recruitment materials to distribute, and they should take part in volunteer recognition events. Ellis also advises agencies to remember that board members themselves are volunteers despite their legal and fiduciary responsibilities, and attempts should be made to link board members and direct service volunteers from time to time.

As important as it is for board members to understand the benefits of volunteers, it is more important for paid staff to support volunteer programs. Employees must not feel that volunteers are clients who need attention. Volunteers and staff must be trained to work with each other. Volunteers need to know their scope of authority and when to retreat from interfering with employees or clients.

Organizations that have volunteer programs must also decide whether they need to add a position, such as a volunteer coordinator, to administer the volunteer program or if existing employees can assume the responsibilities. According to Farr (1983, p. 18) major program management responsibilities include:

- Obtaining and maintaining support for the volunteer program
- Developing, monitoring, and evaluating the volunteer program budget

- Keeping key officials informed about the scope of volunteer services
- Establishing and monitoring program goals
- Assigning volunteer responsibilities and monitoring results
- Recommending policy changes or action steps to top management to maintain, improve, or expand the volunteer effort

A variety of administrative tasks need to be taken care of as well. Someone needs to recruit volunteers, provide training and orientation, keep records of their attendance and any expenses for which they might need to be reimbursed, secure liability insurance for volunteers or verify their coverage, work with departments to establish the need for volunteers and develop job descriptions, work with agency supervisors to integrate volunteers into their departments or programs, decide how incentives and rewards will be used to motivate volunteers, and keep the volunteers informed about issues that will affect them (Farr, 1983; Fisher & Cole, 1993). Pearce (1993) notes that organizations have less control over the time of volunteers than over employees; thus, there needs to be a large pool of volunteers to accommodate different preferences, talents, and time constraints (Montjoy & Brudney, 1991). For these reasons, more and more organizations that rely on volunteer assistance for executing their missions are hiring volunteer coordinators to assume management and administrative responsibilities.

Orientation and Training

Volunteers should be made familiar with the agency's mission, history, accomplishments, fiscal goals, and strategic plan (Alexander, 1991), as well as what the agency expects from them. It has been suggested that an agency's mission statement be translated into operational objectives, making it easy for volunteers to see how their contributions reinforce the mission (Muson, 1989). Understanding what the agency is about should increase commitment to its programs.

Volunteers need to be trained. Often employees expect them to be clairvoyant and know what to do, how to do it, or what the standard operating procedures are. This is a mistake: volunteers do not necessarily have the same expertise or experience that employees have. On-the-job training time should be devoted to providing instructions, answering questions, and allowing the volunteer to witness and absorb how the agency operates. This experience will reduce volunteers' insecurity about performing new tasks. Those working for social service or public organizations may need to receive training in appropriate laws or policies, such as client confidentiality, what to do in case of an emergency, or how to handle citizens' questions or complaints.

Alexander (1991) found that the organizations with the most formalized training and orientation programs had the least turnover. These programs not only teach volunteers necessary skills; they also serve to clarify expectations and integrate volunteers socially into the organization. Orientation and training programs reinforce agency expectations.

Research studying agency commitment as applied to volunteers indicates that pride and respect in volunteer policies lead to greater commitment and can minimize the reliability problems that often exist with volunteers (Boezeman & Ellemers, 2007).

Volunteer Recognition

Volunteers and the paid staff who supervise them should be recognized for their efforts. Recognition impresses on volunteers and paid staff that the organization appreciates their contributions. Research by Cnaan and Goldberg-Glenn (1991) indicates that volunteers not only give to the organization, but they also derive rewards or satisfactions from volunteering. Some of these rewards and satisfactions are intrinsic, an inherent part of doing the job, such as the satisfaction of task accomplishment, self-development and learning opportunities, self-fulfillment, opportunities for social interactions, and the opportunity to help other people. Other rewards and satisfactions are extrinsic, that is, external to the work. These rewards are reinforcers that are controlled by the agency: tokens of recognition that compliment volunteers for jobs performed well, including letters of appreciation, awards, and pictures or articles about the volunteer published in the newspaper or agency newsletter. Praise from supervisors and the paid staff, the opportunity to train other volunteers, and expanding a volunteer's area of responsibility are some intangible rewards that agencies often bestow on volunteers.

Because individuals volunteer for different reasons, organizations must be prepared to recognize them in a variety of ways. Suggestions made by Boezeman and Ellemers (2007) to enhance pride and respect include providing volunteers with concrete feedback about the success of their efforts—for example, an article in the newsletter describing the amount of money collected or the projects supported. If possible, arrange an informal meeting between volunteers and the individual the agency is serving so volunteers have an opportunity to hear from the beneficiaries what the efforts of volunteers mean to them. Volunteer coordinators can create a supportive environment in which they regularly communicate with volunteers that the agency appreciates their donations of time and effort and inquire whether all is going well or offer them assistance.

Evaluation

Performance evaluations inform volunteers about whether they are meeting the supervisor's and agency's expectations. The evaluation must be job related. Volunteers should be assessed on the tasks they perform, as well as their contributions to the agency. Supervisors and volunteers need to understand each other's expectations and establish specific goals and objectives to use as evaluation standards. A schedule should be developed so that the performance evaluation takes place at regular intervals.

The primary purposes of evaluation should be to provide feedback and develop volunteers. Sometimes, however, a volunteer does not meet the agency's expectations. Should this occur, McCurley (1993) recommends that the following six steps be taken:

1. *Resupervise.* You may have volunteers who do not understand the policies of the organization, or they may be testing the rules to see what can be expected.
2. *Reassign.* Move volunteers to different positions. The volunteer coordinator may have misread the volunteer's skills, or the volunteer may not be getting along with paid staff or fellow volunteers.
3. *Retrain.* Send the volunteers back for a second training program. Some people take longer to learn new techniques. Do not let the lack of knowledge lead you to believe new volunteers are not motivated.
4. *Revitalize.* Longtime volunteers may need a rest. They may not be aware they are burned out.
5. *Refer.* Refer volunteers to other agencies more appropriate to their needs.
6. *Retire.* Allow longtime volunteers the dignity to resign.

If these steps do not work, you will have to terminate the volunteer. It is important to have policies in place to ensure consistent termination procedures. Supervisors should be trained in these steps and the documentation that may be required before terminating a volunteer.

Volunteer Protection Act

The Volunteer Protection Act of 1997 provides immunity from lawsuits filed against a nonprofit's volunteer where the claim is that he or she carelessly injured another in the course of helping the nonprofit. The act does not provide immunity to the organization itself. The law applies only to uncompensated volunteers. The immunity is a qualified immunity and protects the volunteer only against claims of negligence, not against claims of gross negligence, willful or criminal misconduct, reckless misconduct, or conscious, flagrant indifference to the rights or safety of the individual harmed by the volunteer. There is, however, no clear distinction between negligence and gross negligence, so anyone who wants to sue a volunteer can allege gross negligence rather than negligence in the complaint. Some states have their own volunteer protection acts. The federal law preempts state laws to the extent that such laws are inconsistent; however, it does not preempt state laws that provide additional protection from liability. Readers should look to see if their state has its own volunteer protection act and what actions it covers.

Service Initiatives

AmeriCorps, Volunteers in Service to America (VISTA), the Peace Corps, and USA Freedom Corps and their programs are examples of national initiatives that promote service to local communities in the United States and in other countries. Participants in these programs may volunteer or receive stipends or low pay. Community Emergency Response Teams, the Medical Reserve Corps, Neighborhood Watch, and Volunteers in Police Service are part of the Citizen Corps housed in the Department of Homeland Security, Office of Domestic Preparedness. These programs rely on community volunteers. Participants in other programs such as AmeriCorps (AmeriCorps, State and National; VISTA; and National Civilian Community Corps) generally serve for one year and receive a stipend for their services and money to further their education. SeniorCorps participants (Retired and Senior Volunteer Program, Foster Grandparents, and Senior Companions) may, depending on the program, receive insurance coverage, a small hourly wage that is tax free, physical accident and liability insurance, and reimbursement for transportation and meals.

Perry and Thomson (2004) refer to stipend or low-pay opportunities as *civic service*. They make a distinction between volunteerism and national service. Civic service is frequent and long-term, not less than four hours per day and twenty hours per week for an extended time. Civic service typically includes below-market pay and addresses problems not served through the market or public policy. It also focuses on more difficult problems than traditional voluntary service, with efforts directed toward alleviating the problem. Some of the identified problems with national service programs are insufficient funding for program development, program continuity, and infrastructure development. There are additional problems due to the complexity of communication and coordination among the various agencies implementing volunteer policy and misplaced expectations about working with volunteers (Brudney & Gazley, 2002; Rehnborg, 2005).

Governing Boards

> Governing boards in the public and nonprofit sectors bear the ultimate accountability for organizational activity and accomplishment; they make policy and provide oversight.

Governing boards in the public and nonprofit sectors bear the ultimate accountability for organizational activity and accomplishment; they make policy and provide oversight (Carver, 1990).

Public Governing Boards

The duties and authority of public governing boards are regulated by ordinances or statutes, while nonprofit governing boards are regulated by the organization's bylaws. Public boards, whether they are elected or appointed, are typically more bound by legal requirements than are nonprofit boards. They are also subject to a greater variety of statutes (Carver, 1990).

Public sector governing boards deal primarily with policymaking, such as planning, personnel or civil service, parks and recreation, zoning and building, and probation and corrections (Baker, 1994, 2006). What differentiates most public sector governing boards from those in the nonprofit sector is that they typically serve in only an advisory capacity; final approval or decisions are made by the legislative body. Governmental board members may be appointed by elected officials or elected directly by citizens. The provisions that govern local government boards and commissions are typically found in the community's ordinances or are required by state statute. Board members play important policymaking roles and serve as volunteers. Baker (2006) found that the motivation to serve on boards and commissions in small cities was due to both individual and contextual factors.

Nonprofit Governing Boards

In nonprofit organizations, directors or trustees typically develop policies relating to the organizations' management. The directors are responsible for ensuring that the public purpose of the nonprofit organization is carried out. Ingram (1988) identifies the basic responsibilities of nonprofit boards:

- Determining the organization's mission and purposes and setting policies for its operation
- Selecting the executive director and evaluating executive performance
- Ensuring effective organizational planning by engaging in long-range planning to establish its future course
- Ensuring adequate resources by establishing fiscal policy and boundaries and seeing that resources are managed effectively
- Determining and monitoring the organization's programs and services
- Enhancing the organization's public image by promoting the work of the organization
- Serving as a court of appeals for employees with grievances
- Assessing its own performance in relation to its responsibilities

Houle (1989, p. 6) defines a governing board as "an organized group of people with the authority collectively to control and foster an institution that is usually administered by a qualified executive and staff."

Board members are volunteers, and like most other volunteers, they join boards for a variety of reasons. Research on the motivations of citizens serving on public sector boards indicates that they expect to receive certain benefits, and there are a number of selective incentives. Baker (1994, citing Clark & Wilson, 1961, and Widmer, 1985) identifies five types of incentives:

1. *Material incentives* are tangible rewards such as the opportunity to advance politically or the opportunity to make professional contacts.
2. *Solidarity incentives* are intangible rewards such as socializing, a sense of group membership, status, and sense of involvement.

3. *Purposive incentives* are intangible and relate to the satisfaction or gratification of working toward the stated goals of the organization.
4. *Developmental incentives* are intangible rewards such as the ability to assume civic responsibility or using one's capabilities.
5. S*ervice incentives* include fulfilling or reducing a sense of civic responsibility; they are focused on relieving or fulfilling one's sense of obligation. Different board members are motivated by different incentives.

Personal enrichment, substantive interest, social and business contacts, and feelings of accomplishment are just some of the reasons that individuals become board members.

Drawing on previous research on board members' motivation to serve, Inglis and Cleave (2006) developed a scale to assess board members' motivations. They identified six components:

1. *Enhancing self-worth* reflects attitudes and behaviors that benefit the individuals serving as board members.
2. *Learning through community* benefits the individual's growth through learning new skills, learning about the community, developing strengths, and making contacts.
3. *Helping the community* reflects motivations to make a difference.
4. *Developing individual relationships* reflects the importance of social relationships with fellow board members.
5. *Making unique contributions to the board* addresses what individuals perceive to be the skills or knowledge they bring to the board.
6. *Self-healing* considers why individuals might be interested in volunteering as a way to deal positively with deeply felt needs.

Board members are volunteers, and like most other volunteers, they join boards for a variety of reasons.

Herman (2005) notes several similarities between board and service volunteers; they are similar in demographics, show the same mix of motives and incentives for volunteering, and often are helped by supportive management practices. There are some differences as well. For elite nonprofits, the community status of their board members may be important in regard to who is nominated and selected as a board member, and since board members are the ultimate authority in their organizations, the employee model of volunteer management is less applicable to them. Unlike service volunteers, board members are less likely to have written job descriptions and policies in regard to their responsibilities, and they are not supervised but encouraged to perform their duties.

Nonprofits that can afford to also typically purchase directors and officers (*D & O*) insurance to protect the organization and board members against indemnification costs and any other costs incurred by directors that would not be covered by the nonprofit. This type of insurance contract agrees to pay on behalf of the directors and officers of the organization any financial losses that arise from claims or lawsuits brought against them for committing some wrongful act.

What should an organization look for in board members? Characteristics identified by O'Connell (1988) and Houle (1989) include distributions in age, sex, location of residence, representatives of the constituency work being served by the organization, political contacts, clientele, expertise, and training in the following areas: personnel, finance, law, fundraising, and public relations. Each board member should have KSAOCs that contribute to the policymaking and oversight responsibilities of the board as a whole.

To select new board members, the existing board or its nominating committee should identify the characteristics needed in new board members. The KSAOCs should relate to the organization's mission and objectives. To determine what KSAOCs are needed, the incumbent board members should be evaluated (Houle, 1989).

Table 5.1 presents a sample grid identifying the match between the relevant criteria and the incumbent board members. Notice that space is permitted to add prospective board members to the grid. The grid identifies five criteria for determining the composition of the board: age, gender, residence, background, and responsibilities:

1. There should be a greater spread in the ages of the members of the board.
2. The board should be representative of the whole community.
3. The board should be evenly divided between men and women.
4. Major ethnic groups should be represented in roughly the same proportion as is found in the population served.
5. Board members should have expertise or substantive knowledge about the programs provided by the agency, or skills in personnel, finance, public relations, law, or building maintenance and acquisition.

This particular board has fifteen members serving three-year terms. Look at the members with expiring terms and determine which characteristics are needed to balance out the board member grid.

TABLE 5.1. GRID FOR MATCHING INCUMBENT AND POTENTIAL BOARD MEMBERS

	Present Board Members	Potential Board Members													
Criteria	A	B	C	D	E	F	G	H	I	J	V	W	X	Y	Z
Age															
Under 35	X	X													
From 35 to 50	X	X													
From 51 to 65	X	X	X	X											
Over 65	X	X													
Gender															
Women	X	X	X	X	X	X									
Men	X	X	X	X											
Residence															
Central city	X	X	X	X											
North side	X	X	X	X											
West side	X														
South side															
Suburbs	X	X													
Background															
Black	X	X													
White	X	X	X	X	X	X									
Hispanic	X														
Asian															
Responsibilities															
Program	X	X	X	X	X										
Personnel	X	X	X	X											
Finance	X	X													
Public relations	X	X	X	X	X										
Legal	X														
Building	X														

Source: Houle, 1989, p. 40. Used by permission.

After reviewing the KSAOCs needed by new board members, the names of possible new members should be identified. These names might be retrieved from a list of people previously considered to be board members: professional people whose names are given to the agency by a board bank sponsored by the United Way or Junior League, other volunteers, and individuals providing professional services to the agency. People associated with the agency, such as clients, employees, or other board members, often recommend prospective board members.

Nonprofits need to be vigilant about recruiting board members committed to serving the organization's best interest. They need to seek members who have special skills they can bring to the board. For example, Seattle Emergency Housing made a point of recruiting a former budget analyst at the United Way to review its financial statements, as well as a city employee with expertise and knowledge about public funding (Knauft, Berger, & Gray, 1991). The Spring of Tampa Bay provides programs and services to victims of domestic violence. Its board of directors has members from the fields of law enforcement, medicine, law (judges and attorneys), accounting, public relations, human resources management, finance, financial planning and general business administration, and community volunteers.

The expertise and competence of board members that a nonprofit needs often change over time. For example, the Tampa Theatre is a movie palace that was built in 1926. After it began to deteriorate in the 1970s, a nonprofit group, the Tampa Theatre, was established to preserve and revitalize it. In 1978, the theater was named to the National Register of Historic Places. At first, since the mission of the nonprofit emphasized restoration and preservation, most of the board members were individuals with real estate, architecture, finance, and construction expertise. Now the emphasis is on programming and community outreach, so board members with different skills are being sought.

Bylaws or statutes usually specify the procedures that should be followed to formally nominate candidates, as well as the selection procedures. After new board members have been selected, they should be provided with an orientation outlining their responsibilities as board members. They should also be informed about the organization's mission, objectives, and administrative and management structures. Brown (2007) found that board development practices lead to strong board members, and strong board members are a predictor of engaged board performance.

Morrison (1994) recommends that the following information be provided to board members:

- Constitution and bylaws
- Organization's mission or purpose statement
- Organization's goals and current plans, strategic and long-range
- Annual report
- Budget and financial report
- Program description and its goals and objectives
- Organization chart (staff names and numbers)
- Committees: their goals and plans, such as fundraising expectations and commitments
- Public relations strategies
- Personnel policies and expectations
- A list with the names, addresses, e-mail addresses, and phone numbers of board members
- Meeting information, with attendance and time requirements
- Minutes from meetings for the previous fiscal year
- Any appropriate procedures governing conduct of meetings
- Any evaluations conducted during the past year

Training and orientation are important for all board members regardless of their professional expertise and experience. Bowen (1994) acknowledges that when people from the for-profit sector join a nonprofit board, they often lack an appropriate frame of reference as to the nature of the missions served by nonprofits. Bowen cites the following example: "A business man on the board of directors for a church kept pushing for 'double-digit' growth no matter what the implications were for the church's capacity to fulfill its mission" (p. 41). Herzlinger (1994) notes that board members may be perplexed about their appropriate roles. Because some board members are intimidated about the talent and professional expertise of the organization's employees, they abandon their oversight role. "How can I tell a symphony orchestra how to play Beethoven? How can I tell a doctor how to operate?" (p. 53). Other board members become overly involved in the organization's work. They feel free to give unsolicited and unwanted counsel on orchestra programs, museum exhibitions, educational curricula, or social service intervention strategies. Some board members pour themselves into fundraising, while others use their appointment for status seeking and social climbing. According to Herzlinger, the role of a board's director is to ensure that the organization's mission is appropriate to its charitable orientation and that it accomplishes its mission efficiently.

Board members must be prepared to assume responsibility for guiding the agency. Bowen (1994) notes that often hard-nosed businesspeople become permissive when serving on a board of directors. He provides an example of the board at a private school with severe financial difficulties that approved a request for new equipment the school could not afford because the board could not say no to its dedicated teachers. In another case, a board of directors felt guilty about the low salary given to the director of a small arts organization, so it granted her permission to take the summer off.

Board members, like other volunteers, should be evaluated on their performance and the contributions they make to the agency. Those who miss meetings or are unprepared when they do attend should be held accountable. The fiduciary and oversight responsibilities of governing boards require individuals who are committed to the agency for the length of their terms. Organizations cannot afford to retain board members who ignore their responsibilities. The board as a whole should also assess its effectiveness. Some examples of instruments available to assist boards in a self-assessment include the following materials: Jackson and Holland's (1998) Board Self-Assessment Questionnaire; the Drucker Foundation Self-Assessment Tool (Leader to Leader Institute, 1998); and the Governance Effectiveness Quick Check (Gill, Flynn, & Reissing, 2005). BoardSource (www.boardsource.org) also has a number of resources that can be used for board evaluation.

Conclusion

Volunteers have become an integral part of public and nonprofit organizations and are critical to SHRM. Despite the belief of some that volunteers take paid positions away from employees, volunteers typically perform tasks that otherwise would not get done or would have to be handled by already overextended employees.

The guidance and support provided to volunteers and incumbent staff are essential to the successful integration of volunteers into the agency, their performance, and the achievement of agency goals. To minimize any conflicts, staff development programs should be provided that communicate the differences in authority and responsibilities between paid staff and volunteers.

Agencies should develop volunteer recruitment strategies to reach individuals whose interests and skills are likely to match the needs of the organization. This is extremely important given the extent of societal changes. Organizations need to be creative in their volunteer assignments and recruitment strategies. To facilitate good staffing decisions, key staff should be involved in the development of job descriptions for the volunteers they will supervise or work with. Volunteers should receive training on how to perform their tasks and on the performance standards of the agency. Board members are different from service volunteers; however, they should undergo development activities and also be evaluated for their contributions.

Agencies alone should not benefit from the use of volunteers. The volunteer experience should provide individuals with opportunities for personal and professional growth.

Exercise 5.1: Voluntourism

Earthwatch Institute (www.earthwatch.org) is a nonprofit that sends volunteers to science-based conservation and cultural projects in fifty-five countries to protect threatened habitats, species, and cultures. Expeditions are two-week contributions of participants' time, money, support, and spirit to professional, peer-reviewed scientific research. Research priorities are based on climate change, endangered species and resources, marine biology and ocean conservation, and threatened traditional cultures. Participants contribute to their room and board, research permits, scientific equipment, off-site staff to coordinate logistics and safety, carbon offsets to neutralize the researchers' footprints, and more. Part of the contribution may be tax deductible. Some of the excursions for 2008 were trips to Africa, Australia, Central America and the Caribbean, Europe, South America, and North America. One of the Africa excursions has Earthwatch teams mapping the locations, movements, and associations of two zebra species in northern Kenya's Samburu region.

Questions

1. Are there volunteer opportunities in your community where volunteers are already willing or might be willing to pay for the opportunity to volunteer? Describe them.
2. What strategies would you use to implement a program to recruit volunteers willing to pay for the privilege of volunteering?

Exercise 5.2: Screening for Terrorists

The Bush administration plans to screen thousands of people who work with charities and nonprofit organizations that receive U.S. Agency for International Development funds to ensure they are not connected with individuals or groups associated with terrorism. The plan has aroused concern and debate among some of the larger U.S. charitable organizations and recipients of U.S. Agency for International Development (AID) funding. Officials of InterAction, representing 165 foreign aid groups, said the plan would impose undue burdens and has no statutory authority.

The program demands for the first time that nongovernmental organizations file information with the government on each officer, board member, key employee, and those associated with an application for AID funds or managing a project when funded. The information is to include name, address, date and place of birth, citizenship, Social Security and passport numbers, sex, and profession or other employment data. The data will be used to conduct national security screening to ensure these persons have no connection to entities or individuals "associated with terrorism." Under an earlier initiative, nongovernmental organizations were required to check their own employees and then certify to AID that they were certain no one was associated with individuals or groups that appeared on applicable governmental terrorist listings.

Questions

1. How might the new policy increase the recruitment, screening, and selection of employees and board members working for nongovernmental organizations that receive AID funding?
2. Do you think the new policy will be effective in screening out individuals and groups associated with terrorism activities? What might be some unanticipated HRM consequences? Explain your answer.

Source: Pincus (2007).

Chapter Questions

1. Based on your reading, what are some of the organizational benefits associated with having volunteer programs? What are some of the organizational disadvantages associated with having volunteer programs? Do you believe the benefits outweigh the disadvantages? Explain your answer.
2. In small groups, choose three volunteer programs that you are familiar with based on your own experience or Internet research, and evaluate their strengths and weaknesses. What challenges do the organizations face based on the types of services they provide? Which organization is likely to have a successful volunteer program? What recommendations would you make to improve the least successful program?

Online Activities

1. Visit the Web sites of the City of Virginia Beach and the Girl Scouts of America. What types of volunteer positions are available at the two organizations? Do they have similar application forms and screening requirements? Which Web site do you think is more effective in attracting volunteers? Explain your answer.
2. Visit the Minnesota Council of Nonprofits Web site. What resources are available for volunteer programs? If you were asked to develop a volunteer program for an organization, what HRM practices would you implement?

PART TWO

METHODS AND FUNCTIONS OF HUMAN RESOURCES MANAGEMENT

Strategic human resources management (SHRM) depends on the successful integration and execution of human resources management (HRM) methods and functions. The chapters in Part Two explore the importance of job analysis, recruitment and selection, performance evaluation, compensation, benefits, training and career development, collective bargaining, and information systems.

Chapter Six discusses the importance of job analysis. A job analysis is a systematic process of collecting data for determining the knowledge, skills, abilities, and other characteristics (KSAOCs) required to successfully perform a job and make judgments about the nature of a specific job. Information collected through a job analysis is applied to most HRM activities, such as recruitment and selection, development of compensation systems, human resources planning, career development and training, performance evaluation, risk management, and job design. The nature of work—how tasks, behaviors, and responsibilities are assigned to different jobs and how different jobs relate to one another—is explained.

Recruitment and selection are examined in Chapter Seven. Strategic human resources management depends on the successful recruitment and selection of qualified individuals. Recruitment is the process of attracting qualified candidates to apply for vacant positions within an organization. Selection is the final stage of the recruitment process, when decisions are made as to who will fill those positions. In public and nonprofit organizations, the recruitment and selection of competent employees are critical responsibilities because people are central to delivering the programs and services that constitute these organizations' reason for existence.

Selection techniques used to hire applicants must comply with federal laws and guidelines and be job related. They must not unfairly screen out protected-group members for reasons unrelated to the job.

The importance of performance management is addressed in Chapter Eight. Performance evaluations provide management with essential information for making strategic decisions on employee advancement, retention, or separation. Evaluation links training and development with career planning and an agency's long-term human resource needs. Used to support job analysis and recruitment efforts, performance evaluations are an important component for forecasting the KSAOCs available within the organization.

Chapter Nine explains the development and maintenance of compensation systems. Compensation is the largest expense of public and nonprofit organizations: from 60 to 80 percent of the operating budget goes to employees' salaries and benefits. The design, implementation, and maintenance of compensation are therefore important parts of SHRM. Decisions about salaries, incentives, benefits, and quality-of-life issues are important in attracting, retaining, and motivating employees. Strategic decisions about pay levels, pay structures, job evaluation, and incentive pay systems influence the ability of an organization to compete in the marketplace, attract the most qualified and competent applicants, and retain its most talented and productive employees. Compensation systems are influenced by local, state, and federal laws and by external, internal, and employee equity considerations.

Benefits are part of the compensation system and are commonly referred to as indirect compensation. Benefits are an important part of the compensation package. An attractive benefit package can assist in the recruitment and retention of qualified employees. Chapter Ten discusses some of the more traditional benefits offered by employers, such as health insurance, retirement pensions, and paid time away from work, in addition to less traditional benefits such as child and elder care, flexible scheduling, and educational assistance. Changing demographics, family needs, and employee priorities require a greater range of employer-provided benefits than what was offered in the past.

The demands placed on organizations keep changing, and technology has taken on much of the mentally and physically repetitive tasks that employees once performed. Positions today require employees to possess greater skills as they assume more challenging responsibilities. Jobs have become less specialized, forcing employees to work in teams to deliver services. New equipment and technology, the enactment of new laws and regulations, fluctuations in the economy, and the actions of competitors are just some of the variables that influence change. As organizations keep changing, they must implement training and development programs to ensure that their staff have the necessary KSAOCs to confront these new challenges. Chapter Eleven discusses training and career development. Developing a comprehensive, long-range training program requires an SHRM plan and a recognition that employees are an organization's most valuable resource. Training and development must become integrated into the core HRM functions.

Labor-management relations is an important component of SHRM. To remain competitive, management and unions have had to rethink their adversarial relationship and work together to creatively resolve problems and develop solutions that benefit both labor and management. Chapter Twelve explains the legal framework governing collective bargaining in the public and nonprofit sectors and provides some examples of the different types of benefits unions have negotiated for their members consistent with workforce and workplace changes. Mental health and substance abuse benefits, child care benefits, incentive awards, employee individual development plans, and flexible work schedules are just some nontraditional benefits that have been negotiated.

The effect of information technology on strategic human resources management is presented in Chapter Thirteen. Technological changes such as the increased use of computers, information systems, databases, telecommunications, and networking have changed the way agencies are structured and work is organized and managed. Organizations need to recruit, hire, and provide training to individuals who have the skills and motivation to adapt to technological changes. The last chapter discusses the HRM challenges for public and nonprofit organizations.

CHAPTER SIX

JOB ANALYSIS

After you read this chapter, you should be able to:

- Understand the importance of job analysis to strategic human resources management (SHRM)
- Understand what a job analysis is
- Discuss the different SHRM purposes and uses for job analyses
- Discuss commonly used methods to conduct a job analysis
- Explain the different types of information about performing a job that can be identified through job analysis techniques

For organizations to remain competitive, they must accurately identify and forecast their human resources needs. They must assess past trends, evaluate their current situation, and project the human resources they will need to meet the requirements of their strategic plans. Before informed decisions can be made about recruitment and development needs, compensation plans, training and career development objectives, performance management systems, and job design, data must be collected and analyzed. The technique used to acquire the data necessary to make informed decisions is called *job analysis*.

A job analysis is a systematic process of collecting data for determining the knowledge, skills, abilities, and other characteristics (KSAOCs) required to perform a job successfully and make judgments about the nature of a specific job. This analysis identifies a job's activities, behaviors, tasks, and performance standards; the context in which the job is performed; and the personal requirements necessary to perform a job, such as personality, interests, physical characteristics, aptitudes, and job-related knowledge and skills. Each position is also analyzed in terms of its relationship to other positions in the organization.

Chapter Two emphasized the need for human resources management (HRM) departments to assist their organizations in improving organizational effectiveness. Strategic job analyses are integral to strategic human resources management (SHRM) planning. Strategic job analyses recognize that most jobs will not remain stable but will change to meet future demands.

Job analyses provide the foundation for most HRM activities. Following is a brief introduction to each area of activity:

◆ ◆ ◆

- *Recruitment and selection.* Job analysis identifies the KSAOCs required for each position. It identifies the minimum education, certification, or licensing requirements. It also identifies the essential tasks and responsibilities of the job. This information identifies the skills of the people the agency recruits and hires. A job analysis is critical when an organization uses preemployment examinations for selection and promotion. Tests must be job related; the knowledge, skills, abilities, personality variables, and constructs to be tested need to be identified through an up-to-date job analysis. An organization does not know what knowledge, skills, and abilities to test for unless it knows what competencies are required for successful performance.
- *Developing compensation systems.* Compensation is typically related to a job's requirements, such as education, the skills and experience needed to perform the job, and whether the employee is working in hazardous conditions. A job analysis provides a standardized procedure for systematically determining pay and other benefits across the organization. It provides all employees with a basis for gaining a common understanding of the values of each job, its relationship to other jobs, and the requirements necessary to perform it.
- *Human resources planning, career development, and training.* Job analysis information can help employers design training and career development

programs by identifying the skills required for different jobs. Identifying the knowledge, skill, and responsibility requirements of each job makes it possible to train and develop employees for promotional opportunities. Available information helps all employees understand promotion and transfer requirements and recognize career opportunities.

- *Performance evaluation.* Performance standards should be derived from what employees actually do on the job. A job analysis identifies the tasks and responsibilities that employees perform in the course of their jobs. Areas of accountability can be identified and evaluation standards developed.
- *Risk management.* A job analysis can be used to identify job hazards such as exposure to flammable materials or complicated machinery. Employers should use this information to develop training programs to alert employees to possible dangers. Included in this are health, safety, and security issues.
- *Job design.* Jobs are arranged around a set of work activities designed to enable the organization to carry out its mission. External and internal changes, however, often force organizations to rearrange or restructure work activities. The traditional tasks associated with a particular job change over time; a job analysis is necessary to identify and accommodate these changes.

◆ ◆ ◆

This chapter discusses the legal significance of job analysis, the types of information obtained through a job analysis, the factors to consider when designing a job analysis program, and some of the advantages of strategic job analysis and generic job descriptions. The chapter concludes with a look at some of the job analysis techniques commonly used in the public and nonprofit sectors.

Legal Significance of Job Analysis Data

To demonstrate the validity and job relatedness of an employment test, the Uniform Guidelines on Employee Selection Procedures (1978) require that a job analysis be conducted.

The test's content, criteria, and construct test-validation strategies must be based on a thorough and up-to-date job analysis. Employers must show that the requirements established for selecting workers are related to

> To demonstrate the validity and job relatedness of an employment test, the Uniform Guidelines on Employee Selection Procedures (1978) require that a job analysis be conducted.

the job. When used as the basis for personnel decisions such as promotions or pay increases, performance evaluations are also considered to be examinations and fall under the same rigorous scrutiny as employment tests. Furthermore, the Americans with Disabilities Act defines a qualified applicant as one who can perform the essential functions of the job. Essential functions are the primary job duties intrinsic to the position; they do not include marginal or peripheral tasks that are not critical to the performance of the primary job functions. It is important that positions be analyzed to identify these functions. The applicant must then satisfy the prerequisites for the position and be able to perform the essential functions of the job with or without reasonable accommodation.

The most common reasons for conducting a job analysis are to gather information so that a job description can be written, job specifications can be identified, and the job can be placed within a job family classification. A job family is a collection of jobs that require common skills, occupational qualifications, technology, licensing, and working conditions. A job description is a summary of the most important features of a job. It states the nature of the work and provides information about tasks, responsibilities, and context. Information typically found in job descriptions includes job title, job family, job summary, task statements, reporting relationships, and job context indicators.

The Americans with Disabilities Act does not require employers to develop written job descriptions. However, a written job description that is prepared before advertising or interviewing applicants for the job should be reviewed to make sure that it accurately reflects the actual functions of the job. The Equal Employment Opportunity Commission and the Civil Rights Division of the Department of Justice recommend that job descriptions focus on the results or outcomes of a job function, not solely on the way it is customarily performed. This is because a person with a disability may be able to accomplish a job function, with or without a reasonable accommodation, in a manner that is different from the way an employee who is not disabled may accomplish the same function.

Job specifications contain information about the KSAOCs of the position. Whereas each job description is specific to a particular job, job specifications may be more general. They contain the minimum qualifications that a person should possess in order to perform the job.

Job Analysis Information and Methods

Job analysis is used as the basis for many HRM activities. However, different types of job analysis information, instruments, and procedures lend themselves to different purposes. The first steps in conducting a job analysis are to define the purpose behind the analysis and then to determine what information is required.

Job Analysis Information

Different types of information are collected during a job analysis, and a variety of methods can be used. Information is most commonly collected on job activities, educational requirements, types of equipment or tools used, working conditions, supervisory or management responsibilities, interpersonal or communication skills, agency contacts, external contacts, and the KSAOCs. *Knowledge* is the information required for the position. It can be factual, procedural, or conceptual and is related to the performance of tasks, such as a general knowledge of accounting principles or of fund accounting as used in nonprofit organizations. *Skills* are the observable competencies required to perform the particular tasks of the position, such as the ability to input data accurately at one hundred characters per minute or to diagnose and repair personal computers. *Abilities* are the applicant's aptitudes for performing particular tasks—what the applicant is able to do and how well—such as the ability to prepare and make presentations or to read city maps. *Other characteristics* include attitudes, personality factors, or physical or mental traits needed to perform the job.

Methods of Collecting Job Data

Job analysis information can be obtained through a variety of methods. Data collection depends on the nature of the positions, the number of incumbents in and supervisors of the positions being analyzed, the geographical dispersion of jobs, and the time available, as well as the type of information needed and the purpose of the analysis. The job analyst and the agency supervisors must work together to determine the most effective method for collecting information. The job analyst can be an employee from the HRM department, an employee working for a consulting firm hired to perform job analysis studies, or, in a small organization, a support staff employee such as the administrative assistant to the city administrator or executive director of a nonprofit agency. Following are the most common methods used for data collection:

◆ ◆ ◆

- *Interview.* The analyst interviews the incumbent performing the job, the immediate supervisor, or another subject matter expert (SME), or a combination of all three, about the essential functions of the position.
- *Questionnaire.* Subject matter experts are asked to complete an open-ended questionnaire. The job incumbent usually is asked to complete the questionnaire first, and then the supervisor is asked to review it to add anything that may have been neglected or to clarify statements made by the incumbent. Exhibit 6.1 provides an example of a job analysis questionnaire.

Exhibit 6.1. Job Analysis Questionnaire

Name:________________________ Date Completed:__________

Job Title:__________________________________

1. Please specify the percentage of your total time spent in performing each task.

Work that is performed daily:

Essential Activities	***Tasks***	***Percentage of Time***

2. Indicate by X the organizational level of people in the agency and in other organizations with whom you come into contact. Also indicate the primary means by which you contact these individuals.

Within Agency (Employees of Agency)

_______ Contact mainly within own department or office.

_______ Regular contact with other departments or offices furnishing and obtaining information.

_______ Regular contact with other departments or offices, requiring tact and the development of utmost cooperation.

_______ Regular contacts with major executives on matters requiring explanations and discussions.

Means of Contact

_______ Personal conversation _______ Telephone _______ Letter
_______ E-mail _______ Other (specify)

Outside Agency (Nonemployees)

_______ Regular contact with persons outside the organization, involving effort that necessitates a great deal of tact and diplomacy.

_______ Regular contact with others by presenting data that may influence important decisions.

_______ Regular contact with persons of high rank, requiring tact and judgment to deal with and influence these people.

Means of Contact

_______ Personal conversation _______ Telephone _______ Letter
_______ E-mail _______ Other (specify)

3. What types of errors are possible on your job, and what would be the consequences of such errors in terms of additional expense to the organization, rework, or loss of goodwill?

• *Structured checklist.* This is another form of questionnaire. The SMEs are asked to respond to information presented on the checklist. They then check the responses most appropriate for their positions. Exhibit 6.2 presents an example of a structured checklist.

Exhibit 6.2. Structured Task Questionnaire

For each question, three responses are required:

A. Indicate the *frequency* with which this function is performed in this position.
B. Indicate how *important* this function is to the position.
C. Indicate whether *knowledge* of this function is essential for a newly hired employee in this position.

A	B	C
Frequency	Importance	Knowledge
0 = Never	0 = Not applicable	0 = Not required for job
1 = Rarely	1 = Not important	1 = Essential for newly hired employee
2 = Sometimes	2 = Somewhat important	2 = Not essential at hiring; can be learned on the job
3 = Often	3 = Important	
4 = Very Often	4 = Very Important	

Typing

A	B	C
Frequency	Importance	Knowledge
0 1 2 3 4	0 1 2 3 4	0 1 2

1. Type/keyboard letters from handwritten rough drafts.
2. Type/keyboard letters to students, faculty, staff, applicants, or outside individuals or companies.
3. Type/keyboard inventory reports or budget reports.
4. Type/keyboard monthly status reports.
5. Type/keyboard general office forms (such as purchase requisitions, work orders, travel vouchers, printing requisitions).
6. Type/keyboard course materials, transparencies, syllabi, or tests for faculty.
7. Compose various letters and memos without written or verbal instructions. Compose letters and memos from simple written outline of verbal instructions.
8. Proofread for spelling, grammar, and punctuation on all correspondence and reports.
9. Type/keyboard or edit manuscripts or drafts for supervisor.
10. Prepare manuscripts for publication, including correction of errors and consultation on other editing matters.
11. Lay out format and spacing for tables, charts, or other illustrations in preparation for typing.

- *Observation.* The analyst observes the incumbent performing the job and records what he or she sees. This method works primarily for jobs in which activities or behaviors are readily observable. This method would not work well for intellectual or cognitive processes.
- *Diary or log.* Employees are asked to keep track of and record their daily activities and the time they spend on each.
- *Critical incident technique.* Job experts generate a list of good and poor examples of performance that job incumbents exhibit. The purpose is to gather information regarding specific behaviors that have been observed, not develop judgmental or trait-oriented descriptions of performance. These behaviors are then grouped into job dimensions. The final list of job dimensions and respective critical incidents provides information about a job and the behaviors associated with success or failure. A critical incident should possess four characteristics: it should be *specific*, focus on *observable* behaviors that have been exhibited on the job, describe the *context* in which the behavior occurred, and indicate the *consequences* of the behavior.
- *Combination of all methods.* Depending on the purpose of the job analysis and the targeted jobs, it may be necessary to use a combination of all of the methods introduced here. Not all jobs lend themselves to observation. Many public and nonprofit incumbents sit behind desks, use personal computers, and talk on the telephone. An analyst can observe those behaviors but will not understand the cognitive processes that accompany them or the requisite educational requirements and knowledge that may be specific to each position.

◆ ◆ ◆

Many organizations have a variety of positions, from very skilled to nonskilled. For example, a local government may have city planners, experts in computer applications, budgeting and finance personnel, clerk-typist positions, and groundskeeper and laborer positions. The analyst may use different methods of data collection for different positions. For example, the groundskeeper and laborer positions may not require reading and writing skills. To ask incumbents who may lack those skills to complete an open-ended written questionnaire may not provide the analyst with useful information. Instead, interviews and observation might be more appropriate data-collection techniques. The city planner, however, might be asked to complete a questionnaire, followed by an interview to clarify any jargon or statements that the analyst does not understand. A follow-up interview also allows the incumbent to add information that she or he may have forgotten when completing the questionnaire.

In large organizations with many incumbents in the same position or in state or federal organizations with geographically dispersed locations, the analyst may want to meet with a small number of incumbents and supervisors and ask them questions or have them fill out an unstructured questionnaire. The analyst may then develop a structured questionnaire based on the information provided, distribute it to all of the incumbents who hold that position, and then analyze the data for common work activities and responsibilities.

Designing a Job Analysis Program

Why are you collecting job information? For what purpose will the data be used? The answers to these questions are important because different purposes require different information. For example, if the job analysis is to serve as the basis for determining compensation, the analyst would need to obtain information about educational requirements and level of experience and training. However, if the analysis is to serve as the basis for developing performance appraisal instruments, the job analyst will need to identify levels of task proficiency.

Another consideration is that employees may be sensitive to some of the purposes behind the job analysis. For example, employees are more likely to be more concerned about a job analysis when it will be used to develop a compensation system than when the information will be used to develop training and orientation material for new employees. Employees are thus likely to emphasize different information depending on the purpose of the analysis.

The analyst should work with representatives of the organization to determine the most effective method and procedures for collecting information. It is important for the analyst to understand how the organization operates and the best time to obtain information from incumbents and supervisors because not all jobs or tasks require the same intensity at the same time or for forty hours a week. Different tasks are likely to be performed on different days or at different times of the month or year. Also, some jobs have busy cycles during which the incumbents cannot be interrupted to visit with an analyst or take the time to complete an extensive questionnaire.

The following factors should be taken into consideration when deciding on the most effective way to collect information:

◆ ◆ ◆

- *Location and number of incumbents.* Will a particular method or procedure enhance or restrict data collection because of a job's location? Will it be hazardous or too costly for an analyst to observe the job being performed? In the public sector, many jobs are geographically dispersed throughout the city, state, or country. It might be too expensive and time-consuming for an analyst to visit and interview, for example, all of the child-protective investigators across a state. Asking the investigators to complete a questionnaire instead would be more feasible.
- *Work conditions and environment.* Would work need to shut down during interviews because of a dangerous working environment? Would the incumbent or analyst be at risk if work were disrupted? Are there distractions in the work environment, such as noise, heat, hazardous materials, or risk management requirements, that would impair the data collection?
- *Knowledge, technology, and personal factors.* Do the knowledge, technology, or personal characteristics of the incumbents lend themselves to a particular method or procedure? Not all jobs or aspects of jobs are conducive to observation. A teacher's classroom performance can be observed. But what about the preparation? What would an analyst see? Can the thought processes or the knowledge required to prepare a lesson be observed? Other factors to consider are whether the job consists of routine or unpredictable tasks and whether the complexity of the job favors a particular method. Will the SME prefer a particular method? Are there peer or organizational factors that may influence whether a procedure may be effective? For example, will a group interview inhibit employees from speaking up because they are intimidated by the presence of others? If supervisors and incumbents are asked to collaborate, will the supervisor dominate the conversation with the analyst?

◆ ◆ ◆

After considering the factors just presented, the jobs to be studied need to be identified and the types of instruments that will be used to obtain relevant data and information chosen. Management should notify the incumbents and supervisors in advance that a job analysis will be undertaken and explain to them the purpose or purposes behind the endeavor. The quality of the data collected depends on assistance from SMEs.

Job Descriptions and Job Specifications

Often the information obtained from a job analysis is used to develop a job description and its job specifications. A job description identifies the tasks, duties, and responsibilities of a job. The job specifications list the KSAOCs individuals need to possess to perform a job successfully. Most job descriptions contain the following information.

- *Identification of the job position.* This provides the job titles, reporting relationships, department, and location. It may also include the job code, pay grade, exempt or nonexempt status under the Fair Labor Standards Act, and Equal Employment Opportunity Commission classification.
- *General summary.* This is a brief statement of the general responsibilities and components that make the job different from others.
- *Essential functions and duties.* This lists the essential functions and duties, It identifies the major tasks, duties, and responsibilities performed.
- *Job specifications.* This provides the qualifications needed to perform the job successfully. Usually the KSAOCs are noted; the education and experience needed; physical requirements and working conditions. Exhibit 6.3 provides two examples of job descriptions.

Exhibit 6.3. Example Job Descriptions

MANAGER OF A HOUSING DEVELOPMENT

Job Title	Manager Housing Development
Job ID	20289
Full-/Part-Time	Full-time
Regular/Temporary	Regular
Salary Range	$61,648 to $88,634 annual salary

Position Information

Manage the Multifamily Housing Development Division of the Community Planning and Economic Development Department

Job Duties

Manage, supervise, plan, administer, and monitor complex financing programs and various projects designed to improve or redevelop affordable housing stock in the city.

Supervise staff, establish and communicate assignments, and monitor performance.

Provide technical guidance in the area of housing development.

Identify training needs of staff, and initiate appropriate action.

Prepare and monitor program budgets, implementation plans, and program activities.

Provide underwriting expertise and analysis for housing development projects.

Coordinate project activities with other city departments and outside organizations, resolving a variety of project management and financial issues.

Develop policies on housing issues, including preservation of low-income subsidized housing and homelessness issues, and create strategies for implementation.

Provide analysis and implementation of low-income housing tax credit and other developer incentives to encourage private investment in affordable housing projects.

Negotiate redevelopment contract terms and conditions.

Develop, implement, and use a variety of programs and financial mechanisms to assist single-family or multifamily housing development, stabilization, and development.

Prepare and present reports, including city council reports.

Act as a liaison with city staff, council, the federal Department of Housing and Urban Development, state agencies, and other organizations regarding single-family or multifamily housing development.

Make presentations and handle community relations for housing development.

Required Education

Bachelor's degree in public administration, finance, urban planning, a related field or equivalent. A master's degree in public administration, business administration, or a closely related field is preferred.

Required Experience

Eight years of experience in management related to residential development, property, and finance are required. Professional or managerial experience

Exhibit 6.3. Example Job Descriptions (*continued*)

with local government, nonprofit community development organizations, or real estate development is preferred.

An equivalent combination of related education and experience may be considered.

Other Requirements

Supplemental application: There may be supplemental questions that must be answered and submitted with your application to complete this process. These questions will be e-mailed to you after the posting deadline.

Background Check

The city has determined that a criminal background check and qualifications will be checked for this position.

Other Qualifications

Successful completion of various appraisal and mortgage banking courses from recognized accredited organizations.

Knowledge of real estate development, finance, equity raising, asset management, property management, and design.

Knowledge of city, state, and federal development and financing programs and related policies and procedures.

Excellent verbal and written communication skills.

Ability to plan, organize, and delegate work and to supervise and evaluate the work of technical staff. Involved with administering complex programs and projects.

Ability to establish and maintain effective working relationships with a diverse clientele and at all levels of city government.

Knowledge of budgeting and project financing principles and practices.

AA/EOE

The city is an Affirmative Action/Equal Opportunity Employer

Account Clerk II

Job Title	Account Clerk II
Job ID	20277
Full-/Part-Time	Full-time
Regular/Temporary	Regular
Salary Range	$15.76 to $21.85 per hour

Job Duties

Analyze extensive data, ensuring accuracy.

Prepare records that deal with complex payrolls, accounting, and bookkeeping procedures.

Receipt cash, credit card, and electronic payments into accounting system.

Prepare daily deposits for armored car delivery to bank.

Process levied assessments, including calculating cost, determine coding, receipt payment. Balance daily cash receipts to system reports.

Extensive processing of requisitions/receivers, internal and external billings, and journal entries, ensuring a high degree of accuracy.

Prepare records that deal with accounting or bookkeeping procedures and complex payrolls.

Assist in audits of financial documents and ensure that documents covering the same financial information match or that appropriate adjustments are made.

Audit general ledger interface and accounts receivable and payable interface between software programs.

Identify problems, and relay information to the proper authority.

Process online receivable transactions.

Process all accounts payable, including contracts using online financial transactions and supporting documentation for payable, purchasing, and billing transactions.

Verify and distribute bills and invoices to proper expenditure accounts.

Code and prepare invoices for payment.

Compute cost, including distribution of labor, equipment rentals, materials, and overhead according to funds, projects, divisions, and departments.
Receive, calculate, verify, and submit monthly mileage reports for processing.

Respond to internal and external questions about billings, and resolve any questions or problems.

Audit, identify discrepancies, and correct biweekly time reports for accurate reporting of sick leave, vacation, funeral, military, and other authorized leave, compensatory time earned and used, and shift differential premium pay and regular hours.

Assist employees in completing forms, online registration, and other documents that relate to personnel and payroll, including tax documents, first report of injury, and leave requests.

Perform tasks on a personal computer and online accounting system.

Exhibit 6.3. Example Job Descriptions (*continued*)

Required Education
High school diploma or equivalent. Postsecondary education in entry-level accounting, finance, or closely related field is desired.

Required Experience
Three years of basic accounting or bookkeeping experience.

Equivalency
An equivalent combination of related education and experience may be considered.

Background Check
The city has determined that a criminal background check and qualifications will be checked for this position.

Other Qualifications
Knowledge of department and city policies and procedures and of computers.

Knowledge of payroll processing and procedures, accounting principles and procedures, and bookkeeping.

Knowledge of office procedures practices and policies.

Proficient in use of a personal computer and an online accounting system (Excel preferred).

Meet deadlines and work under pressure.

Strategic Job Analysis

Advances in information technology have changed many public and nonprofit organizations. Positions are being redefined to mesh better with new missions and services. Organizations have become less hierarchical as many managerial responsibilities have been transferred to employees and work teams. Positions have become more flexible in the attempt to capitalize on improved information management capabilities as well as the changing characteristics of employees. Today many employees are expected to plan and organize their own work. One result of these changes is that employees are expected to perform a variety of complex tasks that go beyond formal job descriptions. Positions today are more flexible than in the past and contingent on changing organizational and job conditions.

Traditional job analysis tends to focus on the KSAOCs required for performance of a position as it currently exists or as it has existed in the past. However, if agencies want to prepare for future changes, they must integrate into the job analysis strategic issues that may affect jobs in the future. To adopt a future-oriented approach to job analysis, agencies should convene a panel of SMEs to discuss the types of issues that are likely to challenge positions as well as the organization in the future. Recommended SMEs include job incumbents, managers, supervisors, strategic planners, human resources staff, and experts in a technical field related to the job to be analyzed. After potential future issues have been identified, tasks and KSAOCs need to be revised in anticipation of changes. Implementation of this strategic job analysis process can assist HRM practitioners by anticipating and forecasting future organizational needs.

Sanchez and Levine (1999) use the term *work analysis* instead of *job analysis*. They believe that the analysis of work should serve to propel the change process, whereas the word *job* serves to define job boundaries and make them rigid. They note that the circumstances and situations that once influenced traditional job analysis are changing. For example, at one time, many jobs were defined by a division of labor. Tasks were routine and broken down into distinct elements. Today, most public and nonprofit employees are professionals, and tasks have been replaced by cross-functional responsibilities. Changing responsibilities require employee flexibility. Employees are more involved in planning and controlling their own work. For organizations adapting to change, job descriptions are likely to be short-lived, so there needs to be a system of continuous work analysis. The shift to teamwork and self-managed groups requires that greater emphasis be placed on interactive activities.

Organizational citizenship behaviors and contextual performance have become more important as employees interact with a greater variety of people. Managing the emotional aspects of work, such as displaying sensitivity to culturally different individuals, is important. Emotional stability and other personality attributes have received little attention in conventional job analysis when compared with cognitive and technical aspects of the job. However, interpersonal, team, and customer-oriented attributes can be decisive in many of today's work assignments and in such cases should be acknowledged.

Not only may organizations want to review the way they analyze work, but they may also want to focus on the level of general characteristics important for success in the organization's culture and for dealing with change. For example, the focus could be on general categories of competencies important for success, such as adaptability, self-motivation, and trainability, in addition to job context and specific technical skills. The job description could be on a broader set of KSAOCs instead of on specific tasks or behaviors.

Competency Modeling

Competency modeling is a method of collecting and organizing job information and worker attributes into broad competencies. *Competencies* are descriptions of the characteristics and qualities that a person needs to possess to perform a job successfully. A competency model is a set of competencies that are necessary for effective performance, and they typically cover a broader range of jobs than traditional job analysis. Many organizations adopt a critical set of core competencies that are required of organization members across all jobs and all levels. Brannick, Levine, and Morgeson (2007) discuss competency modeling in the context of managerial positions.

Competency modeling is a method of collecting and organizing job information and worker attributes into broad competencies.

Bartram (2005) has identified eight competencies for managerial positions:

- *Leading and deciding*, described as telling other people what to do and deciding what action to take
- *Supporting and cooperating*, described as working well with other people and being a team player
- *Interacting and presenting*, described as persuading others and possessing social confidence and presentation skills
- *Analyzing and interpreting*, described as effectively analyzing problems and being comfortable with data
- *Creating and conceptualizing*, described as dealing effectively with change and moving things forward according to the larger environment
- *Organizing and executing*, described as planning to meet objectives and ensuring customer satisfaction
- *Adapting and coping*, described as handling pressure and bouncing back after setbacks
- *Enterprising and performing* described as focusing on results and understanding finances (p. 138).

Exhibits 6.4 and 6.5 provide examples of competencies identified for Canadian public managers (Bourgault, Chairf, Maltais, & Rouillard, 2006) and from the American Cancer Society, Florida Chapter.

Exhibit 6.4. Competencies of Canadian Public Managers

Openness of new governance described as recognizing that traditional public policymaking and service delivery methods are changing due to new approaches to the role of government, citizens' desire for greater participation in public management, the increased availability of information, new technologies, and the public's changing needs. Listen, consult, and act with citizens and groups, without losing sight of the public interest and democratic rules.

Political savvy described as nonpartisan public service; managers are expected to analyze the political environment in which the public administration operates, the aspirations of politicians, the growing complexity of the policy-making process, and the domestic and international forces that bear on the development and implementation of policy. The ability to provide politicians with loyal, frank, objective and non-partisan advice, based on the most comprehensive and available information. Know and accept role in relation to elected officials.

Strategic and tactical skills described as understanding the working of government, the foundations and processes of the public administration and their own agency. Interpret the context before suggesting and deciding on an action. Assess the impact of policies on actors in their environment. Manage proactively and know how to position the organization based on the situation. See their organization's multiple dimensions and can seize opportunities that result from complexity and change. Innovate, while managing the associated political risk.

Vision and innovation described as needing to be open-minded and to be creative when faced with problematic situations. Be prepared intellectually and emotionally to consider new ideas and emerging phenomena. Use innovative approaches to accomplish goals, encourage experimentation and new working methods.

Managing complexity, adaptability and continuous learning described as able to read the changing environment and adapt actions to the changing and conflicting demands. Look for opportunities for learning and development and strive to provide support for democratic governance.

Leadership described as being alert to changes that can improve their agency's performance. Promote change and encourage others to embrace it. Make difficult decisions, even when they cause discontent, and try to rally people around those decisions. Their authority rests in part on their ability to persuade and inspire others. They are critical, question the status quo, and do not like new ideas just for their novelty. Possess strong organizational skills, know where they are going and able to capitalize on their strengths

Exhibit 6.4. Competencies of Canadian Public Managers (*continued*)

and those of the people around them. Not afraid to challenge preconceived notions.

Emotional intelligence described as being able to handle their own emotions, reactions and impact on others, including subordinates, peers, superiors and others outside their administrative units. Sensitive to others' emotions and take them into account when handling difficult matters.

Human resources management described as showing respect for and interest in people, support employees in their work, are able to win and keep trust, help employees work independently, and motivate them to improve their performance. Pay attention to managing diversity, striving to leverage differences and take advantage of each individual's specific characteristics. Are frank and open, unafraid of difficult decisions concerning personnel, and resolve conflicts quickly. Able to recognize, reward and dismiss employees and deal with any performance problems.

Knowledge management described as building knowledge within public organizations for the development of public policy and programs. Encourage openness to new thinking and to new developments in the field that relate to the agency's activities. Concerned about managing and integrating knowledge.

Applying ethical values described as possessing the ability to withstand pressures from political sources, deregulation, devolution when placed in situations in which decisions cannot be based on clear rules and formal codes. Promote ethical conduct and pay attention to ethical issues. Provide superiors with full and timely information.

Communication and negotiation described as listen, disseminate, connect, exchange and negotiate within their administrative unit, their ministry, the larger government and other government units, nonprofits, business and social groups. Know how to talk to the media, public and elected officials. Develop, articulate and project a clear and coherent vision to their people. When partnering with other organizations such as nonprofit and for-profit businesses to apply and deliver services, need to be skillful and effective negotiators.

Technological savvy described as staying abreast of the possibilities that new technologies and new information technologies create for public administration modernization, cost reduction, easier access to public services, redesign of delivery methods, and facilitate transactions between public and government. Take a proactive stance; identify changes to internal structures, operating methods, and requirements concerning access to information and privacy.

Managing performance, risk and enterprise described as producing results while respecting laws, regulations, and citizen's expectations. Encourage enterprise and initiative on the part of employees, identify the risks associated with decisions and projects under consideration and assess the probability and magnitude of those risks.

Partnering and networking described as recognizing the opportunity for working with organizations of all types in order to enhance the development of public policy and programs and the delivery of public services. Initiate partnerships and build networks and able to elicit support and active involvement of partners; open to differences, work as part of a team, delegate and empower.

Source: Bourgault, Chairf, Maltais, & Rouillard (2006, pp. 94–103).

Exhibit 6.5. American Cancer Society Competencies

ACHIEVES RESULTS

CRM

Keeps constituents in mind when identifying direction and execution of plans and priorities.

Actively looks for ways to increase level of constituent satisfaction.

Keeps staff constituent-focused.

Builds Capacity

Visionary thinker.

Recognizes that today's decision affects tomorrow's outcomes.

Makes analytical, data-based decisions.

Increases Expectations

Establishes challenging performance goals and standards for staff.

Leads people to achieve organizational results.

Constantly looks for ways to improve individual and group performance.

COMMANDS RESPECT

Takes a Stand

Speaks out on issues within the management team, even when the view is unpopular; *but* actively supports Florida Division.

Makes tough staff and organizational decisions.

Exhibit 6.5. American Cancer Society Competencies (*continued*)

Disagrees Without Being Disagreeable

Confronts conflict situations honestly and directly.

Manages conflict effectively without personalizing it.

Action Oriented

Is decisive.

Strives for brevity, clarity, and the simple solution when solving complex problems.

Advocates for staff equity/fairness.

BUILD WINNING TEAMS

Attracts Talent

Attracts, selects, and values high-caliber people with diverse backgrounds and experience.

Develops People

Provides timely, candid feedback on performance via written performance evaluations, memos, letters, etc.

Constructively coaches staff to improve performance.

Instills a meritocracy by tying rewards to results.

Delegates Authority

Delegates fully and holds people accountable for outcomes.

Provides latitude to accomplish goals while staying within guidelines and limitations.

Builds Alliances

Cultivates active relationships inside and outside of one's function and encourages staff to do so.

Actively fosters collaboration with other organizations to further our Mission.

INSPIRES TRUST

Organizational Credibility

Openly shares information with others as appropriate.

Always puts the interests of ACS [the American Cancer Society] ahead of one's personal agenda.

Communicates an exciting vision of our impact and our future.

Is true to those not in the room.

Personal Credibility

Maintains composure and professional demeanor, especially under pressure.

Delivers what is promised.

Acknowledges one's own mistakes and limitations.

Deflects credit for accomplishments to those who are responsible.

Demonstrates unqualified loyalty and inspires commitment to our mission and values.

Models stewardship for donated dollars.

Sets high personal standards and acts as role model for professionalism.

Models volunteer/staff relationships in accordance with our polices.

Job Analysis Techniques

A variety of job analysis approaches have been developed over the years. These approaches gather information on job content and worker characteristics that are common to jobs across a wide spectrum. They might describe how the incumbent does the job, the behaviors that are required to perform the job, or the activities that are performed. Let's look at some of the common approaches used.

Position Analysis Questionnaire

The Position Analysis Questionnaire (PAQ), developed by researchers at Purdue University, is a structured job analysis questionnaire consisting of 187 worker-oriented job activities and work situation variables divided into six categories:

1. *Information input.* Where and how does the worker get the information that is used in performing the job?
2. *Mental processes.* What reasoning, decision-making, planning, and information-processing activities are used in performing the job?

3. *Work output.* What physical activities does the worker perform, and what tools or devices are used?
4. *Relationships with other people.* What relationships are required in performing the job?
5. *Job context.* In what physical and social contexts is the work performed?
6. *Other job characteristics.* What activities, conditions, or characteristics other than those already described are relevant to the job?

The PAQ items are rated using different scales, including importance, amount of time required, extent of use, possibility of occurrence, applicability, and difficulty. It is scored by a computer, and a profile for the job is compared with standard profiles of known job families, enabling the comparison of one job to another. The quantitative nature of the PAQ enables it to be used for evaluating job worth and for identifying applicable exams for screening applicants.

Department of Labor Procedure and Functional Job Analysis

The Department of Labor Procedure (DOL) and Functional Job Analysis (FJA) are comprehensive approaches that concentrate on the interactions among what an employee does with respect to data, people, and things (see Table 6.1). In addition, the FJA considers the goals of the organization, what workers do to achieve those goals in their jobs, level and orientation of what workers do, performance standards, and training content.

TABLE 6.1. DEPARTMENT OF LABOR WORKER FUNCTIONS

Data	People	Things
0 Synthesizing	0 Mentoring	0 Setting up
1 Coordinating	1 Negotiating	1 Precision working
2 Analyzing	2 Instructing	2 Operating-controlling
3 Compiling	3 Supervising	3 Driving-operating
4 Computing	4 Diverting	4 Manipulating
5 Copying	5 Persuading	5 Tending
6 Comparing	6 Speaking-signaling	6 Feeding-offbearing
	7 Serving	7 Handling
	8 Taking instruction and helping	

Comprehensive Occupation Data Analysis Program

The Comprehensive Occupation Data Analysis Program is a task inventory developed for U.S. Air Force specialties by the Air Training Command. Detailed task statements are written to describe the work. Each statement consists of an action, an object of the action, and essential modifiers. Job incumbents are asked to indicate the relative amount of time they spend on each task. Responses are then clustered by computer analysis into occupational groupings so that jobs with similar tasks and the same relative time-spent values are listed together.

Job Element Method

The purpose of the job element method, developed by Ernest Primoff of the U.S. Office of Personnel Management, is to identify the behaviors and accompanying achievements that are significant for job success. A combination of behavior and achievements is referred to as an element. Elements may include job behaviors, intellectual behaviors, motor behaviors, and work habits.

A panel of SMEs identifies tasks significant to the job and then the KSAOCs necessary to perform the job. At this stage, the job tasks are turned into job elements. For example, the task "writes computer programs to perform statistical analyses, interprets the data, and writes reports" is transformed into the element "ability to write computer programs to perform statistical analyses, interpret data, and write reports."

The SMEs then rate the elements on four factors (Primoff, 1975, p. 3):

1. *Barely acceptable.* What relative portion of even barely acceptable workers are good in the element?
2. *Superior.* How important is the element in picking out the superior worker?
3. *Trouble.* How much trouble is likely if the element is ignored when choosing among applicants?
4. *Practical.* Is the element practical? To what extent can we fill our job openings if we demand it?

The ratings on these four factors are analyzed to identify the elements with the greatest potential for selecting superior applicants. The premise behind the job element method is that the same elements may traverse different tasks and different jobs. The federal government uses this method to establish selection standards and to validate selection examinations (Primoff & Eyde, 1988).

Occupational Information Network

The Occupational Information Network (O*NET) is a database compiled by the U.S. Department of Labor to provide basic occupational data. Its framework is organized around six sets of descriptors: worker requirements, experience requirements, worker characteristics, occupational requirements, occupation-specific requirements, and occupation characteristics. The information is available online (http://www.onetcenter.org/overview.html) and can be used to develop job descriptions, job specifications, and career opportunity information.

Contextual Performance

Contextual performance refers to aspects of performance unrelated to specific tasks. These include activities directed at enhancing the interpersonal and psychological environment that facilitates task completion. Borman and Motowidlo (1993) note that contextual activities are different from tasks or job performance. Whereas task activities contribute directly to the technical or core of an agency's or department's production of goods and services, contextual activities contribute to the social environment. Task activities may differ across jobs, and contextual activities are common to many, if not all, jobs. Task activities are also associated with skills or abilities, while contextual activities are associated with motivational or personality variables. Some examples of contextual behaviors are coming to work on time, working overtime on short notice when unexpected problems arise, helping others when needed, minimizing or solving conflicts within the work group, and training or mentoring newcomers (Guion & Highhouse, 2006). In an attempt to identify behaviors associated with contextual performance, researchers have developed personality-based job analysis instruments.

Personality-Based Job Analysis

Raymark, Schmidt, and Guion (1997) developed an instrument based on twelve personality dimensions: general leadership, interest in negotiation, achievement striving, friendly disposition, sensitivity to others, collaborative work tendency, general trustworthiness, adherence to work ethic, attention to details, desire to generate ideas, tendency to think things through, and emotional stability. Other instruments used to identify personality measures are the Self-Descriptive Index (Guion, Highhouse, Reeve, & Zickar, 2005), the International Personality Item Pool (Goldberg, 1999), the NEO Job Profiler and NEO Job Personality Inventory (Costa, McCrae, & Kay, 1995), and the Position Classification Inventory (Gottfredson & Holland, 1994).

Team-Based Job Analysis

As working in teams has become more important, job analysis questions and measures need to be developed to identify the job elements and competencies for successful collaboration and teamwork. The following issues are important in understanding what is required to successfully perform a job:

- *Task interdependence.* Within the team, jobs performed by team members are related to one another.
- *Goal interdependence.* Work goals come directly from the goals of the team.
- *Interdependent feedback and rewards.* Performance evaluations are strongly influenced by how well the team performs.
- *Communication and cooperation between groups.* Teams cooperate to get the work completed on time.

For a comprehensive compilation of different types of job analysis techniques and job analysis studies across a variety of occupations, refer to *The Job Analysis Handbook for Business, Industry, and Government* (Gael, 1988).

Conclusion

Forecasting human resources needs is a critical component of SHRM. Organizations must assess trends, evaluate their current situation, and project their human resources needs. Before decisions can be made on recruitment and selection or training and development objectives, organizations need to audit the skills and positions of their incumbent employees. This audit will provide information on the inventory of KSAOCs and positions available within the agency and will call attention to any KSAOCs or positions that may be missing. Jobs change, and the KSAOCs required to perform them also change. To remain competitive, agencies must keep abreast of changing skill and position requirements.

Not only is a job analysis required for the planning and development of recruitment and selection strategies and for planning training and development programs, but it also provides the foundation for other HRM functions. A job analysis is essential for the development of compensation systems, identifying job-related competencies that can objectively evaluate employees' performance, restructuring work activities, and assessing risks in the workplace. An up-to-date job analysis is required to validate the job-relatedness of other human resources functions.

Despite the importance of a job analysis, Guion and Highhouse (2006) offer some warnings that should be heeded. Different sources of information may yield different information, at least some of it wrong. Observing one incumbent rather than another may get biased information. An unusually effective worker may do different things with different resources. People with strong verbal skills can describe tasks and resources more clearly than others—and perhaps say more to embellish their jobs.

Job analysis tends to yield static descriptions of "the way we've always done it." Job analysis typically describes the job as it is, not how it might be, ought to be, or will be in the future. Job analysis should, but rarely does, include planning for future contingencies and alternatives.

Job analyses rarely recognize alternative ways to do the job or qualify for it. Most jobs can be done in more than one way. More attention should be given to if-then hypotheses: if an applicant can be expected to do the job one way, then one set of attributes will provide the best predictors, but if the applicant is likely to do it differently, then a different set of attributes may be better.

Job analysis is typically descriptive, not prescriptive. It might often be useful to describe effective ways to do a job. Differences in information from high performers and low performers can highlight the actions and personal resources that lead to effectiveness.

No one method of job analysis is clearly superior to another. For personnel research, the purpose of job analysis is to understand the job well enough to form sensible, rationally defensible hypotheses about the characteristics of people that predict criterion variables of interest. That purpose is not likely to be optimally met by any one method or if one uses any method or set of methods uncritically.

Exercise 6.1: General Manager and Chief Executive of the Walter E. Washington Convention Center Resigns

The general manager and executive director of the Walter E. Washington Convention Center resigned from her position after two-and-a-half years to spend more time with her family.

An official who chairs the authority said members had talked about the pressure to move the convention center to "the next level of competition." The board wants to bring more retail, conventions, and businesses, including banquets, to the facility. The board, however, thought the performance of the chief executive was satisfactory and was not dissatisfied with her performance.

Question

1. Before hiring a new general manager and chief executive, a job analysis should be conducted. What job analysis method or methods would you recommend to identify the most important KSAOCs for the position at the Washington Convention Center?

Source: Woodlee & Haynes (2008).

Exercise 6.2: Caseworkers Often Face Tremendous Difficulties

In Washington, D.C., which has the highest child poverty rate in the country, it is not uncommon for caseworkers working with children to face armed drug dealers and stoned parents, homes crawling with cockroaches, and kids with scabies. An average caseload of twelve can mean dealing with fifty to seventy people, including parents and siblings. A caseworker may get a parent into rehab, help pay family bills, and obtain furniture, food, and clothing. A caseworker may also take children to the doctor and celebrate their birthdays.

According to a General Accounting Office study in 2003, the average tenure of caseworkers nationwide is less than two years, mainly due to high caseloads, the risk of violence, low pay, and insufficient training. In Washington, D.C., a caseworker's annual salary is approximately $40,000.

Question

1. Based on a job analysis, develop the job specification for a Washington, D.C., caseworker. What are the qualifications a caseworker needs to perform the job effectively? What are some of the KSAOCs needed? Include in your analysis the following items:
   - Education, degrees, or certificates
   - Skill requirements
   - Experience
   - Personal requirements
   - Mental and physical requirements
   - Working conditions
   - Job hazards

Source: Dvorak (2008).

Chapter Questions

1. In small groups, discuss the methods by which a job analysis can be completed. Compare and contrast these methods, noting the pros and cons of each. Which method of job analysis would be more effective for capturing the KSAOCs of the position each group member holds now or a job held in the past? Discuss why you selected the job analysis method that you did.
2. Discuss why the American with Disabilities Act has heightened the importance of job analysis activities.
3. Discuss why strategic job analysis is important for organizations to remain competitive. How important are strategic job analyses for SHRM activities? Explain your answer.

Online Activities

1. Visit the O*Net Web site (http://online.onetcenter.org/) and conduct a skills search for your position. Are the skills identified by O*Net similar to the skills you possess?
2. Identify five job titles and their job descriptions that are used for classifying positions in your agency or an agency you are familiar with. Visit the Dictionary of Occupational Titles Web site. Are the job titles and descriptions for the positions you identified consistent with the position descriptions in your agency? In what ways are they similar? How are they different? Which title and description appears to be most accurate?

CHAPTER SEVEN

RECRUITMENT AND SELECTION IN THE PUBLIC AND NONPROFIT SECTORS

After you read this chapter, you should be able to:

- Understand the importance of recruitment and selection to strategic human resources management
- Understand the recruitment techniques that public and nonprofit organizations use
- Discuss how technology is changing recruitment and selection procedures
- Understand the tests and techniques used in selection
- Understand legal concerns in the recruitment and selection process

The need to adapt to rapidly changing situations requires agencies to recruit and select qualified individuals. Strategic human resources management (SHRM) provides agencies with the opportunity to use recruitment and selection to influence the operational strategy of public and nonprofit organizations. Recruitment is the process of attracting qualified candidates to apply for vacant positions within an organization. Selection is the final stage of the recruitment process, when decisions are made as to who will be selected for the vacant positions. Both recruitment and selection require effective planning to determine the human resources needs of the organization. The organization must determine its immediate objectives and future direction, and it must forecast its employment needs to align them with the organization's strategies.

To fill positions, agencies have a variety of options. They can recruit new employees, promote or transfer incumbent employees who possess the skills necessary for the vacant positions, or provide training or educational support to lower-level or paraprofessional employees in anticipation of future needs.

The recruitment and selection of qualified and competent employees is critical for public and nonprofit agencies because mission-driven agencies are dependent on their staffs. It is people who deliver the programs and services that public and nonprofit stakeholders expect; therefore, planning for and selecting qualified and competent employees must be done with strategic purpose.

Vacancies arise when employees are promoted or transferred to different positions within the agency or when people retire or leave to seek employment elsewhere. Some departments or agencies may expand into new service or program areas, requiring additional staff. Recruitment is an ongoing process in most organizations; however, often it is not planned and therefore is less successful than it could be. For recruitment to be successful, planning is essential. Recruitment efforts must be consistent with the agency's mission. Employers must understand how to determine the job requirements and where to seek and how to screen applicants so that qualified and competent individuals are selected.

This chapter discusses internal and external recruitment, applicant screening, selection methods, preemployment testing under the Americans with Disabilities Act, and executive and managerial recruitment and selection. An explanation of employment-test-related measurement terms is also provided.

Recruitment

As noted in Chapter Two, recruitment must be tied to the organization's mission, and attempts should be made to anticipate the agency's future personnel needs. A SHRM plan facilitates an agency's ability to accomplish its objectives. This may mean hiring individuals who possess knowledge, skills, abilities, and other characteristics (KSAOCs) that are different from those of incumbent employees. This makes it possible for an agency to implement a wide range of strategies within a short time frame in response to external demands.

Before recruitment for candidates begins, the human resources management (HRM) recruiter and the unit manager should review the qualifications needed for the vacant position or positions. This review enables them to identify the KSAOCs they will be looking for in the applicants, and it will guide them in developing an accurate job bulletin or advertisement. They should also identify different career patterns that can fit within the department or agency's framework. Many prospective employees have different expectations, needs, and interests from previous generations, which means agencies must offer a wider variety of employer-employee relationships and recruit differently (U.S. Office of Personnel Management, 2006).

There is good news for public and nonprofit employers and prospective employees. In 2007, Congress enacted the College Cost Reduction and Access Act of 2007, which makes college more affordable. That part of the act received much attention. The law also contains a measure that provides special relief to those who enter the public and nonprofit sectors. The Education for Public Service Act allows graduates with direct federal loans and consolidated federal loans to obtain immediate reductions in their monthly payments as well as loan forgiveness after ten years in public service. A public sector job is defined as a full-time job in which the employer is a federal, state, or local government agency or intergovernmental authority, or an organization that is described in Section 501(c)(3) of the Internal Revenue Code of 1986 and exempt from taxation under Section 501(a) of such act.

Internal Recruitment

Public sector agencies often look at current staff first to fill vacancies. In fact, many public agencies give extra credit or points to employees already working for the organization. In some cases, there may be collective bargaining agreements in place that stipulate that incumbent employees should receive preferential consideration. Preference for incumbent employees may also exist in many nonprofit agencies in which program stability and connections to the community and funding sources are important. In these cases, employers first consider the internal labor market.

For internal recruitment to work, agencies need to be proactive and incorporate strategic planning into their human resources practices. Organizations need to track the KSAOCs needed for the various jobs within the organization. Employees who possess those needed skills, whether administrative, managerial, or technological, should be identified. Human resources

For internal recruitment to work, agencies need to be proactive and incorporate strategic planning into their human resources practices.

management departments and department managers should work together and make workforce projections based on the current level of employee skills. They should review transfers, retirements, promotions, and termination patterns and do succession planning in order to identify individuals who might fill positions when an incumbent leaves. This requires keeping track of and updating the records of each employee's KSAOCs and the demands required of each position. A human resource information system can sort employee data by education, career interests, work histories, occupation fields, and other factors.

Many organizations favor internal recruitment because administrators have the opportunity to review and evaluate the KSAOCs of internal applicants prior to selection. Choosing internal candidates also enables agencies to recoup the investment they have made in recruiting, selecting, training, and developing their current employees. Promoting qualified incumbent employees rewards them for their performance and signals to other employees that the agency is committed to their development and advancement.

Before organizations limit recruitment efforts to internal recruitment, however, other factors should be considered. Some positions in public and nonprofit organizations require specialized skills that may not be found within the agency, and for such positions it may be necessary to recruit and hire from outside. Organizations with homogeneous workforces—that is, agencies composed of all women, men, or Caucasians, for example—should also consider outside recruitment to increase the demographic diversity of their staff. Another important reason for the organization to consider external recruitment is when it wants to change its internal culture. Applicants hired from outside are not hampered by sacred cows, relationships with colleagues, or the agency's history.

External Recruitment

External recruitment is the seeking of qualified applicants from outside the organization. Typically, the agency would seek qualified applicants from the relevant labor market, defined by the skills required for the position and the location (geographical region) where those skills can be found. The nature of specific occupations or jobs often demarcates the labor market. Local labor markets, for example, are small areas, cities, or metropolitan statistical areas. Laborer, office and clerical, technical, and direct service provider positions are often filled from the local labor market. It is common for federal, state, and local governments and nonprofits to recruit clerical and trade employees, such as maintenance or custodial personnel, from the local labor market. Applicants for these positions are typically abundant, and the salaries that accompany the positions preclude relocating new employees.

Regional labor markets are larger. They usually comprise a particular county, several areas of a state, or even the entire state. Depending on the skill supply in the region, technical, managerial, and professional workers, as well as scientists and engineers, may be recruited from a regional labor market. Agencies in the New England area, for example, can use the regional labor market to recruit applicants for all kinds of positions because of the large number and variety of colleges, universities, and industries located there.

State, local, and nonprofit agencies use the national labor market when critical skills are in short supply locally. Scientists, engineers, managers, professionals, and executives are most likely to be sought at the national level. The federal government, for example, recruits nationally through regional offices for all of its professional positions.

Public and nonprofit organizations need to develop a recruitment strategy. Decisions need to be made about when and where to look for qualified applicants when action needs to be taken. In some organizations, vacancies are posted, but there is no recruitment plan, which is necessary in a competitive job environment. Agencies need to anticipate their future needs and actively and creatively promote the opportunities available in their organizations. Internships, co-ops, and on-the-job training should be integrated into the recruitment and selection process (Ban & Riccucci, 1993; U.S. Merit Systems Protection Board, 2003b, 2008).

Recruitment planning and strategies at the federal and state levels are typically directed by central personnel offices and for large local governments by centralized human resources or civil service offices. It would be remiss to generalize any more than that because many changes are taking place at all levels of government in regard to recruitment and selection. The federal government and many states have delegated responsibility for recruiting and examining new employees to the agencies. This has resulted in some creative techniques. The State of Missouri has gone to Second Life, the three-dimensional virtual world, to recruit employees for information technology positions, assuming that the site gets visited by individuals in their mid-twenties and thirties interested in technology (Hanson, 2007).

Despite the well-deserved criticism of centralized personnel offices, they have begun to change with the times. Technology has made information more accessible to job seekers. Personal-computer-based kiosks provide job seekers with current job information at the touch of a finger. At the federal level, job seekers can access USAJobs, an automated employment information system in which all federal jobs are announced by telephone, fax, personal computer, and touch-screen kiosks. This system includes vacancy announcements and application forms and is available around the clock. Applicants can search for job opportunities using a variety of criteria, such as job title, key word, agency location, and pay. They can create a federal résumé, store it on the site, and in some instances use it to apply for multiple federal jobs (U.S. Merit System Protection Board, 2008). The U.S. Merit System Protection Board surveyed new employees to determine if different recruitment strategies attract different types of applicants. It compared the responses of new employees under thirty years of age to those over thirty years of age. For both groups, the largest number of survey respondents found out about their job through a friend or relative. New employees thirty years and older relied on the Internet, using USAJobs and agency Web sites. New employees under thirty years of age relied on college-related sources such as job fairs and college placement offices. Federal agencies can access USACareers, an automated package that they can use to help employees affected by downsizing to determine training needs, develop career paths, and find new jobs.

Recruiting for Local Governments and Nonprofits

Recruitment efforts for local governments and nonprofit organizations should begin with a review of the competencies and skill levels of the positions that need to be filled. After these elements have been identified, the government or agency needs to develop a recruitment plan and target the local, regional, or national labor market. Clerical, trade, and technical positions can typically be filled by the local or regional labor market. Executive, scientific, and medical positions such as executive directors of nonprofits, directors of development, city managers, police chiefs, and directors of large departments such as personnel, community development, public health, and finance may be recruited nationally. Some national recruitment sources used by the public and nonprofit sectors are general professional journals and newsletters such as the *PA Times*, *International City Manager's Association (ICMA) Newsletter*, *IPMA-HR Nonprofit Times*, and the *Chronicle of Philanthropy*. They are also available in digital versions.

Job boards such as www.monster.com, jobsonline.net, and www.indeed.com provide places for employers to post jobs or search for candidates. Web sites are another recruitment vehicle.

Exhibit 7.1 presents a list of organizations for locating employment in the public and nonprofit sectors.

Exhibit 7.1. Resources for Job Seekers

Chronicle of Philanthropy, www.philanthropy.com
Nonprofit Times, http://www.nptimes.com
Charity Channel, http://charitychannel.com
Campus Compact, http://wwwcompact.org/jobs/nonprofitjobs.php
Action Without Borders, www.idealist.org
Foundation Center, http://fdcenter.org/opnd/jobs
Association of Fundraising Professionals, www.afpnet.org
Young Nonprofit Professionals Network, www.ynpn.org
Craigslist, http://www.craigslist.org/npo/
Opportunity Nocs, http://www.opportunitynocs.org/jobseekerx/SearchJobsForm.asp
Guidestar, www.guidestar.org
Energ!ze, http://www.energizeinc.com
Nonprofit Oyster, http://www.nonprofitoyster.com/
National Council of Nonprofit Associations, http://www.ncna.org/
Nonprofit Jobs Cooperative, http://www.nonprofitjobscoop.org
Community Career Center, http://nonprofitjobs.org
Deep Sweep, http://www.deepsweep.com
Nonprofit Career Network, http://www.nonprofitcareer.com/
Americans for Arts Job Bank, http://www.artistplacement.org
Arts Journal, www.artsjournal.com
Diversity at Work, www.diversityjobs.com
indeed, http://www.indeed.com/
Bizjournals, http://www.bizjournals.com/
Human Service Career Network, www.hscareers.com
Social Work Job Bank, www.socialworkjobbank.com
Opportunity Knocks, http://content.opportunityknocks.org
USAJobs, http://www.usajobs.gov/

Today, most public entities and nonprofits post open positions and accept applications on their Web sites. Posting has become so pervasive that the Office of Federal Contract Compliance Programs issued an Internet applicant final rule that addresses record keeping by federal contractors and subcontractors about the Internet hiring process and the solicitation of race, gender, and ethnicity of "Internet applicants." An Internet applicant is defined as an individual who satisfies the following criteria:

- The individual submits an expression of interest in employment through the Internet or related electronic data technologies.
- The contractor considers the individual for employment in a particular position.
- The individual's expression of interest indicates that he or she possesses the basic qualifications for the position.
- The individual at no point in the contractor's selection process prior to receiving an offer of employment from the contractor removes himself or herself from further consideration or otherwise indicates that he or she is no longer interested in the position. (http://www.dol.gov/esa/regs/compliance/ofccp/faqs/iappfaqs.htm)

If a contractor uses the Internet to advertise a position but requires all individuals to complete a paper application form, the individuals who apply will not be considered Internet applicants. It is not the method of advertising a job that determines the applicability of the Internet applicant rule. Rather, the determining factor is whether the expression of interest in employment was made through the Internet or related electronic data technologies.

When advertising is part of the recruitment process, it should be written in a manner that will attract responses from qualified individuals and deter responses from those who are not qualified. It is important for the advertisement to focus on the job qualifications required for the position so that only candidates with qualifications matching the requirements of the position are attracted to apply. An advertisement that is too expansive, including everything but the kitchen sink, may discourage qualified candidates from applying. Be accurate and realistic when posting a job advertisement.

To comply with the Americans with Disabilities Act, employers should inform applicants on an application form or job advertisement that the hiring process includes specific selection procedures (for example, a written test; demonstration of job skills such as typing, making a presentation, or editing a report; or interview). Applicants should be asked to inform the employer within a reasonable time period prior to the administration of the selection procedure of any reasonable accommodation needed to take a preemployment examination, accommodate an interview, or demonstrate a job skill. Employers may request from the applicant documentation verifying the need for an accommodation.

To ensure compliance with equal opportunity requirements, it is important for agencies to scrutinize their recruitment procedures for practices that may result in discrimination. For instance, the recruitment strategies used should not exclude certain groups. With the increase in recruitment over the Internet, it is important that organizations realize that not all applicants may have ready access to computers. It is also important that Internet and Web site advertisements indicate a commitment to diversity (Rubaii-Barrett & Wise, 2007).

The Equal Employment Opportunity Commission (EEOC) bans the use in recruitment of preferences based on age, race, national origin, religion, or sex. Some organizations, however, undertake targeted recruitment: they make deliberate attempts to recruit protected-class members who have been identified as absent from or underused in an agency. Nonprofits that provide services to particular constituency groups, such as persons with AIDS, unwed mothers, or senior citizens, may deliberately target applicants from those groups during recruitment.

As noted in Chapter Three, the Immigration Reform and Control Act of 1986, as revised in 1990, prohibits the employment of unauthorized aliens and provides civil and criminal penalties for violations of this law. The law prohibits the initial or continued employment of unauthorized aliens but also employment discrimination on the basis of national origin or citizen status. The purpose of this provision is to discourage employers from attempting to comply with the prohibition against hiring unauthorized aliens by refusing to hire applicants who are foreign looking in appearance or have foreign-sounding names.

The U.S. Citizenship and Immigration Services revised Form I-9, which is used to verify employment eligibility in the United States. It updated the form in response to the Illegal Immigration Reform and Immigrant Responsibility Act of 1996, which mandated a reduction in the number of documents that employers may accept from newly hired employees. Employers should use the revised form (Rev. 06/05/07) for individuals hired on or after November 7, 2007.

Employers may apply for temporary H-1B visas for temporary foreign workers. H-IB visas allow U.S. employers to employ foreign guest workers in specialty occupations. A specialty occupation requires theoretical and practical application of a body of specialized knowledge along with at least a bachelor's degree or its equivalent. For example, architecture, engineering, mathematics, physical sciences, social sciences, medicine and health, education, business specialties, accounting, law, theology, and the arts are specialty occupations.

There is a cap of sixty-five thousand workers per year, though Congress has varied it. Universities and nonprofit and government research entities are exempt from the cap. The position the foreign national is being hired for must require a minimum of a bachelor's degree in a specialty occupation, and the person being hired must possess the bachelor's degree or its equivalent. The employer must pay the employee the prevailing wage for employees working in a similar position for the employer and attest that the employee will not displace any other U.S. employees. H-1B visa holders may change jobs as soon as their employer files an approval petition, and they are not restricted to their current geographical area. The law is enforced by the U.S. Citizenship and Immigration Services within the Department of Homeland Security. Noncompliance may result in fines up to ten thousand dollars for each unauthorized alien employed, as well as imprisonment for up to six months for a pattern or practice of violations. Federal contractors may be barred from federal contracts for one year.

Screening Applicants

Once the organization has communicated its need to fill positions and applicants have responded, it moves on to screening the applicants to identify those with the requisite KSAOCs.

Employment applications are often the first step in the screening process. Applicants fill out a form asking them to answer a variety of questions. The questions must not violate local, state, or federal employment discrimination laws. The rule followed by the EEOC, state agencies, and most courts is that if the employer asks a question on an employment application form, it is assumed that the answer is used in the hiring process. If the question does not pertain to the job applicant's qualification for the job in question, the question may be held illegal if it has a disparate impact on a covered group. When developing an application, an organization should refer to the state's fair employment laws to eliminate any potential discriminatory questions. Questions about age, race, gender, and disability are permitted only when responding is voluntary and the information is required for record-keeping purposes. Equal employment opportunity data should be collected by the personnel office and should not be used to screen out applicants.

Most applications are generic and not tailored for any one position. They usually provide limited space for applicants to provide detailed information about relevant work or educational experience. A supplemental questionnaire should be developed that asks questions related to the specific job to facilitate the screening process.

After individuals apply for a position, the applications need to be screened to identify a list of qualified applicants and eliminate unqualified applicants. This process is different for each position. It is not uncommon for a large urban government that is recruiting for firefighters to receive hundreds of applications. Positions typically inundated by applicants use multiple screening procedures to pare down the number of candidates. The first screen is to weed out applicants who do not meet the minimum requirements, such as age (for example, law enforcement positions require applicants to be at least twenty-one years old), level of education, or required certification. The second screen might eliminate applicants who lack the requisite experience.

For administrative or professional positions, which usually have more stringent education and experience requirements, there are likely to be fewer applicants. To reduce the number of applicants to the most qualified, it is important to have preestablished criteria to facilitate the screening. Requiring previous experience as a city planner or community development specialist might be one standard. Previous financial management experience with a budget of two million dollars might be another. To screen résumés, an instrument such as a checklist might be developed to keep track of the relevant experience and education required. Anybody who has spent time reading many résumés knows that after the first ten or so, fatigue sets in. You become less attentive as the review progresses. A checklist keeps you focused on the salient KSAOCs.

Background investigations have become more common, and not only for public safety and Homeland Security positions. Employees and volunteers working with children must undergo a background investigation and have their fingerprints reviewed by law enforcement agencies to screen out pedophiles or individuals with criminal histories. City managers and other executives often have their backgrounds investigated. Employers are concerned with the reliability of the applicant's behavior, integrity, and personal adjustment. They may also be scrutinized by a consumer reporting agency. The information may contain the applicant's credit history, along with employment history, income, driving record, arrests and convictions, and lifestyle. A consumer report is virtually any information on an applicant that is compiled from a database by a consumer reporting agency and provided to the organization. The Fair Credit Reporting Act (1970), as amended, regulates the organization's acquisition and use of consumer reports on job applicants.

The Internet has created informal means, not necessarily sanctioned by the agency, to screen applicants. Conducting a Web search on Google may provide news reports, press releases, or even blogs that may disclose personal characteristics of the applicant. Visits to social networking sites such as MySpace, Facebook, and Xanga have also been used to ascertain if there are pictures or comments made by the applicant that might embarrass the agency.

Employment screening techniques and tests must comply with the general principles and technical requirements of the Uniform Guidelines on Employee Selection Procedures (1978), which apply to public, for-profit, and nonprofit organizations. Preemployment testing is used to measure the KSAOCs of applicants and predict their ability to perform a job. It is an attempt to standardize the screening process and determine whether applicants possess the characteristics necessary to be successful on the job. Along with the Uniform Guidelines, the Principles for the Validation and Use of Personnel Selection Procedures, developed by the American Psychological Association, Division of Industrial and Organizational Psychology (1987), broadly define tests as a variety of instruments or procedures used in the selection or promotion process.

Following are some of the selection techniques commonly used in employment settings, as well as alternative approaches. *Cognitive ability and aptitude tests* are designed to reflect the general and the specific capabilities and potentials of the individual applicant by measuring verbal, quantitative, nonverbal, and oral skills, or motor functions such as mechanical ability, numerical aptitude, finger dexterity, or perceptual accuracy. They are used to determine whether applicants possess the aptitude to learn the KSAOCs required in the position.

Achievement tests are designed to measure the degree of mastery of specific material to assess whether an individual has profited from prior experience and learned specific materials. Most of the items on achievement tests assess whether the individual possesses specific knowledge of concepts considered critical for a job. Trade tests are examples of this type.

Personality inventories are designed to assess a person's typical behavioral traits and characteristics by measuring such traits as dominance, sociability, self-control, or introversion and extroversion. Some of the more common personality tests used in the public sector are the Minnesota Multiphasic Personality Inventory, the California Psychological Inventory, and the Edwards Personal Preference Schedule. They are used when interpersonal skills are key to successful performance.

Interest inventories are designed to predict job choice behavior rather than job performance by ascertaining the occupational likes and dislikes of the individual and indicating the occupational areas that are most likely to be satisfying to that person. They are used to make a compatible person-job match.

Experience and training (E & T) rating is a procedure that quantifies the education, experience, training, achievements, and other relevant data that applicants provide on job applications and questionnaires. Points are assigned to applicants based on the number of years of experience, education, and training relevant to the position. Experience and training exams are often referred to as unassembled examinations.

Structured oral exams are used to evaluate job requirements that are not easily assessed by paper-and-pencil measures, such as interpersonal, oral communication, and supervisory skills. Although the specifics of the exams may differ, all structured oral exams share similar components. They are based on a job analysis that captures the critical KSAOCs necessary for the position. The questions are job related, and all applicants are asked the same questions. Rating scales are used to evaluate the responses, and the raters receive training prior to conducting the examination. Structured oral exams are used a great deal in the public sector.

Work sample or performance tests require applicants to demonstrate that they possess the necessary skills needed for successful job performance. Applicants are asked to perform tasks that are representative of actual job activities. For example, applicants applying for the position of editor of a nonprofit newsletter may be asked to write and edit copy, and applicants applying for a training position could be required to prepare and present a training module.

To screen applicants for multisystemic therapy positions, some social service agencies require a master of social work degree and several years of experience working with families. Therapists work primarily with parents or caregivers, as well as the youth and their network of extended family, peers, school, and community toward positive behavioral outcomes. The position requires the ability to apply analytical and systemic principles and processes to clinical skills with families and to collaborate as a team member with families, a clinical team, and other community care providers.

After résumés have been screened, eligible applicants interested in the position must demonstrate their clinical and interpersonal skills by answering behavioral-based questions to assess their personal character, ability to think systematically, conceptualization skills, and counseling skills. The applicants are interviewed by a team of therapists and a supervisor, and are provided with scenarios of family situations that they will encounter on the job. For example:

> This family consists of a single mother and her two sons, ages eleven and twelve. There have been chronic problems in school, which resulted in their being placed out of the home in the past. Mom has a poor relationship with the school personnel and is fearful about talking with them. Since their return home, the children have begun acting out behaviorally again in the school (arguing with the teacher, not following rules, refusing to complete schoolwork, and so on). What would be your focus with the mother?

Anne Goldych Dailey uses this screening procedure to hire new employees because she found that possession of an M.S.W degree did not guarantee strong interpersonal and clinical skills. She believes that to be successful in this position, therapists also need to engage people and establish effective relationships. Such skills are not always obvious in a traditional interview situation. Although the scenario simulations may be stressful for some candidates, the ability to function in stressful situations is key to effective performance. The client population is families raising challenging youth who have not been successful in multiple areas of their lives and are heading to or returning from residential placement. Therapists are autonomous, spending most of their time in the field and not under direct supervision.

In-baskets are written tests designed to simulate administrative tasks. The in-basket exercise consists of correspondence designed to be representative of the job's actual tasks. A set of instructions usually states that applicants should imagine that they have been placed in the position and must deal with the memos and other items that have accumulated in their in-basket. The test is used to measure such skills as task prioritization, written communication, and judgment.

Leaderless group discussions assess attributes such as oral communication, leadership, persuasiveness, adaptability, and tolerance for stress. Applicants are assembled to work on solving a problem that requires cooperation. For example, they may be asked to compose a statement in response to charges that the agency's employees are treating clients unfairly, or they may be asked to work on a problem involving competition, such as deciding how to allocate a limited amount of money among a number of community projects. Nobody is designated as the group leader. Assessors evaluate the individual applicant's participation in the group's discussion.

Assessment centers are special selection programs that rely on performance tests. The purpose of an assessment center is to obtain multiple measurements of key job dimensions by using a variety of instruments, such as role-playing exercises, in-baskets, leaderless group discussions, paper-and-pencil tests, and other written exercises. Judgments about each applicant's behavior are made by assessors who are trained in the scoring of each exercise. Assessment centers are frequently used to select administrators and supervisors, who need skills in such areas as leadership, planning, and decision making. In the public sector, assessment centers are commonly used for the selection of city managers and the promotion of public safety managers.

Biodata selection procedures require that applicants complete a questionnaire that asks for biographical information. Questions may include topics such as level of education, demographic profile, work experience, interests and social activities, habits, hobbies, family history, attitudes, values, achievements, and personal characteristics. Individuals are selected based on whether their answers to the questions are related to job success. Schmidt and Hunter (1998) reported mean biodata validity coefficients of .35 and .30 against job and training success, respectively. As a result of the high predictability, the ease of administration of biodata instruments, and diminished adverse impact, the use of biodata has increased in both the public and private sectors.

Drug testing has become commonplace for reasons of on-the-job safety. Drug-dependent employees are more likely than nondependent employees to be involved in workplace accidents. Decreased productivity, increased absenteeism, and threats to fellow employees' or clients' safety are some of the problems manifested by substance abusers (Office of National Drug Control Policy, 2001). Consequently, many organizations have instituted drug testing as part of preemployment screening. It is important to note that applicants do not have the same rights as employees. Although applicants for a position may be tested for substance abuse at the organization's request, organizations do not necessarily have the right to test employees who are already on the payroll.

Lie detector exams are permitted in certain circumstances. The Employee Polygraph Protection Act of 1988 prevents employers involved in or affecting interstate commerce from using lie detectors. It is unlawful for employers to require prospective employees to take lie detector tests or for employers to use test results or a worker's refusal or failure to take a test as grounds for failure to promote, discharge, or discipline. The law does not, however, apply to the federal government, state or local governments, or any political subdivision of a state or local government. Other exemptions include individuals or consultants working under contract for federal intelligence agencies; makers and distributors of controlled substances; and security companies whose business involves the protection of currency, financial instruments, or vital facilities or materials.

The right of a public employer to require a public employee to take a lie detector test may be limited by state statute. Federal law and most state laws prohibit questions about religion; political, racial, and union activities; and sexual and marital matters. Subjects must be informed of their rights, and written consent must be obtained before administering the test. The test results must remain confidential, and only licensed, bonded examiners may be used. Polygraph exams are used primarily for law enforcement and public safety positions.

Honesty and integrity tests are lawful under the Employee Polygraph Protection Act of 1988 and most state polygraph laws. There are two kinds of honesty and integrity tests: overt and personality. Overt tests deal with attitudes toward theft or admission of theft or other illegal activities. Personality tests do not look at honesty per se but at a variety of counterproductive work behaviors such as impulsiveness, nonconformance, and dislike of authority. A review of the literature on selection indicates that integrity tests produce a 27 percent increase in predictive validity over general cognitive ability alone (Schmidt & Hunter, 1998).

Physical ability tests are used when a significant level of physical activity is involved in performing the job. In the public sector, physical ability tests are used most often in the selection of law enforcement and public safety officers, such as police officers, firefighters, corrections officers, and park and conservation safety officials. Physical ability testing has replaced height and weight requirements, which were often used to screen applicants, resulting in adverse impacts on women and Hispanics, and they were difficult to defend as being job related. Agencies have turned instead to physical ability tests that were developed to replicate the physical tasks necessary to perform specific jobs (Arvey, Nutting, & Landon, 1992; Hughes, Ratliff, Purswell, & Hadwiger, 1989).

Preemployment Testing Under the ADA

Congress intended the ADA to prevent discrimination against individuals with hidden disabilities such as cancer, heart disease, mental illness, diabetes, epilepsy, and HIV infection or AIDS. Employers are permitted to ask applicants about their ability to perform job functions, but they may not ask about disabilities before a job offer has been made. Once a conditional job offer has been made, however, the employer may require a medical examination and make disability-related inquiries. Employers may ask applicants to describe or demonstrate how they would perform job-related tasks with or without reasonable accommodation. If the examination screens out an individual with a disability as a result of the disability, the employer must demonstrate that the exclusionary criterion is job related and consistent with business necessity. The employer must also show that the criterion cannot be satisfied and the essential job functions cannot be performed with reasonable accommodation.

Medical examinations are procedures or tests that seek information about the existence, nature, or severity of an individual's physical or mental impairment or that seek information regarding an individual's physical or psychological health. Following are some of the guidelines established by the EEOC to determine whether a procedure or test is a medical examination:

- The procedure or test must be administered by a health care professional or someone trained by a health care professional. The results of the procedure or test must be interpreted by a health care professional or someone trained by a health care professional.
- The employer must administer the procedure or test for the purpose of revealing the existence, nature, or severity of an impairment or to determine the subject's general physical or psychological health.
- The procedure or test may be invasive (for example, drawing blood, testing urine, or analyzing breath).
- The procedure or test may measure physiological or psychological responses of an individual only if the results determine the individual's ability to perform a task.
- The procedure or test must be one that is normally administered in a medical setting (a health care professional's office, a hospital).
- Medical diagnostic equipment or devices may be used for administering the procedure or test.

Physical agility and physical fitness tests, in which applicants demonstrate their ability to perform actual or simulated job-related tasks, are not medical examinations. These tests measure applicants' ability to perform a particular task; they do not seek information concerning the existence, nature, or severity of a physical or mental impairment or information regarding an applicant's health. They may be administered at the preoffer stage.

Psychological examinations such as aptitude tests, personality tests, honesty tests, and IQ tests are intended to measure applicants' capacity and propensity to perform a job successfully and are not considered to be medical examinations. Psychological tests that result in a clinical diagnosis and require interpretation by a health care professional are considered medical examinations and are prohibited at the preoffer stage.

Interviews

Interviews are often the deciding factor in who gets hired for a position. This is unfortunate because interviews are a subjective selection tool. It is easy for interviewers to inject their own prejudices into the selection decision. Another problem with interviews is that job-related questions that can differentiate between successful and unsuccessful employees often are not asked.

Interviews are often the deciding factor in who gets hired for a position. This is unfortunate because interviews are a subjective selection tool.

Successful interviewing requires planning and structure. The components of a structured oral exam should be incorporated into the interview process. Questions related to the dimensions of the job should be asked. The interviewers should agree in advance what competencies the position requires. The focus should be on the KSAOCs that interviews can assess most effectively, such as interpersonal or oral communication skills and job knowledge.

To minimize the subjectivity, the interview process should be structured. The U.S. Merit Protection Board (2003a) and Dixon, Wang, Calvin, Dineen, and Tomlinson (2002) propose the following steps:

1. Develop questions based on a job analysis.
2. Ask effective questions.
3. Ask each candidate the same questions.
4. Use detailed rating scales. Anchor the rating scales for scoring answers with examples and illustrations.
5. Train interviewers.
6. Use interview panels so that more than one person conducts the interview.
7. Take notes.

8. Assess candidate responses objectively, use the rating scales, and use the ratings to score candidates.
9. Evaluate selection decisions based on subsequent employee performance.

Research indicates that team interviews reduce individual interviewer biases about the applicant (Campion, Pursell, & Brown, 1988) and that mixed-race interview panels serve as a check and balance on the evaluation process (Dobbins, Lin, & Farh, 1992).

Interviewers should be trained to accurately receive and evaluate information. Even if a structured interview format is not used, interviewers should still document the candidates' responses to the questions.

Interviewers must comply with the EEOC guidelines concerning preemployment disability-related inquiries. They may not ask about the existence, nature, or severity of a disability, but they may inquire about the ability of an applicant to perform specific job-related functions. Here are some examples of questions prohibited under ADA:

- Do you have a disability that would interfere with your ability to perform the job?
- How many days were you sick last year?
- Have you ever been treated for mental health problems?
- Have you ever filed for workers' compensation?

Here are examples of questions permitted under ADA:

- Can you perform the essential functions of this job with or without reasonable accommodation?
- Please describe how you would perform these functions.
- Can you meet the attendance requirements of this job?
- Do you have the required licenses to perform this job?

The interview should be one of many factors considered when selecting applicants. Not all competent people interview well, and not all jobs require competent interpersonal and communication skills. Many positions use a combination of the screening techniques. For example, it is common for applicants for public safety positions to have to pass a written cognitive ability test, a medical examination and drug screen, a polygraph examination, a background investigation, a physical ability test, and an oral interview before the decision to hire is made. Positions that encompass a lot of responsibility, require time-consuming and expensive training, or in which risk to the organization or public is great typically have more demanding screening procedures.

Testing Issues

Employment tests that measure cognitive ability skills are controversial because they often result in adverse impact on protected-class members. Arvey and Faley (1988) report that African Americans score one to one-and-a-half standard deviations lower than whites. Not only have state, local, and private sector employers found themselves facing litigation, but so has the federal government. In 1979 the Department of Justice signed a consent decree in which it agreed that the Professional and Administrative Career Examination for entry into federal employment would be eliminated. African Americans and Hispanics as groups did not score as high on the exam as white candidates. A class action suit asking for an injunction and a declaratory judgment was filed against the director of the Office of Personnel Management. The plaintiffs alleged that the exam was in violation of Title VII of the Civil Rights Act of 1964 because the test had a disproportionately adverse effect on African Americans and Hispanics and was not validated in accordance with the Uniform Guidelines on Employee Selection (Nelson, 1982). An outcome of the consent decree was the establishment of a variety of selection avenues, such as the outstanding-scholar and cooperative education programs used to hire entry-level federal employees, in addition to the more recent Administrative Careers with America written examination.

State and local governments have found themselves mired in controversy over paper-and-pencil tests and adverse impact. Most large urban police and fire departments have ended up in federal court or having to negotiate consent decrees with the Department of Justice in efforts to remedy the effects of either purposeful discriminatory practices or neutral employment practices such as paper-and-pencil tests, which resulted in adverse impacts against protected class members.

Why are tests used? Organizations that need to distinguish among a large pool of applicants must develop formal, objective methods of screening, grouping, and selecting applicants. Testing is a way to do that. Research on testing has established that cognitive ability tests are equally valid for virtually all jobs and that failure to use them in selection would typically result in substantial economic loss to individual organizations

(Schmidt, 1988). Hunter (1986) found the following evidence in regard to cognitive ability tests:

- General cognitive ability predicts performance ratings in all lines of work, though validity is higher for complex jobs than for simple jobs.
- General cognitive ability predicts training success at a uniformly high level for all jobs.
- Data on job knowledge show that cognitive ability determines how much and how quickly a person learns.
- Cognitive ability predicts the ability to react in innovative ways to situations in which knowledge does not specify exactly what to do.

Measurement Terms and Concepts

Employers need to be familiar with a number of psychometric concepts that pertain to employment testing.

Reliability This concept of *reliability* is concerned with the consistency of measurement. An exam's reliability can be determined through a number of different procedures. *Test-retest* reliability occurs when individuals taking the test score about the same on the test in each administration. If a test is reliable, there should be consistency between two sets of scores for the test taken by the same person at different times. *Split-half* reliability is derived by correlating one part of the exam with another part of it. If the exam is measuring an aptitude reliably, it should do so throughout the exam. *Odd-even* reliability is when a score is computed for all the even-numbered exam items and then correlated with a score derived from the odd-numbered items. *Internal consistency measure* reliability is when each exam item is correlated with every other exam item. *Equivalent-forms* reliability is when different forms of an exam have been constructed. Each version of the exam is administered to the participants, and the two sets of exam scores are correlated.

Validity Is the test or selection instrument measuring what it is intended to measure? *Validity* is the most important characteristic of measures used in personnel selection. Why use a particular test or procedure if it is not predicting or evaluating correctly the most qualified candidates? Validity and reliability are often confused. Reliability is necessary for a test to be considered valid, but it cannot stand alone; just because a test gives consistent results does not mean that it is measuring what it is intended to measure.

Three types of validity are recognized by the Uniform Guidelines on Employee Selection: content, criterion, and construct.

Content Validity Selection instruments and procedures are considered to be content valid if they reflect the KSAOCs considered essential for job performance. If you want to see if, at the time of hire, an applicant possesses a skill or knowledge necessary to perform a job, then content validity is an appropriate validation strategy. The most common example cited is the typing test. How does an employer know if applicants can type eighty words per minute? By requiring applicants to demonstrate their skills by taking a test.

The procedures that need to be followed to develop a content-valid test are as follows. First, a job analysis must be conducted. The KSAOCs and responsibilities required for the position must be discovered. Once they have been identified, they need to be rated for their relevancy, frequency, and importance to the job. It must then be determined whether it is essential for candidates to possess those KSAOCs at the time of hiring or whether they can be learned once the person is on the job. Test items must be written or performance measures must be developed to capture the KSAOCs that are essential at the time of hiring. Then incumbents and supervisors who are familiar with the job (subject matter experts, or SMEs) must evaluate the test items or performance samples to determine whether the test accurately reflects the competencies required by the job. A majority of SMEs must agree that the items are representative of the types of skills, knowledge, and behaviors required for the job.

Content validity is used often in the public and nonprofit sectors. Personnel specialists and managers often possess the skills needed to develop content-valid exams. They can be trained in how to conduct in job analyses and how to work with SMEs to develop selection instruments. Large applicant or incumbent populations are not required, and content-validation studies do not necessarily require consultants or an extensive background in psychometrics. Content-valid exams possess face validity: candidates easily understand how the exam relates to the position. Studies have shown that exams with face validity lead to litigation less often than other types of tests.

Criterion Validity Criterion validity measures whether the test scores (called *predictors*) are related to performance on some measure (called a *criterion*), such as supervisory evaluations or success in a training program. Does the test predict subsequent job performance? The most common example is the correlation of test scores with supervisory ratings of job performance.

There are two types of criterion-related validity: *predictive* and *concurrent.* Both demonstrate a statistical relationship between the test scores and performance measures. What differs is the sample of test takers and the amount of time between taking the exam and obtaining job performance measures. The meaning of this will become clearer as the procedures are explained.

Predictive validity. The procedure for predictive validity studies is as follows. First, a job analysis is conducted to determine the relevant KSAOCs for the position. Based on the KSAOCs, an exam is developed, and candidates are tested for the job using the selection instrument. Next, candidates are selected using some other standard. For example, decisions may be based on letters of reference, the interview, or previous experience.

After the new employees have been working for the organization for six months to one year, job performance measures are obtained. These could be supervisory ratings or performance in a training program. After these measures have been collected, a statistical analysis is conducted to evaluate the relationship between the test and the job performance measure. If the test is to be considered useful for selection, the high scorers on the test should have higher performance ratings and the low scorers on the test should have lower performance ratings.

You are probably wondering why the test is not used to select employees. Why develop an instrument and then ignore it? The test was not originally used to select candidates because to determine whether the test could predict performance, both high and low test scores are needed. If only people who scored high on the test were selected, it would not be clear whether individuals with low scores on the test could be good employees. If individuals with low test scores turn out to be the best performers, then the test is not measuring what it was intended to measure in order to predict which applicants would be most successful on the job. If it is not yet known whether the test is valid, making selection decisions on its results would be premature.

Concurrent validity. Concurrent validity also statistically demonstrates a relationship between the predictor and criterion measure. However, the procedures are different than they are in a predictive validity study. Instead of applicants, incumbents take the examination. Because incumbents are already working for the agency, job performance data can be collected immediately. Then the predictor and criterion data can be correlated, and a relationship between the selection instrument and job performance can be determined.

There are some factors to consider when doing a concurrent validity study. Because job incumbents are being used, it must be recognized that over time, they may have become more proficient in performing the jobs, and hence they might perform better on the exam than applicants. Or they may perform worse: because they are already employed, they may not care about performing well, or they may even resent having to spend the time taking the test.

Concurrent validity studies are conducted more frequently than predictive validity studies because they take less time to administer and are less costly to develop. Also, research shows that their results tend to be comparable to predictive validity studies (Barrett, Phillips, & Alexander, 1981).

Criterion validity studies are used more frequently at the federal or state levels, where large samples can be obtained. At the local level, they are conducted for public safety positions (police and fire), for which hundreds or thousands of applicants are available. They may also be used for positions for which large numbers of people are hired and then sent for specific training, such as to the police or fire academy or to receive specialized training to become Internal Revenue Service agents. The employer is relying on the test to screen in applicants with the cognitive skills likely to be successful in training.

Construct Validity Construct validity is the most theoretical type of validity. Selection instruments are developed or used that measure hypothesized constructs or traits related to successful job performance. Constructs are intangible or abstract characteristics that vary in individuals—for example, intelligence, motivation, aggressiveness, anxiety, honesty, initiative, and creativity. To validate exams designed to measure constructs requires expertise in psychometrics. The existence of personality or character traits that are often abstract and intangible is difficult to establish through a job analysis. The burden is on the employer to prove empirically that the test is valid for the job for which it is being used. Organizations that are considering adopting a test to measure constructs should seek advice from a qualified person (not the test vendor).

Person-Organization Fit

Historically, most of the research on testing and selection has focused on the ability of cognitive ability tests to predict success on a particular job. Recent scholarship has recognized that performance in an organization is influenced by more than cognitive ability. People differ in terms of personality, interpersonal relations, vocational interests, values, orientations, motivations, and perceptions. Each of those individual difference variables affects behavior in organizations (Zedeck, 1996).

Murphy (1996), the editor of *Individual Differences and Behavior in Organizations*, noted that research in industrial/organizational psychology from the mid-1960s to the mid-1980s can be roughly categorized as research on the relationship between scores on written-ability tests and job performance and other research. What was overlooked in scholarship was the relationship between individual employees' behavior in the organization and how their behavior affected the organization's outcomes. Variables such as whether employees work to advance the goals of the organization, the organizational experience, the climate and culture of the organization, the quality of interpersonal relations within the organization, the amount of conflict within the organization, and whether employees identify with the organization are characteristics that are important to job performance.

Murphy (1996) further stated that current theories of job performance suggest that the performance domain is multifaceted and that it is likely to include dimensions that are not highly or even positively correlated. Individual difference domains that contribute to effective job performance include cognitive ability, personality, orientation (values and interests), and affective disposition (mood, affect, temperament). Given today's team-oriented environment, a variety of individual behaviors bear directly on accomplishing the goals of the organization. These include not only individual task performance but also nontask behaviors such as teamwork, customer service, organizational citizenship, and prosocial organizational behaviors. These behaviors may not be included in an individual's job description, yet they are crucial to the effective functioning of the organization. Individual differences in ability, personality orientation, and affective states might affect any or all of these variables. Next we will look at some examples of other variables that often affect performance and are becoming important in HRM selection research.

Practical Intelligence

More than two decades ago, Sternberg (1985) recognized the importance of practical intelligence, defining it as how people deal practically with different kinds of contexts: how they know and use what is needed to behave intelligently at school, at work, or on the streets. He suggested that practical intelligence and tacit knowledge play a role in job success. Practical intelligence is often described as the ability to respond effectively to practical problems or demands in situations that people commonly encounter in their jobs. One's practical intelligence is influenced by the context of the problem or situation (Albrecht, 2007). Practical intelligence is important for success in our society and yet rarely is taught explicitly or tested systematically. The efficacy of using tests that measure practical intelligence or common sense to predict job performance has started to be discussed in the personnel literature. McDaniel, Finnegan, Morgeson, Campion, and Braverman (1997, 2001) found that measures of common sense or practical intelligence are correlated with job performance and cognitive ability. Smith and McDaniel (1997) found that situational judgment measures also correlate with job performance and are influenced by experience, personality, and cognitive factors. Their study provided an observed validity coefficient of .31 across aggregated occupations in the service, engineering, and business sectors.

Adaptability

Adaptive job performance is characterized by the ability and willingness to cope with uncertain, new, and rapidly changing conditions on the job. Personnel must adjust to new equipment and procedures, function in changing environments, and continuously learn new skills. Technological change requires the organization of work-around projects rather than well-defined and stable jobs, which requires workers who are sufficiently flexible to be effective in poorly defined roles. Pulakos, Arad, Donovan, and Plamondon (2000) identified eight dimensions of adaptive performance: (1) handling emergencies or crisis situations, (2) handling work stress, (3) solving problems creatively, (4) dealing with uncertain and unpredictable work situations, (5) learning work tasks, technologies, and procedures, (6) demonstrating interpersonal adaptability, (7) demonstrating cultural adaptability, and (8) demonstrating physically oriented adaptability.

Multiple Intelligences

The theory of multiple intelligences maintains that there are many kinds of intelligences that are not measured through standardized paper-and-pencil tests. Howard Gardner has identified eight-and-one-half intelligences. The eight intelligences are logical-mathematical, linguistic, musical, spatial, bodily-kinesthetic, interpersonal, intrapersonal, and naturalist. Gardner considers spiritual-existential intelligence as half an intelligence because of its perplexing nature (Gardner, 1993, 1999; Gardner & Hatch, 1989).

Emotional Intelligence

Daniel Goleman (1995, 1998) defines *emotional intelligence* as being able to motivate oneself and persist in the face of frustration, control impulses and delay gratification, regulate one's moods, and keep distress from swamping the ability to think, empathize, and hope. He suggests that the focus on logical-mathematical intelligence has neglected an important set of skills and abilities, such as how an individual interacts with people and emotions.

Social Intelligence

Social intelligence is defined by Albrecht (2005) as the ability to get along well with others while winning their cooperation. It is a combination of sensitivity to the needs and interests of others, an attitude of generosity and consideration, and a set of practical skills for interacting successfully with people in any setting. Goleman (2006) suggests that social intelligence is made up of social awareness and social facility. Social awareness encompasses empathy, attunement, empathic accuracy, and social cognition. Social facility includes synchrony, self-presentation, influence, and concern.

Personality Measures

A meta-analysis investigating the relationship of the "big five" personality dimensions: extroversion, emotional stability, agreeableness, conscientiousness, and openness to experience found personality measures to be predictors for some occupations (Barrick & Mount, 1991; Barrick, Mount, & Judge, 2001).

Citizenship Performance and Organizational Citizenship Behavior

Employees may engage in activities that are not directly related to their main task functions but nonetheless are important for organizational effectiveness because they support the organizational, social, and psychological context important for task activities and processes (Borman & Motowidlo, 1993; Borman, Penner, Allen, & Motowidlo, 2001; Organ, 1988; Podsakoff, MacKenzie, Paine, & Bachrach, 2000; Smith, Organ, & Near, 1983; Organ, Podsakoff, & MacKenzie, 2006).

Executive and Managerial Recruitment and Selection

At the federal and state levels, executives are typically appointed to their positions by the chief elected officials or their designees and are referred to as *political executives*. They lack permanent status and retain their positions only for as long as the president or governor desires or until the next election. Often these executives have been referred to the respective executive branches by someone they know, such as a legislator, a professional associate, a campaign worker, a university classmate, or a corporate executive.

At the local level and in nonprofit agencies, the recruitment and selection of city managers or executive directors is usually conducted by search committees. Usually the personnel committees of the city council or board of directors are responsible for the search. They identify the qualifications needed and determine the recruitment strategies to use. Often citizens or clients and representative staff will be asked to participate in the effort.

Search committees who lack the time or expertise to recruit executives may choose to delegate much of the responsibility for directing the recruitment and screening efforts to professional recruitment firms or consultants. An advantage of using professional recruitment firms is that they can devote complete attention to the search process. Unlike council or board members, professional recruiters are not part-time volunteers committed to other jobs. Developing recruitment strategies, placing advertisements, screening résumés and applications, responding to correspondence, verifying references, and conducting preliminary interviews are time-consuming. Professional recruitment firms are knowledgeable about fair employment laws and practices and document the procedures used should allegations of discrimination arise. Their livelihoods and reputations depend on conducting professional and legal searches.

Another advantage in using a recruitment firm is that it can provide an objective viewpoint if internal candidates apply for the position. Board or council members may place loyalty, politics, or familiarity above proficiency. An additional reason to consider a professional firm is that sometimes organizations wish to remain anonymous in the early stages of the recruitment process. Screening applicants through a professional firm retains that anonymity (Ammons & Glass, 1989; Snelling & Kuhnle, 1986).

Even if a professional firm is hired to direct the recruitment and selection process, council and board members should not abrogate their oversight responsibility. They need to work with the firm to identify the professional and personal qualifications required to guide the organization and consistent with the organization's mission. They must determine the strategic challenges facing the organization, where it is, and where it is going (Albert, 2000; Axelrod, 2002; Gilmore, 1993; Stene, 1980). For example, a county health department in fiscal distress might look for an executive with strong financial management skills, or a nonprofit agency having to contend with declining donations due to a former director's scandalous behavior might need to recruit someone known to have integrity and who also possesses successful fundraising experience.

The recruitment and selection process for executive and managerial positions is more complex than for other positions because it is difficult to describe the components of effective job behavior. Taxonomies commonly used to describe executive effectiveness include good planning, organization, communication, leadership, and decision-making skills, as well as industry technical knowledge and management techniques. Competencies more specific to the public sector could include skill in fiscal management and budgeting, council communication, citizen relations, media relations, intergovernmental relations, program development, and the execution of policies and programs (International City/County Management Association, 2001; Wheeland, 1994).

Herman and Heimovics (1989) identified twelve other categories of competencies needed to deal with critical events in nonprofit organizations: developing new programs, recognizing program decline, collaborating, managing mergers, fundraising, lobbying, relating with government officials, responding to personnel actions, developing human resources, leading accreditation efforts, reorganizing, and interacting with the board. Proficiency in one competency does not necessarily mean proficiency in the others. An individual may have excellent communication skills but lack technical knowledge. Someone may have wonderful fiscal management skills but lack the skills necessary for effective council or board relations. The likelihood of a successful recruitment and the selection of a chief executive is increased when the board of directors and incumbent executive work together to create the conditions for a successful leadership transition (Axelrod, 2002).

Because of the vast array of skills needed for executive positions, organizations should use a combination of selection methods. Some of the screening techniques commonly used for executive and managerial selection are in-baskets, leaderless group discussion, assessment centers, performance tests, and structured oral exams. As part of the screening process, prospective city managers and nonprofit executives often meet various stakeholders in addition to board or council members. For city managers, residents, the leadership of community organizations, and employees are asked to meet the candidates. For nonprofits, often funders, clients, and elected officials and public employees in that area who work closely with the nonprofit may be asked to meet the prospective candidates.

For executive selection to be successful, organizations must invest the time and effort to recognize the interrelationships among individual behaviors, managerial effectiveness, and organizational success, and they must plan the search process accordingly (Cascio, 1991).

Conclusion

Organizations periodically need to attract applicants for their existing or future staffing needs. Recruitment is the process of locating qualified candidates. Recruitment strategies should be planned in advance of the agency's needs. Strategic job analyses and audits of positions and employee skills should be updated on a regular basis to determine whether incumbent employees are qualified for promotions or newly created positions. For some positions, depending on the qualifications and experience needed, agencies may prefer to seek applicants from the external labor market.

After applicants submit résumés or employment applications, the organization must use job-related criteria to screen the applicants' qualifications for the positions. Those who do not meet the initial criteria are eliminated from consideration. A variety of selection techniques is available for organizations to use to help assess applicants' skill levels or potential for success. Cognitive ability tests, personality or interest inventories, performance tests, ratings of experience and training, assessment centers, and structured interviews are some of the techniques for evaluating applicants. Organizations must be vigilant that their recruitment and selection procedures do not violate federal, state, or local equal employment opportunity laws.

The recruitment and selection process should not end with the hiring and promotion of employees. Agencies should record their recruitment and selection procedures so they can be evaluated. The evaluation should identify the successes and failures at each step in the recruitment process so that modifications can be made if necessary. Future recruitment and selection strategies should be based on the procedures that attracted the most qualified applicants and the screening techniques that best predicted successful on-the-job performance. Although recruitment and selections are critical, a number of agency factors affect performance. Training and development programs, compensation systems, work design strategies and work schedules, supervisory methods, and performance management systems are also important and must be integrated with one another. Only looking at factors without reviewing them is not likely to bring about desired performance. Organizations need a strategic approach to HRM.

Exercise 7.1: Recruiting Medical Personnel in Southwest Florida

Recruiting and retaining critical care workers in southwest Florida is challenging. The expensive housing market, combined with medical school debt for doctors and college debt for nurses, physical therapists, occupational therapists, and medical technicians, has required hospitals to become creative in their recruitment techniques. Boosting hourly wages, offering signing bonuses, and providing relocation allowances are just some of the techniques used. The NCH Healthcare System offers housing assistance programs. It also owns two hundred apartments for seasonal registered nurses who can stay in them for three months at no cost.

Recruits in critical care positions are eligible for three hundred dollars a month to help with rent up to three years when they commit to staying with the hospital system. The NCH board of trustees approved a budget of three hundred thousand dollars for rental assistance.

Another incentive is a first-time home buyers' assistance of one thousand dollars for current or new recruits in noncritical fields who buy in Lee or Collier county. The loan is forgiven after two years of employment. For critical care workers, the loan is three thousand dollars for a first-time purchase and is forgiven after three years of employment.

More recently, NCH began offering an interest-free loan of $20,000 for seven years to critical care workers toward a first-time purchase. At the end of seven years, the money must be paid back. Current employees are eligible.

Lee Memorial Hospital recruits in the northern markets where the costs of living are similar to southwest Florida. It also recruits nurses and medical technicians from other countries. Another hospital, Physicians Regional, began an in-house training program that enables employees to receive higher wages. Nurses can complete a six-month program and become operating room nurses or emergency room nurses. The hospital offers tuition reimbursement of twenty-five hundred dollars per year at an accredited school for each full-time employee who wants to obtain more education and receive higher wages.

Questions

1. Which of the recruitment strategies noted above would be most attractive to you as a prospective employee? Identify any risks associated with these strategies.
2. What other organizational factors would you want to consider before implementing the recruitment strategies in the exercise?

Source: Adapted from Freeman (2006).

Exercise 7.2: Boomerang Database Used to Recruit Retirees Back to the Labor Force

Boomerang is a new database that allows retirees to list their expertise and interests, while letting California state agencies know they are available. "With the baby boomers retiring in large numbers, we are going to have a big gap between who is leaving and who we can bring in," said Andrew Armani, state director of e-services. "So Boomerang will be a piece of what we are trying to do to remedy that problem."

Organizers of the program plan to promote the effort among the state's four to five hundred thousand retirees. They are working with the state controller's office to publicize the program on pay stubs. A Boomerang newsletter will go out to retirees, and planners are coordinating with CalPERS, the state's public employee retirement system.

Boomerang is easy to use. Most registrant information can be filled in with a mouse click or a pull-down menu: last agency worked for, skills, and experience. Retirees are asked to review a list and check the box for what they want to do. No confidential information is collected. No Social Security numbers or driver's license numbers are needed.

Registrants can also specify their preferred work schedule.

Questions

1. How would you integrate the recruitment of retirees back into service with an agency or department SHRM strategy?
2. What are some additional strategies that public and nonprofit organizations can implement to recruit retirees to work for their organizations?

Source: Adapted from Stone (2008).

Chapter Questions

1. What are some of the risks associated with not staffing an organization correctly?
2. Discuss the strategic recruiting considerations your organization or an organization you may have worked for in the past should address, and why.

Online Activities

1. Does your organization use Internet recruiting? If so, what are the advantages and disadvantages? If your organization does not use Internet recruiting, go online and find an organization that uses Web-based recruitment. What is your opinion of the Web site?
2. Devise a recruitment and selection system for the following positions, and identify the considerations that need to be taken into account:

   - Executive director of a human services nonprofit
   - Budget analyst for a local government
   - City manager
   - Police officer
   - Social worker for a public or nonprofit organization

3. Visit the Web sites of the *Chronicle of Philanthropy*, idealist.org, Action Without Borders, and the Job Corner Alert, Foundation Center. Are there any patterns in regard to the types of positions that are advertised? Compare the advertisements on the Web sites. Are there differences in the information presented?

CHAPTER EIGHT

PERFORMANCE MANAGEMENT

After you have read this chapter, you should be able to:

- Understand the importance of performance management systems to strategic human resources management
- Understand the relationship of motivation to performance management
- Identify the major uses of performance evaluations
- Describe the different types of evaluation instruments and the benefits of each
- Identify the major sources of rater errors when conducting evaluations
- Be able to discuss the legal issues associated with performance evaluations

The increasing demands for accountability made by the stakeholders of public and nonprofit organizations have focused greater attention on performance management. As a result, agencies have begun to reevaluate their performance management systems. Because employees are essential to the delivery of quality services, performance evaluation is a critical component of strategic human resources management (SHRM) in public and nonprofit agencies. The information gleaned from an effective evaluation system can be used to assist agencies in accomplishing their missions. The performance evaluation process also provides feedback to the agency about whether the other human resources management (HRM) functions are working in concert to execute the agency's mission.

Employees are motivated by many factors. An employee's performance is often determined by the level and interaction of ability and motivation, that is, the desire within a person to act in a particular way. Employees are motivated by both intrinsic and extrinsic rewards. Intrinsic rewards are part of the job itself, such as having challenging job tasks, learning new skills, developing additional job knowledge, and assuming increased levels of responsibility. Extrinsic rewards are part of the job situation that is provided by others. They may include the salary and benefits or status that one receives from being employed. An individual may have a routine job that does not lead to the employee's motivation, but the employee may be motivated by the compensation and benefits that he or she receives through being employed.

Performance evaluations provide management with essential information for making strategic decisions about employee advancement, retention, or separation. Evaluation links training and development with career planning and the agency's long-term human resources needs. Used to support job analysis and recruitment efforts, performance evaluations are an important component of evaluating the knowledge, skills, abilities, and other characteristics (KSAOCs) available among the agency's internal supply of labor. Evaluations can be used to assess career advancement opportunities, for succession planning, and to develop compensation and reward systems, as well as to identify deficiencies in incumbent KSAOCs.

Accurate evaluations provide information and feedback to employees. Employees must be informed about the goals and objectives of the agency and the role they play in the agency's success. They must know what standards will be used to judge their effectiveness. Supervisors must communicate to employees their strengths as well as their deficiencies, thus providing the opportunity for employees to correct their weaknesses before serious problems emerge. Through the evaluation process, training and development needs can be identified and addressed.

Performance evaluation systems are indispensable for planning and research. A review of incumbent competencies and KSAOCs may indicate that they lack critical skills that the agency needs, thus necessitating that external recruitment efforts be undertaken or, if time permits, that incumbents be trained and developed. Performance evaluations are also used to validate selection instruments or techniques. There should be a positive relationship between the methods and criteria used to screen employees and successful performance. If there is not, the recruitment and selection system should be reevaluated and changed.

When used in the context of SHRM, performance evaluation should provide feedback to employees, facilitate personnel decisions, and provide information essential for planning and research. Feedback about the effectiveness of other HRM functions can also be obtained through the evaluation process.

Reflecting widespread disappointment in the efficacy of performance evaluation systems, performance appraisal is one of the most researched and written-about topics in the academic and professional HRM literature. Employee (ratee) dissatisfaction with performance evaluation systems has been based on a number of factors. For example, objective performance measures have been lacking; employees have believed that supervisors are often biased in their ratings, and because of this perceived bias, unions have tended to distrust management and prefer that promotions and pay increases be based on seniority; and employees have recognized that many of their performance outcomes are dependent on the efforts of other individuals or groups, which typically are ignored in traditional performance evaluation systems.

Rater dissatisfaction with evaluation systems is also common. Supervisors complain that agencies often promote the use of evaluation systems without devoting the necessary time, supervision, and fiscal resources to make the system work. Raters are expected to evaluate employees and provide feedback without first receiving training, which leaves them ill prepared to coach and counsel their subordinates. Raters also are not held accountable for the accuracy and quality of their ratings, which signals to them that their efforts are better spent elsewhere because upper management is not committed to the process.

Another reason that performance evaluation systems have been heavily researched is that they play an important role in court cases involving promotions, discharges, layoffs, and merit-pay increases. Employees who find themselves the victims of adverse personnel decisions, such as terminations or layoffs, seek redress through human rights agencies and the courts. Employers

> Employers are likely to defuse potential lawsuits or investigations if they can show that performance appraisals are job related and reflect fair and accurate evaluations of performance.

are likely to defuse potential lawsuits or investigations if they can show that performance appraisals are job related and reflect fair and accurate evaluations of performance.

This chapter discusses some of the common theories on employee motivation: how to develop an appraisal program, train raters, prepare documentation and review evaluations, as well as ethical issues in performance appraisal. It also provides examples of performance appraisal techniques and instruments and concludes with a discussion of alternative evaluation practices.

Motivation

Motivation is the desire within a person causing that person to act. According to Rainey (2003), *work motivation* refers to a person's desire to work hard and work well—that is, to the arousal, direction, and persistence of effort in work settings. He notes that the definition is far too simple, however, and leaves unanswered many questions about what it means to work hard and well, what determines a person's desire to do so, and how such behavior can be measured. He states that motivation is an umbrella concept that serves as an overreaching theme for research on a variety of related topics, including organizational identification and commitment, leadership practices, job involvement, and characteristics of work goals. He further notes the variety of words used to describe motivation, which often overlap: *needs, values, motives, incentives, objectives,* and *goals*, for example. Rainey (2003) defines them as the following: A *need* is a resource or condition required for the well-being of an individual. A *motive* is a force within an individual that causes him or her to seek to obtain or avoid some external object or condition. An *incentive* is an external object or condition that evokes behaviors aimed at attaining or avoiding it. A *goal* is a future state that one strives to achieve, and an *objective* is a more specific short-term goal, a step toward a more general, longer-term goal.

Content Theories of Motivation

Content theories of motivation refer to the needs, motives, and rewards that people are attempting to satisfy. They are often referred to as *need* theories of motivation. These theories use personal characteristics or attributes of the individual to explain motivation. Needs are latent internal characteristics activated by a stimulus or objects that a person experiences. The person tries to behave in a way that satisfies an activated need.

Hierarchy of Needs Abraham Maslow's hierarchy of needs (1954) is one theory suggesting that needs can be reduced to five groups of basic human needs whose satisfaction is sought by adults. The lowest-level needs are *physiological needs*: food, water, sleep, and sex. *Safety needs*, which come next, are the desires of a person to be protected from physical or economic harm. *Belongingness and love needs* include the desire to give and receive affection and to be in the company of others. *Esteem needs* address a person's self-confidence and sense of self-worth. The highest-level need is *self-actualization*, which describes the desire for self-fulfillment. As each of these needs becomes satisfied, the next need becomes dominant. Physiological and safety needs are referred to as lower-order needs, and social, esteem, and self-actualization needs are categorized as higher-order needs. According to this theory, people must satisfy needs at the bottom of the hierarchy before high-level needs emerge as important.

ERG Theory Clayton P. Alderfer (1972) proposed a modification of Maslow's hierarchy of needs theory. Alderfer reduces the five need levels to three more general levels: existence needs, relatedness needs, and growth needs (ERG). *Existence needs* are those required to sustain human existence, including physiological and safety needs. *Relatedness needs* are those concerning how people relate to their surrounding social environment, including the need for meaningful social and interpersonal relationships. *Growth needs* relate to the development of human potential, including the needs for self-esteem and self-actualization. This is the highest need category.

Alderfer's model is similar to Maslow's in that in both models, individuals move up the hierarchy one step at a time as a need is met. An unmet need is a motivator. If both lower-order and higher-order needs are unsatisfied, the lower-order needs will be the most important motivators of behavior. Where the theories are different is, according to Maslow, individuals progress up the hierarchy as a result of the satisfaction of lower-order needs. In contrast, ERG suggests that in addition to this satisfaction progression process, there is also a frustration regression process. When an individual is continually frustrated in his or her attempt to satisfy growth needs, relatedness needs will reemerge as a primary motivating force and the individual is likely to redirect his or her efforts toward lower-level needs.

Theory of Needs According to David McClelland (1961), individuals have three primary needs: for achievement, power, and affiliation. A strong need for *achievement* is characterized by a strong desire to assume personal responsibility for finding solutions to problems; a tendency to set moderately difficult achievement goals and take calculated risks; a strong desire for concrete feedback on task performance; and a preoccupation with task and task accomplishment. A low need for achievement is typically characterized by a preference for low risk levels and shared responsibility on tasks. When an employee or manager with high achievement is placed on a difficult job, the challenging nature of the task serves to cue the achievement motive, which activates achievement-oriented behavior. However, if high-need achievers are placed on routine or unchallenging jobs, the achievement motive will probably not be activated. Hence, there would be little reason to expect them to perform in a superior fashion under such conditions. This concept is important for understanding how people respond to the work environment because of the implications for job design. High achievers prefer autonomy and willingly assume responsibilities, while low achievers may withdraw from challenging situations.

A strong need for *affiliation* is characterized by a desire for human companionship and reassurance. People with a high need for affiliation typically possess a strong desire for approval and reassurance from others, a tendency to conform to the wishes and norms of others when pressured by people whose friendship they value, and a sincere interest in the feelings of others.

A strong need for *power* is characterized by a desire to influence others and control one's environment. Employees with a power need try to control or lead those around them. They tend to influence others directly by making suggestions, giving their opinions, and using persuasion. They seek positions of leadership in group activities, and they are usually verbally fluent, often talkative, and sometimes argumentative. Employees with strong needs for power tend to be superior performers and tend to be in supervisory positions. They are often rated by others as having good leadership abilities.

Motivator-Hygiene Theory Frederick Herzberg (1964, 1968) concluded that people have two different categories of needs that are essentially independent of each other and affect behavior in different ways. He found that when people were dissatisfied with jobs, they were concerned about the environment in which they were working. When they felt good about their jobs, this had to do with the work itself.

The first category of needs he referred to as *environment, hygiene, or maintenance* factors: *hygiene* because they describe people's environment and serve the primary functions of preventing job dissatisfaction and *maintenance* because they are never completely satisfied and therefore have to be maintained. Agency policies, supervision, working conditions, interpersonal relations, money, status, and security are referred to as hygiene factors because they are not an intrinsic part of the job but are related to the conditions under which a job is performed. These factors do not contribute to productivity; they only prevent losses in worker performance due to work restriction, which is why they are called maintenance factors. When these factors are adequate, people will not be dissatisfied, but neither will they be satisfied. According to this theory, to motivate people on their jobs, factors associated with the work itself or to outcomes directly related from it, such as promotional opportunities, opportunities for personal growth, recognition, responsibility, and achievement, should be emphasized.

The second category of needs is referred to as *motivators*. Motivators seem to be effective in motivating people to superior performance. These factors involve feelings of achievement, professional growth, and recognition that people can experience in a job. They are called motivators because they appear to have a positive effect on job satisfaction.

Process Theories of Motivation

Process theories of motivation concentrate more on the cognitive and behavioral processes behind motivation. They suggest that a variety of factors may serve as motivators, depending on the needs of the individual, the situation, and the rewards for the work done.

Expectancy Theory

An early model of expectancy theory was developed by Victor H. Vroom (1964). *Expectancy theory* holds that the force to act in a certain way results from a conscious decision-making process undertaken by an individual. The decision to act rests on three sets of perceptions: *expectancy*, *instrumentality*, and *valence*. *Expectancy* is the individual's perception that a certain level of effort is required to achieve a certain level of performance. *Instrumentality* is the strength of the belief that a certain level of performance will be associated with various outcomes such as promotion, pay increase, and the opportunity to telecommute. *Valence* is the attractiveness of the outcomes. In the decision to act, these perceptions are assumed to be combined.

The theory focuses on the following relationships:

- *Effort to performance relationship*. The probability perceived by the individual that exerting a given amount of effort will lead to the desired performance
- *Performance-reward relationship*. The degree to which the individual believes performing at a particular level will lead to the attainment of a desired outcome
- *Rewards-personal goals relationship*. The degree to which rewards satisfy the individual's personal goals or needs and the attractiveness of those rewards for the individual

Equity Theory *Equity theory* is often referred to as social comparison theory (Adams, 1965). Employers and employees enter into an exchange relationship: the employer provides outcomes such as pay, praise, promotions, and benefits, and the employee provides inputs, which is his or her performance.

An employee who perceives that the ratios of outcomes to inputs are about equal is likely to be satisfied with the exchange relationship. The balance of outcomes to inputs is the goal that employees are motivated to achieve. Employees compare themselves to other employees both within and outside the organization. If the employee perceives that the ratio of his or her inputs is less than the ratio of outcomes to inputs for others, the employee may feel underrewarded. Rarely do employees feel overrewarded. Positive outcomes are pay, fringe benefits, a pleasant working environment, friendly coworkers, and intrinsic outcomes of the job itself. Negative outcomes include unpleasant or hazardous working conditions, a monotonous job, and controlling supervision. The perception of inequity creates an internal state of tension that the individual is motivated to reduce, which can be accomplished by changing the inputs. A person can reduce his inputs or efforts or, under conditions of positive outcomes, may increase those inputs.

Goal-Setting Theory Goals that are specific, challenging, reachable, and acceptable to employees lead to higher performance than goals that are unclear, unchallenging, and unattainable (Locke, 1968). High performance results from clear expectations. Employees who are told to do their best do not do as well as those who have specific task goals to reach. Goal-setting theory does not view goals as static. Instead, they are based on the past and some predictions about the future. As circumstances change, goals may need to change. An important element is the ability to change goals after they have been set because circumstances surrounding the goals may have changed.

Goals that are specific, challenging, reachable, and acceptable to employees lead to higher performance than goals that are unclear, unchallenging, and unattainable

Testing the Theories

An analysis of motivational theories has led researchers to conclude that many of these theories are difficult to test. In a public or nonprofit context, goals are not always clear, there are not necessarily reward-performance contingencies, rewards may be scarce, and motivational situations or contexts are often dictated by institutions and embedded in laws, rules, and external expectations (Perry, 2000).

Developing an Evaluation Program

There is little consistency in performance evaluation systems across federal, state, and local governments and nonprofit organizations. At the federal level, the system used to evaluate federal employees was developed to tie performance with pay. Yearly evaluations determine pay increases or bonuses, or both. The approach is different from what it is at the state and local levels, where formal performance evaluation systems often do not exist. In many state and local governments, collective bargaining agreements or civil service systems determine promotions and pay increases. In this environment, if evaluations exist, they are used strictly as communication vehicles.

The performance evaluation systems of nonprofit organizations also vary widely. In many nonprofits, formal appraisal systems do not exist. Health care facilities are known for evaluating direct service providers such as nurses, social workers, and medical assistants on the basis of their individual behaviors and performance, while executive directors and directors of development often receive bonuses or pay increases tied to the organization's financial performance.

The only commonality found in the performance evaluation systems of public and nonprofit organizations is that both the raters and ratees typically dislike having to participate in the evaluation process. Yet despite the reservations expressed about performance evaluation systems, most organizations do undertake some form of appraisal. Because performance evaluations are used for different and sometimes multiple purposes, employees and supervisors must understand why evaluations are being conducted.

The integrity of a performance appraisal system depends on the raters' and ratees' understanding its objective. The following statement is taken from a state agency evaluation instrument for civil service employees:

> The Employee Performance Evaluation is designed to encourage all civil staff members to grow professionally and to reach full potential in their work. Using actual job performance as a basis for discussion, this review provides supervisors and employees with an opportunity to identify developmental needs on a mutual basis. In addition, it supplies a means of defining goals and objectives and the most appropriate course of action to pursue in order to increase competency and accelerate career progression. Supervisors are urged, in the strongest possible terms, to discuss the completion of this form during, as well as, after the evaluation process. This review is a tool of that process, not just the result of it. In this agency, evaluation serves one purpose: employee training and development.

Rater Training

Training is essential for both ratees and raters if performance evaluation systems are to be used in the strategic human resources planning process. Ratees who receive training and understand the evaluation system tend to be more committed to its goals. They should understand why the evaluation is being conducted, how it will be used, and what their role is in the process. Through training, they become aware of the difficulty that raters face in evaluating performance. Training also informs ratees of the levels of performance expected of them.

For evaluations to be as accurate as possible, raters should receive training in the development of performance standards and objectives, goal setting, observation, and recall and documentation skills; they should also learn how to complete the evaluation instruments, how to give performance feedback, and how to avoid rating errors. Because performance appraisals rely on human judgment, which is subject to error, personal biases need to be removed from the rating process. Employees must be rated on the basis of job-related, nondiscriminatory criteria, and the appraisals must accurately reflect job performance. Exhibit 8.1 lists some of the most common rating errors.

Exhibit 8.1. Common Rating Errors

Halo effect: Rating an employee excellent in one quality, which in turn influences the rater to give that employee a similar rating or a higher-than-deserved rating on other qualities. A subset of the halo effect is the *logic error.* In this situation, a rater confuses one performance dimension with another and then incorrectly rates the dimension because of the misunderstanding. For example, an employee demonstrates a high degree of dependability (is never absent or late), and from this behavior, a comparable high degree of integrity is inferred (such as "would never use organization property for personal use").

Central tendency: Providing a rating of average or around the midpoint for all qualities. This is the most common error, and it is a serious one. Since many employees do perform somewhere around an average, it is an easily rationalized escape from making a valid appraisal.

Strict rating: Rating consistently lower than the normal or average; being consistently overly harsh in rating performance qualities.

Lenient rating: Rating consistently higher than the expected norm or average; being overly loose in rating performance qualities.

Latest behavior: Rating influenced by the most recent behavior; failing to recognize the most commonly demonstrated behaviors during the appraisal period.

Initial impression: Rating based on first impressions; failing to recognize most consistently demonstrated behaviors during the appraisal period.

Spillover effect: Allowing past performance appraisal ratings to unjustly influence current ratings. Past performance ratings, good or bad, result in a similar rating for the current period, although demonstrated behavior does not deserve the rating, good or bad.

Same as me: Giving the ratee a rating higher than deserved because the person has qualities or characteristics similar to those of the rater (or similar to those held in high esteem).

Different from me: Giving the ratee a rating lower than deserved because the person has qualities or characteristics dissimilar to the rater (or similar to those held in low esteem).

Because different organizations evaluate employees for different purposes and use different types of instruments, organizations must provide raters with training relevant to the organization's instruments and objectives. Raters must understand how to use the instruments with which they are provided. In agencies where evaluations are used for training and development purposes, supervisors also need to be trained in how to develop performance objectives and standards, motivate employees to achieve the agreed-on objectives, and counsel employees whose performance is unsatisfactory. In agencies where evaluations are used to substantiate personnel decisions such as promotions, terminations, or pay increases, supervisors must understand how the relationship between the evaluation process and the agency's policies and personnel regulations governs those decisions. They must be able to document that their decisions are based on job-related behaviors or performance. Supervisors may not use the evaluation process as a subterfuge for unjust discrimination.

Because of the sensitive nature of performance evaluations, agencies have a responsibility to train their raters. Training can improve raters' documentation and counseling skills, thereby not only reducing their discomfort but also enabling them to help employees clearly understand what the employees' strengths are and areas that need improvement. Training can teach raters how to describe job-related behaviors and develop performance standards, emphasize the importance of accuracy and consistency in the appraisal process, and provide constructive feedback. Training can be provided through a variety of methods: in workshops conducted in-house by the HRM department or off-site by trainers from universities or consulting firms or video packages tailored to the performance evaluation process.

Who Should Rate?

In most organizations, the employee's immediate supervisor evaluates the employee's performance. This is because the supervisor is responsible for the employee's performance, providing oversight, disseminating assignments, and developing the employee. A problem, however, is that supervisors often work in locations apart from their employees and therefore are not able to observe their subordinates' performance. Should supervisors rate employees on performance dimensions they cannot observe? To eliminate this dilemma, more and more organizations are implementing appraisals referred to as *360-degree evaluations*. Employees are rated not only by their supervisors but by coworkers, clients or citizens, professionals in other agencies with whom they work, and subordinates. The reason for this approach is that often coworkers and clients or citizens have a greater opportunity to observe an employee's performance and are in a better position to evaluate many performance dimensions. Clients or citizens, for example, are a more appropriate source for evaluating such dimensions as the employee's manner of performance, how the employee treated them, or whether the employee answered their questions adequately.

Performance dimensions such as leadership, training and developing employees, communicating agency policies, and delegating and assigning work are responsibilities commonly found in supervisory or management positions. Competence in these dimensions can best be assessed by subordinates who have frequent contact with the supervisor or manager and can observe different aspects of their performance. The South Carolina Department of Archives and History, for example, developed a subordinate appraisal process as a tool for improved communication and feedback between managers and staff. Employees were asked to rate their immediate supervisors on thirty-seven items that fell under five dimensions: communications, managerial support of employees, management skills, leadership, and support of quality improvement (Coggburn, 1998).

Bernardin (1986) notes, however, that some caveats do exist with subordinate evaluations. Like supervisors, subordinates often lack the training necessary to evaluate their managers; ratings may be based on political gains; subordinates may not tell the truth, fearing retaliation from their boss; employees pushed hard may be strict in their ratings; and subordinates may not have a chance to gain an awareness of the larger picture by observing the manager in diverse situations. Despite these difficulties, Bernardin still believes that subordinate appraisals result in useful feedback to managers, reinforce good management behavior, encourage greater attention to subordinate needs, and facilitate needed group changes.

Research conducted by McEvoy (1990) in five public sector organizations suggests that managers would accept the use of subordinate appraisals if the following conditions were met: subordinates were made aware of the requirements of the manager's job, subordinates were asked to rate only the people-oriented dimensions of their boss's performance, the accuracy and fairness of subordinate evaluations were monitored, morale issues were discussed in advance, and the ratings were used primarily for developmental purposes.

Aspects of performance such as providing timely and accurate information to other departments or agencies can often best be assessed by asking the individuals who interact with the employees to evaluate their performance. The absence of complaints does not mean that employees are satisfactorily performing their tasks, so supervisors should not rely on such unreliable indicators. Instead, information should come from the sources that are in the best position to evaluate an employee's performance on specific dimensions.

Many organizations require employees to evaluate their own performance independent of other evaluations. This is referred to as *self-appraisal.* Supervisors and employees complete appraisal instruments and then meet to compare their evaluations. Differences in their perceptions and expectations are clarified, and strategies for improving future performance or developing career goals are discussed. This process is helpful because employees often are aware of performance constraints or have received commendations for their performance that their supervisor does not know about.

Executive Evaluation

The evaluation of city managers and executive directors of nonprofits is typically performed by city councils, board directors, or subcommittees of the board. Again, there is little consistency in evaluation procedures. The International City/County Management Association (ICMA) recommends that as part of the employment contract, the council should attach a statement of performance goals and standards and evaluation procedures. The simplest approach is to specify an annual review and the evaluation of the manager's performance based on goals and standards agreed on by the manager and the council. The city of Troy, Michigan, develops goals that are generic in nature and reflect community values—for example, improved infrastructure in the city. From that goal, a specific objective is developed, such as widening Main Street, and the task is to allocate resources and manpower toward developing a project budget, including design, right-of-way acquisition, and construction (Szerlag, 2005). The city manager would then be evaluated on if and how well the objectives and tasks were met.

Another approach is to use evaluation forms that members of the council complete. Each council member rates the manager on performance dimensions, targeting this person's critical responsibilities, such as budget management, supervision, HRM, relationship with the mayor and council, relationship with employees, public relations, leadership, execution of policy, and community reputation. The evaluations are sent to the mayor, who compiles the data and determines an overall rating. Other recommendations include having the council and manager meet in executive session to evaluate the manager's performance or having the manager, council, and mayor set annual work objectives and goals and evaluate the manager's progress toward the goals. The ICMA recommends that councils provide yearly evaluations but leaves the details to be developed by the council and manager in each city.

City managers are often evaluated on the following competencies:

- Relationship with the council
- Fiscal management
- Planning
- Public relations
- Effective leadership of staff
- Communication
- Interpersonal skills
- Execution of duties

Like the ICMA, BoardSource recognizes that there is not one best technique to evaluate chief executives. Instead, each board must decide which procedures best serve the agency. Four general methods of assessment have been identified by Nason (1993):

◆ ◆ ◆

1. *Intermittent or continuous observation of the chief executive by board members, especially the chairperson.* This method is used mostly in small

organizations in which the board works closely with the chief executive. If problems arise, it is easy to identify the cause and provide remedies. Nason notes, however, that as organizations expand and board members become less involved in the agency's operations, this method may no longer be effective. Should this become the case, the board will have to reanalyze its oversight role and restructure its own performance.

2. *Periodic assessment of the chief executive by the board's chairperson or other board members.* This assessment should reflect the chief executive's performance over the previous year. The evaluation should consider the assessments of other board members, especially those of the chairs of standing committees. Nason believes that board members should not discuss the chief executive's performance with the staff. He claims that "to do so is to risk good morale within the organization and to distort proper lines of responsibility" (p. 5). That statement needs further consideration. Some aspects of the chief executive's performance, such as communicating agency policies, informing employees about changes, delegating tasks and responsibilities, and leadership characteristics, are best evaluated by subordinates. Should subordinate evaluations be used, it is important that employees receive training and be asked to evaluate only relevant dimensions. Information from proximate sources is important because council and board members spend most of their time away from the organization. For evaluating responsibilities such as council and board relations and communication, board members are the most appropriate source. But for other dimensions, such as fiscal management, they may need to rely on an audit prepared by an outside accounting firm or government regulators to verify that the chief executive's fiscal management performance was satisfactory.
3. *Annual board committee review designed to assess the state of the agency and the chief executive's performance.* This is a formal review of the chief executive's goals and accomplishments and is conducted by the executive committee, the personnel committee, or another committee. The standard procedure is for the chief executive to review the accomplishments of the previous year in relation to the goals set and propose goals for the next year. During the evaluation, the chief executive's strengths and weaknesses are identified and discussed, and the evaluation concludes with an agreement about the next year's goals.
4. *Full-dress public assessment of the chief executive, including formal hearings and survey data from an extensive variety of interested parties.* Only a few nonprofit organizations use this approach because it is time-consuming, often

requires an outside consultant to administer the process, and can be an emotionally charged procedure.

◆ ◆ ◆

Regardless of the type of assessment used, chief executives must have advance notice of the board's expectations and the criteria used for the evaluation. Self-assessments by chief executives are recommended because they permit them to review how they have met the responsibilities, expectations, and objectives of the position. Opportunities are provided for chief executives and boards to resolve any differences they might have in their perspectives about the requirements of the chief executive's position and the role of the board in its governance and management functions.

The strategic purpose of the chief executive's evaluation is to strengthen the agency by improving its management. The board's evaluation of the chief executive should assist in improving his or her performance by identifying the executive's strengths and the areas in which improvement is needed. Boards should also support and encourage their executives' participation in professional development activities (Nason, 1993; Pierson & Mintz, 1995).

Nonprofit executives are often evaluated on the following competencies:

- Accomplishment of management objectives
- Program management
- Fiscal management
- Effectiveness in fundraising
- Board relations
- Public image and external relations

Documentation

During the evaluation period, raters should document both positive and negative aspects of job performance. One way to do this is by maintaining employee performance logs. Raters note in the logs any critical behaviors (positive and negative) that employees exhibit. Information such as when an employee volunteered for difficult assignments or received letters of commendation are examples of positive aspects of performance. Noting that an employee failed to submit an assignment by its deadline or submitted inaccurate and incomplete reports are examples of unacceptable performance that should be recorded. By documenting performance throughout the evaluation cycle, raters are able to provide specific feedback and minimize their susceptibility to committing rating errors.

It is important that employees receive feedback throughout the evaluation cycle, not only when it is time to review the formal evaluation. Employees who receive feedback from their raters on a regular basis know how well they are performing their jobs and what improvements might be needed. Poor performers should be receiving feedback on what they can do to improve their performance, and excellent employees should receive positive recognition for performing well. For many employees, positive reinforcement is a powerful motivator that encourages them to sustain excellent performance.

Prior to completing the formal evaluation instrument, raters should retrieve the employee performance logs for inclusion in the evaluation. Raters should be required to justify each rating they give with explicit examples. This corroborates the job relatedness of the evaluation and diffuses allegations of unfairness, prejudice, favoritism, and so on. For employees who must improve their performance, supervisors should recommend some potential strategies for employee development. Raters should provide clear, descriptive, job-related, constructive, frequent, timely, and realistic feedback.

Evaluation Review

It is not enough for raters to complete performance appraisal instruments; they must also review the evaluation with their employees. Employees should play a critical role in the process. They should be given advance notice when the review is scheduled so that they too can prepare. Employees should be encouraged to bring to the review any documentation they feel is relevant, such as letters of commendation or records of accomplished objectives of which their raters may not be aware. Some raters ask their employees to complete a self-evaluation, including relevant documentation, prior to the scheduled review. This puts employees at ease, making them feel that they are part of the process, not just its victim. By asking employees to complete self-evaluations, raters can elicit input from employees about how they rated themselves and why, what accomplishments they are most proud of, and in what areas they believe performance improvement is needed.

In many public and nonprofit organizations supervisors lack the authority to determine the purpose of evaluation. As noted earlier, promotions may be based on competitive examinations and seniority, and pay-for-performance may not exist. In such cases, however, supervisors can use the evaluation process to develop their employees. The evaluation process should open up communication between supervisors and employees and be used to discuss with employees areas for development and the best ways to achieve their goals. A systematic approach to performance appraisal will help employers make sure that they and their employees have the same understanding of the expectations for satisfactory performance.

Ethical Issues in Performance Appraisal

Requiring documentation by raters is critical if employees and supervisors are to believe in the integrity of the process. Longenecker and Ludwig (1990) report that supervisors often inflate or deflate performance appraisals. More than 70 percent of supervisors surveyed admitted that they intentionally inflated or deflated subordinates' ratings for a variety of reasons, such as because they believed that accurate ratings would have a damaging effect on the subordinate's motivation and performance, wanted to avoid airing the department's dirty laundry, wanted to improve an employee's eligibility for merit raises, wanted to reward employees for displaying great effort even when results were relatively low, or needed to avoid confrontation with hard-to-manage employees. Reasons provided by supervisors as to why they often deflate employee ratings included wanting to scare better performance out of an employee, wanting to punish a difficult or rebellious employee, or wanting to encourage a problem employee to leave the organization.

The deliberate distortion of performance evaluations can be discouraged by the organization by not only requiring documentation to substantiate ratings but also by holding supervisors accountable for their ratings. Supervisors should be evaluated on the accuracy and comprehensiveness of the performance appraisals they complete. While inflating performance ratings may be benevolent or discourage conflicts in the short term, the long-term consequences may prove deleterious for the agency. Poorly performing employees may not improve. Or an unforeseen reduction in force might necessitate the layoff of staff. The courts require documentation for dismissals or layoffs to prove that they were based on performance, so inflated evaluations do not demonstrate cause or differentiate the levels of performance of different employees, thus discrediting the supervisor's and agency's credibility.

Another problem with disingenuous evaluations is that when they are used for SHRM, the data they provide are inaccurate. Any decisions made based on the evaluations could prove to be harmful to the future growth and success of the organization by not recognizing liabilities and identifying where the agency needs to acquire talent. Inaccurate evaluations also do not develop individuals (Longenecker & Ludwig, 1990).

Performance Appraisal Techniques

There are three general approaches to performance appraisals: absolute, comparative, and goal setting.

◆ ◆ ◆

- *Absolute* methods evaluate the employee without referring directly to other employees. Instead, employees are evaluated against their own standards. For example, John Doe is evaluated in March and then again in September, and his September evaluation is compared to his March evaluation. The strengths identified in March should have been maintained, and any deficiencies or problems identified in March should have been corrected by September. Absolute evaluations are used most frequently for developmental purposes.
- *Comparative* methods evaluate the employees in one unit relative to everyone else in the group. In March, all of the juvenile probation officers were evaluated on the same performance dimensions and then compared to one another. For example, probation officer A received the highest ratings in accuracy and timeliness of presentencing investigation reports, while probation officer C received the lowest rating for that dimension. Probation officer C, however, received the highest rating for number of clients supervised and number of collateral contacts, while probation officer B received the lowest rating on that dimension. Comparative evaluations are used to differentiate levels of performance across employees.
- *Goal setting* evaluates whether the ratee attained predetermined goals. For example, the supervisor and employee agree that the employee will prepare seven more grant applications in the next five months to

secure a greater percentage of external funding. After five months have passed, the supervisor will evaluate whether the employee met this preagreed-on goal.

◆ ◆ ◆

There are differences not only in the format of evaluation but also in the types of data collected and evaluated. Some evaluations rely on *direct indexes*, or objective data. These indexes can be quantified, such as the number of errors, the number of clients on a caseload, the number of grants that received funding, the number of arrests made, or the number of proposals written. Direct indexes are referred to as objective measures because they do not depend on someone's opinion to be verified. Another type of data commonly used are *subjective measures*, which depend on human judgment and should be based on a careful analysis of the behaviors viewed as necessary for effective job performance. Decision-making skills, the ability to solve problems, and oral communication skills are examples of subjective measures.

The types of data and the performance standards used should be based on a current job analysis. Performance standards should be developed based on the critical tasks and responsibilities of each position. The standards should be measurable through quantifiable or observable methods. Next, an overview is provided of some of the most common types of evaluation instruments used in the public and nonprofit sectors.

Trait Rating

Raters are provided with a list of personality characteristics, such as cooperation, creativity, attitude, and initiative. Raters then assign a number or adjective, such as "average," "above average," or "superior," to indicate the degree to which employees possess those traits. Trait ratings are difficult to defend in court if challenged. They tend to be subjective, and raters often disagree on their definitions and how they should be measured. Trait ratings also are often not related to job performance or relevant behaviors. Someone may have a poor attitude but still be technically proficient. The scales also do not define what is meant by "average" or "superior." Different raters may apply different standards in evaluating the same behaviors. An example of a trait-rating scale is presented in Exhibit 8.2.

Exhibit 8.2. Trait Rating Scale

Name/rank ______________________ Section ______________________

Unit ______________________

Outstanding = 1, Very good = 2, Average = 3, Improvement needed = 4, Unsatisfactory = 5

Judgment ______________	Cooperation ______________
Dependability ______________	Knowledge of work ______________
Work initiative ______________	Public contacts ______________
Quality of work ______________	Supervisory ability ______________
Appearance ______________	Overall evaluation ______________

Behaviorally Anchored Rating Scales

Raters evaluate employees based on a set of behavioral descriptions. The descriptions list various degrees of behavior with regard to a specific performance dimension and identify a range of behaviors from unacceptable performance to outstanding performance. Ratees do not have to actually exhibit the behaviors on the scale; rather, the behaviors serve as a guide to help the rater and ratee understand the level of performance required for an assigned rating. Unlike some of the other instruments, behaviorally anchored rating scales (BARS) rely on employee behaviors—what employees actually do and what is under their direct control.

A problem for many public and nonprofit service providers is that despite their best efforts, unacceptable outcomes often result. For example, a psychiatric client may have a psychotic relapse that requires hospitalization despite the social worker's best efforts to help the client remain in the community. BARS would evaluate the social worker on his behaviors, not on the number of patients needing hospitalization. An advantage to using BARS is that they reduce ambiguity because employees are provided with descriptions of desired levels of performance. They are also accepted by both raters and ratees because both employees and supervisors participate in their development. A disadvantage to BARS is that their development is time-consuming and complex because each dimension requires its own behavioral anchors.

An example of a behaviorally anchored rating scale is presented in Exhibit 8.3.

Essay

The rater writes a narrative essay describing the employee's performance. The weakness in this method is that the evaluation may depend on the writing skills of the supervisor or the amount of time the supervisor takes to complete the evaluation. Another problem is that raters and employees do not necessarily use common criteria.

Productivity Data or Work Standards

Raters evaluate employees on expected levels of output and the quality of output. If employees are to believe that the standards are fair, they should understand how the standards were set.

Management by Objectives

Raters and employees together determine goals or objectives and a plan of action for achieving them that the employee is to achieve during the upcoming evaluation cycle. At a scheduled time, the two participants reconvene and determine whether the goals have been met. The effectiveness of management by objectives (MBO) depends on the skills of supervisors and subordinates in defining appropriate goals and objectives. Often easy objectives are set. Sometimes there is an overemphasis on objectives at the expense of specifying how these objectives are to be obtained. For example, Internal Revenue Service collection agents need to retrieve revenue from delinquent taxpayers but not through illegal or intimidating tactics. Nonprofits must be successful in raising money but not through dishonest fundraising activities.

A typical MBO rating scale is presented in Exhibit 8.4.

Critical Incidents

Raters record actual incidents of successful or unsuccessful performance of work actions. The rater uses these observations to evaluate employee performance. An example of a critical incidents report is presented in Exhibit 8.5.

Exhibit 8.3. Behaviorally Anchored Rating Scale

Job: Lieutenant Investigator
Dimension: Assign and review cases to investigators

________ Superior	Reviews all cases sent to investigations from records section on a daily basis. Assigns cases to investigators on a daily basis, giving clear, verbal instructions about what is expected of them by the supervisor in reference to a particular case. Attaches case assignment log sheet with handwritten scheduled time once a week. Keeps a case management log of all cases assigned.
________ Very good	Reviews all cases sent to investigations. Assigns cases to investigators. Attaches a case assignment log sheet with written instructions. Reviews cases with investigators when necessary.
________ Good	Reviews all cases referred to investigations from the patrol division and records division. Assigns cases to investigators.
________ Needs improvement	Takes several days before reviewing cases. Rarely reviews investigators' work. Assignment of cases to investigators takes several days to a week.
________ Unsatisfactory:	Allows investigators to review all reports given to investigations by the records section and to pick their own assignments. No review of investigators' work.

____

____

____

Rater's signature:

____

Exhibit 8.4. Management by Objectives (MBO) Rating Scale

Position evaluated:	Lieutenant Investigator
Dimension:	Maintaining and updating standard operating procedures manual for the investigations section.
Objective:	Create a documented review procedure for investigations personnel to review Standard Operating Procedures (SOP) Manual.
Type of measure:	Timeliness
Present level:	Manual is reviewed with investigations personnel on a yearly basis, but with no formal documented procedure
Desired level:	Manual to be reviewed with investigations personnel once a year, on a scheduled date, with Captain present. A review form is signed and initialed by each individual investigator, the supervising Lieutenant, and the Captain. Review forms are kept on file with the SOP Manual.
Time frame:	One month

Method used to achieve objective:

1. Create SOP review form and submit it to the Captain for approval.
2. Check with Captain and establish a yearly review date in January.
3. Update manual to include file for review forms.
4. Immediately file completed review forms.

Employee signature:

____

Supervisor signature:

____

Date completed: ____________________ Date of review: ____________

Exhibit 8.5. Sample Critical Incidents Report

Positive	
Date	Employee volunteered for four extra assignments.
Date	Received phone call from professional X commending the assistance given by employee A.
Date	Employee submitted progress report B two weeks ahead of deadline. The report was complete and accurate. Employee exercised independent judgment.
Negative	
Date	Employee failed to submit accurate and complete verification reports. Auditors found deficiencies that warranted a payback.
Date	Employee refused to return phone calls to client, resulting in loss of client.
Date	Employee missed the deadline for the grant proposal submission. This resulted in the agency's not receiving X amount of funds. Program X had to be eliminated.

Personnel Data

Raters tabulate information such as the number of absences or the number of times employees report to work late. The data are used to regulate employees' conformance to organizational policies.

Each of the evaluation instruments has advantages and disadvantages and may be appropriate when used in the correct context. It is important that appraisal instruments are congruent with the objective for the evaluation and suitable for the positions being evaluated. For example, personnel data such as tardiness or absenteeism do not address task proficiency or job-related behaviors. BARS or critical incidents are more appropriate for capturing such behaviors. Personnel data tend to enforce rules and regulations.

Many agencies also make the mistake of believing that evaluation instruments should be uniform across the organization, regardless of the position being evaluated. That is not the case. The evaluation process is valuable only if it is relevant to the position. There must be a direct link between the requirements of the job and the instrument used to evaluate performance. The KSAOCs that some jobs require incumbents to possess will be different from the KSAOCs required in other jobs. For example, nonprofit executive directors or public agency managers need to be evaluated more comprehensively than individuals who perform limited and routine tasks. Performance dimensions such as decision making and oral communication might be relevant for management positions, but less so for trade positions. Because the responsibilities of different jobs within public and nonprofit agencies vary, different instruments or even different evaluation procedures might be needed. Agencies and departments need the flexibility to develop their own performance management and reward systems that improve the performance of both their employees and the agency and department. Policymakers, executives, managers, and employees need to understand that to accomplish this, systems must be updated, revised, and redesigned as job responsibilities and employee abilities change to reflect current organizational performance standards.

Team-Based Performance Techniques

As agencies move to team-based environments that focus on continuous improvement and measuring performance outcomes, traditional performance appraisal techniques are being reexamined, and in some cases there is a movement away from individual appraisals. Gainsharing and team-based pay-for-performance systems have been introduced in many organizations. In these models, team members share the savings from higher productivity or reduced errors and waste. While team goals and objectives are becoming more common, often team members work as individuals collaborating with one another to accomplish the team's goals. Often each team member has a fixed role that is completed independently but contributes to the team's objectives. Team members must be aware of their responsibilities and be challenged by their work. Team members decide which measurements set the standards for performance, and teamwork can benefit when team members are expected to conduct a self-assessment of their own achievement levels and understand the relationship between their performance and the team's success.

Individual goals should be set after the team has set its goals. That way, employee goals can be directly tied to what the team needs to accomplish. Team meetings should be scheduled to discuss the team's objectives and progress made toward them. The purpose of meeting is to identify and remove any barriers that may exist. This also ensures that individual actions do not interfere with team productivity. Task accomplishment is important to teams, but general competencies are important as well. Competencies such as effective communication, demonstrating initiative, volunteering to assist team members, responding to requests for information in a timely manner, and other behaviors and competencies necessary for team success are also critical.

For team-based performance systems to work, team objectives need to be clear. There need to be clear and specific performance objectives. Each team member needs to understand her or his responsibility in relationship to the other team members' responsibilities so confusion is eliminated. It is important to document what has been agreed on and follow up with progress meetings. If necessary, training and development should be provided so that individuals are contributing to the team's objectives.

Gainsharing

Gainsharing is a group incentive plan that distributes gains from improved performance to employees in a department or organization, based on an established sharing formula. Participative management and teamwork are used to develop performance techniques and standards that control costs or units of output. All members of the team, department, or agency benefit from the increased cost savings. Lawler (2000) refers to gainsharing as a management style, a technology for organizational development, and an incentive system. Gainsharing and increases in compensation are discussed in greater detail in Chapter Nine.

Goalsharing

Goalsharing plans, like gainsharing plans, pay bonuses when performance is above a standard. The difference is that goalsharing plans seek to leverage an organization's operational strategy by measuring performance on key strategic objectives. Goalsharing plans can reward things that do not have an immediate or direct-dollar payoff for an organization such as quality or customer satisfaction. A specific bonus amount is tied to achieving performance on the goals that were set. At the end of the year, a different set of measures and standards may be established as part of a new plan, or the old plan may continue. Goalsharing plans are typically used when the external environment is rapidly changing and the organization wants to target a particular kind of performance improvement for a limited time period (Lawler, 2000).

Another strategy that goes beyond financial indicators to evaluate performance and is related to goalsharing is the balanced scorecard (Kaplan & Norton, 1996). Although no one will dispute the importance of financial measures and the importance of operating in the black, financial measures are not always the best indicators of effectiveness in the public and nonprofit sectors. Public and nonprofit agencies often provide services that are not profitable and to citizens and clients who need special and often expensive assistance. The balanced scorecard approach to evaluating performance includes measures such as customer satisfaction, employee satisfaction and quality, in addition to relevant financial measures.

Gainsharing, goalsharing, a balanced scorecard approach, and other team-based quality improvement processes rely on many of the same principles as performance evaluation and are not antithetical to the performance evaluation process. If done correctly, quality improvement processes require the development of performance standards and measures to determine whether the standards have been achieved; they require feedback from multiple sources and the development of an action plan for reaching future goals. What is key to the success of any of these quality improvement and performance assessment systems is not the name of the process used but the HRM policies and rules that support and enhance quality improvement processes in the entire organization. Exhibit 8.6 identifies key questions that management should consider prior to developing a performance evaluation system.

To facilitate change, HRM departments must expand their awareness to ensure that all work focuses on the agency's mission and its stakeholders. Continuous improvement must be integrated into its culture. Mutual respect and teamwork among all levels of the organization are necessary. Quality improvement requires that supervisors give workers more autonomy and allow their participation in decision making. Employee training therefore must extend beyond job or technical skills. Since all workers will be expected to function in a group setting, quality improvement and performance evaluation programs must provide training in group dynamics, problem-solving techniques, and the use of quality improvement tools. Quality improvement processes and performance evaluation systems do not have to be at odds with each other. Evaluation systems can be developed that focus on developing individual job skills that support the group's efforts for quality and productivity improvements. The competitive nature of evaluation can be eliminated by comparing employees to standards instead of to one another.

Exhibit 8.6. Questions to Consider When Developing a Performance Evaluation System

1. How can your agency effectively involve employees and their representatives in redesigning performance management to promote the credibility and acceptance of the system? Have you identified your mutual interests?
2. Does your performance management system include effective performance planning, goal setting, and communications processes that link to your strategic objectives?
3. Should you be developing measures of customer service and group or team performance outcomes that can be used for planning performance and for distributing rewards based on improved performance?
4. Have you given enough attention to planning, measuring, and rewarding internal customer service for your various staff operations and administrative functions?
5. Have you developed collateral processes for establishing performance goals and monitoring performance, and established how these might be integrated into the formal appraisal and reward process?
6. Do you provide ongoing performance monitoring and feedback to employees about their individual and group performance?
7. Are the people who have the best knowledge of the quality and effectiveness of employee performance providing feedback, either for developmental purposes or as input to a performance appraisal? Should you explore using 360-degree assessment where it is appropriate?
8. Do the elements and standards of your employee performance plans capture the results and accomplishments you expect, or do they merely describe the same tasks and process inputs year after year?
9. Are the distinctions you make among levels of performance credible to internal and external stakeholders? How many distinctions can be made credibly, given your culture and the nature of your work?

Source: U.S. Office of Personnel Management (1994, p. 51).

Changing to a quality improvement culture may require the modification of many HRM policies that have become institutionalized throughout the years. Organizations need to analyze their selection, training, development, compensation, and evaluation systems to ensure that they reify the values necessary for quality improvement efforts.

Are Employee Motivations and Management Different in Public and Nonprofit Organizations Than in For-Profit Organizations?

Perry, Mesch, and Paarlberg (2006) conducted a comprehensive review of the literature on motivation. Based on an analysis of the research, they developed thirteen broad propositions:

Financial Incentives

- Financial incentives improve task performance moderately to significantly, but their effectiveness is dependent on organizational conditions.
- Individual financial incentives are ineffective in traditional public sector settings.
- Group incentive systems are consistently effective, but they are not well tested in public sector settings, where measures of organizational performance often are uncertain.

Job Design

- Job design is an effective strategy that enhances performance.
- Job design interventions influence affective outcomes more strongly than behavioral outcomes.
- Moderators and implementation are important influences on the efficacy of job design.

Participation

- Participation has a strong positive impact on employees' affective reactions to the organization.
- Participation has a positive but limited impact on employee performance.
- The promise of participation may lie in improved decision making.

Goal Setting

- Challenging and specific goals improve the performance of employees
- Setting learning goals, as opposed to merely difficult-to-attain goals, may be most effective when tasks are complex.

- The goal-performance relationship is strongest when employees are committed to their goals and receive incentives, input, and feedback related to the achievement of goals.
- Goal setting may face unique challenges in the public sector.

Public service motivation is an individual's predisposition to respond to motives grounded primarily or uniquely in public institutions and organizations (Perry & Wise, 1990, p. 368).

Perry and Wise (1990) organized public service motives into three broad categories: *affective*, *norm-based*, and *rational* motives. *Norm-based* motives are based on social values and norms of what is proper and appropriate and include a desire to serve the public interest, fulfill a sense of duty to the community, and express a unique sense of loyalty to the government. *Affective* motives are rooted in an individual's emotions. Affective motives include a deep belief in the importance of a particular program to society. *Rational* motives are when an individual chooses among a set of possible alternatives and is motivated after an assessment of the potential benefit of each option. Rational motives might include a desire to represent some special interest, or having a personal identification with a program or policy goal, as well as a desire for personal gain and personal need fulfillment (Wise, 2005).

Perry (1996, 1997) developed a multidimensional scale to measure public service motivation. A number of other scholars have conducted research to assess the utility of public service motivation, finding it to be a useful construct in understanding the behavior and attitudes of employees working in public and nonprofit organizations (Alonso & Lewis, 2001; Coursey, Perry, & Brudney, 2008; Brewer, Selden, & Facer, 2000; Bright, 2005, 2007; Crewson, 1997; Houston, 2005; Moynihan & Pandey, 2007; Mann, 2006; Naff & Crum, 1999; Perry, Brudney, Coursey, & Littlepage, 2008; Scott & Pandey, 2005).

Conclusion

Motivation and performance management are closely aligned. Performance management is the process that reviews and measures employee performance. Those who develop performance management systems must understand the factors that contribute to or hinder employee motivation. Performance evaluations should be objective, job-related, and consistent with the organization's mission. When correctly developed and executed, they should enhance the organization's effectiveness. The performance management process provides management with important information for making strategic decisions on employee promotions, training and development activities, compensation decisions, and retention or separation. Employees who are performing at high levels in their positions should be informed as to what career progression paths exist within their organization so that career development activities can be planned. And employees who fail to meet performance standards should be provided with training or, if necessary, be dismissed. In today's competitive environment, nonproductive employees cannot be tolerated.

Performance evaluations are used to support many HRM functions, but because the appraisal process and instruments cannot serve all purposes simultaneously, the organization must decide on the specific objectives it wishes to achieve and then develop the appropriate instruments and performance management system. Regardless of the type of instrument used or the purpose of the evaluation, all raters must be trained.

Many researchers have suggested that traditional performance evaluation systems that focus on individual performance be eliminated and replaced with team approaches. Other researchers believe that individual assessments complement team approaches because they foster individual accountability and identify individual developmental needs that benefit the work team (Masterson & Taylor, 1996).

Exercise 8.1: The HR Director Resigns Immediately

The human resources director of Hernando County, Florida, resigned after hours of negotiations with the new county administrator and following an independent investigation into racial harassment and discrimination in the utilities department. The investigation noted that current policy was followed, but that the policies were outdated.

In addition, a series of audit and follow-up reports since 2000 had told the HR director to tighten up processes and procedures to better protect the county and its employees. The recommendations were never implemented and were included in repeated audit recommendations. The HR department never developed standard operating procedures for the county; instead, each department had its own. The director had also been suspended without pay earlier in the year for storing candidate petition cards in her office, a violation of the county's policy about political activities. Since then, an investigation found that the HR director was soliciting petition cards using her county e-mail.

Questions

1. What performance management processes would you implement to prevent similar problems applicable to all department directors?
2. What additional issues should be addressed?

Sourcs: Behrendt (2008); Dupre's downfall was long time in the making (2008, April 26).

Exercise 8.2: Why Executive Directors Get Fired

According to Richard L. Meyers, director of the Nonprofit Sector Fund at the Eugene and Agnes E. Meyer Foundation in Washington, a communications breakdown is often the reason that an executive director gets terminated. "An important part of an executive director's job is that relationship with the board." One indicator of communications problems is a lack of honest feedback from board members regarding the executive director's performance.

According to a survey Meyers conducted in 2006, 25 percent of executive directors are not getting regular performance reviews from their boards, and even those who are receiving assessments say they are not helpful.

Questions

1. Assume you are an executive director of a nonprofit agency whose board of directors has been inconsistent in regard to evaluating your job performance. How would you encourage the board of directors to become more consistent?
2. Develop a performance evaluation instrument and evaluation procedures to share with the board of directors.

Source: Berkshire (2008).

Chapter Questions

1. Identify the major SHRM issues an agency, department, or supervisor faces in designing a performance management system. What recommendation would you make for addressing them?
2. Can employees in all occupations be evaluated by 360-degree feedback systems? What are some advantages and disadvantages of these systems?
3. In small groups, each member should select an occupation and design a performance management system for the position. Identify what sources would be appropriate for performance feedback and the best way to obtain the feedback.

Online Activities

1. Visit the U.S. Department of Personnel Web site. What performance management strategies are recommended that would be useful for you to develop for your agency or department? How would you adapt them to fit your needs?
2. Search the Internet, and identify three companies that have developed computerized employee performance evaluation systems. Compare and contrast their products. What are the strengths and weaknesses of the different products? What factors would you consider before purchasing a computerized system for your agency?

CHAPTER NINE

COMPENSATION

After you have read this chapter, you should be able to:

- Understand the importance of compensation to strategic human resources management
- Understand basic theories underlying pay systems
- Explain external, internal, and employee equity
- Understand the role that labor markets play in determining compensation
- Explain how to determine the relevant labor market for a specific job
- Discuss what compensable factors are and how they relate to job evaluation

The design, implementation, and maintenance of compensation systems are important parts of strategic human resources management (SHRM). Decisions about salaries, incentives, benefits, and quality-of-life issues are important in attracting, retaining, and motivating employees.

Strategic decisions about pay levels, pay structures, job evaluation, and incentive pay systems influence the ability of an organization to compete in the marketplace to attract the most qualified and competent applicants and retain its most talented and productive employees. Compensation is a topic that most employees are concerned with, yet most of us do not understand the underlying premises that drive compensation systems. What factors, for example, explain the differences in compensation between an administrative specialist working for the federal government in a general salary classification GS-6, step 3, who makes an annual salary of $31,228, whereas a fellow GS-6, step 8, makes $36,108. They perform the same tasks, but the step 3 administrative specialist is more proficient. Or why are the starting salaries for firefighters in adjacent municipalities different? Firefighters in municipality A start at $32,000 per year, while the starting salary for firefighters in municipality B is $36,071 per year. Or what explains the difference between the salaries of executive directors of Boys & Girls Clubs of America at different clubs? The advertised salary range for the executive director of the Boys & Girls Club of Central Maryland, located in Conejo, and that of Las Virgene, California, is $90,000 to $120,000, while the advertised salary range for the executive director of the Boys & Girls Club in Eugene, Oregon, is $42,000 to $52,000.

From an SHRM perspective, employers use compensation to attract, retain, and motivate employees to achieve organizational goals. Employees expect fair remuneration for the services they perform. However, what is often lacking is the understanding that compensation is affected by many factors: employees' expectations and perceptions of fairness, competitive labor market wages, the extent of other benefits provided to employees, the organization's ability to pay, and federal, state, and local laws.

This chapter introduces the concepts of equity, competitive labor markets, and comparable worth, as well as job evaluation methods, the design of pay structures, and federal laws that influence compensation. Indirect financial compensation, more commonly referred to as employee benefits, is discussed in Chapter Ten.

Equity

Individuals have expectations about what they will be paid. They expect fair compensation. The standards that they use to determine whether the compensation they receive is fair are based on perceptions of equity. According to equity theory, employees compare their job inputs and outcomes to the inputs and outputs of other employees performing similar tasks. If they perceive their ratio of inputs to outputs to be equal to those with whom they compare themselves, a state of equity is said to exist. If the ratios are unequal, inequity exists, and employees will believe that they are underrewarded. To develop compensation systems, employers rely on three types of equity: external, internal, and employee.

External Equity

External equity is the standard that compares an employer's wages with the rates prevailing in external markets for the employee's position. What do other organizations pay employees who perform similar tasks and have similar responsibilities? For example, what do other counties pay entry-level budget analysts? What do program directors at nonprofits that provide services to the victims of domestic violence get paid? The federal government and state governments want to know the salary range for chemists with a doctorate working in industry or universities.

External equity is determined by surveying the competitive labor market. Labor markets are identified and defined by some combination of the following factors: education and technical background requirements, licensing or certification requirements, experience required by the job, occupational membership, and geographical location, such as local, regional, or national labor markets (Wallace & Fay, 1988). The labor market reflects the forces of supply and demand for qualified labor within an area. These forces influence the wages required to recruit or retain qualified employees. If employees do not see their pay as equitable compared to what other organizations pay for similar work, they are likely to leave if they have an opportunity.

Local governments seeking to determine relevant employers for wage comparisons typically look at the size of the government's population, the size of its workforce, its urban/rural mix, and its equalized assessed value (EAV), which is the assessed value of real property multiplied by the state equalization factor. (The state equalization factor is a device to provide equity across the state in property tax by equalizing or balancing the property value between jurisdictions.) The EAV is divided by the population to understand per capita wealth. Each state has its own ratio. It is the base against which tax rates are calculated and translates into the government's ability to pay salaries. Using these criteria, small local governments would seek other small local governments with similar features as their reference points rather than large industrial cities.

Nonprofit agencies should also look for comparable organizations. That may be more difficult because nonprofit services and structures evolve in response to a variety of forces. Programs and services often have been developed by the professional staff and board of directors to be consistent with the agency's mission. Programs also evolve in response to local, state, and federal funding opportunities. Nonprofit staffing patterns and the ability to pay employees are subject to a greater variety of influences than the influences found in the public sector. When looking for comparable employers, agencies must seek organizations that provide similar services and are similarly situated in terms of size and structure (including number of employees), revenue sources (size of operating budget and types of grants and contributions received for nonprofit agencies), cash compensation (base and merit pay, increase schedules, and cost-of-living adjustments) and benefits (number of paid holidays, personal days, and sick days; nature and extent of health care coverage; and contributions made to retirement), and position titles and benchmark equivalents (scope of responsibilities, education requirements, years in position, and salaries paid to incumbents). For example, a small community-based social service nonprofit that provides services to those who are developmentally disabled should compare itself with other organizations of the same size and with similar characteristics that provide comparable services. An agency staffed by fifteen employees should not compare itself with a large metropolitan nonprofit hospital. Local governments can use these same characteristics (except for grants and contributions as sources of revenue) to determine comparable employers.

If conducting a survey itself or hiring consultants to do so is not feasible, various government agencies such as the state or federal Department of Labor or commercial firms such as the Bureau of Labor Statistics, the Bureau of National Affairs, and the Commerce Clearing House publish area wage surveys and industry wage surveys, as well as professional, administrative, technical, and clerical surveys. Professional associations and consulting firms also publish salary data. For example, the Child Welfare League of America publishes the salaries of youth service workers. *Nonprofit Times, Guidestar,* and *Chronicle of Philanthropy* also publish studies of management salaries in nonprofit organizations. A recent salary study (Hrywna, 2008, p. 21) found that the mean projected salaries for 2007/2008 (respectively) were as follows:

Executive director/CEO/ president	$116,902/ $119,553
Chief financial officer	$83,212/ $84,020
Program director	$65,925/ $68,066
Development director	$70,568/ $73,725

Major gifts officer	$71,968/ $76,559
Chief of direct marketing	$71,857/ $72,201
Director of volunteers	$43,208/ $42,493
Webmaster	$53,171/ $54,128
Director of human resources	$68,399/ $68,008

The nonprofits with the largest budgets paid executive directors the most.

Internal Equity

Internal equity is the standard that requires employers to set wages for jobs within their organizations that correspond to the relative internal value of each job. Positions that are determined to be more valuable to the organization receive higher wages. Typically high-level employees receive greater compensation than low-level employees.

The internal value of each position to the organization is determined by a procedure known as job evaluation, which determines the worth of one job relative to another. To institute internal equity into its compensation structure, Congress passed the Classification Act of 1923. Prior to the establishment of the system, federal employees were paid according to which agency they worked for, and wages were determined at the discretion of agency management. The lack of procedures and standardization permitted disparities among employees performing the same type of work. Different positions were often given the same title, and similar positions were often given different titles. Pay was not necessarily related to the work performed. The act created the Personnel Classification Board, which mandated that positions be grouped according to similar responsibilities and duties and be compensated accordingly. Employees would be paid according to the value of their work, which would be determined according to the job's compensable factors, such as level of education and amount of experience required, the amount of responsibility, and job hazards. Exhibit 9.1 lists some of the most common compensable factors.

A variety of factor comparison systems are used to determine job value. Compensable factors are identified, weighed, and assigned point values that reflect their weight. Jobs are broken down into their compensable factors and rated along a continuum of points or rank-ordered. After the compensable factors have been rated or ranked, they are summed to derive a total

Exhibit 9.1. Typical Compensable Factors

Each of the compensable factors is defined and a job specification question is noted.

Experience

Experience is the training and development acquired from previous work that is necessary to qualify for a position, plus the training and development on the job that is necessary for proficiency. The requirement for this factor is usually expressed in terms of the time necessary to acquire the experience.

Job specification question: How long should the incumbent have worked in this job or in a closely related job?

Education

Education refers to the basic ability, skill, and intellectual requirements the position demands, normally assumed to have been acquired by attending high school, business school, trade school, college, or graduate school. Referring to periods of formal schooling is convenient when comparing positions; however, the term "or its equivalent" should usually be part of the educational specifications when such reference is made.

Job specification question: What does the job require in terms of formal schooling, training, or knowledge of a specialized field?

Complexity of Duties

This factor is a measure of the variety and difficulty of the work performed and the degree of skill and judgment necessary in performing it. Complexity is found to some extent in all positions.

Job specification question: Does the job require the incumbent to show judgment and initiative and to make independent decisions?

Supervision Received

This refers to the degree to which the work is supervised, guided by practice or precedent, and the requirements of the position for problem solving and decision making.

Job specification question: How closely does the incumbent's supervisor check his or her work and outline specific methods or work procedures?

Supervision Exercised

This factor measures the responsibility for directing the work of others. Its value is determined by the nature and complexity of the work supervised, the degree of responsibility for attaining desired results, and the number of persons supervised.

Job specification question: How many people does the incumbent supervise directly or indirectly?

Mental Demands

This factor appraises the amount and continuity of mental demand required to perform the job. It is a value factor in positions requiring a degree of concentrated mental effort or constant attention to detail.

Job specification question: What degree of concentration is required by the job?

Physical Demands

This factor appraises the amount and continuity of physical effort required to perform the job. It is a value factor in jobs that require the employee to stand, lift, carry, bend, or walk for extended periods.

Job specification question: Are there special physical demands on this job?

Working Conditions

This factor has value in those positions where excessive heat, noise, use of chemicals, poor ventilation, and so forth are elements in the job environment.

Job specification question: Is there anything in the work environment that is unusually hazardous or uncomfortable? If so, what percentage of the time is the incumbent exposed to this?

point value for the job. Positions with higher point values are considered more valuable to the agency.

In 1949, Congress passed the Classification Act of 1949, which established the General Schedule (GS) system. The GS system defines the basic compensation system for nonmanagerial white-collar positions. There are fifteen grade levels, with ranges of pay within each grade. There are approximately 450 categories in the GS, sorted into specialized groups such as finance and accounting, social science, psychology and welfare, engineering and architecture, and physical science. Each grade contains examples of the kind of work performed in jobs that would be assigned to that grade. These examples are referred to as *benchmark positions*. Benchmark positions are jobs with characteristics similar enough to jobs performed in other organizations that can serve as market anchor points using a factor comparison system called the factor evaluation system. Jobs are described and placed in grades on the basis of their duties, responsibilities, and the qualifications required to perform them. Nine factors with different levels and different point values are used to evaluate jobs: knowledge required by the position, supervisory controls, guidelines, complexity, scope and effect, personal contacts, purpose of contacts, physical demands, and work environment. After all nine factors have been evaluated and levels have been established for the position, the points are summed across each factor until an aggregate total is derived. The total points are then compared to a chart, and the position is assigned to a grade.

A problem with this job evaluation system is that the duties and responsibilities of a specific job do not always neatly fit into one grade or job class. The GS has been criticized for its lack of flexibility in supporting individual agency missions, structures, and cultures and for its inability to respond to rapidly changing external conditions. As a result, some federal agencies have received permission to modify the GS by reducing the number of occupational categories and permitting agencies to establish broadbanding systems (Thompson, 2007). (Broadbanding is described later in this chapter.)

Employee Equity

Employee equity is the comparison of pay across employees performing the same or similar work. It focuses on the contributions of an individual worker within a job classification. At issue is what coworkers performing the same job are paid. Are differences in levels of proficiency or contribution reflected in compensation?

Most compensation structures include pay ranges. A pay range exists when one or more rates are paid to employees in the same job. The range permits organizations to pay different wages for differences in experience or differences in performance. A pay range reflects the minimum and maximum that the employer will pay for the position.

Table 9.1 presents the General Salary Pay Scale for federal employees. Each grade has ten pay-level increments. New college graduates usually begin at the base pay for the grade, but the Office of Personnel Management may authorize recruitment at rates above the minimum for jobs in which there are shortages, such as engineers, chemists, and architects.

Pay grades and pay ranges for a city-county library district are presented in Table 9.2. Each of the fourteen pay grades in this salary schedule has six pay-level increments. Employees move up to the next highest level on the anniversary of their employment. After six years, they have reached the top of the salary grade, or "maxed out." Employees at the top of the salary grade can expect to receive only cost-of-living increases in the future.

To design pay ranges, the employer needs to establish the current market rates for benchmark jobs. After the data have been compiled, organizations develop salary ranges to fit their structure. Each salary range should have a midpoint, a minimum, and a maximum. The distance separating a grade's minimum and maximum salaries is called the *grade's range*. The midpoint for each range is usually set to correspond to the external labor

TABLE 9.1. GENERAL SCHEDULE PAY SCALE: ANNUAL RATES BY GRADE AND STEP

Grade	1	2	3	4	5	6	7	8	9	10	Within-Grade Amounts
1	$17,046	$17,615	$18,182	$18,746	$19,313	$19,646	$20,206	$20,771	$20,793	$21,324	Varies
2	19,165	19,621	20,255	20,793	21,025	21,643	22,261	22,879	23,497	24,115	Varies
3	20,911	21,608	22,305	23,002	23,699	24,396	25,093	25,790	26,487	27,184	697
4	23,475	24,258	25,041	25,824	26,607	27,390	28,173	28,956	29,739	30,522	783
5	26,264	27,139	28,014	28,889	29,764	30,639	31,514	32,389	33,264	34,139	875
6	29,276	30,252	31,228	32,204	33,180	34,156	35,132	36,108	37,084	38,060	976
7	32,534	33,618	43,702	35,786	36,870	37,954	39,038	40,122	41,206	42,290	1,084
8	36,030	37,231	38,432	39,633	40,834	42,035	43,236	44,437	45,638	46,839	1,201
9	39,795	41,122	42,449	43,776	45,103	46,430	47,757	49,084	50,411	51,738	1,327
10	43,824	45,285	46,746	48,207	49,668	51,129	52,590	54,051	55,512	56,973	1,461
11	48,148	49,753	51,358	52,963	54,568	56,173	57,778	59,383	60,988	62,593	1,605
12	57,709	59,633	61,557	63,481	65,405	67,329	69,253	71,177	73,101	75,025	1,924
13	68,625	70,913	73,210	75,489	77,777	80,065	82,353	84,641	86,929	89,217	2,288
14	81,093	83,796	86,499	89,202	91,905	94,608	97,311	100,014	102,717	105,420	2,703
15	95,390	98,570	101,750	104,930	108,110	111,290	114,470	117,650	120,830	124,010	3,190

Source: U.S. Office of Personnel Management (2008).

TABLE 9.2. CITY-COUNTY LIBRARY DISTRICT SALARY AND WAGE SCHEDULE

A	$1,691.00	$1,762.00	$1,835.00	$1,912.00	$1,988.00	$2,067.00	Monthly
	20,292.00	21,144.00	22,020.00	22,9440.00	23,944.00	24,804.00	Yearly
	9.72	10.17	10.55	10.99	11.43	11.88	Hourly
B	1,912.00	1,988.00	2,067.00	2,151.00	2,236.00	2,325.00	Monthly
	22,944.00	23,856.00	24,804.00	25,812.00	26,832.00	27,900.00	Yearly
	10.99	11.88	11.88	12361	1285	13.36	Hourly
C	2,151.00	2236.00	2,325.00	2,418.00	2,515.00	2,615.00	Monthly
	25,812.00	26,832.00	27,900.00	29,016.00	30,180.00	31,380.00	Yearly
	12.36	12.85	13.36	13.90	14.45	15.03	Hourly
D	2,418.00	2,515.00	2,615.00	2,721.00	2,829.00	2,940.00	Monthly
	29,016.00	30,180.00	31,380.00	32,652.00	35,282.00	35,280.00	Yearly
	13.90	16.25	16.90	16.90	18.28	19.02	Hourly
E	2,721.00	2,829.00	2,940.00	3,058.00	3,181.00	3,309.00	Monthly
	32,652.00	33,948.00	35,280.00	36,696.00	38,172.00	39,708.00	Yearly
	15.64	16.26	16.90	17.57	18.28	19.02	Hourly
F	3,058.00	3,181.00	3,309.00	3,439.00	3,577.00	3,738.00	Monthly
	36,696.00	38,172.00	39,708.00	41,268.00	42,924.00	44,652.00	Yearly
	17.57	18.28	19.02	19.76	20.56	21.39	Hourly
G	3,439.00	3,577.00	3,721.00	3,872.00	4,026.00	4,187.00	Monthly
	41,268.00	42,924.00	44,652.00	46,464.00	48,312.00	50,244.00	Yearly
	19.76	20.56	21.39	2225	23.14	24.06	Hourly

H	3,872.00	4,026.00	4,187.00	4,354.00	4,527.00	4,707.00	Monthly
	46,464.00	48,312.00	50,244.00	52,248.00	54,324.00	56,484.00	Yearly
	22.25	23.14	24.06	25.02	26.02	27.05	Hourly
I	4,354.00	4,527.00	4,707.00	4,897.00	5,092.00	5,297.00	Monthly
	52,248.00	54,324.00	56,484.00	58,764.00	61,104.00	63,564.00	Yearly
	25.02	26.02	27.05	28.14	29 26	30.44	Hourly
J	4,897.00	5,092.00	5,297.00	5,507.00	5,728 00	5,958.00	Monthly
	58,764.00	61,104.00	63,564.00	66,084.00	68,736.00	71,496.00	Yearly
	28.14	29.26	30.44	31.65	32.92	34.24	Hourly

K	5,07.00	5,728.00	5,958.00	6,195.00	6,444.00	6,699.00	Monthly
	66,084.00	68,736.00	71,496.00	74,340.00	77,652.00	80,388.00	Yearly
	31.65	32.92	34.24	35.60	37.03	38.50	Hourly
L	6,195.00	6,444.00	6,699.00	6,969.00	7,247.00	7,539.00	Monthly
	74,340.00	77,328.00	80,388.00	83,628.00	86,964.00	90,468.00	Yearly
	35.60	37.03	38.50	40.05	41.65	43.33	Hourly

M	6,969.00	7,247.00	7,539.00	7,839.00	8,152.00	8,477.00	Monthly
	83,628.00	86,964.00	90,468.00	94,068.00	97,824.00	101,724.00	Yearly
	40.05	41.65	43.33	45.05	46.85	48.72.94	Hourly
N	7,839.00	8,152.00	8,477.00	8,817.00	9,170.00	9,537.00	Monthly
	94,068.00	97,824.00	101,724.00	105,804.00	110,040.00	114,444.00	Yearly
	45.05	46.85	48.72	50.67	52.70	54.81	Hourly

market. It specifies the pay objectives for employees performing at satisfactory levels. The minimums and maximums are usually based on a combination of the size of the range identified in survey data and judgments about how the ranges fit the organization. These judgments are based on a variety of factors, such as salaries paid by the organization's competition, the organization's culture, and standard salaries across an occupational classification. For example, production and maintenance positions typically have ranges of 20 to 25 percent, whereas professional, administrative, and managerial personnel might have ranges of 40 to 50 percent under certain circumstances. Wider ranges are designed to reflect greater discretion, responsibility, and variations in performance. Pay ranges are useful because they allow an organization to provide a competitive salary and recognize individual differences among employees. Table 9.3 illustrates current market rates and their minimums, maximums, and midpoints for selected benchmark positions in local government.

When establishing pay ranges, employers must look at the degree of overlap in adjacent pay ranges. Overlap is the amount of comparability of pay between pay grades. The amount of overlap between pay grades signifies the similarities in the responsibilities, duties, and KSAOCs of the jobs whose pay ranges overlap. Overlap between pay ranges permits more valuable senior employees in lower-paying jobs to be paid more than new employees in higher-level jobs who have not yet begun to make significant contributions to the organization (Henderson, 1989, 2000). In both Tables 9.1 and 9.2, GS-1 or Grade A employees at steps 5 and above receive higher compensation than GS-2 or Grade B employees at step 1.

When developing a salary structure, you may find that certain jobs in the organization have been underpaid or overpaid. Underpaid positions are referred to as *green-circled* and overpaid positions as *red-circled.* To bring these wages in line with market rates and internal equity standards, underpaid employees should be given pay increases that raise their rates to at least the minimum of the range for their pay grade. The salaries of overpaid employees may need to be frozen until other jobs are brought into line with them. Other options include cutting the wages to the maximum in the pay range for the pay grade, increasing the employees' responsibilities, or transferring or promoting them to positions in which they can be paid their current rate.

Compression Compression results when salaries for jobs filled from outside the organization are increasing faster than incumbent wages (that is, when new employees are paid salaries that are comparable to those of

TABLE 9.3. COMPARABLE MUNICIPAL MARKET STUDY FOR SELECT LOCAL GOVERNMENT POSITIONS

Administrative Classifications	City A	City B	City C	City D	City E	Lowest minimum	Highest minimum	Midpoint
Personal property auditor	$29,287	$44,377		$33,876.98		$29,287.98	$44,377	$33,876.98
Department secretary assessor's office	36,169	24,720	16,720			16,070	36,169	24,720
Finance director	78,780	55,210	59,770	66,797	71,948	55,210	78,780	66,797
Administrative assistant	62,603	39,060	41,060	31,597	53,673	31,597	39,060	
Treasurer	45,719	48,872	43,963	36,620	36,963	68,620	45,719	
City clerk	41,333	44,474	33,846	49,178	65,812	33,846	65,812	44,474
City librarian	53,503			42,930	58,188	42,930	58,188	55,503
Planning director of community development and planning	69,780	45,210	41,128	36,994	53,231	36,994	69,780	42,210
Planner	46,057	38,774	34,445	32,269	44,504	32,269	46,057	38,774
Code enforcement officer	43,313	37,409	38,671	36,290	40,383	36,290	43,313	38,671
Police officer	42,547	34,036	38,529	36,150	40,356	34,036	42,547	38,529
Firefighter	36,071	32,115	32,238	26,582	33,595	26,582	36,071	32,238
Mechanic	42,556	28,361	36,578	37,408	39,824	28,361	42,556	37,408
Utilities clerk	25,848			20,821	24,024	20,821	25,848	24,821

more experienced employees) or the salaries of jobs filled from within the organization. Compression occurs in most public and nonprofit organizations. For example, ten years ago, the starting salary for county probation officers might have been $26,500. Today, probation officers hired ten years ago might be making $40,000, while new probation officers might start at salaries around $36,500. The pay differential between an employee with ten years of experience and a new employee is compressed because of market wages.

Grade Creep Grade creep is a form of classification inflation. That is, supervisors and incumbents request that positions be reclassified to the next highest grade so that the incumbent receives higher compensation despite no change in job tasks or responsibilities. Grade creep typically results when incumbents are at the top of their pay level and no other mechanism exists to increase their pay.

Pay Differentials Employee equity addresses pay differentials within the same position. It recognizes that employees who possess the same job title and responsibilities often perform at different levels of productivity or proficiency, making different contributions to the agency's mission.

The problem with seniority-based differentials [in pay] is that longer tenure does not necessarily translate into more effective performance.

In the public sector, seniority is frequently used to differentiate pay. More senior employees receive higher wages regardless of their performance. For each year of service, employees' salaries are automatically increased to the next grade step to reward their years of service to the organization. This is why the administrative specialist in step 3 receives a lower salary than his coworker at step 8. The problem with seniority-based differentials is that longer tenure does not necessarily translate into more effective performance.

If seniority is the only system in place to differentiate pay, organizations may find it hard to attract and retain competent employees. Employees who believe that their pay is low after comparing their inputs and level of pay to other employees in similar positions will become less motivated over time. Dissatisfied employees are prone to file more grievances, to be absent more frequently, and to search for higher-paying positions elsewhere. Employers must have in place different strategies to address employee equity concerns.

The following sections provide brief descriptions of alternative pay systems that are used to enhance traditional pay systems.

Longevity Pay Longevity pay rewards employees who have reached pay grade maximums and are not likely to move into higher grades. Its purpose is to reduce turnover as well as reward employees for continuous years of service. It may be a percentage of the employee's base pay, a flat dollar amount, or a special step increase based on the number of years the employee has spent with the organization.

Broadbanding or Paybanding There has been a movement away from using a system of many pay grades. Instead, salary grades are being collapsed into broader bands with wider ranges. The use of broadbands or paybands eliminates having to maintain many narrow salary grades. Broadbanding was introduced by the federal government out of frustration with the inflexible federal classification and pay system and to increase flexibility, managerial control, and accountability (Risher & Schay, 1994). Two naval research and development laboratories found it difficult to recruit and retain scientists and engineers, so the laboratories designed a new classification and compensation system that would give their managers the flexibility needed to compete with the private sector. Today, twenty-two federal agencies have implemented paybanding (Thompson, 2007).

Broadbanding grants managers the discretion to offer a variety of starting salaries and reward employees with pay increases or different job assignments as needed to fulfill the agency's mission. Advocates of broadbanding claim that it simplifies pay administration, helps to facilitate career development, creates a performance-driven culture, and links compensation with SHRM.

Skill-Based Pay or Pay for Knowledge In skill-based or pay-for-knowledge pay plans, pay is determined by the number of tasks or jobs or the amount of knowledge an employee masters. It is a compensation system based on paying for what employees can do, for the knowledge or skills they possess. Under skill-based pay, employees can be expected to perform a broad range of duties. Benefits attributed to skill-based pay from an organizational standpoint include developing a cross-trained and more flexible workforce, improving the flow of information throughout the organization, placing an emphasis on the work to be done rather than on the job itself, encouraging the acquisition of skills needed to perform a variety of jobs, and increasing employees' interest in and commitment to their work. Benefits from the employees' perspective include higher motivation, increased job satisfaction, and greater opportunities for increased pay (Feuer, 1987; Gupta, Jenkins, & Curington, 1986; Shareef, 1994, 1998; Thompson & Lehew, 2000; Towers Perrin, 1992). The implementation of skill-based pay is not without problems. Changing a compensation system in the public sector typically requires obtaining the approval of multiple external stakeholders such as legislative bodies and union representatives, as well as the managers or supervisors and employees who will be affected. Employees may be reluctant to give up annual step or cost-of-living increases while developing new competencies (Gupta, 1997; Shareef, 1998, 2002; Thompson & Lehew, 2000).

Thompson and Lehew (2000) provide a comprehensive and critical review of skill-based pay for public organizations. They developed a theoretical model that suggests broadening the framework to include a discussion of environmental contingencies such as threats and crises, competition, and performance pressures; the proximate environment such as the various stakeholders, unions, and elected officials; the design features of the plan such as how radical it is, training opportunities available for employees, and the certification process; and the relevance of those components to organizational contingencies such as workforce characteristics, managerial practices and attitudes, and congruence to skill-based pay.

Organizations that implement skill-based pay need to be aware that wages and salaries will increase as employees learn new skills. And despite the strategic focus of skill-based training, all other HRM systems must be aligned. Performance evaluation systems, training and development systems, communication systems, and record-keeping systems all must change and reinforce the implementation of skill-based pay systems, or the implementation will not be successful (Shareef, 2002). Johnson County, Kansas, the Ventura Regional Sanitation District of Ventura, California, and the metro Regional Government in Portland, Oregon, have implemented skill-based pay practices (IPMA-HR, 2005).

Merit Pay or Pay for Performance Merit pay, or pay-for-performance systems, is grounded in the belief that individuals should be paid according to their contributions. Increases are rewarded on the basis of performance rather than seniority, equality, or need (Heneman, 1992). As logical as that may sound, research over the years has indicated that merit pay systems have not achieved the expected and desired results (Heneman, 1992; Kellough & Nigro, 2002; Kellough & Lu, 1993; U.S. Merit Systems Protection Board, 2006; Perry, 1995; Risher, Fay, & Perry, 1997).

Pay-for-performance systems fall victim to much of the same criticism made about performance evaluations noted in Chapter Eight, as well as additional criticism. Critics claim that the pay-for-performance evaluation process is subjective, that employees are rated by instruments that do not reflect their actual job competencies, that supervisors lack skills to develop performance standards and provide feedback, and that comparing individuals to one another sets up a competitive environment that can be destructive to department or unit cohesion. An additional criticism is that adequate financial resources are not always allocated (U.S. Merit Systems Protection Board, 2006). Even when pay rewards are not restricted, the small percentage of difference between high and low performers typically found in merit systems does not encourage improved performance or reward outstanding employees (Heneman, 1992).

Merit pay systems have been condemned for focusing on compensation rather than improved performance. Research has found that when pay and performance are discussed, employees fail to address the developmental issues and instead focus on not receiving a pay increase or on receiving an increase lower than expected. When provided with constructive feedback in a training-and-development context, employees are likely to accept the information. When feedback is tied to pay increases, however, employees process the information differently. They tend to get defensive, believing that the rater is taking something away from them by not granting a pay increase. Other research indicates that when performance appraisal results determine pay, employees often set lower goals so that they can achieve them (Cascio, 1991; Lawler, 1989).

The concepts of procedural justice and distributive justice must be considered when developing and administering pay-for-performance systems. *Procedural justice* focuses on the perceived fairness of the evaluation procedures used to determine performance ratings or merit increases. For example, what procedures or instruments are used to guarantee a link between pay and performance? *Distributive justice* focuses on the perceived fairness of the rating or increases received relative to the work performed (Greenberg, 1986, 1996). For example, is the rating or increase congruent to the performance inputs? Merit systems that are not developed with these principles in mind will lack the integrity and credibility necessary for employees to perceive that the system can discern and will reward differences in performance.

Heneman (1992) found that for employees to perceive the process as just, five components must exist: performance must be clearly defined, rewards must be communicated to employees, rewards must be made contingent on desired performance, opportunities to improve performance must exist, and the perceived relationship between rewards and performance should be viewed as important as the actual relationship.

To be successful, pay-for-performance must be linked to the strategic mission of the organization, and upper-level management must support the plan. Employees should participate in the development of the plan. This increases their understanding, commitment, and trust in the plan. Organizations must provide training to the raters and hold them accountable for the accuracy of their ratings, and a system of checks and balances is necessary (Heneman, 1992; U.S. Merit Systems Protection Board, 2006; Newlin & Meng, 1991; Perry, 1995; Healy & Southard, 1994; Risher, 2002).

Gainsharing Gainsharing is a team bonus program that measures controllable costs, such as improved safety records or decreases in waste or units of output. Teamwork is encouraged, and all team members are rewarded for controlling costs or improving productivity. Formulas are used to measure costs that are controllable, and these costs are then compared to the costs of a historical base period. When performance improves relative to the base period, a bonus pool is funded. When performance falls short, no bonus pool is created. Employees keep a percentage of the bonus pool, and the organization keeps the rest.

Not all gainsharing plans are the same. The formulas and participative management features need to fit each other as well as the organization. Different situations require different designs. However, some common critical elements are necessary for any plan to succeed. (1) There must be a credible and trusted development process. (2) Employees must believe that improved performance and decreased costs will lead to bonuses; the bonuses must be understandable and large enough to influence performance; and employees must recognize how their behavior can influence the size of the bonus. (3) Employees need to be involved in the process; they must have influence over the measures used to calculate the bonus. (4) There must be appropriate measures, and they must focus on all of the controllable costs.

Measures such as units of output, materials, and supplies must be addressed; otherwise, employees may focus on one cost, leading to its reduction but also to increases in other costs. For example, data processing clerks may produce a greater number of records, but if the number of errors on the records has increased, the effort has been counterproductive. Or public works employees may be able to maintain and landscape more of the city's property in less time, but if the increased productivity results in equipment breakdowns and expensive repairs, then that is counterproductive. The program must be maintained; because missions and environments change, gainsharing formulas and programs must change as well to stay relevant (Lawler, 1989, 2000). Miami-Dade County, Florida; the City of Charlotte, North Carolina; the City of College Station, Texas; Maricopa County, Arizona; the Virginia Beach City Public Schools; and the New Mexico State Personnel Board have gainsharing programs (IPMA-HR, 2006; New Mexico State Personnel Board, 2006).

Goalsharing Goalsharing is another group incentive plan. Payments are linked to the achievement of performance goals, which can also include cost savings (Risher, 2008). Cash awards are a result of the achievement of strategic goals. It is likely to be most effective in an agency or unit that has measurable performance goals.

Closing Thoughts on Equity

Despite an organization's best efforts to ensure equity, a number of factors that affect compensation are outside an agency's control. For example, as positions demand higher skill requirements, organizations can expect to pay more for those skills. If skills are in abundance, then employers can offer less even if those skills are critical to the organization. For instance, school teachers are often paid less than electricians, despite the greater value of teachers to the school, because unions may restrict the number of qualified electricians, thus driving up their salaries, while there are plenty of applicants wishing to be teachers. Or jobs with unpleasant or hazardous working conditions, such as sanitation or public works, might demand higher salaries because they are necessary to attract individuals to those positions.

Developing a compensation system that meets employee and organizational goals requires fine-tuning. Not all employees have the same priorities. Today, quality-of-life issues are also considered important by applicants and employees. To attract and retain employees, organizations need to offer either competitive wages or other benefits deemed important to employees and applicants, such as flexible work schedules, career mobility, a sense of purpose and the opportunity to use their skills, and child care or educational reimbursement programs.

Executive Compensation and Benefits

The compensation and benefits provided to executives in public and nonprofit organizations are often different from the compensation and benefits other employees receive. In the public sector, executives are exempt from civil service protection and serve at the discretion of elected officials. In the nonprofit sector, executives serve at the discretion of the board of directors. Because in both sectors the positions lack security, executives are likely to have negotiated employment contracts that specify the level of compensation and benefits they will receive. Some common benefits found in executive employment contracts are severance protection; moving expenses; health, retirement, and disability insurance; professional association memberships and dues; and paid conference registration and associated expenses such as travel and accommodations.

Executives are hired for their professional experience and expertise. They must often make hard choices and unpopular decisions that run counter to the wishes of the policymaking and governing body. Severance protection allows executives to be free to make those decisions without having to worrying about their financial situation if they are terminated. Severance protection usually includes a fixed amount of salary and the continuance of insurance benefits for a predetermined period of time.

Executives are typically recruited from the national labor market and often relocate to accept a position. Organizations that pay for moving expenses and in some cases provide a housing allowance in jurisdictions where housing is expensive make it easier to attract key executives. Executives will be less likely to relocate if they will continue to lose equity in their homes or if the costs associated with moving are prohibitive.

Because it is the responsibility of executives to guide as well as manage the organization, it is imperative that they have access to training and development activities such as attending conferences and belonging to professional associations. Organizations benefit when their executives are aware of the external forces affecting their agencies and changes in industry standards and practices. Agencies that maintain their competitive posture are led by proactive executives.

In both the public and nonprofit sectors, salaries are determined by surveying what relevant organizations in the external labor market pay for executive positions (Albert, 2000; Stene, 1980). Albert recommends that nonprofit executive salaries should be at the median or above the median of comparable organizations in the area. Board members should assess the agency's resources and offer the best salary and benefits package they can afford.

Concerns about some of the high salaries paid to nonprofit executives have been raised in the light of the financial difficulties facing many nonprofits. However, nonprofit officials and consultants believe that while boards must be sensitive to public perception, they have an obligation to pay salaries high enough to allow them to recruit and retain talented executives who will help an organization operate its programs effectively. Manzo (2004) notes that the real salary scandal is not that executives of nonprofits are paid too much but that most nonprofit employees are paid too little.

Deciding what the compensation of executives should be is difficult. Executives in public, nonprofit, and for-profit organizations may possess the same levels of responsibilities, administer similar-size budgets, and supervise similar-size staffs (public, nonprofit, and for-profit hospitals, for example).

All organizations must be careful that their executive salaries do not come at the expense of lower-level employees, like the examples cited later in the chapter regarding the CEO of Parent/Child Inc. and the KCMC Child Development Corp. All employees should be paid fair wages. Paying low salaries can be self-defeating. After two or three years, employees leave, and agencies need to recruit and train new staff incurring significant costs.

Paying low salaries can be self-defeating. After two or three years, employees leave, and agencies need to recruit and train new staff incurring significant costs.

Federal Laws Governing Compensation

All public and nonprofit employers are required to comply with two federal laws, the Fair Labor Standards Act (FLSA) and the Equal Pay Act.

The Fair Labor Standards Act

The main provisions of the FLSA, enacted in 1938, are minimum wage, overtime pay, equal pay, and child labor rules. On July 24, 2007, the federal minimum wage was raised to $5.85 an hour, to be increased 70 cents each summer until 2009, when it will reach $7.25 an hour.

The FLSA requires that employers keep records of the hours that employees have worked. Its overtime provision requires that employers pay one-and-one-half the regular rate of hourly pay for each hour worked that exceeds forty hours per week.

The FSLA divides employees into exempt and nonexempt workers. *Exempt employees* are not covered by the overtime provisions. They can be expected to work more than forty hours per week without additional compensation. Title 29, Chapter V, Part 541 of the Code of Federal Regulations (1993) defines exempt employees as those who spend 80 percent of their work time performing administrative, executive, or professional duties.

Administrative employees' primary responsibilities consist of performing office-based duties related to the implementation of management policies or general business operations. They customarily and regularly exercise discretion and independent judgment.

Executive employees exercise discretionary decision-making powers and supervise two or more employees. They have the authority to hire and fire employees, make recommendations as to advancement and promotion, and make any other change of status of the employees they supervise.

Professional employees perform duties requiring advanced knowledge acquired through specialized intellectual instruction. Their work is predominantly intellectual and varied in character and is of such character that the output produced or the result accomplished cannot be standardized in relation to a given time period.

Computer-related employees are computer systems analysts, computer programmers, software engineers, and other similarly skilled positions. Their primary duties consist of the application of systems analysis techniques and procedures, including consulting with users, to determine hardware, software, or system functional specifications; the design, development, documentation, analysis, creation, testing, or modification of computer systems or programs, including prototypes, based on and related to user or system design specifications; or the design, documentation, testing, creation, or modification of computer programs related to machine operating systems [E541.1, §541.2, §541.3, §541.4].

Employees are considered to be paid on a salary basis within the meaning of the FLSA if each pay period they receive a predetermined amount that constitutes all or part of their compensation and is not subject to reduction because of the quality or quantity of the work they performed. This means that employers are prohibited from making hourly deductions of pay from exempt employees.

Agencies with restricted budgets should not be tempted to coerce employees to work overtime without pay. The Florida Department of Children and Families (DCF) denied overtime to 126 Palm Beach County abuse investigators. The department employees said their supervisors used fear and coercion to convince them to work overtime without reporting it. An investigation by the U.S. Department of Labor's Wage and Hour Division found the employees averaged more than ten hours a week without pay for thirteen months ("DCF Accused of Coercing Employees to Work Overtime Without Pay," 2007; Chapman, 2007).

In 1985, the Supreme Court ruled in *Garcia* v. *San Antonio Metropolitan Transit Authority* that the FLSA could be applied to state, county, and municipal employees. This meant that public employers could no longer use compensatory time in lieu of dollars and would have to pay overtime. Because of the financial burden this would cause, public agencies petitioned Congress for relief. Congress reacted by amending the FLSA with the Fair Labor Standards Amendments of 1985. Section 7(o) of the FLSA authorizes compensatory time off as a form of overtime. It applies only to public sector agencies. To be legal under the FLSA, compensatory time must be one-and-a-half hours for each hour worked; personnel who are not sworn (that is, public employees other than sworn officers such as police, fire, and corrections) may have no more than 240 hours of compensatory time on the books at any one time, and sworn personnel can accrue no more than 480 hours of compensatory time at any one time. Nonsworn and sworn personnel who reach the limits of 240 and 480 hours, respectively, must receive cash for additional hours of overtime worked or use some compensatory time off before accruing further overtime compensation in the form of compensatory time off.

The 1985 amendment also has special provisions for hospital employees and police and fire officials who typically work nontraditional shifts. Section 7(j) permits the use of a fourteen-day work period (instead of the usual seven-day workweek) in the computation of overtime provisions. Overtime is considered only if an employee works more than eighty hours during the fourteen-day period.

Section 7(k) provides work periods up to twenty-eight days for public safety officials. These officials do not have to be paid overtime until they work more than 212 hours.

Nonprofit employers must comply with the FLSA overtime provision of one-and-a-half times an employee's normal hourly rate of pay for each hour that exceeds forty hours per week. Employees may elect compensatory time in lieu of overtime, but it must be their choice and not imposed by the employer.

Equal Pay Act of 1963

In 1963, the FLSA was amended by the Equal Pay Act, which prohibits unequal pay differences for men and women who are performing equal work on jobs requiring equal skill, effort, and responsibility and performed in the same establishment under similar working conditions. Pay differences between equal jobs can, however, be justified when that differential is based on a seniority system, a merit system, a piece-rate payment system that measures earnings by quality or quantity of production, or any factor other than gender (for example, different experience or different work shifts).

State and Local Government Minimum Wages

State and local governments are not bound by the federal minimum wage. They cannot permit wages lower than the federal minimum wage, but they can require higher wages. Currently, thirty-three states have passed minimum wage laws establishing higher wages than the federal level. Some of the minimum wage increases were passed by state legislatures and local city or county commissions, while other minimum wage increases were approved by voters. (For state minimum wages, go to the U.S. Department of Labor Web site, www.dol.gov).

Living Wages

Living wage is a term often used by advocates to point out that the federal minimum wage is not high enough to support a family. Advocates have attempted to calculate a living wage based on income that would provide for a family's basic needs in a particular community. Living wages are also commonly referred to as wages set by local ordinances that cover a specific set of workers—usually government workers or workers hired by businesses that have received a government contract, subsidy, or grant. The justification behind living wage ordinances is that tax dollars should not be used to support poverty-level jobs.

Without living wage laws, governments can inadvertently contribute to the creation of poverty-level jobs by hiring low-paying subcontractors or giving businesses tax breaks or subsidies to create jobs without any guarantee that the new jobs will pay a fair wage. This creates additional demands on public services and benefits. And because the responsibility of providing income supports and services to low-wage workers is passed on to the government, citizens pay for the services through increased taxes.

Living wage campaigns may differ. Some local laws have been designed to address specific city or county contracts, while others have been planned to cover a variety of public expenditures that include increasing the hourly wages of public employees or temporary employees working for public agencies and employees working for quasi-governmental agencies such as redevelopment authorities, school boards, hospital commissions, convention bureaus, or airports. In some cases, these employers are covered under separate ordinances, and at other times they are included in the definition of public employer. Other workers covered by living wages include employees working for contractors and subcontractors receiving public contracts and tenants of firms who receive economic development assistance. For example, a developer that gets a tax break to build a shopping center is likely to rent space to tenants that employ low-wage workers. The living wage must apply to those tenants and workers. Other ordinances have been extended to agencies or firms that lease city or county property such as businesses in or around airports and marinas where hotels, restaurants, and retail establishments are located.

Some living wage campaigns have exempted nonprofit organizations from its provision. However, as the examples provided indicate, employees at such agencies provide critical services and are often the most in need of a wage increase. Some local government campaigns have addressed nonprofits in different ways. Sometimes the law sets a threshold level to distinguish among nonprofits. The Ypsilanti, Michigan, living wage ordinance exempts nonprofits employing fewer than ten workers; Los Angeles exempted nonprofits if the compensation of their executive officer was less than eight times the lowest wage paid workers in the organization. Washtenaw County, Michigan, proposed a three-year phase-in and allowed nonprofits to petition local governments for either increased funding or special hardship exemptions if no new funds were provided. The cities of St. Paul and Minneapolis, along with the State of Maryland, have also exempted nonprofits from their living wage laws.

The Dane County, Wisconsin, campaign acknowledged the need for the county to increase funding to smaller nonprofits in the human service areas, and efforts in Allegheny County, Pennsylvania, and Santa Cruz, California, have won similar special funding pools. Multnomah County, Oregon's law, while not covering nonprofit social service contracts, committed the county and the Living Wage Coalition to jointly lobbying state and federal sources for increased funding for nonprofits to make living wage coverage eventually possible.

In many nonprofits, the executive director's salary is significantly higher than the employees providing direct services. In San Antonio, Texas, the CEO of Parent/Child Inc. earned ten times the average salary of her teaching staff, who earn $20,500 annually, which is $5,000 below the salaries of preschool teachers in the area. The CEO received a salary of $200,000 and a $200 a month car allowance. In an attempt to resist complying with the city's living wage ordinance, the CEO sent a letter to the San Antonio city manager protesting having to pay the living wage of $8.75 an hour to its employees (Tedesco, 2004). The *San Antonio Star Express* took a closer look at one hundred tax-exempt nonprofits that received Head Start money in 2001. The ten lowest-paid Head Start officials made less than an elementary school principal. The ten highest-paid executives earned salaries that rivaled the U.S. Secretary of Health and Human Services at the time, who earned $171,900 and oversaw a $488 billion budget.

The KCMC Child Development Corp. in Kansas City, Missouri, retained the highest-paid Head Start executive: the CEO earned $307,500 in pay and perks. The *Kansas City Star* reported that Head Start funds were used to lease a Mercedes sport utility vehicle at $600 a month.

The boards of directors approved the contracts. These are egregious examples, but there does need to be balance between what CEOs get paid and direct service providers. Living wage laws often lack the support of community nonprofits, and some have refused government money as a result.

Comparable Worth

Should sign painters and tree trimmers receive higher wages than emergency room nurses? What about state grain inspectors who are at the same job evaluation level as administrative secretaries? If you think no, then you are likely to favor comparable worth as an element to be considered in the development of compensation systems.

Comparable worth is the idea that each job has an inherent value or worth that can be compared to different types of positions across the organization. Jobs of greater inherent value to the organization should be paid more. Comparable worth has been defined as equitable compensation relationships for jobs that, while not the same, have been evaluated as equivalent based on the composite skill, effort, responsibility, and working conditions required. Comparable worth tries to eradicate the pay disparity between jobs that are traditionally female versus jobs that are traditionally male. It argues that jobs associated with women tend to be undervalued and discriminated against in the marketplace—for example, when nurses are paid less than tree trimmers or clerical employees are paid less than male-dominated physical plant employees (*Christensen* v. *State of Iowa*, 1977; *Lemons* v. *City and County of Denver*, 1980).

Opponents of comparable worth claim that pay disparities are the result of supply and demand and that market rates provide impartial values of labor (Taylor, 1989). In 1985, the Court of Appeals for the Ninth Circuit upheld that belief, ruling that salaries resulting from the market system do not amount to deliberate discrimination based on sex *(American Federation of State, County, and Municipal Employees* v. *State of Washington*, 1985; Gaston, 1986; Graham, 1992).

Advocates for comparable worth believe that labor market rates are not entirely objective. There is no going rate for any job. The determination of what wages to pay involves making value judgments and decisions. For example, to determine external equity, the agency decides which organizations should be compared; whether the data should be collected directly, purchased, or taken from government sources; and whether it wants to be a wage leader. It is also responsible for considering other forms of compensation. These decisions are rarely assessed for their discriminatory impact (Elliott, 1985; Taylor, 1989).

It has also been suggested that the compensable factors used during the job evaluation procedure to assign points or rankings often devalue women's work. Treiman and Hartman (1981), Elliott (1985), and Wittig and Lowe (1989) propose that sexual stereotypes and perceptions of gender differences combined with the expectations and experiences of work could influence the nature of job evaluation procedures and outcomes. Historically, female work was devalued, subject to the perception that a woman's income was secondary to her husband's. Blumrosen (1979, p. 435) states that "value systems and perceptions of the job analyst influence what information is collected and therefore what is available in later stages in the process."

Arvey (1986) and Elliott (1985) observe that subjectivity can play a major part in the evaluation process in determining the job factors that are considered to be important and in deciding their weights or points. For example, supervision is a compensable factor beneficial to men, while responsibilities such as planning, coordination, and scheduling (typically female tasks) are usually ignored. Physical strength (required for typically male tasks) is valued, while dexterity and handling multiple tasks simultaneously (required for jobs typically held by females) are not. Other characteristics and responsibilities, such as counseling and teaching, that are common in occupations heavily populated by women are often neglected as compensable factors. Guy and Newman (2004) and Guy, Newman, and Mastracci (2008) note that caring, negotiating, empathizing, smoothing troubled relationships, and working behind the scenes to enable cooperation are required components of many public service positions. Yet these skills are typically excluded from job evaluation forms, job descriptions, and performance evaluations so the work is invisible and uncompensated. They refer to this as emotional labor.

To eliminate these biases, compensable factors must be reevaluated. Otherwise organizations risk incorporating these inequities into future job evaluation procedures.

The federal courts have not recognized comparable worth as a statutory requirement under the Equal Pay Act or Title VII of the Civil Rights Act of 1964. However, various legislative bodies have acted to remedy pay disparities across jobs of similar value to the organization. In 1984, Congress enacted the Pay Equity and Management Act, reflecting the federal government's interest in comparable worth. In 1987, the U.S. Federal Employee Compensation Study Commission Act examined and attempted to promote equitable pay practices within the federal workforce. This legislation was followed by the Federal Equitable Pay Practices Act of 1988, which directed a study to determine the extent to which wages are affected across the board by gender and determine the role this influence may play in the formation of wage differentials between male- and female-dominated jobs (Kovach & Millspaugh, 1990).

Several state and local governments have passed legislation requiring that public jobs be paid according to their worth to the organization. An investigation by the State of Minnesota found that grain inspectors for the state were at the same job evaluation level as administrative secretaries, but they were paid three hundred dollars more per month. Each state job was evaluated using skill, effort, responsibility, and working conditions as the compensable factors. Despite similar internal value scores, men were paid more throughout state positions. To correct the disparity, in 1982 the Minnesota legislature passed a comparable worth law for state employees. The law required equitable compensation relationships between comparable male-dominated and female-dominated jobs.

In 1984, the Minnesota legislature enacted another law, this one requiring other public employers, such as city and county governments, public utilities, libraries, hospitals, and school districts, to develop plans to institute pay equity and implement those plans by 1987 (Aho, 1989; Watkins, 1992). Rhode Island followed in 1990, when it amended its classification and pay plan to authorize classification and pay increases for seventy job categories traditionally held by females.

Although no federal legislation exists that mandates equal pay for comparable worth, the Fair Pay Act and the Paycheck Fairness Act were introduced in Congress.

The Fair Pay Act was introduced by Senator Tom Harkin (D-Iowa) and Delegate Eleanor Holmes Norton (D-Washington, DC) introduced the bill in the House. The act would amend the Fair Labor Standards Act of 1938 to prohibit discrimination in the payment of wages on account of sex, race, or national origin and for other purposes. The bill seeks to end wage discrimination against those who work in female-dominated or minority-dominated jobs by establishing equal pay for equivalent work. The Fair Pay Act makes exceptions for different wage rates based on a seniority system, a merit system, or a system in which earnings are measured by quantity or quality of production, or differentials based on bona fide factors that the employer demonstrates are job-related or further legitimate business interests. It also contains a small business exemption. On July 31, 2008, the House of Representatives passed the Paycheck Fairness Act, H.R. 1338, by a vote of 248–178. However, the White House issued a veto threat.

The Lilly Ledbetter Fair Pay Act fell short of the required sixty votes in the U.S. Senate. The act would have reinstated the reasonable rule for filing claims of discriminatory pay practices that prevailed until the U.S. Supreme Court decision, *Ledbetter* v. *Goodyear Tire and Rubber Co.* (2007). The Court ruled five to four that Lilly Ledbetter, the only female supervisor at a tire plant in Gadsen, Alabama, did not file her lawsuit against Goodyear Tire and Rubber Co. in the time frame specified in Title VII of the Civil Rights Act of 1964. The law requires that a suit be filed within 180 days "after the alleged unlawful practice occurred." Ledbetter argued that she had been discriminated against throughout her career, receiving smaller raises than the men received, and that each paycheck was a new violation. Justice Ruth Ginsburg, joined by Justices John Paul Stevens, David H. Souter, and Stephen G. Breyer, said the decision set up a sometimes impossible barrier: "Pay disparities often occur, as they did in Ledbetter's case, in small increments; only over time is there strong cause to suspect that discrimination at work. . . . Even when unequal pay is discovered, women may be reluctant to go to federal court over small amounts. An employee like Ledbetter, trying to succeed in a male-dominated workplace, in a job filled only by men before she was hired, understandably may be anxious to avoid making waves." Backers of the Senate bill noted that many workers could not be certain what their colleagues were making and would not be able to initiate legal actions within 180 days of the first instance of discrimination. Pay discrimination has long-term consequences. Ledbetter's lower salary over the years she worked for Goodyear Tire and Rubber Co. has resulted in a lower pension and lower Social Security benefits.

Conclusion

Compensation systems should be designed with the intent to attract, motivate, and retain proficient employees. A number of factors determine the salaries paid to public and nonprofit employees: the salaries paid in the external labor market, federal laws such as the FLSA and the Equal Pay Act, and the responsibilities and KSAOCs required to perform the jobs, as well as an agency's ability to pay competitive wages.

Equity refers to the perception by employees that they are being paid fairly. External, internal, and employee equity influence compensation systems. Market factors influence external equity, job evaluation or job worth influences internal equity, and employee equity is said to exist when employees performing similar jobs are compensated based on their individual contributions. Broadbanding, skill-based pay or pay for knowledge, merit pay, and gainsharing are examples of some of the innovations in public and nonprofit sector compensation systems.

Public and nonprofit executives are hired for their professional experience and expertise. They lack job security and serve at the discretion of elected officials or board members. Because of this unique aspect of their employment, executives typically negotiate employment contracts that specify the level of compensation and benefits they will receive. Executives of some nonprofits also receive bonuses on their agency's performance.

Exercise 9.1: Compensation and Retirement Benefits from the United Way of Metropolitan Atlanta

Mark O'Connell was the United Way of Metropolitan Atlanta's chief executive. Two years prior to his retirement he received $1.6 million in cash to supplement his pension, which will be $106,000 a year for life. O'Connell's compensation covered salary, bonus, and unused leave. It nearly doubled over the last decade. In his final year of employment, he collected approximately $446,700, including a car allowance and $70,200 in unused leave. During his last three years in his position, his earnings approached $1.2 million, not counting the lump-sum payment.

In 2003, the United Way of Metropolitan Atlanta laid off twenty-four workers to save $1.4 million after an economic slump hurt fundraising. In 2007, it reduced grants to community nonprofits by 30 percent.

Not all United Ways compensate their CEOs in a similar manner. Some are more generous than others.

Questions

1. If you were a board member on the HRM committee of the United Way of Metropolitan Atlanta, what factors would you use to determine an equitable level of compensation for O'Connell?
2. As a board member, you will need to approve the hiring and salary of O'Connell's successor. What factors should be considered when approving his successor's salary and benefits?

Source: Vogel (2007).

Exercise 9.2: Are There Too Few Troopers for Safety?

Two Florida state troopers are responsible for covering a two-thousand-square-mile county. Florida law enforcement officials and lawmakers have long disagreed over highway patrol staffing levels. Florida has about 1,600 troopers and 150 vacancies. Ten years ago, the highway patrol had 1,740 troopers. In some areas of the state, it is common for one trooper to cover two or three counties during overnight shifts. Crash victims in those areas can wait more than an hour for assistance.

A study conducted more than ten years ago found that Florida needed to add 500 troopers to keep pace with the state's growth.

One lawmaker who sits on the Florida House Policy and Budget Committee wants to hire more state troopers and increase their pay. Troopers generally earn eight to fifteen thousand dollars less than police officers and sheriff deputies.

The Florida State Highway Patrol has become a training ground for individuals looking to get into law enforcement, but then they leave for city or county law enforcement agencies that pay higher salaries.

Question

1. If you were hired to be the director of HRM for the Florida Highway Patrol, knowing that there is a trooper shortage and the salary for state troopers is below what city and county law enforcement agencies pay, what strategic compensation strategies would you develop to recruit, motivate, and retain patrol officers?

Source: Helgeson (2008).

Chapter Questions

1. What type of equity (external, internal, or employee) is most important to you? Explain the reasons.
2. Review current copies of the *ICMA Newsletter*, *IPMA Newsletter*, *Chronicle of Philanthropy*, or *Nonprofit Times*. What positions receive the highest salaries? What factors do you think are most important in determining compensation?
3. In small groups, discuss the compensation policy in the organizations where you work. What is the basis for the policies? Does one organization have a more progressive policy than the others?

Online Activities

1. Visit the U.S. Office of Personnel Management Web site. How many salary schedules exist? Why are there different salary schedules? Does your agency have different salary schedules?
2. Using the Internet, find salary schedules for two local governments, two state governments, and two nonprofit organizations. What are the similarities and differences in regard to salary schedules and compensation policies across the six organizations?

CHAPTER TEN

BENEFITS

After you read this chapter, you should be able to:

- Understand the importance of employee benefits to strategic human resources management (SHRM)
- Explain how employee benefits are important components of SHRM
- Distinguish between required benefits and discretionary benefits
- Describe strategies to improve the quality of work life in public and nonprofit organizations
- Describe strategies to improve the quality of life of public and nonprofit employees

The preceding chapter on compensation provided an overview of salaries and wages, the direct financial compensation provided to employees for their contributions to the organization. But wages constitute only part of the compensation package. This chapter addresses indirect compensation, more commonly referred to as *benefits*.

The emphasis in compensating employees should be on the total compensation package, not just on direct wages or salary. Benefits are a critical ingredient in creating an accurate compensation picture. The importance of benefits should not be underestimated; an attractive benefits package can assist in the recruitment and retention of qualified employees. Traditional benefits such as health insurance, retirement pensions, and paid time away from work, combined with less traditional benefits such as child and elder care, flexible scheduling, and educational assistance, are critical for attracting qualified applicants, encouraging loyalty and long-term employment, and motivating and rewarding incumbent employees.

Employee benefits often reach 40 percent of total compensation costs. Medical insurance premiums are the highest-cost single benefit. Research conducted by the Kaiser Family Foundation and the Health Research and Educational Trust found that premiums for employer-sponsored health coverage rose an average 7.7 percent in 2006. Premiums increased more than twice as fast as workers' wages (3.8 percent) and overall inflation (3.4 percent). Family health coverage now costs an average of $11,480 annually, with workers paying an average of $2,973 toward those premiums (Kaiser Family Foundation, 2006). Paid time off, vacations, holidays, and sick leave combined account for about one-third of all benefits.

Employees often think of benefits as entitlements and not as compensation. In reality, the only entitlements are the benefits required by federal or state laws, such as employer contributions to Social Security and Medicare or state pension plans, unemployment compensation, and workers' compensation. Aside from these, employers have tremendous discretion in deciding what types of benefits to provide. This chapter discusses the variety of benefits that organizations may choose to offer, as well as the quality-of-life and quality-of-work issues that are becoming more prevalent in today's workplaces.

Required Benefits

All employers are required to contribute to Social Security, Medicare, unemployment compensation, and workers' compensation benefits. Public employers may be required by federal or state statutes to offer additional benefits, such as retirement or disability. The benefits provided by nonprofits are determined and approved by the board of directors.

Social Security

Social Security provides retirement, disability, death, survivor, and Medicare benefits for those beyond age sixty-five. The Social Security system was established in 1935; however, public and nonprofit employers and employees could decline to pay Social Security taxes and earn no credit toward Social Security benefits. The Social Security Amendments of 1983 made Social Security coverage mandatory for all employees of nonprofit organizations as of January 1, 1984. Coverage was extended to nonprofit employees working for organizations that had previously terminated coverage, as well as to employees who had never been covered by Social Security. The 1983 amendments included a special section that provided for nonprofit employees fifty-five years and older to be considered fully insured for benefits after acquiring at least twenty quarters of coverage.

The Social Security Act originally excluded state and local governments from coverage because of the concern that taxation of these governments by the federal government might be unconstitutional. The act was subsequently amended in the 1950s to permit state and local governments to choose coverage for employees not already covered under a retirement system. After five years of participating in the Social Security system, state and local governments could choose to repeal their action and terminate coverage of their employees. This was changed in 1983 by the Social Security Amendments Act, which eliminated the right of state and local government employers to withdraw from the system. Another change came in 1986 when the Budget Reconciliation Act amended the Social Security Act and required all individuals hired by a state or local government to be covered by the Medicare segment of the program and subject to employer and employee payroll taxes. As of July 2, 1991, all state and local government employees (except police officers) not covered by a retirement program were required to participate in the full Social Security program. Federal employees hired on or after January 1, 1984, are covered by Social Security and are subject to full Social Security taxation.

Social Security provides four kinds of benefits: old-age or disability benefits, benefits for the dependents of retired or disabled workers, benefits for the survivors of a worker who dies, and the lump-sum death benefit.

Medicare

Funding for Medicare comes partially from payroll taxes, known as FICA (Federal Insurance Contributions Act) taxes. FICA comprises the Social Security tax and Medicare tax. The rate of the Medicare tax is 2.9 percent. Employers withhold 1.45 percent from their employees and match it with another 1.45 percent. There is no wage base for the Medicare portion of the FICA tax. Both the employer and the employee continue to pay Medicare tax, no matter how much is earned.

Unemployment Compensation

Unemployment compensation, established as part of the Social Security Act of 1935, was designed to provide a portion of wages to employees who have been laid off until they obtain another job. The employer pays into the unemployment compensation fund at a rate based on the average number of former employees who have drawn benefits from the fund. The fund is primarily financed through a payroll tax paid to the state and federal governments based on employees' wages. The employer pays state and federal unemployment taxes. Each state determines its own waiting period for eligibility, level of benefits provided, and the length of time that benefits are paid.

Workers' Compensation

Workers' compensation is an employer-financed insurance program that provides compensation to employees who are unable to work because of job-related injuries or illness. Most states have their own workers' compensation laws and are responsible for administering their own programs. For this reason, the levels of protection and the costs of administering the programs vary by state. Some features that all of the programs have in common are the following (Commerce Clearing House Business Law Editors, 1992, p. 8):

- Workers receive benefits for accidental injury; wage loss, medical, and death benefits are provided.
- Fault is not an issue; if the employee was somewhat or entirely at fault in the injury, the employee still has the right to receive workers' compensation benefits.
- In exchange for the assurance of benefits, the employee (and the employee's dependent family members) gives up the right to sue the employer for damages for any injury covered by a workers' compensation law.
- Responsibility for administering the system usually resides with a state board or commission. Employers are generally required to insure their workers' compensation liability through private insurance, state insurance funds, or self-insurance.

Independent contractors are not considered to be employees and do not have to be covered under the workers' compensation policy of the organization that hired them. Most state workers' compensation agencies apply the same test as the Internal Revenue Service (IRS) for determining whether a contractor is truly independent and not just called so by an employer who does not want to match the contractor's Social Security contributions or deduct and withhold income taxes. To decide whether a contractor is independent, the IRS examines the relationship between the worker and the organization. Evidence of behavioral control, financial control, and the type of relationship are considered.

Behavioral control covers facts that show whether the business has a right to direct and control how the work is done through instructions, training, or other means. *Financial control* covers facts that show whether the organization has a right to control the business aspects of the worker's job. This includes the extent to which the worker has unreimbursed business expenses, the extent of the worker's investment in the business, the extent to which the worker makes services available to the relevant market, how the organization pays the worker, and the extent to which the worker can realize a profit or incur a loss. *Type of relationship* covers facts that show written contracts describing the relationship the parties intended to create; the extent to which the worker is available to perform services for similar businesses; whether the business provides the worker with employee benefits, such as insurance, a pension plan, vacation pay, or sick pay; and the permanence or impermanence of the relationship.

The contractor should probably be covered under the organization's workers' compensation policy if the contractor can be fired or quit without any contractual liability; the contractor is reimbursed for business and travel expenses; the contractor performs the task in person, on company property, and during set hours; the contractor is paid by the hour, week, or month rather than the job; and the organization provides the contractor with tools or equipment. The state's workers' compensation agency should be contacted for verification.

In most states, unpaid volunteers are not considered to be employees and typically are not covered by workers' compensation. But in some states, there are exceptions for police and fire volunteers, and other volunteers may be covered under special circumstances.

Military Leave

Reserve and National Guard units called to active duty have rights with respect to the retirement and health benefits provided by their employers.

The Uniformed Services Employment and Reemployment Rights Act of 1994 strengthens and clarifies the Veterans' Reemployment Rights Statute. A fact sheet and interactive computer program, the USERRA Advisor, has been developed by the Department of Labor's Veterans' Employment and Training Service to provide information as to the rights and responsibilities of individuals and their employers under the act (U.S. Department of Labor, http://www.dol.gov/vets/programs/userra/userra_fs.htm).

Discretionary Benefits

Public and nonprofit employers recognize that to be competitive, they need to offer additional benefits beyond those mandated by law. Research indicates that integrated benefit programs lead to increased productivity and decreased turnover, increased effectiveness of recruitment and retention programs, and employee loyalty to the organization (Cayer, 2003; Cayer & Roach, 2008; Coggburn & Reddick, 2007; Champion-Hughes, 2001; Daley, 2008; Durst, 1999; McCurdy, Newman, & Lovrich, 2002; Reddick & Coggburn, 2007; Roberts, 2000, 2002, 2004).

Research indicates that integrated benefit programs lead to increased productivity and decreased turnover, increased effectiveness of recruitment and retention programs, and employee loyalty to the organization.

Pensions

Pensions provide retired or permanently disabled employees with income throughout the remainder of their lives. In the public sector, different classes of employees are often covered by different pension plans. For example, teachers, police, and firefighters have pension plans separate from those of other general employees. Some states have separate pension plans for judges and legislatures. Police and firefighters may retire with full benefits at a younger age and with fewer years of service than other employees.

Prior to 1984, the retirement plan covering most civilian federal employees was the Civil Service Retirement System (CSRS); employees covered by CSRS were excluded from paying Social Security taxes. The Social Security Amendments of 1983, however, required that federal employees hired after December 31, 1983, be covered by Social Security. A new retirement plan, the Federal Employees Retirement System (FERS), was established by Congress on June 6, 1986, and went into effect on January 1, 1987. Most federal employees hired after January 1, 1987, are covered by FERS, and employees covered under CSRS were given the opportunity to join FERS.

Like state and local government retirement systems, the federal government also has different age and years-of-service criteria that permit certain groups of employees to retire early and with full benefits. Law enforcement officials, firefighters, air traffic controllers, military reserve technicians, and defense intelligence Senior Executive Service (SES) and senior cryptologic SES are some of the positions eligible for early retirement.

Fidelity's Tax Exempt Workplace Savings Tracker found that 55 percent of nonprofit employees surveyed say they have a pension plan, but 57 percent of those worry that their pension benefits will be reduced or discontinued. This is because many for-profit organizations, government, and nonprofits have been phasing out pension plans in favor of 401(k) and other deferred compensation retirement plans (Panepento, 2007a). However, many smaller nonprofits, such as grassroots or social justice organizations, traditionally have not offered retirement plans. In an effort to provide activists, advocates, and social justice organizers some future security, the National Organizers Alliance in 1997 received start-up funds from the John D. and Catherine T. MacArthur Foundation, the Jessie Smith Noyes Foundation, Unitarian Universalist Veatch Program at Shelter Rock, Albert List Foundation, Wieboldt Foundation, Norman Foundation, and the Public Welfare Foundation to establish and implement a retirement program (Billitteri, 1999). Today the coalition's 401(k) plan contains approximately $10 million in assets and manages upward of a thousand accounts. More than 120 nonprofit employers offer the plan. Some agencies offering the plan are staffed by two or three people, while others employ up to twenty. The start-up fee for employers is four hundred dollars, and their yearly administrative fee is also four hundred dollars, which includes the annual cost for the first two employees enrolled in the program. For all additional workers, the charity pays twenty-seven dollars per worker. The program requires employers to contribute a minimum of 5 percent of their employees' salaries into their 401(k) plans each year and must contribute even if their workers do not contribute themselves ("Updating a Program," 2007).

Defined-Benefit and Defined-Contribution Pension Plans

Two types of pension plans are commonly found in the public and nonprofit sectors: defined-benefit and defined-contribution plans.

A *defined-benefit plan* is a pension plan that specifies the benefits or the methods of determining the benefits at the time of retirement but not the level or rate of contribution. The benefit amounts to be paid are determined by a formula that weighs the retiree's years of service, age, and salary history. An advantage of defined-benefit plans is that employees and employers can estimate the probable size of their pension benefits by assuming retirement dates and salary histories. Because taxpayers back public pensions, they are guaranteed.

In *defined-contribution plans*, the employer guarantees that specified contributions, usually a percentage of annual salary, will be deposited to employees' accounts every year that they work. These accounts are invested. Employees are provided with a variety of investment options from which to choose. When they retire, they receive lifetime payments or annuities, with the size determined by the amount on deposit, the interest rate earned on funds in the account, and the length of time during which the annuity is expected to be paid. The employee, the employer, or both may contribute to the pension plan.

A variety of employer-assisted defined-contribution pension plans are available to employees. The most common are 401(k), 403(b), and Section 457 plans, which are set up by employers and funded by employees. Employers design the plan and handle the automatic payroll deductions and paperwork. Employees make contributions and assume the investment risk and responsibility. As part of the Pension Protection Act of 2006, agencies may invest their employees' retirement savings in 401(k) plans without being held liable for losses. Under the new rules, employees could be enrolled in a employer-sponsored retirement program unless they opt out of it. Employers may match part or all of a worker's contribution. No federal agency guarantees the solvency of these plans. The 401(k) plans are used primarily in the private sector although they are available to nonprofits, and 403(b) plans are typically used by nonprofit organizations that are exempt under Section 501(c)(3) of the Internal Revenue Code. Public schools and colleges may also provide 403(b) retirement plans for employees. Section 457 plans are offered to employees of state and local governments and nonprofit organizations as a supplement to other defined-benefit and defined-contribution plans. Contributions remain assets of the employer until they are distributed to the participant and are vulnerable to creditors if an employer goes bankrupt. Money is held in a trust, a custodial account, or an annuity contract.

Defined-contribution pension plans are becoming more popular as more employers have realized the expense and long-term liabilities associated with funding defined-benefit plans. Some states, including Illinois and Florida, are now providing state employees with the option of enrolling in a defined-contribution plan instead of requiring them to become part of the defined-benefit pension. In Florida, the annual employer contributions will be 9 percent for most employees, and law enforcement will receive employer contributions of 20 percent due to their more generous pensions.

Vesting

Vesting occurs when contributions made to a retirement plan belong to the employee. For most defined-benefit pension plans, an employee who leaves the organization retains the nonforfeitable right to those benefits on retirement. However, an employee may be required to wait until retirement before receiving the benefits. Most defined-contribution pension plans allow the employee to take the accrued amount when they leave the organization in a lump-sum payment that is taxable.

Vesting standards for nonprofit and private organizations were amended as part of the Tax Reform Act of 1986. New minimum standards went into effect in 1989 that enable employees to become fully vested in their pension plans after five years of service, or they may be 20 percent vested after three years of service, 20 percent for each year thereafter, and 100 percent after seven years of service.

In the public sector, wide variations exist as to when employees are entitled to vested benefits. In some plans, employees are required to work five years before benefits are guaranteed. Other plans require ten years of plan participation before vesting occurs. Employees considering employment in another organization covered by a different retirement system should find out whether they meet the minimum requirement for vesting.

Retirement systems at the federal, state, and local levels have special provisions for public safety officers. They can retire at an earlier age with full benefits after shortened working careers.

The Employee Retirement Income Security Act of 1974 (ERISA) safeguards the pensions of nonprofit and private sector employees. ERISA sets minimum standards to ensure that employee benefit plans are financially sound so that employees receive the benefits promised by their employers. ERISA does not cover plans established or maintained by government entities or churches. Three federal government agencies share responsibility for the administration and enforcement of ERISA provisions: the U.S. Department of Labor, the Internal Revenue Service, and the Pension Benefit Guaranty Corporation.

Health Insurance

Health insurance is the most frequently provided benefit and the benefit that receives the most attention. The number of people without health insurance rose to 46 million in 2007 (DeNavas-Walt, Proctor, & Smith, 2008).

Health insurance is offered by all state governments and by 99.5 percent of local governments, but by only 62 percent of all organizations nationally (Reddick & Coggburn, 2007). Given that the costs of health insurance rose more than twice the rate of employees' wages and overall inflation in 2006, most managed care plans have been designed to focus on controlling costs. The most common are health maintenance organizations (HMO), preferred provider organizations (PPO), point of service (POS), and high-deductible health plans (HDHP). Each type of plan has advantages and disadvantages. With an HMO plan, employees must receive their health care from an HMO physician. If they do, their expenses are typically covered in full. With a PPO plan, employees have lower deductibles and coinsurance if they use physicians or hospitals in the preferred provider network. With a POS plan, employees are reimbursed at a lower rate for services received outside the network; they also have a primary care physician who must approve visits to specialists and hospitals. An HDHP plan typically has a single deductible of at least one thousand dollars and a family deductible of at least two thousand dollars annually (Reddick & Coggburn, 2007). Some employers offer health saving accounts, which allow employees to have a savings or investment account for money put aside to cover health care costs. The money is excluded from taxable income. If the money is withdrawn and used for health expenses, it is never taxed.

The types of health insurance programs and the amounts that employees and employers contribute to the plans vary. Keeping track of them and figuring out the best plan takes some research and asking questions.

The Consolidated Omnibus Budget Reconciliation Act of 1986 (COBRA) was enacted to provide employees with the opportunity to temporarily continue receiving their employer-sponsored medical care insurance under the employer's plan if their coverage otherwise would cease due to termination, layoff, or other changes in the employment status. COBRA covers employers of twenty or more employees, except for the federal government and religious organizations. Many states have their own versions of COBRA to cover small employers. COBRA enables former employees, spouses, and dependents to purchase insurance coverage for a limited amount of time after leaving the organization. COBRA also applies to divorced, separated, or widowed spouses, and it extends Medicare coverage to state and local government employees.

The Health Insurance Portability and Accountability Act of 1996 allows employees to switch their health insurance plan from one organization to another to get new heath coverage, regardless of preexisting health conditions. The legislation also prohibits group insurance plans from dropping coverage for a sick employee and requires them to make individual coverage available to people who leave group plans. In April 2003, the privacy component of the act became activated. Employees working for pharmacies, hospitals, clinics, health insurance companies, and other health care organizations have an obligation to protect a patient's privacy, and organizations must make sure that health data are secure and private.

Mental Health Care In an effort to encourage individuals to seek mental health treatment, the Mental Health Parity Act was passed into law in 1996. The act provided that beginning in January 1998, health insurance plans must provide the same coverage for mental illness as for physical disorders. It requires that group health plans provide parity for treatment of mental illness. The 1996 Mental Health Parity Act established parity for annual and lifetime dollar limits (dollar-based caps on coverage applied either annually or over an enrollee's life). This left health plans free to continue imposing lower caps on covered inpatient days and outpatient visits, as well as higher cost sharing and deductibles that apply only to mental illness treatment. Critical provisions in S558 are the expansions of the 1996 law to include prohibitions on unequal limitations on day or visit limits and financial limitations. Another key provision requires that this parity standard for mental illness treatment be measured against "substantially all" medical-surgical coverage, and not just a portion of medical-surgical benefits.

Forty-one states have their own mental health parity laws that differ in terms of their scope and requirements. Employers and employees should review the mental health parity laws in the state where they reside to see what coverage is provided.

Genetic Nondiscrimination Act In April 2008, the U.S. House of Representatives and the U.S. Senate passed the Genetic Nondiscrimination Act, and President Bush signed it on May 22, 2008. The act prohibits employers from discriminating against employees and applicants on the basis of genetic information and bans the collection of genetic information except in limited circumstances. The EEOC will be developing regulations to enforce the law, which is expected to take effect eighteen months after it is signed.

Retiree Health Benefits Many public sector employers offer health benefits to retirees. Retirement health benefits are also often offered to employees in unionized organizations and to high-ranking executives in the nonprofit and private sectors. A study conducted by the Pew Center on States found that $370 billion is needed for future retiree health care and other nonpension benefits such as dental and life insurance. Many local governments are facing deficits as well, and some have discontinued retiree health care benefits (Chan, 2008; Gelbart, 2008; Prah, 2007).

Additional Health Benefits More insurance programs are also beginning to offer dental, optical, and prescription drug benefits in addition to traditional medical coverage.

Disability Benefits Insurance

Disability benefits are paid to employees who become disabled before qualifying for regular or early retirement benefits. Generally, disability benefits insurance provides a monthly benefit to employees who cannot work for an extended period of time due to injury or illness. Some employees, however, are not insured for long-term disability but are eligible for an immediate disability pension through their retirement plans. In most instances, long-term disability payments are a fixed percentage of predisability earnings. Most plans distinguish between disability attributed to an accident on the job, which pays higher benefits and has fewer requirements with respect to years of service, and disability that is not job related.

Paid Time Away from Work

Most employers grant employees paid sick leave, vacation days, holidays, and personal days. Employers are not obligated to grant these benefits, and they vary across organizations.

In many public organizations, employees who accumulate their sick and vacation days are able to cash them in for compensation when they retire.

This policy is meant to discourage capricious time away from work and to reward employees for their commitment to the organization. However, many organizations are rethinking this policy because accrued time becomes an unfunded liability for the agency. When a police sergeant in Tampa, Florida, recently retired, he left with seventy thousand dollars compensation for his unused sick and vacation time. Workers employed by the City of Tampa, Florida, may accumulate sick and vacation leave. Specifics vary according to the job position and union contract, but generally employees can carry over up to 240 hours of vacation time from one year to the next. Any accumulation above 240 hours is converted into sick time hours. When they retire, they are entitled to half of their accumulated sick leave, up to 240 hours of annual leave, and half the rest of their accumulated annual leave. The amount of money they receive is based on the final hourly rate they were earning, not when the time was accrued.

Hillsborough County, Florida, eliminated a similar policy in 1997. Employees hired after February 1, 1997, who leave the county do not get paid for any unused hours. They can convert up to four days of unused sick time into vacation time each year. When they leave the county, they are paid for up to 320 hours of unused vacation time. Bernards Township in New Jersey provides a limit of fifteen thousand dollars that can be paid out to nonunion employees. Organizations that provide this benefit need to understand and plan for its fiscal implications when employees leave the organization.

Education Programs

The Council for Adult and Experiential Learning (2004) surveyed HRM professionals across the United States about the educational assistance benefits available at their organizations. Results were obtained from 1,304 organizations. Nearly 86 percent of the organizations agree that education and tuition benefits are important as a strategic investment. The respondents cited increases in employee retention and productivity as the two most important reasons for offering tuition and other education benefits.

Many public and nonprofit organizations provide tuition reimbursement to employees for additional education if the employee receives a B or better grade for the course. While some smaller or undercapitalized organizations may not be able to afford to offer these benefits, most employers are able to assist their employees in other ways. Employers have the discretion to establish flexible work schedules to accommodate an employee's class schedule. For example, if an employee is attending classes at night, the employee can be allowed to leave earlier that day to travel to class. Some employers may not be able to afford college tuition; however, they may be able to afford to purchase textbooks that can become the property of the organization once a class is completed. When appropriate, an employer can substitute tuition for attending conferences out of town. Often the cost of a college class for a semester of learning is less than a conference registration fee, hotel, meals, and transportation expenses, not to mention the employee's time away from work.

Employers can provide information to their employees on the tax credits and deductions sanctioned by the IRS that are available to help offset the cost of higher education. For example, the Hope Credit provides up to $1,650 credit per eligible student, available only until the first two years of postsecondary education are completed. The Lifetime Learning Credit provides up to $2,000 credit per return, and there is no limit on the number of years a lifetime learning credit can be claimed based on the same student's expense. It is available for all years of postsecondary education and for courses taken to acquire or improve job skills. It is available for an unlimited number of years; students do not need to be pursuing a degree or other recognized education credential; it is available for one or more courses; and the felony drug conviction rule that disqualifies otherwise qualified students from receiving financial assistance does not apply. The Lifetime Learning Credit may be limited by the amount of a student's income and the amount of tax liability.

Quality-of-Work and Quality-of-Life Issues

Changes in family structures and employee priorities have encouraged the evolution of a variety of employer-provided benefits. Employers wishing to compete for highly skilled employees believe that quality-of-work and quality-of-life benefits can give them a competitive edge.

Employers wishing to compete for highly skilled employees believe that quality-of-work and quality-of-life benefits can give them a competitive edge.

Quality-of-life and quality-of-work benefits have become very important in organizations' ability to attract and motivate employees. Many nonprofits are unable to compete in benefits such as child care, dental care, or tuition reimbursement, so to remain competitive, they tend to offer health insurance and lots of flexibility as a way to assist employees in balancing work and family.

Preston (1990) found that the opportunity to perform a variety of work and to enhance one's skill development has been instrumental in attracting women to nonprofit organizations. Many women choose to work in nonprofits despite the often lower pay they provide in order to take advantage of the opportunities they offer. Organizations should not overlook the importance of quality-of-work and quality-of-life enhancements in motivating employees.

Flexible Benefits

As early as the 1970s, private sector organizations recognized that different family structures necessitate different employee benefits (Johnson, 1988; Wallace & Fay, 1988). Conventional employee benefit plans were designed to serve the needs of the family structure that was dominant during the 1940s and 1950s: a working father and his dependents (a wife who stayed at home with small children). Today, families have changed, and so have their needs. Current family structures often include a single parent, multiple generations, and domestic partnerships. Continuing increases in dual-career and single-parent families will likely result in a continued demand for a variety of elder and child care services.

Some solutions have been employer-sponsored group insurance plans that provide lower premiums, or flexible spending accounts that enable greater flexibility in the types of services that benefits will pay for (Daley, 1998; Kossek, DeMarr, Backman, & Kolar, 1993).

In the past, wives often took care of elderly parents or in-laws and children. Today there are many single-parent families or families in which both spouses work full-time, and they are unable to care for their children or parents during their working hours. Thus, many benefit plans now have provisions for elder and child care. Employees with small children may need child care, employees with elderly or infirm parents may prefer elder care, and employees without any dependents might opt for other benefits, such as dental care.

Child and elder care responsibilities have an impact on job performance as well as financial costs. Research has found that caregiver responsibilities result in the excessive use of the phone at work, lateness, and unscheduled time off. Employee time spent on caregiver responsibilities affects productivity, absenteeism, turnover, and morale (Nelson-Horchler, 1989). A survey conducted by the National Alliance of Caregiving and Evercare, a division of UnitedHealth Group, found that family members responsible for caregiving often spend on average about $5,500 a year in caregiving expenses, in addition to the physical and emotional stress that already exists (Evercare and National Alliance of Caregiving, 2007).

An emerging issue in all sectors is the provision of domestic partnership benefits to employees. Such benefits extend workplace benefit coverage to unmarried heterosexual or gay couples. One way to support employees and make them feel part of the organization is to recognize and respect alternative families. Health insurance, sick leave, bereavement leave, pension plans, life insurance benefits, and access to employee assistance programs are some of the benefits that have been extended to domestic partners. Typically, couples qualify if they are living together and are jointly responsible for their financial well-being (Gossett & Ng, 2008).

Employee Assistance Programs

Employee assistance programs are another important type of employer-provided benefit. Marital conflicts, alcohol and substance abuse, family stresses, AIDS, and other health-related concerns are some of the problems that come to work with employees. These problems often result in lower employee productivity and morale and may also lead to legal liabilities and high financial costs for the employer. EAPs provide counseling services for employees and their families. In the past, the focus of EAPs was on alcoholism and drug-related problems. The services of EAPs have since expanded to include counseling for marital problems, drug abuse, mental illness, financial stress, and the improvement of employer-employee communications.

EAPs also address such issues as prevention, health and wellness, employee advocacy, and the dysfunctional workplace. Employees with stressful lives are absent more often, resulting in lost productivity. Wellness programs are designed to improve employees' physical and psychological health, thus decreasing the occurrence and severity of medical problems and lowering the costs and number of medical claims (Hyland, 1990). Accident prevention classes, smoking cessation seminars, weight control and nutrition programs, stress management workshops, and on-site exercise programs are also an outgrowth of EAPs. The largest use of EAPs, however, is still for drug or alcohol addictions. Employers have increasingly become involved because alcohol and drug testing is required for many employment positions.

Alcohol and Drug Testing

Substance abuse is a pervasive problem in the American workforce. Alcohol and drug abuse are cited for decreases in productivity and increases in work-related accidents. To combat substance abuse in the workplace, legislators, judges, and regulatory agencies have passed laws or rendered decisions that regulate substance abuse testing in the workplace.

In 1986, President Reagan signed Executive Order 12564, which required federal agencies to set up programs to test workers in sensitive positions for illegal drug use and to establish a voluntary drug testing program for all other employees. In 1988, Congress passed the Drug-Free Workplace Act. The act required federal contractors and grantees who receive more than twenty-five thousand dollars in government business to certify that they would maintain drug-free workplaces. Organizations that did not comply with the requirements of the act could have their payments suspended and lose governments contracts for up to five years.

Nonprofit organizations that are the recipients of federal funds in excess of twenty-five thousand dollars are required to comply with the Drug-Free Workplace Act. State and local governments may also require government contractors to comply with drug abuse prevention efforts. In addition, nonprofits receiving state or local funds, or both, are expected to comply with state regulations.

Nonprofit employees employed under a collective bargaining agreement may be subject to an employer-imposed drug and alcohol testing policy. In 1989, the National Labor Relations Board ruled that the drug testing of employees was a mandatory subject of collective bargaining but the drug testing of applicants was not (Johnson-Bateman Company, 1989). This decision was reversed by the Seventh Circuit Court in the case of *Chicago Tribune* v. *National Labor Relations Board* (1992). The court held that the newspaper could rely on its broad management rights clause to implement a drug testing program on a unilateral basis. The management rights clause gave the employer the exclusive right "to establish and enforce reasonable rules and regulations relating to the operation of the facilities and employee conduct."

Public employees have been insulated by the U.S. Constitution from the capricious use of drug testing. They have challenged drug testing on grounds that it violates the Fourth Amendment's prohibition against reasonable search and seizure. The Supreme Court rendered two decisions on this issue in 1989. In *Skinner* v. *Railway Labor Executives Association* (1989) and *National Treasury Employees Union* v. *Von Raab* (1989), the Court ruled that public employers may require drug testing when a compelling government interest exists that overrides the employee's right to privacy. The Court upheld drug testing when the public's health and safety is at risk or for law enforcement occupations that are involved in drug interdiction activities.

The Fourth Amendment is not applicable to nonprofit and private organizations, which may be restricted by state constitutional provisions, state and local laws regulating drug testing, collective bargaining obligations under the National Labor Relations Act, and federal and state laws prohibiting employment discrimination on the basis of disability. It is important that employers review these laws and regulations before instituting drug testing policies.

The Omnibus Transportation Employee Testing Act, passed by Congress in 1992 and revised in 2005, requires alcohol and controlled substances testing of employees in safety-sensitive jobs in transportation, regardless of which sector they work in. Any employee required to hold a commercial driver's license or who performs other covered safety-sensitive functions is subject to testing. The law requires postaccident and random testing, as well as testing when there is a reasonable suspicion that employees are under the influence of controlled substances.

All organizations should establish alcohol and substance abuse policies, and supervisors should be trained to identify warning signs and instructed to refer employees to EAPs for further evaluation. Some of the common signs of alcohol and substance abuse are mood swings, slurred speech, memory loss, and drowsiness. There may be a decrease in productivity, or increased absenteeism, tardiness, and workplace accidents. Supervisors should be educated in substance abuse issues; they should know how to identify problems and what assistance programs are available to employees.

Alcohol and drug testing policies should provide for written notice to employees that testing will be conducted, explain the procedures that will be used in the testing, employ a chain of custody so that samples are not lost or switched, confirm positive tests with more sensitive tests, and ensure the confidentiality of test results. After an employee has completed rehabilitation and is ready to return to work, the organization should require written documentation from a health care professional that the employee is in recovery and is no longer using drugs or alcohol.

Flexible Job Environment

Changing family structures have focused attention not only on the need for variety in employer-provided benefits but also on the need for more flexible workplace policies. Employers must acknowledge that family life and work have changed, leading to increased stress on employees as they strive to balance the demands of work and family life. Employees who cannot manage these conflicting demands are often less productive, absent more often, and have lower morale.

To better meet the needs of their employees, many organizations have developed flexible work structures. Flextime, voluntary shifts to part-time work, job sharing, flexible leaves, compressed workweeks, and work-at-home or telecommuting opportunities are some of the strategies used to alleviate work and family conflicts.

Another issue affecting morale and motivation at work is career plateauing, or the inability to move up in the organization. As public and nonprofit agencies are confronted with fewer promotional opportunities, more employees have reached career plateaus. To keep employees motivated, organizations must institute HRM policies that focus on the contributions employees can make to the organization without being promoted. Techniques such as job rotation, job enlargement, skill-based pay, and midcareer breaks have been used to maintain employee motivation.

Job rotation allows workers to diversify their activities. Employees perform a variety of tasks by moving to a new activity when their current tasks are no longer challenging or when the work schedule dictates it. They are thus provided with a range of experience that broadens their skills, provides them with a greater understanding of other activities within the agency, and prepares them to assume more responsibility. Job enlargement increases the scope of a job by increasing the number of operations required in it. The job becomes more diverse and challenging because more tasks must be completed. Knowledge or skill-based pay can be used to keep employees motivated by keeping them engaged in learning new skills. Employees are not promoted to a higher-level position, but they are still able to perform new skills and assume new responsibilities.

Typically, midcareer breaks or sabbaticals have been considered one of the benefits of academia. However, many other organizations have begun to realize the benefits of time spent away from work, and some foundations are willing to provide support for sabbaticals.

Not all organizations can afford to give paid leaves to employees, so some have developed alternatives, such as unpaid leave with a guarantee of a job on return or unpaid leave but with tuition reimbursement to defray the costs of schooling.

Outplacement Assistance

Layoffs due to economic hardship, consolidations, mergers, reorganizations, changes in management, and the relocation or elimination of specific positions or programs have resulted in offering outplacement assistance as a benefit. Some of the outplacement assistance benefits include assistance in developing résumés, referrals to employment agencies, and skill and aptitude testing.

Conclusion

Employer-provided benefits play an important role in SHRM. Most organizations offer a variety of benefits, ranging from those mandated by law, such as Social Security, unemployment compensation, and workers' compensation, to those that are optional, such as pensions, health insurance, paid time away from work, educational programs, and a variety of quality-of-life and quality-of-work programs.

The types of benefits that employers provide are key to attracting quality applicants, encouraging loyalty and long-term employment, and motivating and rewarding incumbent employees. The literature on organizational culture and employee retention indicates that different human resources strategies result in different psychological climates that foster varying levels of commitment and retention among employees. This is especially true in the public and nonprofit sectors, where there is often less opportunity for higher pay. Flexible and competitive benefits are one way of attracting candidates and retaining workers (Reddick & Coggburn, 2007). In an analysis of voluntary turnover in state governments, Selden and Moynihan (2000) found that the most significant factor in reducing voluntary turnover is the provision of on-site child care. Flexible benefits that are sensitive to employee needs have the advantage of creating a work climate conducive to high levels of employee commitment, satisfaction, and morale.

Exercise 10.1: Supporting Adoption in Carmel, Indiana

Carmel, Indiana, recently approved a plan to offer each of its five hundred city employees up to five thousand dollars in adoption costs per child, with a maximum of ten thousand dollars per employee. The benefit would cover expenses such as agency and placement fees, court costs, and medical expenses for the birth mother and child. This money would come from the city's employee health care account. Carmel runs its own health insurance program with a third-party administrator. The city's director of human resources, Barbara Lamb, said her department thought about the initiative for a few years: "We're always looking for things we can do in our never-ending quest to make our benefits package as attractive as possible."

Some, however, question whether city employees should receive help from taxpayer dollars. Carmel City councilman Eric Seidensticker said he does not view adoption as an insurance issue, especially not one that should come from city funds. "Just because other companies provide the benefit doesn't mean it's fiscally responsible."

As of 2006, 45 percent of employers offered adoption benefits, according to a survey of 916 employers sponsored by the Dave Thomas Foundation for Adoption, a nonprofit that pushes to increase the number of adoptions nationwide.

Gloria Hochman, communications director for the National Adoption Center, an adoption advocacy group, said that offering adoption assistance benefits is a smart move for employers. Because not many employees take advantage of the option, it provides a relatively low-cost way of making the company a more attractive place to work.

Questions

1. What are the advantages and disadvantages of offering adoption benefits to employees? Is this benefit consistent with SHRM? Explain your response.
2. Do you think employers should offer benefits that apply to a subset of employees and not the general workforce? Explain your position.

Sources: Jarosz (2007); City of Carmel Adoption Assistance Program (2008, January).

Exercise 10.2: Depression Reported by 7 Percent of the Workforce

Government officials tracked depression within twenty-one major occupational categories. They combined data from 2004 through 2006 to estimate episodes of depression within the past year. The information came from the National Survey on Drug Use and Health, which registers lifetime and past-year bouts with depression.

Depression leads to $30 billion to $44 billion in lost productivity annually. Overall, 7 percent of full-time workers battled depression in the past year. Almost 11 percent of personal care workers, whose jobs include child care and helping the elderly and severely disabled with their daily needs, reported depression lasting two weeks or longer.

Workers who prepare and serve food—cooks, bartenders, waiters and waitresses—have the second highest rate of depression among full-time employees: 10.3 percent. Health care workers and social workers were tied at 9.6 percent.

A caveat to the study is that the job categories grouped were quite broad, with employees grouped in the same category with little in common, such as arts, media entertainment, and sports. And a child care worker has a different job from a nursing aide helping an elderly person.

These are the rates of depression per category:

Personal care and service: 10.8%	Transportation and material moving: 6.4%
Food preparation and serving related: 10.3%	Mathematical and computer science: 6.2%
Community and social services: 9.6%	Production: 5.9%
Health care practitioners and technical: 9.6%	Management: 5.8%
Arts, design, entertainment, sports, and media: 9.1%	Farming, fishing, and forestry: 5.6%
Education, training, and library: 8.7%	Protective services: 5.5%
Office and administrative support: 8.1%	Construction and extraction: 4.8%
Building and grounds cleaning and maintenance: 7.3%	Installation, maintenance, and repair: 4.4%
Financial: 6.7%	Life, physical, and social science: 4.4%
Sales and related: 6.7%	Engineering, architecture, and surveyors: 4.3%
Legal: 6.4%	

Questions

1. A significant number of workers responding to the survey were employed in occupations dominated by nonprofit and public service providers. Knowing the incidence of depression in those occupations, what SHRM strategies would you implement to assist the workers?
2. What benefits would you want to promote and implement to attempt to minimize the number of employees suffering from depression?

Sources: Substance Abuse and Mental Health Services Administration (SAMSA) (2007); Freking (2007).

Chapter Questions

1. Why are benefits an important component of SHRM?
2. You have been asked by the HRM director to review the existing benefits program and make recommendations for improvements to the program for the employees in your agency. What factors should you consider, and why?

Online Activities

1. In a small group, each member should select a state, then the groups should discuss the similarities and differences across the states and compare and contrast the workers' compensation policy for each state. Which state provides the best benefits from an employee's perspective? For more information on workers' compensation visit: www.law.cornell.edu/topics/workers_compensation.html.
2. Visit the Employee Benefit Research Institute's Web site. As an employee, what topics discussed concern you the most, and why? From an employer's perspective, what topics concern you the most, and why? Are they the same or different?
3. In the wake of corporate scandals, many private sector employees are finding their pensions at risk, and many public sector pension funds hit by declines in the stock market are underfunded. Visit the Pension Rights Center Web site and the Pension Benefit Guaranty Corporation Web site, and develop a list of five questions to ask your pension administrator about the solvency of your future pension.

CHAPTER ELEVEN

TRAINING AND DEVELOPMENT

After you have read this chapter, you should be able to:

- Define training and discuss why a strategic human resources management (SHRM) approach is important in today's environment
- Define development, and discuss why an SHRM approach is important in today's environment
- Describe different training delivery methods
- Explain the methods used to evaluate training and development activities
- Explain the role of the HR staff in designing and implementing career development programs
- Understand why it is important to integrate career development programs with other HR programs such as performance management, training, selection, and compensation

The demands placed on public and nonprofit organizations keep changing. Agencies are threatened with budget cuts and reductions in staff, while citizens and clients are requesting increases in the level of services or new services. Retiring baby boomers are taking with them the knowledge they have acquired over the years, often leaving less experienced employees to provide services. Changes in technology are requiring new skills. Jobs are requiring employees to assume more challenging responsibilities. The downsizing of managerial staff in many organizations has required that first-level supervisors possess conceptual and communication skills in addition to their technical and applied skills. Higher-level managers must develop skills that will enable them to understand the external environment and develop organizational strategies. Organizations use training and development to improve the skills of employees and develop their capacity to cope with the constantly changing demands of the work environment. Agencies that wish to provide high-quality services must develop strategies to maximize their human resources.

Change has become an inevitable part of organizational life, and organizations must learn how to manage it. Public and nonprofit agencies need to help employees deal with change. Strategic training and development activities must be planned for if agencies are going to thrive.

Technology is being used to communicate with many people across large geographical areas, eliminating the need to be nearby for personal interactions. Demographics are changing; for example, senior citizens are now a significant percentage of the population, and there has been an increase in the number of racial and ethnic minorities employed in public and nonprofit agencies. Jobs have become less specialized, forcing employees to work in teams to deliver services, and productivity needs to be improved despite declining personnel and financial resources.

Changes in goals, the purchase of new equipment, the enactment of new laws or regulations, fluctuations in the economy, increased pressures from stakeholders, and the actions of competitors are some variables that influence change. Today you often find four generations of workers with different priorities and career objectives working together in a unit: traditionalists (those born between 1920 and 1945), baby boomers (born between 1946 and 1964), Generation Xers (born between 1965 and 1980) and millennials (born between 1981 and 2000). Each generation has different characteristics in regard to their training and development needs, as well as their learning styles. As traditionalists and baby boomers begin to retire, departments need to make sure they have employees who can pick up the knowledge and skills that will be lost. They need strategies to retain their knowledge.

As the demands on organizations keep changing, it is critical that organizations implement training and development activities to ensure that their staffs have the requisite knowledge, skills, abilities, and other characteristics (KSAOCs) to confront these new challenges. Training can be targeted to help employees learn new job-specific skills, improve their performance, or adjust their attitudes and behaviors. Often people possess the skill and knowledge to perform the job, but they lack the motivation to exhibit their abilities. Often the need for training results from agency-wide changes. When agencies offer new services, need to comply with new laws or regulations, confront a merger or reductions in staff, or need to learn new technology, an agency-wide training effort is needed. Changes need to be anticipated; training and development needs should be identified, planned for, and budgeted. Developing a comprehensive long-range training program requires a strategic human resources management (SHRM) plan and the recognition that in today's knowledge economy, employees are the most valuable resource. If knowledge is the primary economic enabler, workforce skills are the real capital (Harris, 2001). Agencies wishing to be viable must develop strategies to maximize their human capabilities. Training and development must be integrated into the core human resources management (HRM) functions.

Training and development has been defined as "a planned effort by an organization to facilitate the learning of job-related behavior on the part of its employees" (Wexley & Latham, 1991, p. 3). Training and development programs seek to change the skills, knowledge, or behaviors of employees. Programs may be focused on improving an individual's level of self-awareness, increasing an individual's competence in one or more areas of expertise, or increasing an individual's motivation to perform his or her job well. Sometimes training is targeted to special issues, such as English as a Second Language (ESL), stress management, time management, risk management, health and safety, and customer service. At other times, there may be a need for methods to improve team effectiveness, such as helping teams increase their skills for effective teamwork or assisting them in understanding the dynamics of interpersonal relationships and group behaviors.

It is important to note the word *planned* in Wexley and Latham's definition. Training and development efforts need to be thought out, and the following questions need to be answered:

- How can we develop a comprehensive training plan to address the needs of managers, elected officials, support staff, direct service providers, volunteers, and board members?
- What methods can we use to assess our agency's training needs?
- How can we design and implement the training program?
- What training delivery methods will we use?
- How will we demonstrate that the training budget was well spent?

This chapter first presents the fundamental steps in training. Next, career development is defined, managerial and executive development are discussed, and examples of training and development efforts that have been implemented in public and nonprofit organizations are presented.

The Training Process

The training process consists of the following fundamental steps: developing objectives; developing the curriculum, including determining which methodologies and techniques to use; delivering the training, including a discussion of learning styles; and evaluating training.

Needs Assessment

The first step in the training process is to determine the specific training needs. A need can be defined simply as the difference between what is currently being done and what needs to be done. This difference can be determined by conducting a needs assessment of the skills and knowledge currently required by the position and those anticipated as necessary for the future. A needs assessment is critical to discerning whether performance deficiencies can be eliminated by training. Without a needs assessment, it is possible to design and implement a training program as the solution to a problem that is not related to a training deficiency.

For example, it comes to the attention of higher management that one supervisor rates women and minorities lower than he rates white males, and the ratings are not based on job-related performance criteria. The supervisor is sent to performance evaluation training, where he is exposed to common rating errors and the need for unambiguous performance standards, timely feedback, and so on. Despite the training, the supervisor refuses to use job-related performance criteria when he evaluates his female and minority staff. Performance evaluation training did not resolve the problem; the ratings were deliberately lowered because of prejudice, not because the supervisor lacked knowledge of performance evaluation techniques.

A true needs assessment would have discovered that the problem was different from what was originally thought and that the solution may require a different kind of training. In this case, the supervisor was not deficient in skills; rather, it was his attitude and behaviors that needed to be modified. Multicultural diversity training or training on employment discrimination would have been more appropriate. A needs assessment must be accurate if training is to be successful.

Organizations can determine training needs through a variety of techniques. A strategic job analysis performed prior to the needs assessment is useful. The job analysis should identify the KSAOCs that incumbents need to perform their jobs effectively today and in the future. Surveys and interviews with incumbents and supervisors; performance evaluations that identify performance deficiencies; criticisms or complaints from clients, staff, or personnel in agencies working with employees; changes in pending laws or regulations or operating procedures; and requests for additional training by incumbents can all provide clues as to what training is needed.

The training required to provide the needed KSAOCs should be divided into training that can be learned on the job and training that requires formal instruction. For example, some jobs require certification or licenses mandated by state or federal regulations. More and more states are requiring, for instance, that substance abuse counselors be state certified. In Missouri, paramedics are required to pass a state written exam and attend refresher courses every three years. In New York State, nonprofit residential facilities for delinquent or status offender youths are required to comply with a regulation that new employees must receive training on the HIV virus and AIDS within fifteen days of being hired. In these examples, training is provided by experts outside the agency. Training to acquire other KSAOCs can be provided on the job. Having supervisors explain new policies and procedures or train employees on how to use new equipment can be part of any training plan.

Developing Training Objectives

Training objectives are statements that specify the desired KSAOCs that employees will possess at the end of training. They do not include those things the trainee is expected to know or be able to do before the training. The objectives provide the standard for measuring what has been accomplished and determining the level of accomplishment. For training objectives to be useful, they should be stated as specifically as possible—for example:

> Recreation assistants will be able to apply basic first aid to injured participants, such as cleaning and bandaging scraped knees and elbows.

Supervisors will be able to explain the agency's sexual harassment policy to employees.

Receptionists will be able to transfer and route calls on the new telephone communication system without disconnecting callers.

The development of training objectives should be a collaborative process incorporating input from management, supervisors, workers, and trainers to ensure that the objectives are reasonable and realistic. Three determinants to account for proficiency in any performance component are declarative knowledge or factual knowledge, which is the understanding of things one must do; procedural knowledge, or skill in knowing how to do them; and motivation, or the direction, degree, and persistence of effort in doing them (Guion & Highhouse, 2006).

The development of training objectives should be a collaborative process incorporating input from management, supervisors, workers, and trainers to ensure that the objectives are reasonable and realistic.

Developing the Curriculum

After assessing the training needs and developing objectives, a training curriculum must be developed. Before developing the content and the manner of presenting the information, an analysis of the trainees must be done. This step is critical because trainees often prescribe the kind of training that is likely to be effective. Some of the relevant issues to examine include the following:

- What are the participants' levels of education? For example, classroom instruction may be intimidating for employees with limited formal education.
- What are participants' expectations? Will all participants come to the training with the same concerns?
- What are participants' knowledge levels, attitudes, and relationships with one another?
- Are participants prepared to receive technical instruction?
- Is the training voluntary or imposed from above?
- If the training is mandatory, will the participants be threatened by it?

The answers to these questions will provide some guidance to trainers in developing the curriculum. The curriculum should provide the necessary information and be developed to maximize the imparting of KSAOCs. A number of training techniques can be used to facilitate learning. Informal training, on-the-job, and formal training are the types of training typically used in most public and nonprofit organizations. Other-directed training refers to training methods in which one or more trainers assume responsibility for all instruction processes. Self-directed training refers to training methods where the trainees use workbooks, CD-ROMs, or other methods to target specific skills or knowledge relevant to the job, but the individual is responsible for completing the instruction. Technology-assisted instruction can include elements of both other-directed and self-directed instruction.

One of the first decisions is whether to provide on-the-job instruction or off-the-job classroom instruction, or a combination of the two. On-the-job instruction takes place while the employee is working at the job site. It is usually provided by supervisors, who instruct subordinates in the correct way to perform a task, such as filling out new purchase order requisitions. In another example, a representative from the information technology department demonstrates how to load and set up a new software package.

On-the-job training is useful when employees are expected to become proficient in performing certain tasks or using equipment found at their workstations. Because the training is directly related to the requirements of the job, transferring skills is easier. Employees learn by doing the job, and they get immediate feedback as to their proficiency. Another example of on-the-job training is job rotation, in which employees move from job to job at planned intervals, either within their departments or across the organization. For example, many organizations train managers by placing them in different positions across the agency so that they gain a broad perspective of its operation. To retain the knowledge and skills of retiring workers, some organizations have developed mentoring and shadowing programs to allow younger workers to see experienced workers in action. Another strategy is to encourage older workers to discuss how they carry out projects and what they have learned from their successes and failures. Some organizations have created blogging forums that employees can use to share knowledge, and others have developed communities of practice: a group that comes together to share information about a common problem, issue, or topic. It is a way by which to store and transmit knowledge from one person or a group to another. Another method is using critical incident interviews or questionnaires to document how difficult cases were handled, which also helps to create an institutional memory.

Some KSAOCs are difficult to teach at the work site, so off-site training is necessary. For example, training caseworkers in counseling and listening skills is difficult to do at their desks because other employees not involved in the training would be distracted by the instruction. Off-site training provides an alternative to on-the-job training; employees receive training away from their workstations. In addition to avoiding disruptions to the normal routine at the job site, off-site training permits the use of a greater variety of training techniques.

Discussion of some other common training techniques follows.

Lecture In a lecture format, a trainer presents material to a group of trainees. Lectures have been criticized because the information in them flows in only one direction: from trainer to trainees, who tend to be passive participants. Differences in the trainees' experiences, interests, expertise, and personalities are ignored. Lectures are limited to the transfer of cognitive material. Wexley and Latham (1991) report that lectures are beneficial when they are used to introduce new information or provide oral directions for learning tasks that eventually will be developed through other techniques. Lectures are readily adaptable for use with other training techniques.

Role Playing Role playing gives trainees the opportunity to practice interpersonal and communication skills by applying them to lifelike situations. Participants are expected to act out the roles they would play in responding to specific problems that they may encounter in their jobs. Role playing can be used in a variety of contexts. Law enforcement academies use it when training officers in how to interview crime victims, such as sexually abused children, or witnesses to a crime. Role playing is frequently used in supervisory training in which participants are asked to counsel a problem subordinate who is suspected of having a substance abuse problem.

Case Studies In case studies in training, participants analyze situations, identify problems, and offer solutions. Trainees are presented with a written description of a problem. After reading the case, they diagnose the underlying issues and decide what should be done. Then, as a group, they discuss their interpretations and understanding of the issues and the proposed solutions.

Experiential Exercises Experiential exercises simulate actual job or work experiences. Learning can be facilitated without the cost and risks of making mistakes while on the job. For example, health and safety agencies use experiential exercises to train employees in disaster and emergency planning.

Audiovisual Methods Videos are often used for training in a variety of contexts: to educate employees on legal topics such as sexual harassment, hiring disabled applicants, and using progressive discipline; to teach interpersonal and communication skills; and to simulate situations, for example, a grievance arbitration hearing, permitting trainees to view the process, hear witnesses testify, see the behavior of management and union representatives, and learn how arbitrators conduct proceedings. Videos can be used to demonstrate particular tasks, such as the procedures to follow when apprehending a suspect or extinguishing a chemical fire. They are often used in orientation sessions to present background information on the agency's history, purpose, and goals. This use eliminates the need for trainers or supervisors to repeat themselves for all new employees and ensures that the same information is always presented.

Trainees may also be videotaped. They may be asked to make a presentation or provide performance feedback to colleagues. They may then view the videotape to identify their strengths and weaknesses related to the topic. An advantage of video is that it provides the opportunity to slow down, speed up, or stop the video to review specific activities and ask and answer questions. A disadvantage is that videos can be expensive to purchase or make.

Videos may also be used to disseminate information to a large number of people. Public Health Seattle and King County have launched *Business Not as Usual: Preparing for Pandemic Flu*, a twenty-minute training video to help advance local preparedness efforts. The video has been developed to help businesses, government agencies, and community-based organizations prepare for the ongoing threat of what could be a catastrophic worldwide event. "It's essential that businesses, government, and social service agencies can continue to provide critical services to the public during a severe pandemic flu, which will last for months," said King County executive Ron Sims. "We developed this video to inspire and support local businesses and organizations in their preparations" ("Washington Counties Create," 2008).

Created to assist workplace leaders and staff in their pandemic flu planning efforts, the video describes the threat of pandemic flu and what life might look like during an outbreak. It also shows the benefits of being ready and provides practical tips for creating a plan. "Buildings are left standing, and the roads remain open, but the health impacts of a severe pandemic flu will be felt throughout our community," said David Fleming, director and health officer for Public Health Seattle and King County. "Everyone will need to change how we do business when a pandemic flu comes, so it's important that everyone prepares now."

The video profiles community leaders who share their experience in preparedness. The cast includes local leaders from Washington Mutual, Food Lifeline, Puget Sound Energy, Harborview Medical Center, the Chinese Information and Service Center, and the Seattle Fire Department. King County executive Ron Sims and public health experts also offer their knowledge and experience in disaster preparation. The video is available online at www.metrokc.gov/health/pandemicflu/video. A free DVD can also be ordered, which includes helpful planning materials ("Washington Counties Create," 2008).

Programmed Instruction and Computer-Based Training Programmed and computer-based instruction are self-teaching methods designed to enable trainees to learn at their own pace. Training materials are developed about a specific content area, such as grant writing; learning objectives and instructional goals are specified; and information and training materials are assembled for employees to read and use for practice. At their own pace, employees read the materials or practice the competencies required by the training objectives and then demonstrate what they have learned.

An example of programmed instruction is the *Study Guide for a Budgeting Guide* on a CD-ROM that contains exercises and review questions to reinforce understanding of the strategies and concepts in the book, *A Budgeting Guide* (International City County Managers Association, 2007), which provides an overview of the basic principles of local government budgeting.

Computer-based training uses interactive exercises with computers to impart job skills. Training materials are on the Web or compact disks. Employees read information, instructions, and diagrams or other graphics on the computer screen and then respond accordingly.

An example of computer-based training was developed by the Ohio Secretary of State's Office in collaboration with local boards of elections, Help America Vote Act (HAVA) partners, Pew Charitable Trusts, and the JHET Foundation to developed a poll-worker training program available to all boards of elections in the state. The online training program provides basic information to all poll workers, including voter identification requirements and instructions relating to provisional balloting, as well as information on Ohio's voting systems. The content for all eighty-eight counties is the same, providing uniformity in training standards. However, each board of elections can add tracking features to confirm poll worker participation

("E-Vote: Ohio Unveils Online Poll Worker Training Program," 2008). (You can view the training program at http://www.ohioelectiontraining.com.)

Community Resources Nonprofit and public agencies should be aware of the many community resources that are often available to provide training for nominal costs or even for free. Many health care facilities offer workshops on topics that are targeted to specific clientele groups, such as adolescent or elderly depression, sex abuse, or substance abuse. Chapters of Planned Parenthood offer seminars on boosting self-esteem and preventing teenage pregnancies. Hospice associations offer training on the issues associated with death and dying, and various professional associations also sponsor training classes. Managers and HRM departments need to be on the lookout for relevant community-based training opportunities.

E-learning and Technology New technologies have made it possible to reduce the costs associated with delivering training to employees. New training, delivery, and instruction methods include distance learning, simulations, virtual reality, expert systems electronic support systems, and learning management systems. Digital collaboration is the use of technology to enhance and extend employees' abilities to work together regardless of their geographical proximity. It can include electronic messaging systems, electronic meeting systems, online communities of learning organized by subject where employees can access interactive discussion areas and share training content, Web links, and document handling systems that allow interpersonal interaction. Other technology-based training uses streaming video, simulations, and virtual reality.

Streaming Media Improvements in streaming media technology have made videoconferencing and Webcasting less expensive and more accessible to an increasing number of public and nonprofit organizations. *Streaming media* refers to multimedia distributed over telecommunications networks. Teleconferencing and Webcasts are two training methods that use streaming media. Teleconferencing refers to the synchronous exchange of audio, video, and text between two or more individuals or groups at two or more locations. Two-way video cameras and fiber-optic networks are able to transport interactive live images across large geographical distances.

Webcasting consists of classroom instruction provided online through live broadcasts. It can be live or delayed and requires that individuals have access to computers with streaming video capabilities. The International City/County Management Association (ICMA) provides professional development opportunities through Webcasts and often archives its presentation on CD-ROMs for interested individuals who cannot participate in the live events.

IPMA-HR (International Personnel Management Association for Human Resources) refers to its Webcasting seminars as Webinars, short for Web-based seminar. Webinars are live, interactive ninety-minute seminars that allow attendees to listen to the presenter, view the session presentation online, and ask questions. To participate, all that is needed is a telephone to access the audio portion of the Webinar and a computer with a separate Internet connection to access the visual portion.

Advantages of this method of training include the reduction in time lost in travel to training sites and increased uniformity of training; moreover, the number of individuals who can join in Webcasts is limited to the size of the room.

Simulators Anybody who has taken a driver's education course probably remembers the driving simulator that replicated a car's dashboard, gas, and brake pedals. Simulators are used to bring realism to training situations. For many jobs, like law enforcement, on-the-job training can be too dangerous, such as training police officers when to discharge firearms. So equipment and scenarios that replicate the shadows and noises of alleys are used to train police officers not to overreact. Fire departments use burn buildings, which are designed to withstand repeated fires, to give firefighters opportunities to practice rescue attempts while battling heat and smoke. It would be too expensive and dangerous to burn vacant or decayed buildings. New procedures can be attempted without the risk of endangering human lives.

Virtual Reality Virtual reality is a computer-based technology that provides trainees with a three-dimensional learning experience. Using specialized equipment or viewing the virtual model on a computer screen, trainees move through simulated environments and interact with their components. This allows trainees to experience the perception of actually being in a particular environment.

Police officers in Memphis, Tennessee, who are part of the crisis intervention team (CIT), are trained to interact with mentally ill citizens who may pose a risk to themselves, a police officer, or the community. Members of CIT receive training through virtual hallucination software, which lets trainees step inside the world of mentally ill persons and gives police officers insight into their state of mind. Through earphones and special viewing goggles connected to software, the officer can see and feel what a mentally ill person might experience during an emergency situation.

During training, the officers are asked to perform a task while wearing the earphones and peering into the apparatus. The commands are hardly distinguishable amid various voices and virtual images the software bombards the officer with. This helps officers realize that when they are dealing with someone with a mental illness of that nature, the person might not hear their commands. According to Sam Cochran of the Memphis Police Department and CIT coordinator, "It is one thing for a person to articulate that he is hearing voices and maybe seeing things, but if you don't really understand what that means, or experience what that means, you don't really understand the complexities of trying to interact with an individual who may be experiencing that" (McKay, 2007, p. 38).

Training for public safety is not the only use of virtual reality. Lowes Hotels uses Virtual Leaders, a program that helps participants learn how to be effective in meetings, such as in building alliances or how to get a meeting agenda approved. As trainees attend the simulated meetings, what they say or do not say results in scores that relate to their influence in the meetings (Borzo, 2004; Hoff, 2006).

Multimedia training combines audiovisual training methods with computer-based training, CD-ROM, e-interactive video, the Internet, video, virtual reality, and simulations. It integrates text, graphics, animation, video, and audio, and often the trainee can interact with the content as in virtual reality simulations. Some of the advantages of multimedia training are that it is self-paced, interactive, has consistency of content and delivery, offers unlimited geographical accessibility, can provide immediate feedback, and appeals to multiple senses. It can also be used to test and certify mastery, and provides privacy to the trainee.

Some agencies use blended learning, which combines face-to-face instruction with technology-based delivery and instruction methods. An advantage to blended learning is that it provides more social interaction: learners learn together and discuss and share insights. Live feedback from peers is often preferable to feedback received online.

Considerations for Using Technology Training Advantages of technology training are cost savings due to training accessible to employees at their home or office, the reduced number of trainers needed, and the reduced costs associated with employees traveling to a training location. Some of the disadvantages are that it is expensive to develop, may be ineffective for certain training content, and in some cases can be difficult and expensive to quickly update.

The training methods often depend on what KSAOCs need to be learned or practiced. Another consideration is the best way for the participants to absorb the information. Millennials are likely to be the most comfortable with technology-based training. It is likely that many of their college courses were taught online or in a blended format. To them, a computer is an assumed part of life. Their learning preferences tend toward teamwork, experiential activities, structure, and the use of technology (Oblinger, 2003).

Each training method has advantages and disadvantages that need to be weighed in relation to time constraints, staff resources, the agency budget, targeted audience, and desired outcomes.

Delivering Training

Other issues must be addressed in addition to curriculum. Should the training take place for short periods of time spread over many days (referred to as *distributed practice*), or should it encompass long periods over fewer days (*massed sessions*)? The answer depends on the tasks being trained. At what time of day should the training take place? What size group should be involved? The answer depends on the information being presented or the skills that need to be taught, as well as the aptitudes of the participants and the techniques used. Failing to consider any of these factors can negatively influence the results of training efforts.

In order to arrange the training program to facilitate learning, a number of variables need to be taken into account: the content and amount of information to be learned, whether there is a need for sequencing for the training sessions, whether participants need to practice what they have learned, retention and transfer issues, and whether trainees need the opportunity to practice the trained tasks on the job.

The delivery of the training program is the stage where the trainers and the participants converge. At a well-organized work site, the employees selected for training understand what the objectives of the training are, what they can expect, and how the training will benefit them. This can be connected to the job or to their personal life since adults value relevance to their lives. Patricia Murray, a trainer with the New York State Office of Children and Family Services, notes that one of the most common training errors is not to recognize that the participants are adults with life and work experiences. Murray recommends providing an agenda with training objectives so that participants will know where the training is headed and what methods and techniques will be used. She also

One of the most common training errors is not to recognize that the participants are adults with life and work experiences.

recommends that trainers incorporate the group members' experience into the training. A useful model to consider is that of Kolb (1984), which is based on adults learning from their experience. It is up to the trainers to create a climate in which individual learning styles are recognized and considered in the delivery of the content. This is especially important for employees who resist training or perceive it as a punishment rather than an opportunity.

Research on successful training programs shows that training programs should be designed to address not only substantive content or material but also how people learn, and therefore it needs to incorporate different learning strategies (Agochiya, 2002). Affective learning includes changes in attitudes (affect deals with feelings or emotions). Skill-based learning is the development of procedural knowledge (such as knowing how to make a pizza) that enables effective performance. Cognitive learning refers to the acquisition of different types of knowledge.

As the workforce becomes more diverse, there will be more variation in employees' ability to learn, their learning styles, their basic literacy skills, and their functional life skills. It is more important now than in the past for training to take individual backgrounds and needs into account. Adult learners see themselves as self-directed and expect to be able to answer part of their questions on the basis of their own experiences. Instruction tailored to adult learners allows the trainees the opportunity to participate in the process. The role of the training instructors is to facilitate learning; they use questions, guide the trainees, and encourage two-way communication between the instructor and the class, as well as communication among the class's participants.

Evaluating Training

An evaluation of the training program is necessary to determine whether the training accomplished its objectives. Unfortunately this is often the most neglected aspect of training, especially in the public sector (Bramley, 1996; Sims 1998). Evaluation improves training programs by providing feedback to the trainers, participants, and managers, and it assesses employee skill levels. Evaluations can be used to measure changes in knowledge, levels of skills, attitudes and behavior, and levels of effectiveness at both the individual and agency levels.

Kirkpatrick (1998) identifies four primary levels at which training programs can be evaluated. The first level is measuring the participants' reactions to the training program. He refers to this step as a measure of customer satisfaction. Participants are asked to answer questions such as, "Was the trainer knowledgeable?" "Were the materials and information provided relevant?" "Will the information you learned assist you in performing your job?" Data are gathered through the use of surveys distributed at the conclusion of the training session. Asking these questions provides information on the training program's content and the trainer's skill. (Trainers refer to this step as a "smile meter.")

According to Kirkpatrick (1998), learning has taken place when one or more of the following occurs: attitudes are changed, knowledge is increased, and skills are improved. The second level of evaluation measures whether learning has occurred as a result of attending the training. Did the participants acquire the skills or knowledge embodied in the objectives? Did the training impart the KSAOCs that were deemed important? To determine whether learning took place, participants can be tested on the information presented, follow-up interviews can be conducted, skill demonstrations can be required, or case studies can be developed that test the competencies that were intended to be taught. It is important to note that the methods used should be selected on the basis of the level of mastery desired.

The third level of evaluation seeks to measure the extent to which on-the-job behavioral change has occurred due to the participants' having attended the training program. Evaluation activities are aimed at determining whether the participants have been able to transfer the KSAOCs they learned in training to their jobs. Measurement at this stage is more difficult; it requires supervisors to collect work samples or observe employees' performance. Another technique is to use performance evaluations designed to measure the new competencies.

Kirkpatrick (1998) acknowledges that for change to occur, four conditions must be met: the employee must have a desire to change, must know what to do and how to do it, must work in the right climate, and must be rewarded for changing. Kirkpatrick notes that a training program can accomplish the first two requirements, but the right climate is dependent on the employee's immediate supervisor. Some supervisors may prevent their employees from doing what was taught in the training program; others may not model the behaviors taught in the training program, which discourages employees from changing; some supervisors may ignore the fact that employees have attended the training program, and thereby not support employees' efforts to change; others may encourage employees to learn and apply their learning on the job; and finally some supervisors may know what the employees learned in the training and make sure that the learning transfers to the job. To assist in creating a positive climate so that learning transfers to the job, supervisors should participate in the development of the training program.

The fourth condition, that the employee must be rewarded for changing, can include the feelings of satisfaction, achievement, proficiency, and pride that can occur with successful change. Extrinsic rewards such as praise from the supervisor, recognition from others, and possible merit rewards or promotions can also result.

If the training did not accomplish what it was intended to, the HRM department should assess the conditions the trainee returns to by trying to determine what the problem was and working with line managers to make the necessary changes. Such an assessment could begin with the following questions: What gets in the way? Does the employee who just received training on a new computer system have to go back to the same old equipment? Does the employee reenter a crisis situation and have to revert to the way things were always done? Often so-called training problems are not training problems at all; they are environmental problems. Some of the most common constraints that can hinder the transfer of training on the job are a lack of job-related information provided in the training, inappropriate tools and equipment, lack of needed materials and supplies, and job-relevant authority. For training to be most effective, the organization's culture must support training and hold its supervisors accountable for providing a climate in which employees can transfer what they have learned to their jobs.

The fourth level of evaluation attempts to measure the final results that occurred because employees attended the training. Ideally, training is linked to improved organizational performance. At this level, evaluation is concerned with determining what impact the training has had on the agency. Satisfactory final results can include fewer grievances filed against supervisors, greater employee productivity, a reduction in the number of client complaints, a decrease in workplace accidents, increased dollars raised through fundraising, improved board relations, and less discrimination in the workplace. Some final results are easier to measure than others. For example, the dollars raised from fundraising activities, the number of workplace accidents, or the number of grievances filed can be easily quantified and compared to times before the training. Other final results, like eliminating discrimination, changing attitudes and behaviors, and improving leadership and communication, are less tangible and more difficult to measure. Such results will have to be evaluated in terms of improved morale and attitudes.

Although Kirkpatrick (1998) identifies only four levels of analysis, he emphasizes that as a final step, organizations must determine whether the benefits of the training outweigh its direct and indirect costs. Phillips and Stone (2002) refer to this as level five: return on investment. The results from training programs should be converted to monetary values so cost-benefit analyses can be conducted to determine if a training program should be continued. Examples of direct costs include expenses for instructor fees, facilities, printed materials, and meals. Indirect costs include the salaries of participants who are away from their regular jobs. Has there been a reasonable return on this investment? In other words, was the training worth its costs? Did it accomplish what it was designed to accomplish? Training evaluation reports should present a balance of financial and nonfinancial data.

The potential benefits from evaluating training programs include improved accountability and cost-effectiveness for training programs, improved program effectiveness (Are programs producing the intended results?), improved efficiency (Are they producing the intended results with a minimum waste of resources?), and information on how to redesign current or future programs. Training must be tied to the strategic objectives of the organization. With today's emphasis on outcome measurement, it is critical that training programs be designed to enhance individual, unit, and organizational performance.

Career Development

Fitzgerald (1992) defines training as "the acquisition of knowledge and skills for present tasks, which help individuals contribute to the organization in their current positions . . . . To be successful, training must result in a change in behavior, such as the use of new knowledge and skills on the job" (p. 81). Career development, however, provides the employee with knowledge and skills that are intended to be used in the future. The purpose of career development is to prepare employees to meet future agency needs, thereby ensuring the organization's survival.

Career development is used to improve the skill levels of and provide long-term opportunities for the organization's workforce. Career development programs provide incumbents with advancement opportunities within the organization so that they will not have to look elsewhere.

Taking the time and spending resources to develop employees signals to them that they are valued by the agency. As a result, they become motivated and assume responsibility for developing their career paths (Fitz-enz, 1990).

The focus of career development plans is where the agency is headed and where in the agency incumbents can find future job opportunities. Employees and supervisors should produce a development plan that focuses on employee growth and development. The plan should have measurable development objectives and an action plan. For example, supervisors should review their employees' skills with the job descriptions of higher-level positions within the same job family or of positions within the organization to which the employee might be able to cross over. By comparing employees' skills with the skill requirements of other positions, the employees and supervisors can determine what experience and training might still be needed for advancement or lateral movement. Supervisors should direct employees to relevant training opportunities and, when possible, delegate additional tasks and responsibilities to employees so that they may develop new competencies.

A number of career development programs can be found in the public and nonprofit sectors. Some of them focus on moving employees from clerical or paraprofessional positions into higher-paying administrative jobs. Others focus on developing supervisory and management skills. Examples of some of the programs follow.

Many years ago, the State of Illinois instituted a career development program, the Upward Mobility Program, as part of a master agreement between the American Federation of State, County, and Municipal Employees and the state. Employees can work toward advancement in five major career paths: data processing, office services, accounting, human services, and medical. Employees receive individual counseling to inform them of the career opportunities available and guide them in developing their career plans. Participants take proficiency exams or complete required education and training programs designed to provide the skills and knowledge needed for advancement. The program covers all tuition costs and most mandatory registration fees for classes taken at public institutions and up to $390 a credit hour for undergraduate courses and $435 for master's courses at private universities. When all necessary training and education has been completed, employees are given special consideration when bidding on targeted titles.

Two career tracks are available: credential and certificate. The credential track is for positions that require specific degrees and licenses, such as social worker, licensed practical nurse, or child protective associate investigator.

Employees meet with Upward Mobility Program counselors to discuss the education required for the chosen position. When the employees obtain the necessary degree or license, they are issued a credential.

The certificate track is for positions that require employees to pass written proficiency exams before they can enroll in specific courses. The exam identifies which classes, if any, are required. Employees take courses related to the sections of the exam in which they did not demonstrate proficiency. After employees complete the required course work, they are retested. After they demonstrate proficiency in all segments of the exam, they are issued a certificate. The certificate gives an employee priority for the next vacancy in that title in any agency, even if the title is in another bargaining unit job. Seniority prevails should two or more employees with certificates apply for the same position (State of Illinois, 2008).

Managerial and Executive Development

Problem-solving skills, initiative, the ability to function as a team player, interpersonal skills, and the creativity to seize opportunities are some of the critical skills managers and executives of public and nonprofit agencies need to guide their agencies. Technical experience and competence are no longer enough; public and nonprofit organizations need leaders with the vision to direct and guide their agencies as city, state, and federal funding are cut and donations cannot make up the difference.

Montgomery County, Maryland, estimates that 50 percent of its senior managers will be eligible for retirement in 2010 (Ibarra, 2006; Turque, 2006), and as a result it developed the Manager Development Program (MDP), with the theme "preparing tomorrow's leaders," to enhance the leadership competencies of potential county managers and the occupational mobility of county employees. Faced with impending retirements and the loss in workforce skills and knowledge, the MDP focuses on five leadership competencies: customer service excellence; cultural diversity and inclusiveness; responsiveness and accountability; high standards and ethical behavior; and teamwork, cooperation, and collaboration. (Exhibit 11. 1 presents the definitions.)

The Management Development Program Application package is completed by a candidate, who submits it to his or her immediate supervisor, who submits it to the division manager, who then submits it to the department director. After review, the department director submits it to the Office of Human Resources, which turn submits it to the Leadership

Exhibit 11.1. Montgomery County, Maryland, Leadership Competencies

Customer Service Excellence: requires a commitment to serve others by discovering and meeting or exceeding their needs. This means focusing one's effort on the needs of customers (both internal and external) and partnering with customers to provide the most appropriate value-added services. Individuals who demonstrate this competency employ a determined, proactive approach in responding to the needs of customers and enhancing the quality of the services or products delivered.

Cultural Diversity and Inclusiveness: requires appreciating, respecting, and involving others who may be diverse in some respect, including but not limited to race, religion, sex, disability, age, national origin, sexual orientation, and other protected categories. This competency relates to being sensitive and valuing the unique qualities of each person with whom the employee interacts. This ensures that all employees are afforded equal employment opportunities and all clients/residents are provided equal access to County services and information regardless of their inclusion in any of the aforementioned protected categories. This competency includes compliance with the letter and spirit of the County's EEO and workplace harassment policies.

Responsiveness and Accountability: requires applying the full range of capabilities to successfully accomplish individual and group tasks or assignments in a timely manner. This is demonstrated by responding to challenging circumstances with a positive manner, by applying considerable forethought and commitment. It includes being objective in how you receive and utilize your personal skills and abilities, and the degree to which you accept full responsibility for your actions. Responsiveness and Accountability also include self-managing behaviors such as time and resource management, the organization and prioritization of tasks, timeliness of actions, and balancing multiple work demands.

High Standards and Ethical Behavior: requires doing things in compliance with quality workplace principles and procedures that improve the quality of products or services and result in improvements to measurable and nonmeasurable outcomes. Personally seeks ways to continuously improve process to increase efficiency and/or improve the quality of products and services. This often exceeds the minimal requirements established for tasks or assignments.

Teamwork, Cooperation, and Collaboration: requires actively contributing to the maintenance of cooperative and productive working relationships with subordinates, peers, and managers both in and outside your own department/office, including external customers and partners. It is being part of a team, working to accomplish group or project goals and, ultimately, the County mission . . . as opposed to working separately and/or competitively.

Source: Montgomery County, Maryland, 2008. Used by permission of Montgomery County, Maryland.

Council Selection Panel, responsible for confirming that the MDP candidates meet the program eligibility criteria; assesses applications against the program criteria; and selects the MDP finalists. The Leadership Council Selection Panel conducts a brief interview of each MDP finalist. Candidates are selected based on their demonstrated leadership potential.

Once candidates are selected, individual leadership development plans are created that outline each participant's specific developmental activities. The plans are to be completed within eighteen months of selection. The candidates participate in formal training consisting of courses in the county's supervisory development training track and also attend the Leadership Institute. Each participant and his or her mentor design an experiential learning component—an assignment organized outside the participant's department. The participants are also responsible for self-directed development opportunities that may include participating in additional workshops or training, professional readings, conferences, participating in Toastmasters, getting involved in community volunteer activities, and becoming involved in projects beyond the scope of their immediate jobs (Montgomery County, Maryland, http://www.hca.montgomerycountymd.gov/content/ohr/ResourceLibrary/files/MDP%20Summary.doc).

The Senior Executive Service (SES), established by the Civil Service Reform Act of 1978 and effective as of July 1979, is designed to improve the executive management of the government and to select and develop a cadre of highly competent senior executives with leadership and managerial expertise. Critical leadership competencies expected of SES executives include expertise in leading change, leading people, being results driven, possessing business acumen, and the ability to build coalitions (see Exhibit 11.2).

Exhibit 11.2. Leadership Competencies Expected of Senior Executive Service Executives

Leading Change

Continual Learning. Grasps the essence of new information; masters new technical and business knowledge; recognizes own strengths and weaknesses; pursues self-development; seeks feedback from others and opportunities to master new knowledge.

◆ ◆ ◆

Creativity and Innovation. Develops new insights into situations and applies innovative solutions to make organizational improvements; creates a work environment that encourages creative thinking and innovation; designs and implements new or cutting-edge programs/processes.

◆ ◆ ◆

External Awareness. Identifies and keeps up to date on key national and international policies and economic, political, and social trends that affect the organization. Understands near-term and long-range plans and determines how best to be positioned to achieve a competitive business advantage in a global economy.

◆ ◆ ◆

Flexibility. Is open to change and new information; adapts behavior and work methods in response to new information, changing conditions, or unexpected obstacles. Adjusts rapidly to new situations warranting attention and resolution.

◆ ◆ ◆

Resilience. Deals effectively with pressure; maintains focus and intensity and remains optimistic and persistent, even under adversity. Recovers quickly from setbacks. Effectively balances personal life and work.

◆ ◆ ◆

Service Motivation. Creates and sustains an organizational culture that encourages others to provide the quality of service essential to high performance. Enables others to acquire the tools and support they need to perform well. Shows a commitment to public service. Influences others toward a spirit of service and meaningful contributions to mission accomplishment.

◆ ◆ ◆

Strategic Thinking. Formulates effective strategies consistent with the business and competitive strategy of the organization in a global economy. Examines policy issues and strategic planning with a long-term perspective. Determines objectives and sets priorities; anticipates potential threats or opportunities.

◆ ◆ ◆

Vision. Takes a long-term view and acts as a catalyst for organizational change; builds a shared vision with others. Influences others to translate vision into action.

Leading People

Conflict Management. Identifies and takes steps to prevent potential situations that could result in unpleasant confrontations. Manages and resolves conflicts and disagreements in a positive and constructive manner to minimize negative impact.

◆ ◆ ◆

Leveraging Diversity. Recruits, develops, and retains a diverse high-quality workforce in an equitable manner. Leads and manages an inclusive workplace that maximizes the talents of each person to achieve sound business results. Respects, understands, values, and seeks out individual differences to achieve the vision and mission of the organization. Develops and uses measures and rewards to hold self and others accountable for achieving results that embody the principles of diversity.

◆ ◆ ◆

Integrity/Honesty. Instills mutual trust and confidence; creates a culture that fosters high standards of ethics; behaves in a fair and ethical manner toward others; and demonstrates a sense of corporate responsibility and commitment to public service.

◆ ◆ ◆

Team Building. Inspires, motivates, and guides others toward goal accomplishments. Consistently develops and sustains cooperative working relationships. Encourages and facilitates cooperation within the organization and with customer groups; fosters commitment, team spirit, pride, trust. Develops leadership in others through coaching, mentoring, rewarding, and guiding employees.

Results Driven

Accountability. Assures that effective controls are developed and maintained to ensure the integrity of the organization. Holds self and others accountable for rules

Exhibit 11.2. Leadership Competencies Expected of Senior Executive Service Executives (*continued*)

and responsibilities. Can be relied upon to ensure that projects within areas of specific responsibility are completed in a timely manner and within budget. Monitors and evaluates plans; focuses on results and measuring attainment of outcomes.

◆ ◆ ◆

Customer Service. Balancing interests of a variety of clients; readily readjusts priorities to respond to pressing and changing client demands. Anticipates and meets the needs of clients; achieves quality end products; is committed to continuous improvement of services.

◆ ◆ ◆

Decisiveness. Exercises good judgment by making sound and well-informed decisions; perceives the impact and implications of decisions; makes effective and timely decisions, even when data is limited or solutions produce unpleasant consequences; is proactive and achievement oriented.

◆ ◆ ◆

Entrepreneurship. Identifies opportunities to develop and market new products and services within or outside of the organization. Is willing to take risks; initiates actions that involve a deliberate risk to achieve a recognized benefit or advantage.

◆ ◆ ◆

Problem Solving. Identifies and analyzes problems; distinguishes between relevant and irrelevant information to make logical decisions; provides solutions to individual and organizational problems.

◆ ◆ ◆

Technical Credibility. Understands and appropriately applies procedures, requirements, regulations, and policies related to specialized expertise. Is able to make sound hiring and capital resource decisions and to address training and development needs. Understands linkages between administrative competencies and mission needs.

Business Acumen

Financial Management. Demonstrates broad understanding of principles of financial management and marketing expertise necessary to ensure appropriate funding levels. Prepares, justifies, and/or administers the budget for the program area;

uses cost-benefit thinking to set priorities; monitors expenditures in support of programs and policies. Identifies cost-effective approaches. Manages procurement and contracting.

◆ ◆ ◆

Human Resources Management. Assesses current and future staffing needs based on organizational goals and budget realities. Using merit principles, ensures staff are appropriately selected, developed, utilized, appraised, and rewarded; takes corrective action.

◆ ◆ ◆

Technology Management. Uses efficient and cost-effective approaches to integrate technology into the workplace and improve program effectiveness. Develops strategies using new technology to enhance decision making. Understands the impact of technological changes on the organization.

Building Coalitions

Influencing/Negotiating. Persuades others; builds consensus through give and take; gains cooperation from others to obtain information and accomplish goals; facilitates "win-win" situations.

◆ ◆ ◆

Interpersonal Skills. Considers and responds appropriately to the needs, feelings, and capabilities of different people in different situations; is tactful, compassionate, and sensitive, and treats others with respect.

◆ ◆ ◆

Oral Communication. Makes clear and convincing oral presentations to individuals or groups; listens effectively and clarifies information as needed; facilitates an open exchange of ideas and fosters an atmosphere of open communication.

◆ ◆ ◆

Partnering. Develops networks and builds alliances; engages in cross-functional activities; collaborates across boundaries; and finds common ground with a widening range of stakeholders. Utilizes contacts to build and strengthen internal support bases.

◆ ◆ ◆

Exhibit 11.2. Leadership Competencies Expected of Senior Executive Service Executives (coutinued)

Political Savvy. Identifies the internal and external politics that impact the work of the organization. Approaches each problem situation with a clear perception of organizational and political reality; recognizes the impact of alternative courses of action.

◆ ◆ ◆

Written Communication. Expresses facts and ideas in writing in a clear, convincing, and organized manner

Source: U.S. Office of Personnel Management. Senior Executive Service (2008).

An example of an executive development program in the nonprofit sector is one developed by the YMCA of the USA's national headquarters. Senior managers at the YMCA's 1,966 affiliates across the country nominate people who demonstrate leadership potential to the national headquarters, which selects the participants. This program is designed to develop nonwhite leaders from within the organization. The YMCA assigns participants to a senior-level leader who will coach them through a twelve- to eighteen-month set of courses, retreats, and tests to prepare them to take the next step up the organizational ladder, usually to a chief executive or executive director position (Anft, 2007).

Conclusion

Training is the systematic process by which employees learn the KSAOCs necessary to do their jobs. It is typically associated with improving the performance, knowledge, or skill of employees in their current positions. Career development is viewed as a continuous process consisting of evaluating abilities and interests, establishing career goals, and planning developmental activities that relate to employees' and the organization's future needs. Organizations must recognize the importance of both training and career development planning and provide career enhancement and developmental opportunities.

Given the advances and greater availability in technology, employees and agencies have a greater variety of training methods to select from. E-learning and technology-based training have become more common.

For technology training to be effective, it needs to be designed with good learning principles, match the agency's technology infrastructure, and have top management support. Additional factors to consider include the budget and resources to develop and support the use of new technology, whether trainees are geographically dispersed and whether travel costs related to training are high, whether trainees are comfortable using technology, whether employees have difficulty making the time for scheduled training programs, and if there is sufficient time for practice, feedback, and assessment. Traditional training methods such as classroom instruction and behavior modeling can be delivered to trainees rather than requiring them to come to a central training location.

Once organizations have put together career development programs, they must maintain and update these programs. Career development should be linked with other HRM strategies, such as succession planning, performance evaluations, quality management initiatives, and new-employee orientation. Managers should be held accountable for developing their individual employees. Providing feedback and coaching to their staff should be one of their main responsibilities.

Agencies that are serious about training and career development should continue to monitor, evaluate, and revise their training and career development programs. To be successful, training and career development programs need to be fully integrated with the organization's strategic focus and SHRM system. Increased skill acquisition will be effective only if agencies accurately identify and predict the types of KSAOCs and positions that will be required. If career paths are identified, training and development programs must be used to move employees along the path. New approaches to training need to be considered, and organizational reward structures should encourage individual growth and development that benefits both the employee and the organization. New technologies have influenced the delivery of training, training administration, and training support.

Exercise 11.1: Improving Leadership Prospects for Women at Jewish Charities

Advancing Women Professionals and the Jewish Community was created in 2001 to help eliminate the gender gap in leadership, open up executive training programs to more women, and put pressure on Jewish groups to adopt flexible work schedules that help both men and women better balance their work and family obligations.

A study in 2003 found that although women made up 70 percent of Jewish federations' professional staffs, only two of the forty largest federations were led by women. One of the obstacles to women's advancement identified in the study was the misperception that women are not tough enough to lead, yet women who exhibit toughness are seen as too abrasive. Federation leaders also questioned women's ability to solicit major annual gifts from men. Another barrier was that weak HRM systems could not give women enough support in balancing their work and personal obligations.

Women working in Jewish organizations are recruited to participate in an executive development program at the Mandel Center for Leadership Excellence at Columbia University. The participants are full-time professionals working in Jewish federations in mid- to senior-level positions and are a step or two away from CEO consideration. The participants are required to complete a two-year program that connects Jewish values to leadership skills, develops management abilities, and provides coaching from executives from large federations.

Question

1. If a similar development opportunity were available to you, would the organization you work for encourage you to participate in it? Would you be willing to complete a two-year program in addition to your work responsibilities and other personal responsibilities you might have?

Source: Siska (2007).

Exercise 11.2: Training First Responders in Water Rescue

Different county governments have different training protocols for rescuing individuals who fall out of a boat, slip off a bridge, or drive into a pond. Some rescuers jump in. Others do not.

In one case, an off-duty paramedic saw a car go into a pond and called for help; he was not trained to do any more. An ambulance arrived, but no one on it was trained to perform a water rescue either. They had to wait for firefighters to arrive; and then it was too late: the man drowned. Paramedics in that county were not trained to perform rescues, because water rescue training was not offered at emergency medical school. As a result of this incident, the department decided to make some changes: ambulances will add flotation devices and rope lines as standard equipment so first responders can throw them to people in the water and pull them to shore if necessary.

Neighboring local governments have paramedics who perform water rescues. In those communities, every paramedic, emergency medical technician, and firefighter has been cross-trained and can perform water rescues.

Questions

1. If you were the department director, are there other strategies you would implement besides adding rescue equipment to ambulances in an attempt to prevent another drowning when an ambulance arrives on the scene?
2. Think about your current job or a job you have held in the past. In what skills would you like or have liked to be cross-trained in? Develop a training and development plan for you. What KSAOCs are you seeking? Through what methods of delivery would you acquire them? How long do you think it would take to become cross-trained? How expensive would it be for you or the organization you work for?

Source: Morelli (2007).

Chapter Questions

1. Discuss why training must be a strategic imperative in public and nonprofit organizations.
2. What kinds of analyses need to be made to determine the training needs of an organization, individual employees, or an entire unit?
3. In small groups, share your experiences with training. What are some of the advantages and disadvantages of the training methods and delivery discussed in this chapter? Do you think employees of different generations have different training preferences? Explain why.

Online Activities

1. Visit the American Society for Training and Development Web site. What training topics are discussed there? Which topics are the most interesting to you? Explain why. Do you believe there is a need for a professional society devoted to training and development activities?
2. Visit the Web sites of the International City/County Management Association and the NPO Net: For and About Chicago Area Nonprofits. What kinds of professional development programs are available through those organizations? Which development programs would you be most likely to participate in, and why? What types of training and development methods are most consistent with your learning style?

CHAPTER TWELVE

LABOR-MANAGEMENT RELATIONS

Collective Bargaining in the Public and Nonprofit Sectors

After reading this chapter, you should be able to:

- Understand the elements of labor-management relations and collective bargaining and their importance to strategic human resources management
- Describe what a union is and why employees join unions
- Understand the differences in collective bargaining rights for federal employees, state and local employees, and nonprofit employees
- Understand trends and issues in labor-management relations

The economic, technological, social, cultural, and legal changes affecting the workplace have provoked changes in labor-management relations. The current economic distress, leading to threats of downsizing and privatization, along with the public's concern about waste and inefficiency, requires that unions and employers reexamine their structure and systems to see how they can provide more effective services. To remain competitive, management and unions must adopt new approaches and attitudes for resolving conflicts. Together, they must creatively resolve problems and develop solutions advantageous to both.

Collective bargaining has been defined as a process that obligates management and union representatives to negotiate in good faith in an attempt to reach an agreement concerning issues that affect employees. While many employers dislike having to recognize and negotiate with employee unions, other employers appreciate the continuity and stability that collective bargaining can bring to an organization. Issues that have been negotiated and are part of a collective bargaining agreement are often resolved for the length of the contract. Collective bargaining encompasses the execution, interpretation, and enforcement of the negotiated contract.

This chapter presents the legal framework of collective bargaining, beginning with the history of private sector collective bargaining, because the laws permitting public employee unionism are often patterned after those granting private sector employees the right to bargain; furthermore, nonprofit collective bargaining is governed by the same laws and rulings as collective bargaining in the private sector. This history is followed by an overview of the laws relevant to collective bargaining in the nonprofit and public sectors and then discussion of the concepts and practices that constitute the collective bargaining process, including bargaining unit determination, the selection of a bargaining representative, unfair labor practices, the obligation to negotiate, union security devices, the scope of collective bargaining, management rights, impasse resolution, striking, and grievance arbitration. Distinctions between public and nonprofit labor relations are noted, and the chapter concludes with a discussion of the future of collective bargaining.

The History of Private Sector Collective Bargaining

Private sector labor-management relations were initially governed by the National Labor Relations Act of 1935 (NLRA). The NLRA permitted employees to organize and join unions for the purposes of collective bargaining. It addressed the rights of employees in the areas of union security agreements, picketing, and striking. Employer unfair labor practices were defined, as were the criteria for an appropriate bargaining unit, the selection of a bargaining representative, and the enforcement of the act. Under this law, employers were required to bargain in good faith with employee unions and could be cited for unfair labor practices if they attempted to interfere with the establishment of such unions. The NLRA established the National Labor Relations Board (NLRB) as the administrative agency responsible for enforcing the provisions of the act.

In 1947, Congress amended the NLRA with passage of the Labor-Management Relations Act (LMRA), which articulated union unfair labor practices. In 1959, Congress passed the Labor-Management Reporting and Disclosure Act, which established a bill of rights for union members, specifying internal union election procedures and financial reporting disclosure requirements for unions and union officers. It also added restrictions on picketing, prohibiting "hot cargo" clauses, and closed certain loopholes in the LMRA. (*Hot cargo agreements* are contract provisions in which the employer promises not to handle products that the union finds objectionable, because they have been produced by nonunion labor or at a plant on strike.) These three acts have been consolidated and are now referred to as the Labor-Management Relations Act, 1947, as amended. Federal and state governments are excluded from coverage by the act. Nonprofits became covered in the 1970s.

The NLRB can direct elections and certify results only in the case of employers whose operations affect commerce. The LMRA applies to any employer or unfair labor practice affecting commerce. Therefore, the statute has a broad scope, covering most employers (Feldacker, 1990).

Because the courts have broadly interpreted "affect commerce," the NLRB could theoretically exercise its powers to enforce the act for all employers whose operations affect commerce. However, the board has chosen not to act in all cases. In 1950, it decided to distinguish between businesses that interrupt the flow of interstate commerce and those that are so small that a dispute would probably have no impact on the flow of commerce. It set monetary cutoff points, or standards, that limit the exercise of its power to cases involving employers whose effect on commerce is substantial. The board's requirements for exercising its power or jurisdiction are called *jurisdictional standards* or *jurisdictional yardsticks*. These standards are based on the yearly amount of business done by the employer or the yearly amount of its sales or purchases. The standards are stated in terms of total volume of business and are different for different kinds of enterprises (Commerce Clearing House, 1990; Feldacker, 1990; National Labor Relations Board, 1991). Exhibit 12.1 presents the board's current jurisdictional standards.

Exhibit 12.1. National Labor Relations Board Jurisdictional Standards in Effect as of July 1990

Nonretail businesses	$50,000 total annual revenues
Office buildings	$100,000 total annual revenues
Retail enterprises	$500,000 total annual volume of business
Public utilities	$250,000 total annual volume of business or $50,000 direct or indirect outflow or inflow
Newspapers	$200,000 total annual volume of business
Radio, telegraph, television, and telephone enterprises	$100,000 total annual volume of business
Hotels, motels, and residential apartment houses	$500,000 total annual volume of business
Transportation enterprises, links, and channels of interstate commerce	$50,000 total annual income
Transit systems	$250,000 total annual volume of business
Taxicab companies	$500,000 total annual volume of business
Private universities and colleges	$1,000,000 gross annual revenues
Symphony orchestras	$1,000,000 gross annual revenues
Law firms and legal assistance programs	$250,000 gross annual revenues
Employers that provide social services	$250,000 gross annual revenues
Privately operated health care institutions, defined as hospitals, convalescent hospitals, health maintenance organizations, health clinics, nursing homes, extended care facilities, or other institutions devoted to the care of the sick, infirm, or aged	$250,000 total annual volume of business

Nursing homes, visiting nurses' associations, and related facilities associations	$100,000 total annual volume of business Regarded as single employer in that annual business of all association members is totaled to determine whether any of the standards apply
Enterprises in the Territories and the District of Columbia	Jurisdictional standards apply in the Territories; all businesses in the District of Columbia come under National Labor Relations Board jurisdiction
National defense	Jurisdiction is asserted over all enterprises affecting commerce when their operations have a substantial impact on national defense, whether or not the enterprises satisfy any other standard

Collective Bargaining in Nonprofit Organizations

Originally the NLRB excluded nonprofit employers from NLRA coverage. However, in the 1970s, the board asserted jurisdiction over nonprofits that had a "massive impact on interstate commerce" or those that met certain financial criteria, such as nursing homes with revenue over $100,000, visiting nurses' associations, and similar facilities as applied to profit-making nursing homes (Drexel Homes, 1970).

In August 1974, Congress amended the LMRA to bring nonprofit health care institutions under the law's coverage. At that time, Congress added Section 2(14), which defines "health care institutions" to include hospitals, nursing homes, and other health care facilities without regard for whether they are operated for profit. The health care amendments indicated that Congress had no objection to bringing nonprofit employers under federal labor law.

Two years later, in 1976, the NLRB began to treat nonprofit and charitable institutions the same way it treated businesses operated for profit. If a nonprofit employer was sufficiently involved in the interstate flow of money or goods and a labor dispute might disrupt that flow of commerce, the board would take jurisdiction. The board established a jurisdictional standard of $250,000 annual revenue for all social service agencies other than those for which there is another specific standard application for the type of activity in which the organization is engaged. For example, the specific $100,000 standard still applies for a nursing home (Feldacker, 1990).

The NLRB asserts jurisdiction over nonprofit service organizations that provide services to or for an exempt governmental agency such as Head Start, child care services, and medical clinics supported by state or federal funds (Feldacker, 1990). Some of these agencies have argued that they are excluded by the NLRA by the exemption for government agencies. The board holds that such agencies are covered by the act, even though they are government funded, if they retain independence in labor-management matters, such as establishing the wages, hours, and working conditions of their employees. The sole standard for taking jurisdiction is whether the contractor has "sufficient control over the employment conditions of its employees to enable it to bargain with a labor organization as its representative." The board looks closely at the nature of the relationship between the government institution and the contractor.

An interesting issue of jurisdiction surfaced in *National Labor Relations Board* v. *Catholic Bishop of Chicago* (1979). The Supreme Court held that the NLRB cannot assert jurisdiction over church-operated schools because such jurisdiction would violate the First Amendment establishment of freedom of religion and the separation of church and state. The Court held that the religious and secular purposes of church-sponsored schools are so intertwined that the board's jurisdiction would unconstitutionally introduce the board into the operations and policies of the church.

The board does, however, assert jurisdiction over church-operated, nonprofit social agencies such as nursing homes, hospitals, and child care centers because they function essentially the same as their secular counterparts: they receive government financial support, they are regulated by the state along with other nonprofit social agencies, and their activities only tangentially relate to the sponsoring organization's religious mission (Feldacker, 1990).

Collective Bargaining in the Federal Government

The Civil Service Reform Act of 1978 (CSRA) governs labor relations in the federal sector. It covers most employees of the executive agencies of the United States, including the Library of Congress and the Government

Printing Office. The exclusions include federal employees working for the Government Accountability Office (GAO), Federal Bureau of Investigation (FBI), National Security Agency (NSA), Central Intelligence Agency (CIA), Federal Labor Relations Authority, Federal Service Impasses Panel, Tennessee Valley Authority (TVA), Foreign Service of the United States, U.S. Secret Service and U.S. Secret Service Uniformed Division, Department of State, U.S. Information Agency, and Agency for International Development and its successor agency or agencies, the U.S. Postal Service, and employees engaged in administering a labor-management relations law. TVA employees and postal employees are covered by other statutes. TVA employees are covered by the Employment Relationship Policy Act of the New Deal and have been covered since 1935. The Postal Reorganization Act of 1970 granted collective bargaining rights to postal employees under the NLRA. However, unlike private sector employees, postal employees are denied the right to strike. Employees working for the GAO, FBI, NSA, and CIA have no statutory authority to engage in collective bargaining.

With the creation in 2003 of the Department of Homeland Security, many federal employees who had collective bargaining rights saw those rights slip away. On January 7, 2002, President Bush issued Executive Order 13252 that prevented unions from organizing the following subdivisions in the Department of Justice, citing national security concerns: U.S. Attorneys' Offices, Criminal Division, INTERPOL-U.S. Central Bureau, the National Drug Intelligence Center, and the Office of Intelligence Policy and Review. James M. Loy, the head of the Transportation Security Administration, successfully blocked attempts to unionize airport screeners, also citing that collective bargaining rights could jeopardize national security. Both the Senate and the House have introduced bills to grant screeners collective bargaining rights. At this time, however, the rights do not exist.

Title VII of the CSRA enacted the provision known as the Federal Service Labor-Management Relations Statute, which created the Federal Labor Relations Authority (FLRA) to administer and enforce the CSRA. The FLRA is governed by three bipartisan members who are appointed by the president with the advice and consent of the Senate. The members are appointed for staggered five-year terms.

Dissatisfied parties may appeal rulings made by the FLRA to the U.S. Court of Appeals. The authority of the FLRA is similar to the NLRB. It determines appropriate bargaining units, supervises and conducts union elections, conducts hearings and resolves allegations of unfair labor practices, prescribes criteria and resolves issues relating to determining a compelling need for agency rules or regulations, resolves exceptions to arbitrators' awards, and takes such other actions as are necessary and appropriate to administer the provisions of Title VII of the CSRA.

Federal employees may not bargain over wages and benefits or prohibited political activities. The scope of negotiable issues is more restrictive for federal employees than for employees at other levels of government, nonprofits, and the private sector. For example, federal employees may not strike. In 1980, President Reagan fired striking air traffic controllers.

Collective Bargaining in State and Local Governments

Many states have passed legislation that grants state and local government employees the right to participate in collective bargaining with their employers. Other states permit public employees only the right to "meet and confer" with a public employer. Still other states lack statutes that permit or recognize the right of public employees to join unions or bargain with public employers. The duty to meet and confer provides unions with the right to discuss with the public employer proposals establishing the terms and conditions of employment. However, employers are free to ignore the views of the unions and make unilateral decisions as to the terms and conditions of employment.

Many state statutes are referred to as *comprehensive statutes*. These statutes are modeled after the Labor-Management Relations Act, 1947, as amended. Like the LMRS, they guarantee public employees the right to join or form labor unions or refrain from joining unions; they also establish procedures for the selection of employee representatives, define the scope of bargaining and unfair labor practices, address union security provisions, permit or prohibit strikes, prescribe remedies to resolve contract negotiation impasses, provide mechanisms for contract grievance resolution, and establish an administrative agency to oversee the law. These statutes are referred to as public employee relations acts (PERAs).

Concepts and Practices of Collective Bargaining

This section provides explanations of the issues introduced in the preceding overview, along with specific examples to illustrate the concepts of collective bargaining as they are applied in the federal, state, and local governments and in the nonprofit sector. For purposes of this discussion, all of the labor-management collective bargaining acts—private or nonprofit (LMRA), federal (LMRS), and state (PERAS)—will be referred to generically as labor-management relations acts.

Labor-management relation acts designate or create agencies to provide oversight of the acts and to administer relations among employers, employees, and unions. The NLRB governs private and nonprofit labor relations, and the FLRA provides oversight for the federal government. Although the names of these administrative agencies tend to vary across the states (New Jersey's version is the Public Employment Relations Commission, the Illinois version is known as the Illinois State Labor Relations Board, and Florida calls its board the Public Employee Relations Commission), they are often referred to as public employee relations boards (PERBs).

Unit Determination

The labor-management relations acts generally define the procedures for designating the employees' representative or union. Before a union can represent a group of employees, the constituency of the group must be determined. The group of employees that can potentially be represented by one representative at the bargaining table is called the *appropriate bargaining unit.* The acts contain guidelines for the determination of the appropriate unit and procedures for determination.

The labor-management relations acts exclude some general categories of employees from a bargaining unit. For example, managerial and confidential employees are excluded as a matter of policy because their interests are more closely aligned with management than with the bargaining unit. Managerial employees are employed by an agency in positions that require or authorize them to formulate, determine, or influence the policies of the agency. Confidential employees are those who assist the individuals who formulate, determine, or execute labor policy. Included in this category are employees who have access to information about labor relations or who participate in deliberations of a labor relations nature and are required to keep that information confidential from the labor organization representing a bargaining unit.

Professional and technical employees, and in some cases supervisors, may also be excluded from an overall bargaining unit, but they are still entitled to representation as their own units. A supervisor is an individual who has the authority to, in the interests of the agency, hire, direct, assign, promote, reward, transfer, furlough, lay off, recall, suspend, discipline, or remove employees and to adjust their grievances or recommend such action. However, there is an exception in the case of nurses as supervisors. On October 3, 2006, the NLRB ruled that nurses with full-time responsibility for assigning fellow hospital workers to particular tasks are supervisors under federal labor law and thus not eligible to be represented by unions. In the *Oakwood Healthcare, Inc. and International Union United Automobile, Aerospace and Agricultural Implement Workers of America (UAW), AFL-CIO* (2006) decision, the board changed course and now interprets Section 2(11) in a way that makes it easier for health care employers to argue that charge nurses are statutory supervisors who should not be included in a bargaining unit of registered nurses. The *Oakwood* decision focused primarily on three of the Section 2(11) factors: assign, responsibly direct, and independent judgment. This decision may have broad applications to supervisory employees in all private industries that fall under the Labor-Management Relations Act, 1947, as amended.

Professional employees perform work of a predominantly intellectual, nonstandardized nature. The work must require the use of discretion and independent judgment, and knowledge that is customarily acquired through college or university attendance. Technical employees perform work of a technical nature that requires the use of independent discretion and special training. They may have acquired their training in college, in technical schools, or through on-the-job training.

Public safety officers often receive special treatment. Some states have separate statutes for police officers and firefighters, and others include them in municipal or general statutes. Some states have statutes that require police officers to be in units composed only of police officers, and others require the same for firefighters. This special treatment is meant to ensure the community's safety. In an effort to standardize collective bargaining for public safety officers, on July 17, 2007, the House of Representatives passed the Public Safety Employer-Employee Cooperation Act by a vote of 314 to 97. It requires all state and local governments to engage in collective bargaining with their police, fire, and EMS personnel. The act would establish a national collective bargaining system for personnel to be governed by the FLRA. If enacted, state legislatures would have time to pass or modify their own public safety collective bargaining statutes. If those statutes meet certain minimum criteria as outlined in the act, the FLRA would abstain from exercising jurisdiction over those particular states. If, however, a state does not pass or amend its statute to be compliant, the FLRA would exercise direct jurisdiction over the state's public safety collective bargaining. In the Senate, the Public Safety Employer-Employee Cooperation Act was introduced by Senators Judd Gregg (R-New Hampshire) and Ted Kennedy (D-Massachusetts) as S. 2123. If supported by the Senate and signed into law by President Bush, it would establish a national system of minimum collective bargaining standards for most of the nation's public safety officers, including law enforcement officers, firefighters, and other emergency service personnel employed by state and local governments.

Selection of a Bargaining Representative

The labor-management relations acts also contain specific procedures for selecting an exclusive bargaining representative. *Exclusive recognition* is the term applied when one union has the right and responsibility to speak on behalf of all employees in the bargaining unit. Voluntary recognition by the employer is the easiest way of designating a union. It is available only if the union can demonstrate support by a majority of employees in the unit, usually achieved by having employees sign recognition cards authorizing the union to represent them in collective bargaining.

If voluntary recognition is not achieved or it is challenged by a claim of majority representation by another representative organization, a secret ballot election may be held to select the exclusive bargaining representative. The administrative agencies have the authority to regulate these representation elections, which are also subject to judicial review. Some states insist that a secret ballot election be held to determine employee representation. A union that has been voluntarily recognized by the employer as the exclusive representative possesses the same rights as a union that has been certified through a formal certification election.

The procedures for a certification election are similar across the nonprofit, federal, and state sectors. Unions must request that employees in the proposed unit sign recognition cards authorizing the union to represent them. The union must obtain a "show of interest" by the unit members, which is not less than 30 percent for nonprofits, the federal government, and the majority of states. However, if the employer chooses not to voluntarily recognize a union, an election will be held. If the union receives 51 percent of the votes, it will be recognized as the exclusive representative.

Union Security

Labor-management relations acts contain provisions for union security devices that address the degree to which unions can compel union membership or mandate the payment of dues to support their activities. Most contracts in the nonprofit and private sectors contain some kind of union security provision, and union security provisions are articulated in each state's public employee relations act. Neither the LMRS nor the Postal Reorganization Act of 1970 permits any form of required membership as a condition of employment. Federal employees are free not to join unions. The different types of union security provisions are explained in the following paragraphs.

Most contracts in the nonprofit and private sectors contain some kind of union security provision, and union security provisions are articulated in each state's public employee relations act.

Closed Shop Under a closed shop agreement, an employer was not permitted to hire anyone who was not already a member of the union. Closed shop arrangements became illegal in the private sector under Section 8(a)(3) of the Labor-Management Relations Act, 1947, as amended. These arrangements have always been prohibited in the public sector because they infringe on the employer's prerogative in determining employment standards, as well as restrict the selection of new employees.

Union Shop Under a union shop provision, all unit employees are required to join the exclusive bargaining representative after being hired. An employer operating under this agreement may hire employees who are not members of the union. However, the nonunion employees must join the union within the period specified in the agreement, which is usually thirty days, and remain a member of the union as a condition of continued employment. Compulsory membership by a certain date after employment prevents free riders: employees who are not union members but benefit from union negotiations without paying their share of the union's operating expenses. Free riders are a particular problem in the federal government, where union shops are prohibited.

Agency Shop Under an agency shop agreement, all unit employees, whether or not they are union members, are required to pay a service fee to the exclusive bargaining representative. The service fee is designed to make nonmembers pay their share of the expense of representing all of the unit employees.

Fair Share The fair share provision resembles the agency shop provision in that employees must pay a proportion of regular union dues to cover the exclusive representative's costs for collective bargaining. However, unlike agency shops, nonbargaining activities are not funded by nonunion members.

Maintenance of Membership Under maintenance-of-membership provisions, employees are not required to become union members. However, those who join a union must remain members and pay membership dues to the union until the contract expires.

Dues Checkoff Because unions depend on the fees collected from employees for their support, they must have a reliable and continuous system for collecting membership dues. A dues checkoff mechanism permits unions to collect fees from employers, who withhold the union dues from the employees' paychecks and forward the funds to the union. This is a more efficient process than collecting fees from individual members. Dues checkoff is typically combined with one of the other union security provisions.

Right-to-Work States The following states are known as right-to-work states: Alabama, Arizona, Arkansas, Florida, Georgia, Idaho, Iowa, Kansas, Louisiana, Mississippi, Nebraska, North and South Carolina, North and South Dakota, Tennessee, Texas, Utah, Virginia, and Wyoming. According to right-to-work laws, individuals cannot be forced to join or pay dues to a labor union. Furthermore, no worker need be a union member to acquire or retain employment. In the nonprofit and private sectors, Section 14(b) of the LMRA permits states to outlaw various forms of union security provisions: "Nothing in this Act shall be construed as authorizing the execution or application of agreements requiring membership in a labor organization as a condition of employment in any State or Territory in which such execution or application is prohibited by State or Territorial law." This provision means that an employer can reject a union's demands for the recognition of union security arrangements that are illegal under state law.

Unfair Labor Practices

Labor-management relations acts enumerate specific unfair labor practices that may be committed by the employer, the union, or both. Unfair labor practices are actions by either the employer or the union that interfere with employees' exercise of statutory rights. The administrative agencies generally have exclusive jurisdiction to hear unfair labor practice suits filed by an employee, the employer, or the union, which is subject to limited judicial review.

Unfair labor practice provisions are intended to protect the rights of employees, unions, and employers by prohibiting discrimination, interference, and coercion by both employers and unions. For unions, unlawful activities would constitute interference with the employer's management duties and rights. Charges of employer discrimination, interference, and coercion often pertain to the rights of employees to engage in union activity and the rights of unions to represent their members.

The Scope of Collective Bargaining

The scope of collective bargaining constitutes which subjects are negotiable. Specific topics have generally been classified on a case-by-case basis into three types: mandatory, permissive, and illegal.

Mandatory Topics Mandatory topics of bargaining are topics that the laws (whether private, nonprofit, federal, or state) require management and labor to bargain over. Either side can bargain to impasse on a mandatory topic if they can demonstrate that they made a good-faith effort to reach agreement on it. Mandatory topics in both the nonprofit and for-profit sectors typically include wages, salaries, fringe benefits, and working conditions. Mandatory topics for federal employers and employees are restricted to conditions of employment that affect working conditions, including personnel policies, practices, and other matters, whether established by rule, regulation, or otherwise. Federal employees may not bargain over wages or fringe benefits.

The statutes that permit collective bargaining by public employees vary in what they consider to be mandatory topics of bargaining. For example, Massachusetts has a requirement that

> the employer and the exclusive representative shall meet at reasonable times, including meetings in advance of the employer's budget-making process, and shall negotiate in good faith with respect to wages, hours, standards or productivity and performance, and any other terms and conditions of employment, including without limitation, in the case of teaching personnel employed by a school committee, class size and workload but such obligation shall not compel either party to agree to a proposal or make a concession; provided however that

in no event shall the right of any employee to run as a candidate for or to hold elective office be deemed to be within the scope of negotiation [Massachusetts General Laws Annotated, Chapter 150E, Section 6].

Notice that this law requires negotiation over standards of performance and productivity, and class size and workload for teachers, as well as the more standard issues. Some states, such as Nevada, are even more explicit in defining and articulating mandatory subjects.

Permissive Topics A permissive topic is a matter related to optional policy that may be bargained over if there is mutual agreement between labor and management, but neither side may unilaterally insist on such bargaining. Neither management nor labor has to bargain over permissive topics. In many states, permissive topics of bargaining include insurance benefits, retirement benefits, productivity bargaining, and grievance and discipline procedures. Permissive topics in the federal sector under Section 7106 include, at the election of the agency, work projects, tour of duty, or the technology, methods, and means of performing work. Education benefits could be considered a permissive topic. Because they are not wages, hours, or working conditions, they would not be considered mandatory topics. However, the employer and union could elect to negotiate them.

Deciding whether an issue is mandatory or permissive has generally been accomplished on a case-by-case basis. Administrative agencies and the courts have devised varying and flexible tests rather than establishing fixed rules. The decision is difficult because many issues affect both the terms and conditions of employment and management policymaking. Examples of this dilemma surface frequently in teaching and social work. Teachers want to negotiate issues such as class size, curriculum, teaching loads, and nonteaching duties and responsibilities. Social workers want to bargain over caseload, treatment alternatives, or the process of deciding what services are appropriate for clients. These issues address working conditions, but they are also dimensions of management policy.

Illegal or Prohibited Topics Illegal or prohibited topics cannot be bargained, and any agreement to bargain with respect to illegal topics will be void and unenforceable. Instead, illegal topics typically must be resolved through the legislative process. Examples of illegal or prohibited subjects of bargaining at the federal and state levels are the negotiation of the organization's objectives, how the objectives should be implemented, the agency's organizational structure, and employment standards. Issues regarding retirement, job qualifications, selection, placement, promotion criteria, and the functions of the civil service commission or merit system are often excluded from bargaining in the public sector. The Iowa Public Employee Relations Act specifically excludes the public retirement system from the scope of mandatory bargaining. Other states exclude the merit system. Illegal topics for nonprofit and private organizations could include a closed shop union security provision or contract terms in violation of state or federal laws. For example, contract clauses that permit unions to discriminate against persons of color or against members of certain religious groups would be illegal because they violate Title VII of the 1964 Civil Rights Act and many state fair employment practice acts.

Employer and Management Rights

The missions of public sector organizations are decided by legislative bodies. The managers responsible for the performance of these functions are accountable to those legislative bodies and ultimately to the people. Major decisions made in bargaining with public employees are inescapably political because they involve critical policy choices. The matters debated at the bargaining table are not simply questions of wages, hours, and vacations. Directly at issue are questions of the size and allocation of the budget, tax rates, the level of public services, and the long-term obligation of the government. These decisions are political in the sense that they are to be made by elected officials who are politically responsible to the voters. They are generally considered legislative decisions and not subject to delegation (Edwards, Clark, & Craver, 1979). Therefore, public sector employers tend to have more discretion than nonprofit or private sector employers in exercising their management rights.

Impasse Resolution

When management and labor are unable to agree to contract terms, an impasse occurs. Third-party intervention often becomes necessary to help resolve their differences. Three procedures are commonly used to resolve impasses: mediation, fact finding, and arbitration.

Mediation When a bargaining impasse occurs, either one or both of the parties may request mediation: the introduction of a neutral third party into the negotiation process to assist the bargaining parties in resolving their differences. Mediators often meet with the parties individually at first to discover the conflict. They then encourage the parties to resume bargaining. Mediators may suggest compromise positions that bridge the gap in negotiations, or they may act as intermediaries to persuade the parties that their proposals are unrealistic. Mediators serve only an advisory role. They have no power to compel the settlement of disputes. Mediation findings are not binding unless approved by both parties in the dispute.

Fact Finding Fact finding involves holding an adversarial hearing at which each side presents its position on the issues in dispute. The fact-finding body studies the evidence presented at the hearing and then makes recommendations for a final settlement.

Fact-finder recommendations are not binding on the parties. However, these recommendations are often made public, and the threat of unfavorable publicity can make both sides more willing to reach a negotiated settlement. Fact finding is grounded in the belief that public opinion will encourage the parties to accept the fact finder's report so as not to appear unreasonable.

Interest Arbitration Interest arbitration is the procedure used when mediation and fact finding have not resolved bargaining impasses. An arbitrator will hold an adversarial hearing and, based on the evidence presented, determine the terms of the final agreement. Arbitration resolves conflicts without the use of a strike. State and local governments typically use arbitration as a substitute for permitting the right to strike. Only statutes may compel the use of arbitration to conciliate contract disputes. The courts lack jurisdiction to compel arbitration in the absence of statutory authority. To discourage routine reliance on arbitration, many statutes impose the cost of arbitration on the parties.

Interest arbitration has been criticized for intruding on local government sovereignty. The third party is unaccountable to the voters or elected officials, yet makes decisions that affect the employer-employee relationship. To avoid this concern, many statutes require that arbitration decisions be approved by a majority of the appropriate legislative body.

Public sector arbitration varies across the states, and there are several forms. *Compulsory binding arbitration* requires that any dispute not settled during negotiations must end in arbitration. Arbitrators are free to make awards based on the evidence presented. The arbitrator is free to take any reasonable position and is usually inclined to make a decision that accommodates the positions of both parties in order to create a realistic and effective agreement.

Final-offer arbitration permits each party to submit proposals, or final offers, to arbitration. There are two types of final-offer arbitration: final offer by issue and final offer by package. In final-offer-by-package arbitration, the arbitrator must select either the union's or the employer's final offer on all of the disputed issues. The arbitrator may not modify the proposals or compromise on the two offers. This procedure assumes that each side will make reasonable offers to prevent the arbitrator from selecting the other party's final package. In final-offer-by-issue arbitration, the arbitrator selects either side's final offer on an issue-by-issue basis. The arbitrator is free to select the most reasonable position on each issue. The arbitrator's decision may reflect a combination of employer and union offers. Arbitration by issues gives the arbitrator more flexibility in developing an agreement because the award may incorporate proposals from both sides. This method has been criticized for possibly producing compromise awards that eliminate some of the risk by going to arbitration.

An arbitrator's decision tends to be final and is limited to issues within the permissible scope of collective bargaining. The determination of an issue outside the scope of bargaining will be viewed as a decision made beyond the jurisdiction of the arbitrator and will therefore be reversed. All mandatory topics of bargaining are considered to be within the scope of compulsory arbitration. Nonmandatory topics of bargaining generally are not considered to be within the scope of arbitration unless both parties agree to submit the topic. Most arbitration statutes contain specific criteria that arbitrators must consider in making their decisions. In addition to guiding arbitrators, these criteria facilitate judicial review.

Strikes

Nonprofit employees are permitted to strike; however, most public employees do not have a legally protected right to strike. Federal employees are prohibited from striking, and currently ten states—Alaska, Hawaii, Illinois, Minnesota, Montana, Ohio, Oregon, Pennsylvania, Vermont, and Wisconsin—have laws that permit some public employees the right to strike. However, there is little consistency across the states in which employees are covered and in the conditions that permit them to strike.

Among states that permit strikes by public employees, a clear delineation is made between employees who are permitted to strike and those prohibited from striking. Most states limit permission to employees who are not responsible for the public's welfare. The state of Alaska, for example, divides its employees into three classes. Employees who are prohibited by law from striking must go to arbitration to resolve negotiation impasse. Such employees are those whose services may not be lost for even the shortest time; police, fire, and hospital employees are in this class. In the second class are employees who might strike until there is a threat to public safety and welfare, at which point a court may enjoin the strike and order arbitration. In the final class are all other employees who may strike after a majority vote. Other employees may engage in strikes if there has first been an attempt at mediation with the employer and if a majority of employees in the unit vote by secret ballot to authorize the strike.

In most states that permit public employee strikes, a set of stipulations must be adhered to before a strike is considered allowable. For example, Hawaii state statutes permit strikes for nonessential employees in a bargaining unit if the unit has no process for binding arbitration. Before these employees may strike, they must comply with impasse procedures, sixty days must be allowed to elapse after the fact-finding board publishes its recommendations, and the unit must give a ten-day notice of intent to strike. Still, the Hawaii Labor Relations Board retains the right to set requirements to avoid danger to public health or safety.

In Montana, nurses in public health care facilities are permitted to strike only if written notice is given thirty days in advance and no other health care facility within a 150-mile radius intends to strike or is engaged in a strike. These limitations to strike permit the public employer to take action to prevent the strike or prepare for the absence of public workers. If the restrictions concerning strikes are not adhered to, public employers have the right to certain disciplinary actions toward the union and the striking employees.

Even where strikes are permitted, many state statutes grant courts the authority to issue injunctions or restraining orders if the strike presents a danger to public health or safety. If a strike is enjoined by the courts, violation of the court order could result in civil contempt penalties for the union and employees.

Grievance Arbitration

Grievance arbitration occurs when labor believes that management has violated the terms of a labor contract and files a grievance. In grievance arbitration, a neutral third party is asked to resolve the disagreement that could not be settled by the involved parties. A hearing is held that enables the parties to present evidence and testimony that support their respective positions on the case. After reviewing all of the evidence presented, the arbitrator renders a decision based on the merits of the case. The decision tends to be final and legally binding on both parties.

The scope of an arbitrator's authority is usually negotiated and stated in the collective bargaining agreement. A commonly negotiated clause authorizes the arbitrator to resolve all disputes concerning the application or interpretation of the contract, but it prohibits the arbitrator from adding to or subtracting from the express terms of the agreement in formulating an award.

Grievance arbitration is undertaken as the last resort in settling disputes because it is expensive. Direct costs involve the expenses associated with preparing the case and the arbitrator's fee. Indirect costs involve all the time spent away from work by the grievant, supervisor, union representative, witnesses, and other associated employees. The contract usually specifies which party will be responsible for paying the arbitrator's fee. It is common for labor and management to equally share the cost of an arbitration proceeding. Because sharing the costs makes it less expensive for the union to extend the grievance and appeal process until arbitration, some agreements require that the losing party pay all of the fees associated with arbitration. Holding the losing party responsible for all of the costs should provide the party whose grievance is weak with an incentive to settle at a lower level in the proceedings, and it should encourage the union to screen cases carefully.

Grievance arbitration is expressly authorized by statute for the nonprofit and private sectors. The LMRA requires that all contracts contain a grievance resolution procedure. This requirement is also found in section 7121 of the Federal Service Labor-Management Relations Statute and in most state statutes.

Public Sector Distinctions

Public sector collective bargaining has been influenced by underlying beliefs and organizational structures not found in the private sector. The principle of government sovereignty and the doctrine of illegal separation of powers are two examples of such beliefs. The *sovereignty doctrine* emanated from the tradition that the "king could do no wrong" and could be "sued" only if the king gave his consent. In the United States, the citizens are sovereign. Only the electorate has the right to set the conditions under which the public employees work. Government cannot cede any of its powers to a nonelected group, and a public sector union has been defined as such a group (Guiler & Shafritz, 2004). The *doctrine of illegal separation of powers* forbids a government to share its powers with others. It has been used most frequently to limit the scope of mandatory topics of bargaining. Opponents of public sector collective bargaining have noted a fundamental conflict between collective bargaining and these doctrines because government has a responsibility to act on behalf of all citizens, not just union members, and the public interest should not be subjugated to the political struggles between unions and government.

> Public sector collective bargaining has been influenced by underlying beliefs and organizational structures not found in the private sector.

Another belief unique to public sector collective bargaining is that public employees have no right to withhold services from their fellow citizens. For many public sector jobs, such as police and firefighting, no competitive market exists. Machines cannot provide those services, and consumers cannot turn to other suppliers of the service.

Public sector contract negotiations tend to be more difficult due to the diffusion of authority that exists in the public sector. The executive branch of government is responsible for the day-to-day administration of public organizations and contract negotiations. It is the legislative branch that has responsibility for the budget and the final authority to legitimize a settlement. Because members of public unions are also voters, they often attempt to influence the collective bargaining process by lobbying the people who are dependent on them for reelection.

For these ideological and structural reasons and because many people did not see the need for unionization, the legal framework for public sector collective bargaining lagged behind that of the private sector. Job protection was granted to public employees through civil service systems. Selection, retention, and promotion were based on merit qualifications. Over the years, civil service systems expanded to include job classification, salary administration, and the administration of grievance procedures, training, and safety. Public sector employees had protections usually not found in the private sector. The impetus for change surfaced when proponents for bargaining contended that civil service systems were often inflexible: they were unable or unwilling to respond to demands for wage and fringe benefit adjustments and changes in working conditions that typically required legislative adjustment (Kearney & Carnevale, 2001).

Changes in the Legal Framework

In 1959, Wisconsin enacted the first state statute permitting municipal employees the right to form, join, and be represented by labor organizations. Three years later, President Kennedy issued Executive Order 10988, which granted federal employees the right to join and form unions and to bargain collectively. The order established a framework for collective bargaining and encouraged the expansion of collective bargaining rights to state and local government employees. Kearney and Carnevale (2001) outlined the demise of the sovereignty doctrine: beginning in 1976, the federal courts have ruled that the First Amendment's freedom of association prohibits states from interfering with public sector employees' right to join and form unions (*Atkins* v. *City of Charlotte*, 1969; *Keyeshian* v. *Board of Regents*, 1967; *Letter Carriers* v. *Blount*, 1969; *McLaughlin* v. *Tilendis*, 1968). These decisions invalidated the sovereignty doctrine, contributing to the growth of unions.

The Supreme Court held in *Smith* v. *Arkansas State Highway Employees, Local 1315* (1979), however, that nothing in the Constitution requires public employers to either recognize or collectively bargain with public employee unions. Employees can form and join unions without the benefit of protective legislation, but public employers are not compelled to recognize or bargain with unions (Dilts, 1993). Public employers are required to bargain only under laws that mandate bargaining. The duty to bargain can be imposed only by statute.

Collective bargaining does occur, however, in states that do not provide statutory protection and procedures. For example, in Arizona, local governments have passed protective ordinances to permit de facto bargaining. Indiana permits de facto bargaining, and in Louisiana and West Virginia, state courts have in effect permitted collective bargaining in limited applications (Dilts, Boyda, & Scherr, 1993). There have also been a number of recent changes. A 2007 Missouri Supreme Court decision, *Independence-National Education Association* v. *Independence School District* (2007), held that Missouri public employees have the right to bargain collectively. Missouri was previously a "meet and confer" state.

Governor Bill Ritter of Colorado signed an executive order on November 2, 2007, authorizing partnerships for all state government employees. Executive Order D 028 07 allows employees to choose an organization to represent them in discussions with the state regarding a variety of workplace issues. These certified employee organizations (they are not called *unions*) are able to engage managers in discussions about ways to identify and implement efficiency measures and eliminate waste and redundancies; improve customer satisfaction, such as reducing waiting times; enhance employee recruiting, training, and retention; and improve workplace safety. Issues relating to pay, discipline, and termination proceedings will still be handled by the state, although the certified employee organizations can participate in wage discussions. The purpose of the executive order is to establish the framework for employee partnerships in service of a smarter, more effective, more efficient, and more accountable state government for the citizens of Colorado. Limitations on the scope of partnership agreements include not requiring any executive branch department to negotiate with respect to matters constitutionally and statutorily delegated to the State Personnel Board or the statutory function of any department or agency, or related to the Public Employees' Retirement Association. Terms for resolving disputes, including disputes over the interpretation and application of a partnership agreement, are included. Dispute resolution agreements may include nonbinding mediation or fact finding, or both, but may not include binding arbitration. Partnership agreements shall contain an agreement not to strike or engage in or threaten a strike, work stoppage, work slowdown, sickout, or other similar disruptive measure against the State of Colorado or any of its agencies. Violations of the provision may result in decertification of the certified employee organization, with payroll deductions of any membership dues ended.

Limitations of Civil Service

With the growth of government, public agencies became larger, more impersonal, and more dominated by civil service regulations and boards. This depersonalization of public service has served to isolate and alienate individual employees. Employees looked to unions for support. Civil service or merit systems were no longer perceived to be neutral advocates for employees. In many cases, merit systems were viewed as alternative forms of favoritism, reifying employers' subjective biases.

The need to reconcile collective bargaining and the merit system has been recognized by public sector unions. Jerry Wurf, former president of the American Federation of State, County, and Municipal Employees (AFSCME), saw both the merit system and collective bargaining as legitimate in government labor-management relations. AFSCME's International Constitution lists among the union's central objectives "to promote civil service legislation and career service in government" (Wurf, 1974). In fact, the early years of AFSCME's history were part of the movement to reform government and advocate for the enactment of civil service laws. Merit systems existed in only eleven states. Civil service was viewed as a means to end political kickbacks and protect members who might be fired because of political behavior.

Today it is common to find both unions and civil service systems in public organizations. However, many statutes have management rights clauses that limit the scope of mandatory topics of bargaining. Some statutes state that in conflicts, civil service regulations take precedence over contract terms.

To regain their influence, the unions have refocused their energies on issues of the new and diverse workforce. The numbers of females and minority members in the public workforce have increased. Issues such as pay equity, comparable worth for equitable job classifications, health and safety protection, training and retraining, quality-of-work life, job enlargement, and broader job classifications in many contracts have replaced the previous emphasis on wages, seniority, and work rules.

Nonprofit Sector Distinctions

Unions and nonprofit organizations are not typically linked together in most people's thoughts. That may be because many nonprofits are small and do not meet the NLRB's jurisdictional standards. Another reason may be that nonprofit agencies often respond to new societal needs and thus become desirable places to work even if salaries are lower and working conditions are less comfortable than in more established institutions. Rape crisis and domestic violence centers, agencies that provide support and respite services to parents of special needs children, hospices for the terminally ill, and homes for people with AIDS are some of the services provided by voluntary agencies. Other nonprofit organizations that often pay their employees lower salaries include cultural, social, and educational institutions, day care centers, social welfare agencies, and health care facilities.

The research on unionization and nonprofits has tended to focus on social workers and health care professionals. The dismantling of human service programs under President Reagan in the 1980s resulted in less job security and a decline in real wages. During this time, there were also changes in working conditions. There has been increasing pressure toward greater productivity and a decreasing influence in policymaking that has led to declines in professional autonomy (Benton, 1993; Hush,

1969; Sherer, 1994; Tambor, 1973, 1988a, 1988b). For human service professionals, unionization has been viewed as a vehicle for defending professional autonomy and improving working conditions. Unions have sought to expand the scope of bargaining to include such issues as agency-level policymaking, agency missions, standards of service, concerns about job satisfaction, as well as malpractice and professional liability insurance, legal representation of workers, sabbatical leaves, minimum required training, workload issues, advanced training sessions, in-service training, conferences, degree programs, licensing examination assistance, and remuneration for enhanced education (Tambor, 1988b).

Human service workers are not the only employees of the nonprofit sector who have joined unions. The International Brotherhood of the Teamsters represents nonprofit bargaining units that include hospitals, nursing homes, and health care facilities, as well as Masonic homes, retirement communities, Goodwill Industries, and the Association for Advancement of the Blind and Retarded. Bargaining unit employees run the gamut: social workers, teachers, secretaries, housekeepers, nurses, dietitians, cooking staff, dishwashers, groundskeepers, maintenance activity aids, stock clerks, paramedics, emergency medical technicians, X-ray technicians, accountants, receptionists, cashiers, mechanics, painters, electricians, youth care workers, vehicle drivers, and dispatchers. The Communications Workers of America also represents a large number of workers employed by such nonprofit agencies as museums, housing authorities, social service and health care agencies, libraries, and foundation organizations. AFSCME represents employees who work in the areas of health, social welfare, child care, home care, mental health, and community and educational services, and the Service Employees International Union (SEIU) represents thousands of employees working in health care, long-term care, and public services.

Nonprofit Agency Employees (American Federation of State, County, and Municipal Employees [AFSCME], 1988), a publication that promotes unionization, addresses the similarities between public and private nonprofit employees: both look for recognition, dignity and respect, and decent wages and improved benefits. Private nonprofit employees work in highly stressful occupations for salaries that may not be commensurate with the responsibilities and complexities of their jobs. Employees of nonprofits share many of the same desires as their public sector counterparts: better pay and benefits, contract language protection, career mobility, and safer work environments. Yet the vast majority of these workers have no union representation. AFSCME has taken the position that to win better working conditions and benefits, nonprofits need the clout of union representation.

Hush (1969) and Tambor (1973) observed that the unionization of nonprofits challenges the traditions that voluntary agencies have defined for themselves: altruistic roles and the denial of self-interest as wage earners. The impact of a union contract operating as the authority in place of the board of directors, personnel committee, or administrative staff members seems to contradict the values of openness, dignity, and communication often associated with nonprofits. For the boards and administrators of volunteer agencies, union interest among staff represents a threat to existing relationships. Nevertheless, more and more nonprofit employees are seeking union support. Nonprofit administrators, boards of directors, and personnel committee members must work with their staff to develop progressive and relevant HRM policies.

While unionization in the for-profit sector has decreased in part due to the downward shift in the number of manufacturing, construction, and transportation employees, there has been an increase in the number of professional employees and service industry employees who are joining unions. Professional employees such as medical doctors, legal aid attorneys, archivists and assistant curators at museums, social workers, nurses, and orchestra musicians are examples of some occupational groups that have unionized in nonprofit organizations. Many employees have viewed unionization as a way to defend their professional autonomy, improve working conditions, and maintain or improve their economic security.

Another rapidly growing group of union members are graduate student assistants and adjunct faculty members at many universities. Graduate student assistants, in exchange for tuition, teach classes or conduct research and are paid a stipend. Some universities provide minimum health benefits to them. But they often have little or no control over the number of hours they work. Adjunct faculty members are paid according to each course they teach. Many adjuncts have a full-time teaching load; however, their salary is significantly lower than full-time faculty members or instructors, and they do not receive health or retirement benefits.

Professional and service sector workers are turning to the old-line blue-collar trades to protect their interests. These unions have experience in contract negotiations as well as substantial financial and technical resources, and they realized that if they want to remain viable, they must follow job growth. Job growth is in the service sector for both higher-paid technical and professional positions as well as low-paid service workers such as custodians, nursing assistants, and child care workers. Twenty-three unions are actively involved with the AFL-CIO Department for Professional Employees. Actors, doctors, engineers, journalists, librarians, musicians, nurses, performing artists, athletes, teachers, university faculty, and attorneys are some of the examples of professional employees represented by unions (http://www.dpeaflcio.org/). The United Auto Workers, Local 2110, Technical, Office and Professional Union, represents employees with thirty contracts covering over thirty thousand workers in universities, publishing, museums, law firms, and other offices. It represents teachers, secretaries, administrators, editors, computer operators, librarians, museum curators, typesetters, and graphic artists, among many others. Local 2110 has taken a lead in organizing women and workers in New York nonprofits who have never been organized before. It has won benefits such as child care, flextime, job classification, domestic partner benefits, and family leave. It represents workers at Columbia University, New York University, the American Civil Liberties Union, the Museum of Modern Art, Technical Career Institutes, Barnard College, Teachers College, the National Council of Churches, Bronx Museum of the Arts, and the New-York Historical Society.

As this book is being written, educators, facilitators, and costumed interpreters at the Lower East Side Tenement Museum in New York City are in the process of organizing. They lead tours of the tenement, educate visitors about the immigrant and labor history of the Lower East Side, and portray the historical figures who once lived in the tenement. They work on a per-diem basis with no guaranteed hours and no benefits. They do not receive regular raises, even to keep up with the cost of living. The employees have decided to form a union with Local 2110 of the UAW in order to bargain with the museum management over these and other issues (http://2110uaw.org/tenement_museum.htm#).

Other arts groups associated with the UAW are the National Writers Unions and the Graphic Artists Guild. The staffs at the New-York Historical Society, the Whitney, the Guggenheim, and the San Francisco Museum of Modern Art are also unionized. The Florida Orchestra averted a strike in its fortieth anniversary season. The musicians, who were working without a contract, and management disagreed over the pay scale and length of the season. The orchestra board proposed cutting salaries by 8 percent. The orchestra had a deficit of $665,000 and anticipated losing $550,000 in state and local government grant money. In December 2007, the musicians voted to ratify a three-year contract. The musicians' base salary was reduced, but they will receive raises in years two and three of the contract. The season has been cut by four weeks plus a week of paid vacation in

2007–2008. Five staff positions were cut from management as well (Fleming, 2007a, 2007b, 2008; Loft, 2007a, 2007b).

The impact of competition and organizational restructuring has become an issue in nonprofit organizations. Contracts have called for employers to notify employees of impending layoffs and offer voluntary leaves of absences to employees before reducing their hours. In other circumstances, unions have been called on to defend professional autonomy and improve working conditions. Collective bargaining has expanded the scope of labor negotiations to include such issues as agency-level policymaking, agency missions, standards of service, and professional judgment. Other negotiated topics have been coverage for malpractice and professional liability insurance, legal representation of workers, workload issues, the provision of in-service training, financial assistance for licensing examinations, and remuneration for enhanced education. Professional employees in both the public and nonprofit sectors are joining unions due to changes brought about with privatization and the shift toward managed care not only in the health care field, but also in the provision of social welfare services. As more public services become privatized and former public employees enter nonprofit agencies, nonprofit managers can expect to see an increase in union activity.

Privatization of Public Services

The movement toward the privatization of public services was acknowledged by AFL-CIO president John Sweeney in 1995 when he spoke to the California Association of Public Hospitals. He projected that 1.7 million health care workers could lose their jobs as a result of proposed cuts in Medicare and Medicaid. He expressed concern that an increasing number of public sector service workers, such as technicians, nurse aides, and nurses working in hospitals, nursing homes, home health agencies, ambulatory clinics, blood banks, public health programs, and health maintenance organizations, could lose their jobs as more health care services become privatized. In fact, in the health care organizations, unions are visible and vibrant. Nurses in West Virginia, Kentucky, and California have gone on strike in 2008 in protest over working conditions, lack of professional input, and wages.

Regardless of whether public health services become privatized, many unions have already adopted an aggressive posture to organize public, private, and nonprofit health care facilities. As health care jobs continue to grow and the salaries for many of the paraprofessional and service positions remain stagnant, unions probably will be aggressive in attempting to recruit new members. Not only is the American Nurse Association actively organizing health care employees; so are unions not typically associated with health care, such as the United Automobile Workers; United Food and Commercial Workers; Retail, Wholesale and Department Store Unions; American Federation of State, County, and Municipal Employees' International Union; SEIU; and the American Federation of Teachers. For example, eleven different unions within the AFL-CIO represent nurses.

The increasing privatization of social and human services will also affect the growth of unions in nonprofit organizations. As more and more public services become privatized and former public employees enter nonprofit agencies, nonprofit managers can expect to see an increase in union activities.

Former state and local government employees such as social workers, case managers, mental health therapists, psychologists, and juvenile justice workers are attractive targets for union organizing activities. Workers in these positions often are responsible for caseloads that exceed the recommended maximums stated in professional standards, confront stressful situations daily, are required to work overtime on a regular basis, and often lack adequate health and retirement benefits.

Conclusion

Union contracts with public and nonprofit agencies recognize that new issues have emerged and that labor-management understanding and cooperation are important. The uncertainty of many workplace changes has shaken the confidence of many employees that their jobs are secure and their wages will remain competitive. Uncertain economic times, decreases in health care benefits for many workers, an increase in the temporary workforce, and reduced or lost pensions have contributed to increased insecurity in the labor market that is now affecting many public and nonprofit organizations. Changes in the labor market coupled with ineffective and sometimes arbitrary and unfair management often lead employees to unionize when they feel threatened.

The future of the labor movement will hinge on its ability to reach out to new constituencies and collectively develop a new agenda for political action. Women, persons of color, and new immigrants typically work in the service sector and might benefit by joining a union. The AFL-CIO, SEIU,

UAW, and AFSCME, among others, have reframed their platforms to emphasize such issues as wage stagnation, employment insecurity, and the growing economic inequality between workers and owners. They are talking about corporate responsibility, democracy in the workplace, and worker rights. Other important issues being discussed are universal health care, continuing education and retraining, and making child care available to low-wage earners. Unions have begun to emphasize the need for greater racial, gender, and class equality and improving the political and economic status of workers and their communities. Moving beyond the traditional subject matters of collective bargaining such as wages, hours, and working conditions, these new issues focus attention on the needs for affordable and safe day care, maternal leave benefits, an increased ability to work flexible hours, the elimination of sexual harassment and discrimination in the workplace, and eliminating the exploitation of immigrant workers.

Unions have sought to expand the scope of bargaining to include such issues as agency-level policymaking, agency missions, standards of service, coverage for malpractice and professional liability insurance, legal representation of workers, workload issues, the provision of in-service training, financial assistance for licensing examinations, and remuneration for enhanced education. New employee benefits, including the introduction of labor-management committees, the provision of mental health and substance abuse benefits, child care benefits, employee individual development plans, incentive awards, counseling for tests, alternative work schedules, safety precautions such as guidelines covering the use of video display terminals, and tax-sheltered annuities are also finding their way in collective bargaining agreements.

When employees choose to join unions, increased compensation and benefits are not the only reasons. Often there are concerns about effective management and the quality of the workplace climate. Market-based health care reforms are having a negative impact on the environment in which registered nurses work. They have been replaced with less qualified and less expensive personnel such as licensed practical nurses and technicians. Patient staffing ratios have also been increased. Some of the reforms, many nurses believe, threaten the quality of patient care, and many nurses believe that joining a union will help them gain greater control over patient care. Collective bargaining allows professionals the ability to demand that the standards of their profession be respected and enforced. The threat of losing control over their environment is a factor in the decision to vote for union representation (www.uannurse.org). Nurses with a negative perception of the climate are more likely to vote for a union in a representative election than nurses who perceive their work climate positively (Clark, Clark, Day, & Shea, 2000).

Registered nurses are not the only nonprofit employees who view unionization as a way to have a voice in decision making. Research by Peters and Masaoka (2000) found that nonprofit staffs have an expectation of participatory management. Pro-union staff were concerned about the lack of professional HRM practices, a lack of effective supervision, unfairness in the assignment of workloads, and the lack of diversity in their organizations. Some of the respondents believed that unionization was a way to call attention to inexperienced and unqualified management, as well as bring about more effective leadership.

For public and nonprofit organizations that are not yet unionized, it is important to have a progressive HRM system in place that respects employees. Examinations, performance appraisals, promotions, and merit pay systems must be administered in an equitable and consistent manner. Jobs must be enriched to eliminate tasks that are routine and boring, and career enrichment opportunities must be provided. Employees must feel that their jobs are important and that they are contributing to the mission of the agency. Whether workers join unions depends on their perceptions of the work environment and their desire to participate in or influence employment conditions. Organizations that provide employees with the opportunity to participate in the decision-making process are less likely to be the targets of unionization.

Exercise 12.1: No Union-Related E-Mail

The National Labor Relations Board has ruled that employers have the right to prohibit workers from using the company's e-mail system to send out union-related messages. In a three-to-two ruling, the board held that it was legal for employees to prohibit union-related e-mail as long as the employer has a policy barring employees from sending e-mail for "non-job related solicitations" for outside organizations.

Labor unions argued that e-mail systems have become a modern gathering place where employees should be able to communicate freely with coworkers to discuss work-related matters of mutual concern.

The three NLRB members who voted in favoring of restricting union e-mail stated, "An employer has a basic property right to regulate and restrict employee use of company property. The respondent's communications system, including its e-mail system is the respondent's property."

The two dissenting NLRB members held that the employees' interest in communicating with other employees about union activity and other collective concerns should outweigh the employer's property interest: "The majority erroneously treats the employer's asserted 'property interest' in e-mail—a questionable interest here, in any event—as paramount, and fails to give due consideration to employee rights and the appropriate balancing of the parties' legitimate interests."

Questions

1. Do you agree with the decision made by the National Labor Relations Board in regard to the use of e-mail? Explain your answer.
2. Are there other issues that should have been considered in rendering the decision?

Source: Greenhouse (2007).

Exercise 12.2: Teachers at New York City Catholic Schools Strike

In anticipation of Pope Benedict XVI's arrival in the United States in fall 2007, approximately 350 teachers at Roman Catholic schools from New York City and its northern suburbs went on strike. The teachers are members of the Lay Faculty Association, which represents about 450 teachers at ten schools. The teachers were demonstrating not against the Pope but against low wages, small pensions, and proposed health care premiums that were too expensive. The church teaches economic and social justice, and the teachers saw this as an opportunity to illustrate that this New York diocese does not provide salaries and benefits consistent with what the Pope is preaching. The teachers earn about $44,000 a year, about $25,000 below their public school counterparts.

Questions

1. In your opinion, do you think schoolteachers in general should be allowed to strike over wages and benefits? Explain your answer.
2. Should teachers employed by a diocese have a right to strike? Does the employer make a difference? Explain your answer.

Source: Buckley (2008).

Chapter Questions

1. From an employee perspective, what are three advantages of working in a unionized organization? What are three disadvantages?
2. From a management perspective, what are some advantages of a unionized organization? What are some disadvantages?
3. The U.S. Department of Labor noted that the number of workers belonging to a union grew by 311,000 to 15.7 million in 2007. What factors do you attribute the union growth to?

Online Activities

1. In a small group, have each individual take on the role as spokesperson for the American Federation of State, County and Municipal Employees, the Service Employees International Union, and the American Nurses Association. Each person will then discuss each group's concerns. Use the Web sites of these organizations to research your positions. After each group's positions have been presented, discuss where the interests overlap or are in contradiction. How would an organization address those concerns? Are there any concerns that they would not realistically be able to address?
2. Visit the National Public Employers Labor Association Web site. What are three issues of concern to public employers? Do you think nonprofit employers should be concerned about those issues as well? How would an employer address those issues?

CHAPTER THIRTEEN

STRATEGIC HUMAN RESOURCE MANAGEMENT AND TECHNOLOGY

After you have read this chapter, you should be able to:

- Understand the importance of technology to strategic human resources management
- Discuss what a human resources information system (HRIS) is
- Explain how an HRIS is useful when undertaking human resources planning
- Understand how technology is promoting changes in organizational structures and job design
- Understand why information technology resources policies are important

The changing dynamics noted throughout the book have brought about changes in the way public and nonprofit agencies are organized and managed. Public and nonprofit organizations are using the Internet in innovative ways to deliver services; engage citizens, clients, and volunteers; and improve performance. E-government is enabling organizations to achieve their strategic objectives and improve their administration. To do that, organizations need employees with skills, creativity, and knowledge (Cortés & Rafter, 2007; Podolsky, 2003; Stowers & Melitski, 2003).

Computers and technology now play a major role in the redesign of traditionally routine jobs and are expected to be a major contributor to productivity in the future. North Carolina's Department of Health and Human Services and eighty-five autonomous local health departments collaborated on a statewide enterprise health information system. Besides transmitting data to the state and doing Medicaid billing, local health departments will use the system to determine patient eligibility, capture patients' personal data and medical histories, schedule appointments, and run a variety of management reports tailored to their own needs. Hosted by the state's Office of Information Technology Services, the health information system (HIS) will include a central database with records for anyone who visits one of the local health clinics. All patient information will become available to anyone with the security credentials to view it. For the health departments, a unified database will reduce data entry, saving labor and decreasing error rates. For patients, it will mean better continuity of care because public health department clients often are a transient population. As a Web-based system, the HIS will let health department employees enter data from any location with Internet access. "Right now, most of our health departments have one to five people who do nothing but enter information into the current system. If the health department lab does a test, it will write those results down on paper, and it still goes to the data entry person" (Douglas, 2006, p. 48). The system will be integrated with other medical databases that health departments use, such as the state's immunization registry, so employees no longer have to enter the same data twice. State and local users will also be able to generate a broad range of reports, designing them as needed.

When we think of public organizations and large nonprofits, we think of a hierarchical, centralized structure of specialists who typically rely on a fixed set of standard operating procedures. Today, agencies are flatter and decentralized. These new organizational structures rely on networks of teams and individuals to establish goals and ensure the effective delivery of services. Advances in information technology have assisted in making this possible. In a knowledge- and information-based economy, information technology and systems take on greater importance. Computers and information technology are also being used to design and manage public sector programs. Not only is information technology being used to automate routine tasks, but it is increasingly being used to restructure and integrate service delivery procedures and programs.

The Stanislaus County Superior Court, California, developed a Web-based information system to coordinate efforts of court personnel by collecting case information from the time a case is opened until it is settled by interfacing with the district attorney's office and the Department of Motor Vehicles. When a 911 call comes in, a dispatcher writes a report on that call, and if a police officer is involved, he or she also writes a report. Those reports go to the sheriff's office and then to the district attorney's office. It is then up to the district attorney to file a complaint or sit on the reports until more evidence is collected. The district attorney may hold the reports for up to one year until prosecutors have sufficient evidence to file. If the district attorney's office determines there is sufficient evidence to file a complaint, it files the necessary paperwork, which is integrated with the superior court system. Each case is given a number by which it can be tracked for the remainder of its life. The system can handle cases from any division in the court: traffic, probate, or small claims. It also permits cross-referencing between courts, allowing personnel to access any information on an individual in the system regardless of which court possesses the information (McKay, 2003).

A recent article in the *Tampa Tribune* illustrates how e-mails sent to the City of Tampa's Web site for customer service requests find their way to city employees' BlackBerries during evenings and weekends. Inquiries are delivered immediately to staff who can answer the questions. The City of Tampa tracks its service requests, sending e-mails to residents when action is taken so they know that progress is being made to resolve their problem (Parker, 2007).

Information systems optimize the flow of information and knowledge within the organization and help management maximize knowledge resources. Because the productivity of employees depends on the quality of systems serving them, management decisions about information technology are important to the effectiveness of public and nonprofit organizations.

Information Systems Technology

To understand information systems requires understanding the problems they are designed to solve, their architectural and design elements, and the organizational processes that are needed to accomplish the required tasks. To be able to use an information system, a manager must understand the organization, the management, and the technology dimensions of the system and how they can be used to provide information leading to effective solutions. Computer-based information systems rely on computer hardware and software technology to process and disseminate information. Computers are only part of an information system.

Information systems (IS) technology uses computer hardware, software, storage, and telecommunications technologies. Computer hardware is the physical equipment used for input, processing, and output activities in an information system. The software consists of the detailed preprogrammed instructions that control and coordinate the computer hardware in an information system. Storage technology includes media for storing data, such as magnetic or optical disk, or tape. Telecommunications technology consists of physical devices and software that link the various pieces of hardware and transfer data from one physical location to another. Computers and communications equipment can be connected in networks for sharing voice, data, images, sound, and video. A network links two or more computers to shared data and resources such as a printer.

The capabilities of information technology (IT) can help organizations in a variety of ways (Davenport & Short, 1990):

Transactional capability: IT can transform unstructured processes into routine transactions.

Geographical capability: IT can transfer information with rapidity and ease across large distances, making processes independent of geography.

Automational capability: IT can replace or reduce human labor in a process.

Analytical capability: IT can bring complex analytical methods to bear on a process.

Informational capability: IT can bring vast amounts of detailed information into a process.

Sequential capability: IT can enable changes in the sequence of tasks in a process, often allowing multiple tasks to be worked on simultaneously.

Knowledge management capability: IT allows the capture and dissemination of knowledge and expertise to improve the process.

Tracking capability: IT allows the detailed tracking of task status, inputs, and outputs.

Disintermediation capability: IT can be used to connect two parties within a process who would otherwise communicate through an intermediary (internal or external).

Organizational Change

Information technology can promote various degrees of organizational change. The most common change is the automation or mechanization of routine tasks. However, IT can also be used for higher levels of sophistication, such as reengineering and redesigning business processes, whereby business and work processes are analyzed, simplified, and reconstructed. Processes have two important characteristics: they have defined business outcomes, and the outcomes have recipients, the customers. Customers can be internal or external to the organization. Processes can also occur across or between organizational subunits. Davenport and Short (1990) provide the following examples of processes: investigating and paying an insurance claim, writing a proposal for a contract, creating a marketing plan, developing a new product or service, and ordering goods from a supplier. There are typically five steps in process redesign:

1. Developing a business vision and process objectives to prioritize objectives and set targets
2. Identifying the processes to be redesigned to identify critical or bottleneck processes
3. Understanding and measuring existing processes to identify problems and set baseline performance expectations
4. Identifying IT levers to brainstorm new process approaches
5. Designing and building a prototype of the process to implement organizational and technical aspects

The most likely objectives related to process redesign are reducing costs, reducing the time for tasks to be completed, increasing or improving the quality of output, and empowering individuals and providing them with more control over their output (Davenport & Short, 1990).

Improved work-flow management has enabled many agencies to reduce costs and improve customer service at the same time. Information systems can make organizations more efficient, and information technology can be used to redesign and reshape organizations, transforming their structure, scope of operation, reporting and control mechanisms, work practices, work flows, products, and services. Flatter organizations have fewer levels of management; lower-level employees are given greater decision-making authority, and employees may work away from a manager. Information systems make information available to line workers so they can make decisions that managers previously made. Networks of computers have made it possible for employees to work together as a team. Information technologies such as e-mail, the Internet, and videoconferencing allow employees to work from different locations. For example, employees can work remotely from their homes or cars and can collaborate while miles away from the office or other structures, thus vastly expanding organizational boundaries.

Types of Information Systems

There are four main types of information systems, each serving a different organizational level: operational-level systems, knowledge systems, management-level systems, and strategic-level systems.

Operational-Level Systems

Operational-level systems support operational managers by keeping track of the elementary activities and transactions of the organization, such as sales, receipts, cash deposits, payroll, and the flow of materials in a hospital. The principal purpose of systems at this level is to answer routine questions and track the flow of transactions through the organization.

Work-flow systems support agency operations. The Florida Department of Business and Professional Regulations (DBPR) regulates nearly one million businesses and professionals in more than two hundred license categories to protect the health, safety, and welfare of citizens and visitors. State law authorizes the department to establish uniform application forms and certificates for licensure for use by its divisions. DBPR has expanded its online access by implementing electronic attestation (certain forms for license applications require the applicant's signature attesting or swearing that the information provided is correct) and fingerprinting to facilitate online application submission. Electronic attestation eliminates the need for applicants to download, print, notarize, and mail a variety of licensing documents. Electronic fingerprinting is a faster and more efficient system for conducting background checks than the paper fingerprinting card method that requires applicants to manually complete a paper fingerprint card and submit it to a law enforcement agency. Whereas the paper system required one to two weeks processing time, electronic fingerprinting provides results within twenty-four hours of submission.

To replace paper business processes, the department implemented a documents management system that captures, manages, stores, delivers, and preserves documents electronically. By reducing paper and managing license applications and processes electronically, the department hopes to reduce the time it takes for license approvals, license changes, and compliance activities. Electronic documents can be processed more efficiently because they allow different employees to verify license information simultaneously (Office of Program Policy Analysis and Government Accountability, 2007).

Knowledge-Level Systems

Knowledge-level systems support knowledge and data workers in an organization. The purpose of these systems is to help the organization integrate new knowledge into the agency and control the flow of paperwork. Reporting systems support knowledge-level systems. Generating reports is a basic function of most information systems. For example, demographic data can be used to complete required government forms, or a time and attendance system could be used to generate reports on sick time used by different departments to identify those with high absenteeism. In the case of a direct service nonprofit receiving public funds, the hours of services delivered can be reported to receive reimbursements.

Management-Level Systems

Management-level systems are designed to serve the monitoring, controlling, decision-making, and administrative activities of middle managers. Decision-support systems support management-level systems. They go beyond simply reporting information, typically incorporating rules, formulas, or specialized displays that are designed to help end users make decisions. Scheduling and staffing are areas where decision support can be useful. In scheduling, a routine question is how many people should be scheduled for a given time period or particular event. If there are changes in workload or seasonal variations due to increasing or decreasing need for services or attendance at events, it may be helpful to have a model that recommends the number of people in each job category who should be scheduled. Similar questions emerge over the longer term with respect to recruitment and staffing. If increased retirements are expected, what are the knowledge, skills, abilities, and other characteristics (KSAOCs) of people who need to be hired, and how many people should be hired? Other HRM topics such as benefits planning and analysis are good candidates for decision support.

Strategic-Level Systems

Strategic-level systems help senior management address strategic issues and long-term trends in both the agency and the external environment. Executive-support systems support strategic-level systems. Whereas traditional decision-support systems are directed at well-defined, narrowly focused problems, executive-support systems bring together data from diverse sources to help assess broader strategic questions. Strategic human resources management figures into these decisions. When considering the privatization of services, in the case of public sector agencies, or when considering a merger, in the case of nonprofit agencies, labor costs, including pensions and benefits, are usually significant concerns. Having access to timely and accurate information can provide the necessary perspective.

All organizations and departments need to be aware of their revenue and expenditures. All organizations have an accounting function that is responsible for maintaining and managing the agency's financial records, its receipts, disbursements, and payroll expenditures. An accounting information system enables a manager to keep track of the financial assets and flow of funds. It provides a record of transactions for disbursements, receipts, and other expenditures. Most nonprofits, regardless of size, have an accounts receivable system to keep track of money.

For example, nonprofits must keep track of the grants they receive from public and private sources. They must track their donations, gifts, and contributions, which may be cash or noncash. They need to monitor their fees for services and have a system in place for billing and collections. Some nonprofits may have income from investments, membership dues, and special events that need to be accounted for. The information system keeps track of the outstanding bills and can produce a variety of reports. The system supplies information to the general ledger system, which tracks the agency's total cash flow. The financial reports that can be gleaned from the accounting information system can be used to make immediate and strategic decisions.

Information Systems Design

The design of information systems often becomes entangled in the politics of the organization.

The design of information systems often becomes entangled in the politics of the organization. Because information systems potentially change an organization's structure, culture, politics, and work, they are often resisted when introduced. Consequently, to ensure a successful introduction of information technology, the process must be planned. These factors should be considered in systems plans:

- The environment in which the organization functions
- The structure of the organization: its hierarchy, specialization, and standard operating procedures

- The culture and politics of the organization
- The type of organization
- The nature and style of leadership
- The extent and support of top management
- The principal interest groups affected by the system
- The kinds of tasks and decisions that the information system is designed to assist

Information Technology Resource Policies

New Mexico Governor Bill Richardson issued an executive order in July 2003 creating the state's uniform information technology resources policy for state agencies. The policy covers Internet and intranet use by state employees, e-mail, and use of the state's digital network. The executive order permits the state to install software to "monitor and record all IT resources use, including e-mail and Web site visits. Staff shall have no expectation of privacy while on the state's Internet or intranet." The directive also prohibits employees from using IT resources for anything other than official state business. "Any staff members who violate the policy are subject to immediate suspension and termination of access to IT resources, as well as disciplinary action up to and including termination of employment."

Vermont plans to monitor the Internet habits of its state employees. Officials say monitoring ensures employee compliance with workplace regulations and also protects the state's computer network against viruses spread by some Internet sites. State policy demands that employees be notified they are being monitored. Before an employee can log on, a window appears on every computer screen stating that the computer is equipped with monitoring technology ("State to Monitor Workers' Web Habits," 2007).

Protecting an agency's computer system from viruses or spyware is important. When a human resources employee at the Nature Conservancy in Arlington, Virginia, used his laptop to visit a sports Web site, he inadvertently downloaded a spyware program that allowed the software to retrieve personal and financial information about thousands of Nature Conservancy employees from his hard drive: names, home addresses, Social Security numbers, payroll direct-deposit account numbers, bank routing numbers, and benefits and beneficiary information (Stephens, 2007).

Data loss prevention goes by a lot of names: *extrusion prevention, content filtering, information leak prevention*, and *data leak prevention*. The basic tasks of identifying sensitive data, monitoring where they go, auditing who has access to the information, and restricting that access can happen anywhere on networks, including end points, databases, mobile devices, network gateways, and file stores (Wiens, 2007).

NASCIO, an organization that represents state chief information officers and IT executives and managers from state governments across the United States, recommends that states develop a marketing campaign and provide training to make state employees aware of IT security. It also recommends that states include contractors. Whether a contractor will be performing IT or non-IT-related tasks, most contractors will use a state's IT resources, including handling state government information. NASCIO recommends requiring contractors to sign IT security and acceptable-use acknowledgments. Crafting contractual provisions requiring compliance with state IT awareness and training requirements can guard against security incidents that originate from contractors' use of state IT resources (Whitmer, 2007).

Many employees are subject to electronic and other forms of high-tech surveillance. Information technology and systems make the invasion of privacy inexpensive and widely available. Organizations should have policies and procedures in place that govern the use and dissemination of information that may be considered private. This is especially important for employees working in HRM departments who have access to insurance information and medical records.

Adams (1992) identifies some procedures that organizations can implement to secure privacy and maintain confidential information. Employers should train users to handle equipment, data, and software securely; train employees to sign off personal computers after use; not allow passwords to be shared and require that they be changed frequently; ensure that backup copies, data files, software, and printouts are used only by authorized staff; and ensure that software and mainframe applications include a record of any changes and transactions that occur in the system, including when and who performed the changes. In addition, there should be no personal record system whose existence is secret; employees should have the right to access, inspect, review, and amend information about themselves; there must be no use of personal information for purposes other than those for which it was gathered without prior consent of the employees; and the managers of systems should be held accountable and liable for any damage done by systems, their reliability, and security.

Any organization in any industry that has the potential of being involved in litigation in the U.S. federal court system needs to incorporate electronic discovery (e-discovery) requirements. The December 2006 amendments to the Federal Rules of Civil Procedure (FRCP) mandate changes in the way organizations manage their data. Information technology departments need to have knowledge of what information is retained, where data are stored, and how long to keep the data. They also need to have the ability to quickly and accurately respond to litigation hold notices. Public and nonprofit organizations routinely handle large volumes of sensitive records. They are now responsible for e-mail, instant messages, text messages, blogs, personal digital assistants, voice mail, cell phones, laptops, Internet and intranet, Web sites, hard drives, and all forms of digital files, including music, pictures, and video shared using the agency's resources across all forms of digital media. The changes to the FRCP recognize electronic records as a category of documents that are subject to discovery during litigation and are to be retrievable in a "reasonable" amount of time (Milburn, 2007; Search and Electronically Discover, 2007).

Human Resource Information Systems

The HRM function is responsible for attracting, developing, and maintaining the agency's workforce. Human resources identifies potential employees, maintains complete records on existing employees, and creates programs to develop employees' talents and skills,

Strategic-level human resources information systems identify the personnel requirements, such as the skills, educational level, types of positions, number of positions, and cost, for meeting the agency's strategic plans. At the management level, an HRIS helps managers monitor and analyze the recruitment, allocation, and compensation of employees. HR knowledge systems support analysis activities related to job design, training, and the modeling of employee career paths and reporting relationships. HR operational systems track the recruitment and placement of the agency's employees (see Figure 13.1).

Technological advances have not only changed how organizations are structured and work is performed, but have also begun to change the tasks of HRM specialists. Computers are used to perform many of the functions for which employees were once responsible.

FIGURE 13.1. USES OF HUMAN RESOURCES INFORMATION SYSTEMS

HR Planning and Analysis
- Organization charts
- Staffing projections
- Skills inventories
- Turnover analysis
- Absenteeism analysis
- Restructuring costing
- Internal job matching

Compensation and Benefits
- Pay structures
- Wage and salary costing
- Flexible benefit administration
- Vacation use
- Benefits use analysis
- 401(k) statements
- Notification of benefits under the Consolidated Omnibus Budget Reconciliation Act

Equal Employment
- Affirmative action plan
- Applicant tracking
- Workforce utilization
- Availability analysis

Health, Safety, and Security
- Safety training
- Accident records
- Occupational Safety and Health Administration reports
- Material data records

HR Development
- Employee training profiles
- Training needs assessments
- Succession planning
- Career interests and experience

Employee and Labor Relations
- Union negotiating cost
- Auditing records
- Attitude survey results
- Exit interview analysis
- Employee work history

Staffing
- Recruiting sources
- Applicant tracking
- Job offer refusal analysis

A typical HRIS system for employee record keeping maintains basic data, such as the employee's name, age, sex, marital status, address, educational background, salary, job title, date of hire, and date of termination. The system can produce a variety of reports, such as lists of newly hired employees, terminated employees, leaves of absences, employees classified by job type or educational level, or employee job performance levels. Such systems are typically designed to provide data necessary for federal and state record keeping requirements.

Compensation and Benefits

At a higher level of HRIS is the integration of payroll operations with the HRIS and benefits unit in HR. Government regulations and the complexity of benefits in many organizations warrant HRM expertise. Efficiency can be enhanced when payroll and HR systems are interfaced or integrated, because data entry and maintenance can be reduced.

When payroll operations are moved to the HR department, the benefits and compensation expertise of the HR specialists makes certain that benefits plans remain qualified under government regulations, ensures the accuracy of payroll deductions for HR-managed plans, and provides the opportunity to answer employees' questions about pay and benefits, in person or through interactive HRIS technology.

When organizations offer flexible benefits plans to employees, HRIS can be used to communicate information to the employees that can have an impact on the costs of benefits and their administration. Employees can obtain information about the benefits available and make changes in their plans by enrolling in new benefits, adding or changing dependents, changing the amount of monthly savings deducted from paychecks, making a cash withdrawal, taking out a loan, or withdrawing from a plan altogether. In some systems these decisions are supported by a simple "what if?" analysis that shows the employee choices, pension projections, how much would be saved after five years at a certain rate of deduction, and so on.

Direct access to benefits plans and employees' ability to self-enroll or change benefits reduces staffing requirements in the benefits department, eliminates paperwork, and otherwise improves the administration of benefits. New employees who want to know when they are eligible to enroll in a certain plan can find this information without going to the benefits department, a change in dependents covered by health insurance can be made without paperwork, and retirement benefits at different ages can be projected.

Career Planning and Management Staffing Systems

Employees can use the HRIS for career planning and staffing systems. At the simplest level, electronic bulletin boards list basic job posting information and at a more complex level include online position descriptions, job advertisements when openings arise, résumés of all covered employees, knowledge-based assessment modules, and systematic procedures that link qualified candidates and open positions, providing managers with the backgrounds and résumés of employees and applicants who meet the position requirements.

Career planning and staffing systems that are accessible to employees permit their direct involvement in their own career development or movement in the organization. A career development system able to be accessed by employees can provide information about positions at the next level, job descriptions, information about steps in career paths leading to certain positions, training and development activities that may be required, and information about trends in workforce movement, surpluses and shortages, and other career-relevant information. In some systems, the employee can select a training class or another development activity or create an entirely new career plan, subject to authorization, which can also be handled electronically. Most career development is essentially self-development and requires individual motivation, commitment, and clear linkages between individual effort and career results. Extending information through HRIS involves the employees being managed.

Communicating Policies and Procedures

The distribution of agency policies and procedures through technology is less expensive than printing hard copies and distributing them to employees. Changes can be made and communicated in an expedited manner. Information systems permit automatic communication that provides uniformity and consistency of some policies and procedures yet is flexible for audience-specific variations in others. For example, regional pay levels may influence hourly rates, different labor contracts may be in effect in different locations, and paid holidays may vary. However, other policies with respect to nondiscrimination, privacy, and federal legislation such as the Fair Labor Standards Act may apply to all employees, requiring overtime pay and record keeping.

Organizations are using technology to offer quick online access to company policies. Entering the systems, managers and employees can examine company policy with respect to time off, vacations, holiday pay, or infractions leading to discipline. Such things as merit pay guidelines, performance appraisal instructions, access to training programs, and instructions on how to transfer or hire an individual can be provided online.

Employee Participation

Systems access to employees also permits employees to make their views and ideas known to management in a timely, cost-efficient manner. When employee attitudes are important to the organization, the timeliness, accuracy, and identification of different attitudes and perceptions among different types or categories of employees are important. Online employee surveys can eliminate the administration of paper-and-pencil surveys and automatically summarize data and trends such as changes in attitudes that may deserve prompt management intervention. Linked to HRIS data, an automated attitude survey can produce summaries of responses by such groupings as management level, job function, location, or demographic characteristics without manual analysis.

Training and Performance Support

In a complex HRIS, job analysis data, productivity data, skills and competencies information, performance ratings, applicant qualifications, test results, and other types of information relevant to training can be integrated:

- HRIS demographic data can be analyzed to develop audience-specific curricula and training formats that are most effective for different groups.
- Job requirements can be linked to training. This could include competency-based training and assessment.
- HRIS can provide online training courses or provide links to approved vendor-supplied training courses.
- HRIS can analyze the relationships between training and performance ratings, turnover, compensation, and other variables to establish cost-benefit data on specific types of training.
- HRIS can develop new recruitment practices, preemployment tests, and other employment process tools based on analysis of training data and the requirements of positions.

Restructuring Work and Technology Transfer

E-mail, computer-based training and testing, voice-activated systems, and the range of telecommunications technologies do not necessarily lead to improvements in performance or gains in productivity. Integrating employees and technology can be a complex, multifaceted function. For information systems to work, many factors need to be considered and implemented. Job and work-flow analyses should be conducted, qualified people must be recruited and selected, and training and retraining must be provided.

HRIS can also lead to the outsourcing of the HRM function. Many small nonprofits and local governments lack the organizational capacity to develop and administer HRM programs and find it less expensive to outsource HRM functions than hire new employees with expertise and invest in technology. Even large public employers may choose to outsource the HRM function. Florida, for example, entered a deal with an information management firm to handle some of the state's HRM responsibilities. The Florida Department of Management Services decided that replacing and continually updating its HRIS was too expensive. It felt that it would be more cost-effective to outsource some of its HR functions. State employees use a self-service Web portal to manage changes of address, dependents, emergency contacts, marital status, and other personal information. The portal is also used to enroll in benefit programs and access benefit information. As a result of the outsourcing, some state employees were displaced, and others have expressed concerns about the security of records. The state contracted with Convergys, which subcontracted with GDXdata, which used subcontractors in India. State employees were notified that their personal information was sent offshore and processed by companies in India, Barbados, and possibly China, and the security of their information could not be guaranteed. After the uproar from state employees and state officials, Convergys agreed to a one-year credit protection program for state employees with fifty thousand dollars of insurance for any state worker whose bank or credit accounts are raided by identity thieves (Cotterell, 2006).

Electronic Human Resources Management

Electronic human resources management (eHR) is used to enhance human resources processes such as job analysis, recruitment, selection, training, performance management, and compensation. Data can be collected for job analysis from employees and supervisors from online questionnaires. Data can be summarized and job descriptions can be created. Some of the systems can convert the data to a job evaluation form and create job evaluation point scores for use in compensation systems. Many agencies now use Web-based portal systems to post job openings and screen resumes. E-recruiting systems can be used to track applicants and provide them with virtual job previews. Some organizations are using e-selection systems to assess job applicants' KSAOCs, manage applicant flow, and evaluate the effectiveness of selection systems. Some use technology to conduct interviews, personality assessments, and background checks online and use computerized testing to examine candidates' cognitive ability skills.

E-learning is used for a variety of education and training programs. Web-based systems, CD-ROMs, and audio- or videoconferencing can be used at remote locations. E-performance management systems are used to facilitate the writing of performance appraisals. Technology can also track unit performance, absenteeism, grievance rates, and turnover levels over time. E-compensation is used to help agencies administer compensation, benefits, and payroll systems. Technology can assist with providing managers with comparable labor market data, provide managers with a tool to design and model the costs of compensation systems, provide employees with information about benefits, provide employees with self-service systems to select or change benefits, and enable agencies to comply with laws and union contracts.

Strategic Human Resources Management

Human resources information systems applications must go beyond payroll and benefits administration and tracking employee records such as attendance and absences. They must connect to the strategic objectives of the agency to facilitate more effective recruitment and selection, training and development, communication, manpower planning, and other core HR processes. Data assembled and gleaned from an HRIS can be used by managers and workers to analyze problems and make informed decisions.

Human resources information systems applications must go beyond payroll and benefits administration and tracking employee records. They must connect to the strategic objectives of the agency.

Ashbaugh and Miranda (2002) identify the following strategic applications of HRIS:

- *Align HRIS to organizational performance issues.* Use technology to evaluate organizational performance.
- *Improve core business processes.*

- *Develop a human capital inventory.* Organizations can combine information for education and skills tracking and matching, career planning, succession planning, and performance evaluations.
- *Link position control to budgeting.* By integrating HR with the financial planning process, organizations can develop a compensation management program that includes automated position control to serve as a check that a department will not exceed its salary budget and the ability to develop projections or forecasts based on hours, actual expenditures, or staff totals. They can link HR, benefits, and payroll data to the budget planning process that includes the ability to develop "what-if?" analyses.
- *Facilitate labor-management relations.* Providing accurate information and tracking seniority, disciplinary actions, and grievances filed. Data can also be provided for labor negotiations such as pension changes, trend analysis for employee absences and use of sick time, analysis of the costs for overtime, and comprehensive employee benefit costs.

Other strategic applications include having employees update address changes, enroll in training courses, change benefit plans, and disseminate policies. Business intelligence can also be increased by using new technology. Advanced analytical tools, such as online analytical processing, data mining, and executive information systems, provide insight into trends and patterns and can be used to improve the organization's decision-making capability. In an SHRM context, those tools can be used to support HRM decisions.

Managers must deal with new employee issues because the changes brought about by IT require a new kind of employee. Employees need to be more highly trained than in the past as tasks become more automated. They need the skills and ability to work in an electronic environment, the ability to understand and act on new information, and the ability and willingness to learn new software and work-flow procedures.

Conclusion

Computers are used to advertise job vacancies in public places and computer bulletin boards. Citizens can dial in or push appropriate buttons to see which agencies are recruiting and for what types of positions.

Computers have also been used to replace interpersonal screening and interviewing. In computer-assisted screening, applicants are screened over the telephone. A digitized voice asks applicants to respond to a variety of job-related questions, inquiring about work experience, attitudes, interests, and skills.

Many civil service systems have adopted computerized testing. Applicants read questions at a computer screen and use the keypad or mouse to select the correct answer. Tests that require the ability to read, write, and follow oral and visual instructions have been developed that use interactive video and multimedia. The computer scores the exams as soon as the candidates complete them, immediately notifying the candidates of the results.

Staffing activities generate and use considerable information, often in paper forms. Job descriptions, applicant material, résumé correspondence, applicant profiles, applicant flow and tracking, and reports are the types of information necessary for the operation of a staffing system.

Tasks that used to require many human hours of retrieving data from archival files can now easily be performed by computers. Administrative responsibilities such as tracking applicants and employees for equal opportunity and affirmative action goals and timetables are being handled by computers. Computer programs are also being used for salary administration and performance evaluations. Benefits administration is increasingly being done through computer technology. Interactive voice response systems are providing twenty-four-hour access to retirement plan enrollment, savings plan inquiries and enrollment, and medical plan inquiries. With more and more information being compiled into agency databases, it is imperative that security measures be developed that protect sensitive or confidential information such as medical records and employee personnel files.

For all electronic information, written policies in regard to how electronic data is stored, retrieved, and destroyed should be developed to comply with the Federal Rules of Civil Procedure. All employees need to understand what to do to preserve electronic data and what actions to take.

Increases in the uses of information technology require different combinations of skills and other resources. As public and nonprofit organizations confront these challenges, SHRM will become even more important. Innovative strategies will be imperative and necessary to assist organizations to prepare for changing missions, priorities, and programs.

Exercise 13.1: No-E-Mail Fridays

A growing number of employers, including U.S. Cellular, Deloitte & Touche, PBD Worldwide Fulfillment Services, and Intel, are imposing "no-e-mail" Fridays or weekends. The bans typically allow e-mailing clients and customers or responding to urgent matters, but the normal flow of routine internal e-mail is halted. Violators are hit with token fines or called out by the boss. The limits aim to encourage more face-to-face and telephone contact with customers and coworkers, raise productivity, or just give employees a reprieve from the ever-rising e-mail tide.

Managers complain that rather than confronting problems, employees use e-mail to avoid them by passing issues back and forth in long message strings. E-mail reduces face-to-face contact among coworkers and clients, and terse, poorly phrased messages strain those relationships. E-mail is spilling into weekends, tying employees to computers when they should be relaxing.

Questions

1. What is your opinion of "no-e-mail Fridays"? For your job position, would eliminating e-mail on Fridays increase or decrease your productivity?
2. Do you think "no-e-mail Fridays" would enhance the personal contacts between clients, coworkers, or customers?
3. What are some other job-related issues that might arise out of no-e-mail Fridays?

Source: Shellenbarger (2007).

Exercise 13.2: Tracking Workers Through Technology

Employers are increasingly using technology to track workers. Nurses at Wyckoff Heights Medical Center in Brooklyn, New York, carry radio-frequency identification tags that allow their movements to be tracked. Management said the system was used to ensure the quality of patient care, not keep track of nurses who are on breaks.

The town of Babylon, New York, installed global positioning system technology in most of its 250 vehicles, including snow plows and dump trucks.

In New York City, the Bloomberg administration has devoted more than $18 million toward technology to keep track of when city employees come and go, and one agency requires its workers to scan their hands each time they enter and leave the workplace. In New York City, the use of hand scanners is part of CityTime, an effort by the Office of Payroll Administration to automate timekeeping. CityTime will be able to record attendance and leave requests, collect time forms automatically, coordinate timekeeping with the city's payroll system, and allow workers and their supervisors to monitor time, attendance, and leave online. A spokesman for Mayor Bloomberg said the timekeeping project would make payroll administration more efficient. The use of scanners makes it easier for employees to file timesheets and saves the city personnel costs.

Identification devices have supplanted the use of drug tests and polygraph exams in concerns about workplace privacy. New technologies are raising concerns about the control of personal information.

Questions

1. How do you feel about the potential privacy violations these new devices may bring into the workplace?
2. Develop a policy and security procedures so that employees' personal information will not be at risk.

Source: Chan (2007).

Chapter Questions

1. In small groups, describe Web-based human resources information systems you are familiar with. Based on your own experiences and Internet research, evaluate the advantages and disadvantages of employees using a Web-based HRIS. What HRIS services are most convenient for employees?
2. In small groups, discuss how technology has transformed your job. Share with your group members initiatives that your organizations has established to meet the technology challenges.

Online Activities

1. In a small group, use the Web sites of *Governing Magazine, Government Technology Executive News*, and the *Chronicle of Philanthropy*. Have each individual discuss the most recent topics being discussed. After the topics have been presented, discuss where the topics overlap. Do differences exist among the technology topics of public and nonprofit organizations?
2. Using the Internet, conduct research in identifying three HRIS systems and the companies that develop them. Develop criteria to evaluate the systems. Then use these criteria to prepare a presentation summarizing what you believe to be the benefits of each and introducing the companies that developed them.

CHAPTER FOURTEEN

CONCLUSION: CHALLENGES FOR PUBLIC AND NONPROFIT ORGANIZATIONS

The chapters in Part One of this book addressed how society and workplaces have changed and what the strategic human resources management (SHRM) implications of those changes are for public and nonprofit organizations. The chapters in Part Two focused on HRM techniques and practices: job analysis, recruitment and selection, performance evaluation, compensation, benefits, training and development, labor-management relations and collective bargaining, as well as information technology and human resources information systems (HRIS). This chapter summarizes the main points addressed in earlier chapters and discusses how SHRM can be used to help organizations cope with the challenges that lie ahead.

What to Expect

Public and nonprofit organizations are facing reduced budgets that lower funding for social services, health care, education, legal services, and arts and culture programs for the foreseeable future. Instead of expanding programs and hiring new employees, they are facing reductions in force. To cope, they must be prepared to invest time and money in training their current staff. For many agencies, there is likely to be an increase in the use of contingency workers, workers employed on a temporary or part-time basis, and services contracted out to independent contractors.

New cultural and social changes are affecting the workplace. The numbers of female, minority, disabled, and older workers have increased substantially. There may be four generations of employees working for an agency or department. Many of their values are the same as to what they may expect in regard to interesting and challenging work; however, how they work and their comfort with technology may be different. Their learning styles may also be different. Not only have the public and nonprofit workforces become more demographically diverse, but the values of employees have also changed. They want challenging jobs, and they want to exercise discretion in those jobs.

Jobs are changing, and with those changes arise quality-of-life and quality-of-work issues. Employees want to satisfy their important personal needs by working in the organization. In addition to the desire for more autonomy, employees are looking for a better fit between work and family responsibilities. They are seeking alternative work schedules such as flextime, compressed schedules, and part-time employment opportunities so they can spend more time with their families.

The legal environment has changed as well. Public and nonprofit agencies must comply with federal, state, and local laws; with executive orders; with the rules and regulations promulgated by administrative agencies such as the Equal Employment Opportunity Commission and U.S. Department of Labor; and with federal and state court decisions. Equal employment opportunity, compensation, labor relations, and employer contributions to benefits such as retirement plans and pensions, workers' compensation, and unemployment insurance are regulated by law. The legal environment must be monitored because it is always changing. Some of the legislation that was pending before Congress and in state and federal courts at the time this edition was written may become law and change the legal environment.

Technology has changed many jobs and has led to new skill requirements and organizational structures. Changes in information technology have led to modifications in job knowledge and responsibilities. Earlier chapters provided some examples of the uses of technology and how it has and will continue to affect the workplace. The increased use of information technology has changed the way organizations are structured and the way work is organized and managed.

The use of technology can be exciting, but there are some caveats of which employers need to be aware. To eliminate any gaps in gender, race, or age, employers should require technology training for all employees in appropriate job categories. The training programs should be monitored to ensure that all eligible employees participate. Training in computer skills is not enough; stereotypes that suggest that women, persons of color, individuals with disabilities, and older workers are incapable of learning new technology should be purged from the workplace.

All of these forces have implications for managing public and nonprofit organizations. Many jobs have been changed or eliminated, and employees must constantly upgrade their knowledge, skills, abilities, and other characteristics (KSAOCs). In some instances, upgrading incumbent employees' KSAOCs is not enough; organizations must recruit and hire people with advanced skills. In order to survive, public and nonprofit organizations need employees who can help them provide high-quality mission-related services. To be assured of this, they must link their HRM functions to the short- and long-term priorities of the organization.

Public and nonprofit organizations are subject to the capriciousness of funding, financial support, and market positions, in addition to public and political support that often vacillates. The demands placed on public and nonprofit organizations keep changing. Across both sectors is recognition that organizations need to restructure their HRM systems because they are often unable to attract and retain energetic and competent personnel. They need to reengineer management systems to best use their workforces to facilitate improvements in the quality of their services and workforce productivity.

Alternative service delivery programs require new skills. Employees and organizations can no longer possess tunnel vision or overspecialization. To be effective requires a breadth of knowledge, an interest in learning, and a willingness to tap the knowledge of others (Bozeman & Straussman, 1990). The immediate SHRM implication is that agencies must identify the KSAOCs needed both now and in the future, and they must audit their organizations to determine whether incumbent employees already possess those KSAOCs or can develop them through training and development activities. If neither of these is the case, then HRM departments must work with department managers and line personnel to develop recruitment and selection strategies. Managers and employees need to think about the future and prepare for impending changes.

The requirement for flexibility and speed of response to market changes is likely to continue. This has implications for the practice of SHRM. Agencies need to invest in their workforces and ensure that their members have sufficient security. Employees who fear losing their jobs will resist innovations. Instead, agencies should provide learning environments, invest in development opportunities, and train and retrain their employees when dictated by changes in technology or demands for service.

As Cohen and Eimicke (2002, p. 11) noted, the "effective public manager of the twenty-first century will need to be creative, innovative, and entrepreneurial, as well as a lifelong learner. Stability, complacency and routine will increasingly be replaced by change, new problems, and new solutions. Get used to it."

Challenges of Strategic Human Resources Management

The demographic characteristics of the labor force have changed. There have been increases in the number of women, racial and ethnic minorities, older employees, disabled, and homosexual and transgendered individuals in the workforce. Organizations must recognize underlying attributes or nonobservable characteristics, such as different learning styles, different working styles and values, and different types of personalities, as well as differences in culture, socioeconomic background, educational background, occupational background, and professional orientation.

To accommodate the changing workforce and to minimize conflict, organizations should promote a greater awareness of diversity issues and cultural differences. It is also important that they audit their human resources functions to ensure that they are free from bias. Recruitment selection, training and development, performance evaluation, and compensation and benefits should be administered in an equitable fashion. To avoid discriminating against the disabled, the essential functions of positions and the KSAOCs necessary for successful performance must be identified.

Under the Age Discrimination in Employment Act, employers can no longer force employees to retire when they reach a certain age as long as they are still capable of performing their jobs. In fact, the U.S. Congress is encouraging individuals to work longer and delay retirement, thereby delaying when they will receive Social Security benefits. Fewer employees retiring at early ages combined with flatter organizational structures results in fewer promotional opportunities and career plateauing. To retain a motivated and energetic workforce, new types of career enhancement opportunities need to be developed to challenge employees. To older employees who arc reluctant to retire, organizations may want to offer part-time work, phased retirements, or early retirement buyouts.

Families are another characteristic that differentiate workers. Many employees in the public and nonprofit sector are parents who need greater flexibility in work schedules and work patterns to accommodate family responsibilities. Flexible work arrangements are needed for parents to care for young children or in some cases for employees to care for their parents. More opportunities should be available for part-time work, and there should be greater variety in benefits programs, such as child care and elder care. Benefits packages should recognize alternative families and different priorities.

Alternative scheduling now being used in many public and nonprofit organizations includes job sharing, flextime, and a compressed workweek (a full week's work is compressed into fewer than five days). Working at home or telecommuting are other options.

Change in Skill Requirements

More and more jobs in the public and nonprofit sector are of a professional nature, requiring higher levels of education and fewer jobs requiring routine tasks. Technology has taken on much of the workplace's mentally and physically repetitive tasks. Jobs today require employees to possess greater skills as they assume more challenging responsibilities. Organizations need to acquire the skills necessary for coping with the challenges brought on by today's competitiveness.

Organizations need to acquire the skills necessary for coping with the challenges brought on by today's competitiveness.

Accompanying the change in competitiveness are changes in the way organizations are evaluated. Critical performance standards are *efficiency*, defined as the ability to produce higher volume with the same or fewer resources; *quality*, defined as matching products or services to a human need with a consistent conformance to standards; *variety*, defined as providing choices to suit diverse tastes and needs; *customization*, defined as tailoring goods and services to individual clientele; *convenience*, defined as developing user-friendly products and services and delivering them with high levels of customer satisfaction; and *timeliness*, defined as delivering innovations to customers, making continuous improvement, and developing new applications quickly (Carnevale & Carnevale, 1993).

These new performance standards require improved skills and competencies for employees throughout the organization, regardless of position. Skills deemed to be necessary include the academic basics, such as proficiency in reading, writing, and computation; self-management skills, such as self-esteem, motivation, goal-setting ability, and willingness to participate in career development activities; social skills, such as interpersonal, negotiation, and teamwork skills; communication skills, such as the ability to listen and communicate clearly; and influencing skills, or leadership abilities (Carnevale & Carnevale, 1993).

Today's jobs require an educated workforce with advanced knowledge. Training needs to be continuous; alternative training methods such as interactive videos and individual training modules can be used. Employees need to be trained not just for the positions they already hold but also for future jobs and KSAOCs. Training must be available for all employees regardless of their level in the organization.

As skill requirements increase, job tasks often become less specific. In such situations, job requirements become more flexible and overlapping, making the development of standardized examinations more difficult. Due to changes in the workplace and the rapid changes in technology that necessitate a high degree of change and evolution, it will become necessary to develop selection examinations that capture a variety of KSAOCs. More accurate selection techniques need to be used, using many of the advanced techniques identified in Chapter Seven, to evaluate not only technical skills but also interpersonal or leadership skills. Selection techniques will have to assess many of the skills associated with organizational citizen behaviors, adaptability, and flexibility. Employees will need to possess initiative, judgment, decision-making skills, leadership abilities, interpersonal skills, and other competencies often neglected during the selection process.

Conclusion

The underlying belief of strategic human resources management is the conviction that public and nonprofit employees are important assets to an organization and critical for the organization's success. Human resources representatives should be part of the strategic planning process, along with representatives from other departments. After strategies are formulated, human resources specialists, department directors, line managers, employees, and, in unionized organizations, union representatives should collaborate with one another to develop programs, policies, job tasks, and responsibilities that are compatible with the organization's overall strategies.

References

Adams, J. S. (1965). Inequity in social exchange. In L. R. Berkowitz (Ed.), *Advances in experimental social psychology* (Vol. 2. pp. 267–299). Orlando, FL: Academic Press.

Adams, L. E. (1992, February). Securing your HRIS in a microcomputer environment. *HR Magazine*, 56–61.

Adams, T. (2006). *Staying engaged, stepping up: Succession planning and executive transition management for nonprofit boards of directors*. Baltimore, MD: Annie E. Casey Foundation. http://www.aecf.org/upload/PublicationFiles/staying%20engaged,%20stepping%20up.pdf.

Adarand Constructors v. *Pena*. (1995). 515 U.S. 200.

Advisory Committee on Student Financial Assistance. (2001). *Access denied: Restoring the nation's commitment to equal educational opportunity*. Washington, DC: Author.

Agochiya, D. (2002). *Every trainer's handbook*. Thousand Oaks, CA: Sage.

Aho, K. (1989). Achieving pay equity. *American City and County*, *104*, 14–15.

Albert, S. (2000). *Hiring the chief executive: A practical guide to the search and selection process* (Rev. ed.). Washington, DC: National Center for Nonprofit Boards.

Albrecht, K. (2005). *Social intelligence: The new science of success*. San Francisco: Jossey-Bass.

Albrecht, K. (2007). *Practical intelligence: The art and science of common sense*. San Francisco: Jossey-Bass.

Alderfer, C. P. (1972). *Existence, relatedness, and growth: Human needs in organizational settings*. New York: Free Press.

Alexander, G. D. (1991, February). Working with volunteers: No pain, no gain. *Fund Raising Management*, 62–63.

Alonso, P., & Lewis, G. B. (2001). Public service motivation and job performance: Evidence from the federal sector. *American Review of Public Administration, 31*, 363–380.

American Civil Liberties Union (ACLU). (2004). Pentagon agrees to end direct sponsorship of Boy Scout troops in response to religious discrimination charge. http://www.ACLU.Org/Religion/Discrim/16382prs20041115.html.

American Federation of State, County, and Municipal Employees v. *State of Washington*. (1985). 770 F.2d 1401.

American Federation of State, County, and Municipal Employees. (1988). *Nonprofit agency employees: Working for people, not for profit.* Washington, DC: AFL-CIO.

American Psychiatric Association. (2000). *Diagnostic and statistical manual of mental disorders* (4th ed.). Arlington, VA: American Psychiatric Association.

Ammons, D. N., & Glass, J. J. (1989). *Recruiting local government executives: Practical insights for hiring authorities and candidates.* San Francisco: Jossey-Bass.

Anderson, L. M., & Baroody, N. B. (1992, August). Managing volunteers. *Fund Raising Management, 23*, 43–45.

Anft, M. (2007). Inching to the top: Nonprofit managers who are minorities search for a quicker way of the ladder. *Chronicle of Philanthropy, 20*(1), D4–D6.

Arline v. *School Board of Nassau County*. (1987). 479 U.S. 8937.

Aronson, A. H. (1974). State and local personnel administration. In United States Civil Service Commission (Ed.), *Biography of an ideal.* Washington, DC: Government Printing Office.

Arvey, R. D. (1986). Sex bias in job evaluation procedures. *Personnel Psychology, 39*, 315–335.

Arvey, R. D., & Faley, R. H. (1988). *Fairness in selecting employees* (2nd ed.). Reading, MA: Addison-Wesley.

Arvey, R. D., Nutting, S. M., & Landon, T. E. (1992). Validation strategies for physical ability testing in police and fire settings. *Public Personnel Management, 21*, 301–312.

Ashbaugh, S., & Miranda, R. (2002). Technology for human resources management: Seven questions and answers. *Public Personnel Management, 31*(1), 7–20.

Atkins v. *City of Char1otte*. (1969). U.S. Dist. Ct. 296, F. Supp.

Auslander, J. (2007, December 10). Santa Fe casts wide net for new police officers. *Santa Fe New Mexican.* http://license.icopyright.net/user/viewFreeUse.act?fuid=NjI4MzI2.

Axelrod, N. R. (2002). *Chief executive succession planning: The board's role in securing your organization's future.* Washington, DC: BoardSource.

Baker, J. R. (1994). Government in the twilight zone: Motivations of volunteers to small city boards and commissions. *State and Local Government Review, 26*, 119–128.

Baker, J. R. (2006). Recruitment to boards and commissions in small cities: Individual versus contextual explanations. *State and Local Government Review, 38*(3), 142–155.

Ban, C., & Riccucci, N. (1993). Personnel systems and labor relations: Steps toward a quiet revolution. In F. J. Thompson (Ed.), *Revitalizing state and local public service:*

Strengthening performance, accountability, and citizen confidence (pp. 71–103). San Francisco: Jossey-Bass.

Barr, S. (2007, October 5). Bill pushes diversity among senior executives. *Washington Post.* http://www.washingtonpost.com/wp-dyn/content/article/2007/10/04/AR2007100402369.html.

Barr, S. (2008, April 21). Election e-mails can end your term in office. *Washington Post,* D01.

Barrett, G., Phillips, J., & Alexander, R. (1981). Concurrent and predictive validity designs: A critical reanalysis. *Journal of Applied Psychology, 66,* 1–6.

Barrick, M. R., & Mount, M. K. (1991). The big five personality dimensions and job performance: A meta-analysis. *Personnel Psychology, 44,* 1–26.

Barrick, M. R., Mount, M. K., & Judge, T. A. (2001). Personality and performance at the beginning of the new millennium: What do we know and where do we go next? *International Journal of Selection and Assessment Performance, 9*(1/2), 9–29.

Bartram, D. (2005). The great eight competencies: A criterion-centric approach to validation. *Journal of Applied Psychology, 90,* 1185–1203.

Behrendt, B. (2008, April 24). HR director resigns position. *St. Petersburg Times.* http://www.tampabay.rr.com/news/local/governemnt/article472049.ece.

Bell, M. P., & Berry, D. P. (2007). Viewing diversity through different lenses: Avoiding a few blind spots. *Academy of Management Perspectives, 21*(4), 21–25.

Benavides, A. D. (2006). Hispanic city managers in Texas: A small group of professional administrators. *State and Local Government Review, 38*(2), 112–119.

Benton, T. (1993). Union negotiating. *Nursing Management, 23,* 70, 72.

Berkshire, J. C. (2007). A Bay Area health charity bridges cultural gap to help new immigrants. *Chronicle of Philanthropy, 20*(1), D13.

Berkshire, J. C. (2008, April 3). A parting of ways. Lack of communication is behind many executive firings. *Chronicle of Philanthropy, 20*(12), 37–39.

Bernardin, H. J. (1986). Subordinate appraisal: A valuable source of information about managers. *Human Resources Management, 25,* 421–439.

Billitteri, T. J. (1999, February 11). A safety net for aging activists: Coalition sets up first pension plan designed for social-justice crusaders. *Chronicle of Philanthropy,* 27–28.

Blumenthal, R. (2007, January 11). Unfilled city manager posts hint at future gap. *New York Times.* http://www.nytimes.com/2007/01/11/us/11managers.html.

Blumrosen, R. G. (1979). Wage discrimination, job segregation, and Title VII of the Civil Rights Act of 1964. *University of Michigan Law Review, 12,* 397–502.

Board of Trustees of the University of Alabama v. *Garrett.* (2001). 531 U.S. 356.

Boezeman, E. J., & Ellemers, N. (2007). Volunteering for charity: Pride, respect, and the commitment of volunteers. *Journal of Applied Psychology, 92*(3), 771–785.

Boris, E. T. (2006). Nonprofit organizations in a democracy: Varied roles and responsibilities. In E. T. Boris & C. E. Steuerle (Eds.), *Nonprofits & government: Collaboration & conflict* (2nd. ed., pp. 1–35). Washington, DC: Urban Institute Press.

Borman, W. C., & Motowidlo, S. J. (1993). Expanding the criterion domain to include elements. of contextual performance. In N. Schmitt & W. C. Borman (Eds.), *Personnel selection* (pp. 71–98). San Francisco: Jossey-Bass.

Borman, W. C., Penner, L. A., Allen, T. D., & Motowidlo, S. J. (2001). Personality predictors of citizenship performance. *International Journal of Selection and Assessment, 9*, 52–69.

Borzo, J. (2004, May 24). Almost human. *Wall Street Journal*, R1, R10.

Bourgault, J., Chairf, M., Maltais, D., & Rouillard, L. (2006). Hypotheses concerning the prevalence of competencies among government executives, according to three organizational variables. *Public Personnel Management, 35*(2), 89–117.

Bowen, W. G. (1994). When a business leader joins a nonprofit board. *Harvard Business Review, 72*, 38–43.

Bozeman, B., & Straussman, J. D. (1990). *Public management strategies: Guidelines for managerial effectiveness*. San Francisco: Jossey-Bass.

Boy Scouts of America and Monmouth Council et al. v. *James Dale*. (2000). 530 U.S. 640.

Boy Scouts of America v. *Wyman*. (2003). United States Court of Appeals Second Circuit, Docket Number 02-9000.

Bramley, P. (1996). *Evaluating training effectiveness* (2nd ed.). New York: McGraw-Hill.

Brannick, M. T., Levine, E. L., & Morgeson, F. P. (2007). *Job and work analysis: Methods, research, and approaches for human resources management* (2nd ed.). Thousand Oaks, CA: Sage.

Branti v. *Finkel*. (1980). 445 U.S. 506.

Brewer, G. A., Selden, S. C., & Facer, R. L. II, (2000). Individual conceptions of public service motivation. *Public Administration Review, 60*(3), 254–264.

Bridges, K., & Cicero, D. (2007). *Preparing for an aging workforce: A focus on New York businesses*. Washington, DC: AARP.

Bright, L. (2005). Public employees with high levels of public service motivation: Who are they, where are they, and what do they want? *Review of Public Personnel Administration, 25*(2), 138–154.

Bright, L. (2007). Does person-organization fit mediate the relationship between public service motivation and the job performance of public employees? *Review of Public Personnel Administration, 27*(4), 361–379.

Brockbank, W., Johnson, D., & Ulrich, D. (2008). *Mastery at the intersection of people and business*. Alexandria, VA: Society for Human Resources Management.

Brown, W. (2007). Board development practices and competent board members: Implications for performance. *Nonprofit Management and Leadership, 17*(3), 301–317.

Brudney, J. L. (1990). The availability of volunteers: Implications for local governments. *Administration and Society, 21*, 413–424.

Brudney, J. L. (1993). *Fostering volunteer programs in the public sector*. San Francisco: Jossey-Bass.

Brudney, J. L. (1999). The effective use of volunteers: Best practices for the public sector. *Law and Contemporary Problems, 62*(4), 219–255.

Brudney, J. L. (2001). Volunteer administration. In J. S. Ott (Ed.), *Understanding nonprofit organizations: Governance, leadership and management* (pp. 329–338). Boulder, CO: Westview Press.

Brudney, J. L., & Gazley, B. (2002). The USA Freedom Corps and the role of the states. *Spectrum: The Journal of State Government, 75*(4), 34–38.

Brudney, J. L., & Kellough, E. (2000). Volunteers in state government: Involvement, management and benefits. *Nonprofit and Voluntary Sector Quarterly, 29*(1), 111–130.

Buckley, C. (2008, April 16). Teachers at Catholic Schools strike ahead of people's visit. *New York Times.* http://www.nytimes.com/2008/04/16/nyregion/16strike.html.

Bullard, A. M., & Wright, D. S. (1993). Circumventing the glass ceiling: Women executives in American state government. *Public Administration Review, 53*, 189–202.

Burlington Industries v. *Ellerth.* (1998). 524 U.S. 742.

California Federal Savings & Loan Association v. *Guerra.* (1987). 479 U.S. 272.

Campion, M. A., Pursell, E. D., & Brown, B. K. (1988). Structured interviewing: Raising the psychometric properties of the employment interview. *Personnel Psychology, 41*, 25–42.

Carnevale, A. P., & Carnevale, D. G. (1993). Public administration and the evolving world of work. *Public Productivity and Management Review, 17*(1), 1–14.

Carnevale, A., & Desrochers, D. (2003). *Standards for what? The economics roots of K–16 reform.* Princeton, NJ: Educational Testing Service.

Carver, J. (1990). *Boards that make a difference: A new design for leadership in public and nonprofit organizations.* San Francisco: Jossey-Bass.

Cascio, W. F. (1991). *Applied psychology in personnel* (4th ed.). Upper Saddle River, NJ: Prentice Hall.

Cascio, W. F. (2000). *Costing human resources: The financial impact of behavior in organizations* (4th ed.). Cincinnati, OH: Southwestern College.

Cascio, W. F., & Boudreau, J. W. (2008). *Investing in people: The financial impact of human resource initiatives.* Upper Saddle River, NJ: Prentice Hall.

Cayer, N. J. (2003). Public employee benefits and the changing nature of the workforce. In S. W. Hays & R. C. Kearney (Eds.), *Public personnel administration: Problems and prospects* (4th ed., pp. 167–179). Upper Saddle River, NJ: Prentice Hall.

Cayer, N. J., & Roach, C.M.L. (2008). Work-life benefits. In C. G. Reddick & J. D. Coggburn (Eds.), *Handbook of employee benefits and administration* (pp. 309–334). Boca Raton, FL: CRC Press.

Champion-Hughes, R. (2001). Totally integrated employee benefits. *Public Personnel Management, 30*(3), 287–302.

Chan, G. (2008, January 8). Huge tab for retiree health: Public employee costs will pass $118.1 billion in next 30 years, state panel finds. *Sacramento Bee.* www.sacbee.com/101/v-print/story/617134.html.

Chan, S. (2007, January 23). New scanners for tracking city workers. *New York Times.* www.nytimes.com/2007/01/23/nyregion/23scanning.html?pagewanted=print.

Chapman, K. (2007, July 7). DCF admits it broke labor laws, agrees to pay overtime backlog. *Palm Beach Post.* http://www.palmbeachpost.com/localnews/content/south/epaper/2007/07/07/s1b_overtime_0707.html.

Chicago Tribune v. *National Labor Relations Board.* (1992). United States Court of Appeals for the Seventh Circuit. Nos. 91–3135, 91–3275, & 91-3317. September 10, 1992.

Christensen v. *State of Iowa,* 563 F.2d 353 (8th Cir., 1977).

City of Carmel Adoption Assistance Program. (2008, January). http://www.ci.carmel.in.us/government/humanresources/hrpdffiles2007/Adoption%20Assistance%20Program.pdf.

Clark, D., Clark, P., Day, D., & Shea, D. (2000). The relationship between health care reform and nurses' interest in union representation: The role of workplace climate. *Journal of Professional Nursing, 16*(2), 92–97.

Clark, P. B., & Wilson, J. Q. (1961). Incentive systems: A theory of organizations. *Administrative Science Quarterly, 6,* 129–166.

Clearwater Police Hispanic Outreach. (2005). Hispanic outreach: Operation Apoyo Hispano. http://www.clearwaterpolice.org/hispanic/index.asp.

Cnaan, R. A., & Goldberg-Glenn, R. S. (1991). Measuring motivation to volunteer in human services. *Journal of Applied Behavioral Science, 27,* 269–284.

Coggburn, J. D. (1998). Subordinate appraisals of managers: Lessons from a state agency. *Review of Public Personnel Administration, 18*(1), 68–79.

Coggburn, J. D. (2007). Outsourcing human resources: The case of the Texas health and human services commission. *Review of Public Personnel Administration, 27*(4), 315–335.

Coggburn, J. D., & Reddick, C. G. (2007). Public pension management: Issues and trends. *International Journal of Public Administration, 30,* 995–1020.

Cohen, S., & Eimicke, W. (2002). *The effective public manager: Achieving success in a changing government* (3rd ed). San Francisco: Jossey-Bass.

Cohn, D. (2003, March 13). Live-ins almost as likely as marrieds to be parents. *Washington Post,* p. A01.

Colavecchio-Van Sickler, S. (2005, March 29). Sheriff orders ink under wraps: There's a new sheriff in town, and he's cleaning up the agency's look. That means no visible tattoos. *St. Petersburg Times.* http://www.sptimes.com/2005/03/29/news_pf/Hillsborough?Shriff_orders_ink_un.shtml.

Colvin, R. A. (2007). The rise of transgender-inclusive laws: How well are municipalities implementing supportive nondiscrimination public employment policies? *Review of Public Personnel Administration, 27*(4), 336–360.

Colvin, R. (2008). Transgendered-inclusive workplaces and health benefits: New administration territory for public administrators. In C. G. Reddick & J. D. Coggburn (Eds.), *Handbook of employee benefits and administration* (pp. 399–414). Boca Raton, FL: CRC Press.

Commerce Clearing House Business Law Editors. (1992). *Workers' compensation manual: For managers and supervisors.* Chicago: Commerce Clearing House.

Connick v. *Myers.* (1983). 461 U.S. 138.

Cook, M. E., LaVigne, M. F., Pagano, C. M., Dawes, S. S., & Pardo, T. A. (2002, July). *Making a case for local e-government.* Albany, NY: Center for Technology in Government.

Cook v. *State of Rhode Island, Department of Mental Health, Retardation, and Hospitals.* (1993). 10 F.3d 17.

Cornelius, M., Corvington, P., & Ruesga, A. (2008). *Ready to lead? Next generation leaders speak out.* Baltimore, MD: Annie E. Casey Foundation, Meyer Foundation, idealist.org, and CompassPoint. http://www.meyerfoundation.org/newsroom/meyer_publications/ready_to_lead.

Cornwell, C., & Kellough, J. E. (1994). Women and minorities in federal government agencies: Examining new evidence from panel data. *Public Administration Review, 54,* 265–270.

Corporation of the Bishop of the Church of Jesus Christ of Latter Day Saints v. *Amos.* (1987). 483 U.S. 327.

Cortés, M., & Rafter, K. M. (2007). *Nonprofits and technology: Emerging research for usable knowledge.* Chicago: Lyceum Books.

Costa, P. T., McCrae, R. R., & Kay, G. G. (1995). Persons, places and personality: Career assessment using the revised NEO Personality Inventory. *Journal of Career Assessment, 3,* 123–139.

Cotterell, B. (2006, March 17). State advises workers of security concern; personal information may have been seen in India. *Tallahassee News Democrat.* www.tallahassee.com/apps/pbcs.dll/article?AID=/20060317/CAPITOL-NEWS/60317037/1.

Council for Adult and Experiential Learning. (2004). *The promise and practice of employer educational assistance programs: 2004 state of the field strategies and trends.* Chicago: Author. www.cael.org.

Coursey, D. H., Perry, J. L., & Brudney, J. L. (2008). Psychometric verification of Perry's public service motivation instrument. *Review of Public Personnel Administration, 28*(1), 79–90.

Cox, T., Jr. (2001). *Creating the multicultural organization: A strategy for capturing the power of diversity.* San Francisco: Jossey-Bass.

Crewson, P. E. (1997). Public-service motivation: Building empirical evidence of incidence and effect. *Journal of Public Administration Research and Theory, 4,* 499–518.

Dailey, R. C. (1986). Understanding organizational commitment for volunteers: Empirical and managerial implications. *Journal of Voluntary Action Research, 15,* 19–131.

Dale, M. (2008). Scouts sue after Philly demands rent or new policy. *Philadelphia Daily News.* www.philly.com/philly/apwires/apnews/nation/20080527_ap_scouts sue afterphillydemandsrentornewpolicy.html?asString=ph.news/nation;!category=nation;&randomOrd=052808121033.

Dale v. *Boy Scouts of America and Monmouth Council Boy Scouts.* (1998). A-2427–9573, N.J. Sup. Ct.

Dale v. *Boy Scouts of America and Monmouth Council Boy Scouts*. (1999). A-195/196–97, N.J. Sup. Ct.

Daley, D. (2008). Strategic benefits in human resources management. In C. G. Reddick & J. D. Coggburn (Eds.), *Handbook of employee benefits and administration* (pp. 15–27). Boca Raton, FL: CRC Press.

Davenport, T. H., & Short, J. E. (1990, Summer). The new industrial engineering: Information technology and business process redesign. *Sloan Management Review*, 11–27.

DCF accused of coercing employees to work overtime without pay. (2007, November 13). *Sarasota Herald Tribune*. http://www.heraldtribune.com/article/20071114/NEWS/71114053_1.

Deal, T., & Kennedy, A. (1982). *Corporate culture*. Reading, MA: Addison-Wesley.

Decker, I. M. (2008). Employee support and development benefits: Generational issues. In C. G. Reddick & J. D. Coggburn (Eds.), *Handbook of employee benefits and administration* (pp. 75–93). Boca Raton, FL: CRC Press.

DeNavas-Walt, C., Proctor, B. D., & Smith, J. (2007). *Income, poverty, and health insurance in the United States: 2006*. Washington, DC: Government Printing Office.

DeNavas-Walt, C., Proctor, B. D., & Smith, J. (2008). *Income, poverty, and health insurance in the United States: 2007*. Washington, DC: Government Printing Office.

Denhardt, K. G., & Leland, P. (2005). Incorporating issues of spirituality into the MPA curriculum. *Journal of Public Affairs Education*, *11*(2), 121–132.

Dilts, D. A. (1993). Labor-management cooperation in the public sector. *Journal of Collective Negotiations in the Public Sector*, *22*, 305–311.

Dilts, D. A., Boyda, S. W., & Scherr, M. A. (1993). Collective bargaining in the absence of protection legislation: The case of Louisiana. *Journal of Negotiations in the Public Sector*, *22*, 259–265.

Dixon, M., Wang, S., Calvin, J., Dineen, B., & Tomlinson, E. (2002). The panel interview: A review of empirical research and guidelines for practice. *Public Personnel Management*, *31*(3), 397–428.

Dobbins, G. H., Lin, T. R., & Farh, J. L. (1992). A field study of race and age similarity effects on interview ratings in conventional and situational interviews. *Journal of Applied Psychology*, *77*, 363–371.

Dothard v. *Rawlinson*. (1955). 433 U.S. 321.

Douglas, M. (2006). Getting it together: Statewide health-care data system in North Carolina will unite county and state health departments. *Government Technology*, *19*(11), 46, 48.

Drexel Homes, Inc., 182 NLRB., No 151 (1970).

Dupre's downfall was long time in the making. (2008, April 26). *St. Petersburg Times*. http://www.tampabay.rr.com/opinion/editorials/article474339.ece.

Durst, S. (1999). Assessing the effect of family friendly programs on public organizations. *Review of Public Personnel Administration*, *19*(3), 19–33

Dvorak, P. (2008, February 17). *Social workers battle heavy caseloads, workplace dangers*. Washington Post, C4.

E-vote: Ohio unveils online poll worker training program. (2008, February 7). http://govtech.com/gt/print_article.php?id=261657.

Edwards, H. T., Clark, R. T., Jr., & Craver, C. B. (Eds.). (1979). *Labor relations law in the public sector* (3rd ed.). Riverside, NJ: Bobbs-Merrill.

El Nasser, H. (2007, November 15). Not your granddad's service club: Organizations update policies to woo busy young people. *USA Today*, 3A.

Elliott, R. H. (1985). *Public personnel administration: A values perspective.* Reston, VA: Reston.

Ellis, S. J. (1995). *The board's role in effective volunteer involvement.* Washington, DC: National Center for Nonprofit Boards.

Ellison v. *Brady*. (1991). 924 F.2d 872.

Elrod v. *Burns*. (1976). 427 U.S. 347.

Evercare and National Alliance for Caregivers. (2007, November). *Evercare study of family caregivers: What they spend, what they sacrifice: Findings from a national survey.* http://www.caregiving.org/data/Evercare_NAC_CaregiverCostStudyFI-NAL20111907.pdf.

Faragher v. *Boca Raton*. (1998). 524 U.S. 75.

Farr, C. A. (1983). *Volunteers: Managing volunteer personnel in local government.* Washington, DC: International City Managers Association.

Feeney, M. K., & Kingsley, G. (2008). The rebirth of patronage: Have we come full circle? *Public Integrity*, *10*(2), 165–176.

Feldacker, B. (1990). *Labor guide to labor law* (3rd ed.). Upper Saddle River, NJ: Prentice Hall.

Feuer, D. (1987). Paying for knowledge. *Training*, *24*, 57–66.

Finding family in a nonmarried world. (2007, January 30). *Christian Science Monitor.* http://www.csmonitor.com/0130/p8s02-comv.html.

Fine, M. G., Johnson, F. L., & Ryan, M. S. (1990). Cultural diversity in the workplace. *Public Personnel Management*, *19*, 305–319.

Finkle, J. (2007, July 29). Impossible job. Here's what you need for it. *New York Times.* http://www.nytimes.com/2007/07/29/arts/design/29fink.html?n=Top/Reference/Times%20Topics/Organizations/G/Getty,%20J%20Paul,%20Museum.

Firefighters Local 1784 v. *Stotts*. (1984). 467 U.S. 561.

Fisher, J. C., & Cole, K. M. (1993). *Leadership and management of volunteer programs: A guide for volunteer administrators.* San Francisco: Jossey-Bass.

Fitz-enz, J. (1990). Getting and keeping good employees. *Personnel*, *67*, 25–28.

Fitz-enz, J. (1996). *How to measure human resources management* (2nd ed.). New York: McGraw-Hill.

Fitz-enz, J. (2000). *The ROI of human performance: Measuring the economic value of employee performance.* New York: AMACOM.

Fitzgerald, W. (1992). Training versus development. *Training and Development Journal*, *5*, 81–84.

Fleming, J. (2007a, October 4). Notes of discord resonate as season begins. *St. Petersburg Times*, 18W-19W.

Fleming, J. (2007b, December 10). Orchestra votes to ratify. *St. Petersburg Times.* http://www.sptimes.com/2007/12/10/Southpinellas/Orchestra_votes_to_ra.shtml.

Fleming, J. (2008, January 29). Orchestra achieves a measure of progress: Though cash flow problems loom, new CEO Michael Pastreich has brought a fresh attitude—and success. *St. Petersburg Times,* 1E, 4E.

Flynn, J. P. (2006, May). Designing a practical succession planning program. *PA Times,* 4, 6.

Freeman, L. (2006, December 17, 2006). Hospitals get creative with recruitment. *Naples Daily News.* http://www.naples.com/news/2006/dec/17/get_creative_recruitment/?local_news.

Freking, K. (2007, October, 14). Depression reported by 7% of the workforce. *Washington Post,* A7.

Gael, S. (1988). *The job analysis handbook for business, industry, and government.* Hoboken, NJ: Wiley.

Garcetti v. *Ceballos.* (2006). 126 S. Ct. 1951.

Garcia v. *San Antonio Metropolitan Transit Authority.* 488 U.S. 889.

Gardner, H. (1993). *Multiple intelligences: The theory in practice.* New York: Basic Books.

Gardner, H. (1999). *Intelligence reframed: Multiple intelligences for the 21st century.* New York: Basic Books.

Gardner, H., & Hatch, T. (1989). Multiple intelligences go to school. *Educational Researcher, 18,* 4–10.

Garry, P. M. (2007, Fall). Constitutional relevance of the employer-sovereign relationship: Examining the due process rights of government employees in light of the public employee speech doctrine. *St. John's Law Review.* http://findarticles.com/p/articles/mi_qa3735/is_200710/ai_n21100611/print.

Gaston, C. L. (1986). An idea whose time has not come: Comparable worth and the market salary problem. *Population Research and Policy Review, 5,* 15–29.

Gay, M. (2008, January 5). Firehouse dispute raises racial tension in St. Louis. *New York Times.* http://www.nytimes.com/2008/01/05/us/05stlouis.html.

Gelbart, M. (2008, January 24). A warning on Philadelphia's pension and health costs. A Pew report says health and pension costs will drain Phils.'s resources to tackle other problems. *Philadelphia Inquirer.* http://www.philly.com/inquire/local/20080124_Warning_oncitys_Quiet_Crisis.html?adString-inq.news/local;category=local;&randomOrd=012408082859.

Gilbert, J. A., & Ivancevich, J. M. (2000). Valuing diversity: A tale of two organizations. *Academy of Management Executive, 14*(1), 93–105.

Gill, M., Flynn, R. J., & Reissing, E. (2005). The governance self-assessment checklist: An instrument for assessing board effectiveness. *Nonprofit Management & Leadership, 15*(3), 271–294.

Gilmore, T. N. (1993). *Finding and retaining your next chief executive: Making the transition work.* Washington, DC: National Center for Nonprofit Boards.

Goldberg, L. R. (1999). A broad-bandwidth, public-domain, personality inventory measuring the lower-level facets of several five-factor models. In I. Mervielde, I. Deary, F. De Fruyt, & F. Ostendorf (Eds.), *Personality psychology in Europe* (Vol. 7, pp. 1–28). Tilburg, Netherlands: Tilburg University Press.

Goleman, D. (1995). *Emotional intelligence: Why it can matter more than IQ.* New York: Bantam.

Goleman, D. (1998). *Working with emotional intelligence.* New York: Bantam.

Goleman, D. (2006). *Social intelligence: The new science of human relationships.* New York: Bantam Books.

Gosport Volunteer Centre. (2008). *Barriers to volunteering.* http://www.gosportvb.force9.co.uk/barriers.html.

Gossett, C. W. (2006). Lesbian and gay men in the public-sector workforce. In N. M. Riccucci (Ed.), *Public personnel management: Current concerns, future challenges* (4th ed., pp. 70–91). New York: Longman.

Gossett, C. W., & Ng, E.S.W. (2008). Domestic partnership benefits. In C. G. Reddick & J. D. Coggburn (Eds.), *Handbook of employee benefits and administration* (pp. 379–397). Boca Raton, FL: CRC Press.

Gottfredson, G. D., & Holland, J. L. (1994). *Position classification inventory.* Odessa, FL: Psychological Assessment Resources.

Graham, M. (1992). The drive for comparable worth: Has it sputtered out? *P.A. Times*, p. 8.

Gratz v. *Bollinger.* (2003). 539 U.S. 244.

Green, J. (2000). Introduction to transgendered issues. In P. Currah & S. Minter (Eds.), *Transgender equality.* New York: National Gay and Lesbian Task Force.

Greenberg, J. (1986). Determinants of perceived fairness of performance evaluations. *Journal of Applied Psychology, 71*, 340–342.

Greenberg, J. (1996). *The quest for justice on the job: Essays and experiment.* Thousand Oaks, CA: Sage.

Greenblatt, A. (2004, December). Sweetheart deals. *Governing*, 20–25.

Greene, M. P. (2007). Beyond diversity and multiculturism: Towards the development of anti-racist institutions and leaders. *Journal for Nonprofit Management, 11*(1), 9–17.

Greenhouse, S. (2007, December 23). Labor Board restricts union use of e-mail. *New York Times*, 22.

Grossman, R. J. (2007, June). New competencies for HR: Researchers have updated the portfolio of competencies for high-performing HR professionals. *HR Magazine.* http://shrm.org/hrmagazine/articles/0607/0607grossman.asp.

Grutter v. *Bollinger.* (2003). 539 U.S. 306.

Guiler, J. K., & Shafritz, J. M. (2004). Dual personnel systems—organized labor and civil service: Side by side in the public sector. *Journal of Labor Research, 24*(2), 199–209.

Guion, R. M., & Highhouse, S. (2006). *Essentials of personnel assessment and selection.* Mahwah, NJ: Erlbaum.

Guion, R. M., Highhouse, S., Reeve, C., & Zickar, M. J. (2005). *The self-descriptive index*. Bowling Green, OH: Sequential Employment Testing.

Gupta, N. (1997). Rewarding skills in the public sector. In H. Risher, C. Fay, & Associates (Eds.), *New strategies for public pay: Rethinking government compensation programs*. San Francisco: Jossey-Bass.

Gupta, N., Jenkins, G. D., Jr., & Curington, W. P. (1986). Paying for knowledge: Myths and realities. *National Productivity Review*, *5*, 107–123.

Guy, M. E. (1993). Three steps forward, two steps backward: The status of women's integration into public management. *Public Administration Review*, *53*, 285–292.

Guy, M. E., & Newman, M. A. (2004). Women's jobs, men's jobs: Sex segregation and emotional labor. *Public Administration Review*, *64*(3), 289–298.

Guy, M. E., Newman, M. A., & Mastracci, S. H. (2008). *Emotional labor: Putting the service in public service*. Armonk, NY: M. E. Sharpe.

Hall, H. (2006a). Planning successful successions: Preparing for a leader's departure can prevent problems. *Chronicle of Philanthropy*, *17*(6), 6, 8, 10.

Hall, H. (2006b). Smooth transitions: Experts offer tips on hiring new leaders. *Chronicle of Philanthropy*, *17*(6), 11.

Hall, H., & Kean, S. (2008). Bracing for tough times: Many charities feel vulnerable as economy slips. *Chronicle of Philanthropy*, *20*(8), 6–7, 11.

Halpern, R. P. (2006, February). *Workforce issues in the nonprofit sector: Generational leadership change and diversity*. Kansas City, MO: American Humanics.

Hammonds, K. H. (2005). Why we hate HR. *Fast Company*, *97*, 40.

Handy, F., & Cnaan, R. A. (2007). The role of social anxiety in volunteering. *Nonprofit Management and Leadership*, *18*(1), 41–58.

Hanson, W. (2007, October 4). *Missouri education office recruits IT staff from Second Life*. http://www.govtech.com/gt/print_article.php?id=151168.

Harris, B. (2001). Training for light speed. *Government and Information Technology*, 8, 46–47.

Harris v. *Forklift Systems*. (1993). 510 U.S. 17.

Harshbarger, S., & Crafts, A. (2007). The whistle-blower: Policy challenges for nonprofits. *Nonprofit Quarterly*, *14*(4), 36–44.

Healey v. *Southwood Psychiatric Hospital*, Cal. 3, 70 FEP 439, 1996.

Healy, B., & Southard, G. D. (1994, April). *Pay for performance*. City of Claremont, California.

Helfand, L. (2007a, February 28). Largo officials vote to dismiss Stanton. *St. Petersburg Times*. http://www.sptimes.com/2007/02/28/news_pf/Tampabay/Largo_officials_vote_.shtml.

Helfand, L. (2007b, March 21). Focus shifts to Stanton record: Criticism of his job as city manager is pushing aside his gender change plans as ammunition against him. *St. Petersburg Times*, 1B, 7B.

Helgeson, B. (2008, January 12). Lawmaker: Too few troopers for safety. *Tampa Tribune*, 1, 8.

Helton, K. A., & Jackson, R. D. (2007). Navigating Pennsylvania's dynamic workforce: Succession planning in a complex environment. *Public Personnel Management*, *36*(4), 335–348.

Henderson, R. I. (1989). *Compensation management* (5th ed.). Englewood Cliffs, NJ: Prentice-Hall.

Henderson, R. I. (2000). *Compensation management in a knowledge based world* (8th ed.). Upper Saddle River, NJ: Prentice-Hall.

Heneman, R. D. (1992). *Merit pay: Linking pay increases to performance ratings*. Reading, MA: Addison-Wesley.

Herman, R. D. (2005). Board members of nonprofit organizations as volunteers. In J. L. Brudney (Ed.), *Emerging areas of volunteering* (pp. 77–91). Indianapolis: ARNOVA.

Herman, R. D., & Heimovics, R. D. (1989). Critical events in the management of non-profit organizations: Initial evidence. *Nonprofit and Voluntary Sector Quarterly*, *18*, 119–132.

Herzberg, F. (1964, January–February). The motivation-hygiene concept. *Personnel Administration*, 3–7.

Herzberg, F. (1968). One more time: How do you motivate employees? *Harvard Business Review*, *46*, 36–44.

Herzlinger, R. E. (1994). Effective oversight: A guide for nonprofit directors. *Harvard Business Review*, *72*, 52–60.

Hinkelman, M. (2008, May 28). Scouts sue the city to stay in $1 HQ. *Philadelphia Daily News*. http://www.philly.com/philly/hp/news_update/20080528_Scouts_sue_city_to_stay_in__1_HQ.html?adString=ph.news/news_update;!category=news_update;&randomOrd=081208115620.

Hoff, J. (2006, May 1). My virtual life. *Business Week*, 72–78.

Hopwood et al. v. *State of Texas et al.* (1996). 84 F.3d 720.

Houle, C. O. (1989). *Governing boards*. San Francisco: Jossey-Bass.

Houston, D. J. (2005). "Walking the walk" of public service motivation: Public employees and charitable gifts of time, blood, and money. *Journal of Public Administration Research and Theory*, *16*, 67–86.

HRO Today. (2007, October). HRO today 2008 resource guide. *HRO Today*, *6*(8), 23–107.

Hrywna, M. (2008, February). Special report NPT salary survey. *Nonprofit Times*, *22*, 21.

Hsieh, C. W., & Winslow, E. (2006). Gender representation in the federal work-force: A comparison among groups. *Review of Public Personnel Administration*, *26*(3), 276–294.

Hudson, D. L., Jr. (2008, January). The Garcetti effect: Government employees fear high court case undermines retaliation protections. *ABA Journal*, 16–17.

Hughes, M. A., Ratliff, R. A., Purswell, J. L., & Hadwiger, J. (1989). A content validation methodology for job related physical performance tests. *Public Personnel Management*, *18*, 487–504.

Hunter, J. E. (1986). Cognitive ability, cognitive aptitude, job knowledge, and job performance. *Journal of Vocational Behavior*, *29*, 340–362.

Hush, H. (1969). Collective bargaining in voluntary agencies. *Social Casework*, *50*, 210–213.

Hyland, S. L. (1990, September). Helping employees with family care. *Monthly Labor Review*, 22–26.

Ibarra, P. (2006, August). The myths and realities of succession planning. *IPMA-HR News*, 13, 15.

ICMA. (2007). *A budgeting guide* (2nd ed.). Washington, DC: Author.

Independence-National Education Association v. Independence School District. (2007). S.W. 3d, 2007, WL 1532737, Mo. Banc.

Inglis, S., & Cleave, S. (2006). A scale to assess board members' motivations in nonprofit organizations. *Nonprofit Management and Leadership*, *17*(1), 83–101.

Ingram, R. T. (1988). *Ten basic responsibilities on nonprofit boards*. Washington, DC: National Center for Nonprofit Boards.

Internal Revenue Service. (2008, June). *IRS Publication 557. Tax-exempt status for your organization*. www.irs.gov/pub/irs-pdf/p.557.pdf.

International City County Managers Association (ICMA). (2001). *Recruitment guidelines for selecting a local government administrator*. Washington, DC: Author.

International Personnel Management Association for Human Resources-HR (IPMA-HR). (2002). *Workforce planning resource guide for public sector human resource professionals*. Washington, DC: Author.

IPMA-HR. (2005). *Personnel practices: Skill-based pay*. Alexandria, VA: Author. http://www.ipma-hr.org.

IPMA-HR. (2006). *Personnel practices: Gainsharing policies*. Alexandria, VA: Author. http://www.ipma-hr.org.

Jackson, D. K., & Holland, T. P. (1998). Measuring the effectiveness of nonprofit boards. *Nonprofit and Voluntary Sector Quarterly*, *27*(2), 159–182.

Jamison, I. B. (2003). Turnover and retention among volunteers in human service agencies. *Review of Public Personnel Administration*, *23*(2), 114–132.

Jarosz, F. (2007, November 24). Carmel will help its employees adopt: City's offer of $5,000 toward adoption costs is unusual for municipalities, advocates say. *Indianapolis Star*, p. Y06.

Jensen, B., & Perry, S. (2008, February 28). A budget squeeze hits charities: Bush's 2009 plan calls for cuts in social services and the arts. *Chronicle of Philanthropy*, 20–23.

Johnson, A. (2007, January 8). FBI seeks women as agents. *Pittsburgh Tribune-Review*. http://www.pittsburghlive.com/x/pittsburghtrib/news/cityregion/print_487495.html.

Johnson, R. E. (1988). Flexible benefit plans. In J. Matzer Jr. (Ed.), *Pay and benefits: New ideas for local government*. Washington, DC: International City Managers Association.

Johnson-Bateman Cp. (1989) 295 NLRB No. 26.

Johnson v. *Santa Clara Transportation Agency*. (1987). 480 U.S. 616.

Kaiser Family Foundation. (2006, September). *Health insurance premium growth moderate slightly in 2006, but still increases twice as fast as wages and inflation*. http://www.hret.org/hret/media/content/EHBSrelease06.pdf.

Kalev, A., Dobbin, F., & Kelly, E. (2006). Best practices or best guesses? Assessing the efficacy of corporate affirmative action and diversity policies. *American Sociological Review*, *71*, 589–617.

Kanter, R. M., & Summers, D. V. (1987). Doing well while doing good: Dilemmas of performance measurement in nonprofit organizations and the need for a multiple-constituency approach. In W. W. Powell (Ed.), *The nonprofit sector: A research handbook* (pp. 154–165). New Haven, CT: Yale University Press.

Kaplan, R. S., & Norton, D. P. (1996). *The balanced scorecard: Translating strategy into action.* Boston: Harvard Business School Press.

Kearney, R. C., with Carnevale, D. G. (2001). *Labor relations in the public sector* (3rd ed.). New York: Marcel Dekker.

Kellough, J. E. (2006). *Understanding affirmative action: Politics, discrimination, and the search for justice.* Washington, DC: Georgetown University Press.

Kellough, J. E., & Lu, H. (1993). The paradox of merit pay in the pubic sector. *Review of Public Personnel Administration, 13*, 45–64.

Kellough, J. E., & Nigro, L. G. (2002). Pay for performance in Georgia state government: Employee perspectives on GeorgiaGain after five years. *Review of Public Personnel Administration, 22*(2), 146–166.

Kessler, G. (2007, December 7). Ex-ambassador criticizes Rice. *Washington Post*, A27.

Kettl, D. F. (2002). *The transformation of governance: Public administration for twenty-first century America.* Baltimore, MD: John Hopkins University Press.

Keyeshian v. *Board of Regents.* (1867). 385 U.S. 589.

Kim, P. S. (1993). Racial integration in the American federal government: With special reference to Asian Americans. *Review of Public Personnel Administration, 13*, 52–66.

Kim, P. S., & Lewis, G. B. (1994). Asian Americans in the public service: Success, diversity, and discrimination. *Public Administration Review, 54*, 285–290.

Kimmel v. *Florida Board of Regents.* (2000). 528 U.S. 62.

Kirkpatrick, D. L. (1994). *Evaluating training programs: The four levels.* San Francisco: Berrett-Koehler.

Kirkpatrick, D. L. (1998). *Evaluating training programs: The four levels* (2nd ed.). San Francisco: Berrett-Koehler.

Klein, K. J., & Harrison, D. A. (2007). On the diversity of diversity: Tidy logic, messier realities. *Academy of Management Perspectives, 21*(4), 26–33.

Knauft, E. B., Berger, R. A., & Gray, S. T. (1991). *Profiles of excellence: Achieving success in the nonprofit sector.* San Francisco: Jossey-Bass.

Kolb, D. A. (1984). *Experiential learning: Experience as a source of learning and development.* Upper Saddle River: NJ: Prentice Hall.

Konrad, A. M., Prasad, P., & Pringle, J. K. (Eds.). (2006). *Handbook of workplace diversity.* Thousand Oaks, CA: Sage.

Kossek, E. E., De Marr, B. J., Backman, K., & Kolar, M. (1993). Assessing employees' emerging elder care needs and reactions to dependent care benefits. *Public Personnel Management, 22*, 617–638.

Kovach, K. A., & Millspaugh, P. E. (1990). Comparable worth: Canada legislates pay equity. *Academy of Management Executive, 4*, 92–101.

Kramer, R. M., & Grossman, B. (1987). Contracting for social services: Process management and resource dependencies. *Social Service Review*, *61*, 32–55.

Kunreuther, F. (2005). *Up next: Generation change and the leadership of nonprofit organizations.* Baltimore, MD: Annie E. Casey Foundation.

Lane, P. (1995, March 13). Partners in public service. *Nation's Cities Weekly*, 12.

Lawler, E. (1989). Pay for performance: A strategic analysis. In L. R. Gomez-Mejia (Ed.), *Compensation and benefits* (pp. 136–181). Washington, DC: Bureau of National Affairs.

Lawler, E. (2000). *Rewarding excellence: Pay strategies for the new economy.* San Francisco: Jossey-Bass.

Leader to Leader Institute. (1998). *The Drucker Foundation self-assessment tool: Workbook and process guide.* http://www.leadertoleader.org/tools/sat/content.html.

Ledbetter v. *Goodyear Tire and Rubber Co.* (2007). No. 05-1074.

Lee, C. (2008, April 25). Bush plan to contract federal jobs falls short: Scope and savings have not met goals. *Washington Post*, p. A01.

Lemons v. *City and County of Denver*, 620 F.2d 228 (10th Cir., 1980).

Letter Carriers v. *Blount.* (1969). 305 F. Supp. 546, D.D.C.

Lewis, G. B. (1988). Progress toward racial and sexual equality in the federal civil service? *Public Administration Review*, *48*, 389–397.

Lewis, G. B. (1994). Women, occupations, and federal agencies: Occupational mix and interagency differences in sexual inequality in federal white-collar employment. *Public Administration Review*, *54*, 271–276.

Light, P. C. (1998). *Sustaining innovation: Creating nonprofit and government organizations that innovate naturally.* San Francisco: Jossey-Bass.

Light, P. C. (1999). *The true size of government.* Washington, DC: Brookings Institution.

Light, P. C. (2000a). The empty government talent pool. *Brookings Review*, *18*(1), 20–23.

Light, P. C. (2000b). *Making nonprofits work: A report on the tides of nonprofit management reform.* Washington, DC: Brookings Institution.

Light, P. C. (2003). *In search of public service.* Washington, DC: Brookings Institution.

Light, P. C. (2008). A government ill executed: The depletion of the federal service. *Public Administration Review*, *68*(3), 413–419.

Lipsky, M., & Smith, S. R. (1989–1990). Nonprofit organizations, government, and the welfare state. *Political Science Quarterly*, *104*, 625–648.

Locke, E. A. (1968). Towards a theory of task motivation and incentives. *Organizational Behavior and Human Performance*, *3*, 157–189.

Loden, M. (1996). *Implementing diversity.* Chicago: Irwin.

Loft, K. (2007a, September 29). Still no deal as orchestra's masterworks season nears. *Tampa Tribune*, Metro 3.

Loft, K. (2007b, October 2). Forty harmonic convergence: Musicians and leaders of the Florida Orchestra wax philosophical as the Tampa Bay area's largest arts groups embark on its 40th season. *Tampa Tribune*, Baylife 1, 3.

Longenecker, C., & Ludwig, D. (1990). Ethical dilemmas in performance appraisal revisited. *Journal of Business Ethics*, *9*, 961–969.

Macduff, N. (2005). Societal changes and the rise of the episodic volunteer. In J. L. Brudney (Ed.), *Emerging areas of volunteering* (pp. 49–61). Indianapolis: ARNOVA.

Mann, G. A. (2006). A motive to serve: Public service motivation in human resource management and the role of PSM in the nonprofit sector. *Public Personnel Management, 35*(1), 33–48.

Manzo, P. (2004, Winter). The real salary scandal: It isn't that some nonprofit CEOs make big bucks. It's that most nonprofit employees are paid too little. *Stanford Social Innovation Review*, 65–66.

Marquis, C. (2003, March 13). Total of unmarried couples surged in 2000 U.S. census. *New York Times*. http://www.nytimes.com/2003/03/13/national/13CENS.html?pagewanted=print&position=...3/13/2003.

Maslow, A. H. (1954). *Motivations and personality*. New York: HarperCollins.

Masterson, S. S., & Taylor, M. S. (1996). Total quality management and performance appraisal: An integrative perspective. *Journal of Quality Management, 1*, 67–89.

Mauriello, T. (2007, May 27). State will be looking for lots of good men, women: Upcoming retirement of about 6 percent of commonwealth work force makes now a good time to apply for state jobs. *Pittsburgh Post-Gazette*. http://www.post-gazette.com/pg/pp/07147/789125.stm.

McCabe, B. C., & Stream, C. (2000). Diversity by the numbers: Changes in state and local government workforces, 1980–1995. *Public Personnel Management, 29*(1), 93–106.

McClelland, D. C. (1961). *The achieving society*. New York: Free Press.

McCurdy, A. H., Newman, M. A., & Lovrich, N. P. (2002). Family-friendly workplace policy adoption in general and special purpose local governments: Learning from the Washington State experience. *Review of Public Personnel Administration, 22*(1), 27–51.

McCurley, S. (1993). How to fire a volunteer and live to tell about it. *Grapevine*, 8–11.

McDaniel, M. A., Finnegan, E. B., Morgeson, F. P., Campion, M. A., & Braverman, E. P. (1997, April). *Predicting performance from common sense*. Paper presented at the 12th annual conference of the Society for Industrial Organizational Psychology, St. Louis, Mo.

McDaniel, M. A., Finnegan, E. B., Morgeson, F. P., Campion, M. A., & Braverman, E. P. (2001). Use of situational judgment tests to predict job performance: A clarification of the literature. *Journal of Applied Psychology, 86*(4), 730–740.

McDonnell Douglas v. *Green*. (1973). 401 U.S. 424.

McEvoy, G. M. (1990). Public managers' reactions to appraisals by subordinates. *Public Personnel Management, 19*, 201–212.

McKay, J. (2003, August). Full court press: Stanislaus County's superior court aggressively pursues information integration. *Government Technology*, 44, 46.

McKay, J. (2007). Mind reader. *Government Technology, 20*(6), 38, 40.

McLaughlin v. *Tilendis*. (1968). 398 F.2d 287.

McPherson v. *Rankin*. (1987). 107 S.Ct. 1561.

Meacham v. *Knolls Atomic Power Laboratory*, No. 06-1505 (2008).

Mergenbagen, P. (1991, June). A new breed of volunteer. *American Demographics, 13*, 54–55.

Meritor Savings Bank v. *Vinson*. (1986). 477 U.S. 57.

Milburn, K. (2007, December). "E" evidence: HR's role in preserving electronic data. *IPMA-HR News, 1*, 5, 15.

Milliken, F. J., & Martins, L. L. (1996). Searching for common threads: Understanding the multiple effects of diversity in organizational change. *Academy of Management Review, 21*, 402–433.

Moe, R. C. (1987). The limits of privatization. *Public Administration Review, 47*(6), 453–460.

Montjoy, R. S., & Brudney, J. L. (1991). Volunteers in the delivery of public services: Hidden costs . . . and benefits. *American Review of Public Administration, 21*, 327–344.

Morelli, K. (2007, November 10). Incident highlights rescue differences: Water work needs special skills. *Tampa Tribune*, 1, 4.

Morrison, E. K. (1994). *Leadership skills: Developing volunteers for organizational success* (3rd ed.). Tucson, AZ: Fisher Books.

Mount Healthy Board of Education v. *Doyle.* (1977). 429 U.S. 274.

Moynihan, D. P., & Pandey, S. K. (2007). The role of organizations in fostering public service motivation. *Public Administration Review, 67*(1), 40–53.

Murphy, K. R. (1996). Individual differences and behavior in organizations: Much more than g. In K. R. Murphy (Ed.), *Individual differences in organizations* (pp. 3–30). San Francisco: Jossey-Bass.

Murray, V., & Harrison, Y. (2005). *Virtual volunteering.* In J. L. Brudney (Ed.), *Emerging areas of volunteering* (pp. 31–47). Indianapolis: ARNOVA.

Muson, H. (1989, March). The nonprofit profit. *Across the Board*, pp. 24–38.

Naff, K. C., & Crum, J. (1999). Working for America: Does public service motivation make a difference? *Review of Public Personnel Administration, 19*(5), 5–16.

Naff, K. C., & Kellough, J. E. (2002). A changing workforce: Understanding diversity programs in the federal government. In M. A. Abramson & N. W. Gardner (Eds.), *Human capital 2002* (pp. 355–410). Lanham, MD: Rowman & Littlefield.

Naff, K. C., & Kellough, J. E. (2004). Responding to a wake-up call: An examination of federal diversity management programs. *Administration and Society, 36*(1), 62–90.

Nason, J. W. (1993). *Board assessment of the chief executive: A responsibility essential to good governance* (4th ed.). Washington, DC: National Center for Nonprofit Boards.

National Academy of Public Administration. (2000). *The case for transforming public-sector human resources management.* Washington, DC: Author.

National Association of Counties. (2003). *Acts of caring award winners.* http://www.naco.org/Template.cfm?Section=Acts_of_Caring_Awards&Template=/cffiles/awards/acts_srch.cfm&YearSelected=2003.

National Center for Charitable Statistics (NCCS). Number of Nonprofit Organizations in the United States, 1996–2006. http://nccsdataweb.urban.org/PubAppa/profile.1.pho?state=US.

National Commission on the State and Local Public Service. (1993). *Hard truths/tough choices: An agenda for state and local reform.* Albany, NY: Nelson A. Rockefeller Institute of Government.

National Labor Relations Board. (1991). *A guide to basic law and procedures under the NLRA*. Washington, DC: U.S. Government Printing Office.

National Labor Relations Board v. *Catholic Bishop of Chicago*. (1979). 440 U.S. 490.

National Park Service. (2008). Volunteers-in-Parks: FY07 annual report. http://www.nps.gov/volunteer/FY02annualreport_final.pdf.

National Treasury Employees Union v. *Von Raab*. (1989). 489 U.S. 656.

Nelson, S. (2007, July). The future of the federal workforce. In *Issues of merit*. Washington, DC: U.S. Merit Protections Board.

Nelson, W. R. (1982). Employment testing and the demise of the PACE examination. *Labor Law Journal, 35*, 729–750.

Nelson-Horchler, J. (1989). Elder care comes of age. *Industry Week, 238*, 54–56.

Nevada Department of Human Resources v. *Hibbs*. (2003). 538 U.S. 721.

New Mexico State Personnel Board. (2006). *Memorandum, government cost savings incentive award procedures*. http://www.spo.state.nm.us/NMState_Documents/Compensation_docs/GovernmentCostSavingsAwardGuidelinesFY2006-%20FINAL.pdf.

Newlin, J. G., & Meng, G. J. (1991). The public sector pays for performance. *Personnel Journal, 70*, 110–114.

Newman, A. (2006, December 27). Many origins but one pledge: To protect and serve the city. *New York Times*. http://www.nytimes.com/2006/12/27/nyregion/27police.html.

Oakwood Healthcare, Inc. and International Union United Automobile, Aerospace and Agricultural Implement Workers of America (UAW), AFL-CIO 348 N.L.R.B. No. 37 (2006).

Oblinger, D. (2003, July–August). Boomers, Gen-Xers, millennials: Understanding the new students. *EDUCAUSE*, 37–47.

O'Connell, B. (1988). *Finding developing, and rewarding good board members*. Washington, DC: INDEPENDENT SECTOR.

O'Connor v. *Consolidated Coin Caters Corporation*. (1996). 517 U.S. 308.

Odendahl, T., & O'Neill, M. (Eds.). (1994). *Women and power in the nonprofit sector*. San Francisco: Jossey-Bass.

Office of National Drug Control Policy. (2001). *The economic costs of drug abuse in the U.S., 1992–1998*. Washington, DC: Author.

Office of Program Policy Analysis and Government Accountability. (2007, November). *DBPR continues to make efforts to streamline processes and improve customer service*. Tallahassee, FL: Author.

Oleck, H. L. (1988). *Nonprofit corporations, organizations, and associations* (5th ed.). Upper Saddle River, NJ: Prentice Hall.

Oncale v. *Sundowner Offshore Service*. (5998). 23 U.S. 75.

O'Neill, M. O. (1989). *The third America: The emergence of the nonprofit sector in the United States*. San Francisco: Jossey-Bass.

O'Neill, M. (1994). *The paradox of women and power in the nonprofit sector*. In T. Odendahl & M. O'Neill (Eds.), *Women and power in the nonprofit sector* (pp. 1–16). San Francisco: Jossey-Bass.

Organ, D. W. (1988). *Organizational citizenship behavior: The good soldier syndrome*. Lanham, MD: Lexington Books.

Organ, D. W., Podsakoff, P. M., & MacKenzie, S. B. (2006). *Organizational citizenship behavior: Its nature, antecedents, and consequences*. Thousand Oaks, CA: Sage.

Osbourne, D., & Gaebler, T. (1992). *Reinventing government: How entrepreneurial spirit is transforming the public sector*. Reading, MA: Addison-Wesley.

Ospina, S., & O'Sullivan, J. F (2003). Working together: Meeting the challenge of workplace diversity. In S. W. Hays & R. C. Kearney (Eds.), *Public personnel administration: Problems and prospects* (4th ed.). Upper Saddle River, NJ: Prentice Hall.

Page, P. (1994). African-Americans in the senior executive service. *Review of Public Personnel Administration*, *14*, 24–51.

Page, S. E. (2007). Making the difference: Applying a logic of diversity. *Academy of Management Perspectives*, *21*(4), 6–20.

Panepento, P. (2007a, February 8). Nonprofit workers fall short in retirement saving. *Chronicle of Philanthropy*. http://philanthrophy.com/free/articles/v19/i08/08002801.htm.

Panepento, P. (2007b, October 18). Big environmental group faces challenges after its leader abruptly steps down. *Chronicle of Philanthropy*, *20*(1), 30.

Parker, G. (2007, October 31). Government business on the go. *Tampa Tribune*, 1, 4.

Partnership for Public Service. (2005). *Federal brain drain*. Washington, DC: Author.

Partnership for Public Service. (2006, December). *Develop an effective strategic human capital plan: A process overview for federal executives*. Washington, DC: Author.

Pearce, J. L. (1993). *Volunteers: The organizational behavior of unpaid workers*. New York: Routledge.

Perry, J. L. (1995). Compensation, merit pay, and motivation. In S. W. Hays & R. C. Kearney (Eds.), *Public personnel administration: Problems and prospects* (3rd ed., pp. 121–317). Upper Saddle River, NJ: Prentice-Hall.

Perry, J. L. (1996). Measuring public service motivation: An assessment of construct reliability and validity. *Journal of Public Administration Research and Theory*, *1*, 5–22.

Perry, J. L. (1997). Antecedents of public service motivation. *Journal of Public Administration Research and Theory*, *2*, 181–197.

Perry, J. L. (2000). Bringing society in: Toward a theory of public service motivation. *Journal of Public Administration Research and Theory*, *10*(2), 471–488.

Perry, J. L., Brudney, J. L., Coursey, D., & Littlepage, L. (2008). What drives morally committed citizens? A study of the antecedents of public service motivation. *Public Administration Review*, *68*(3), 445–458.

Perry, J. L., Mesch, D., & Paarlberg, L. (2006). Motivating employees in a new governance era: The performance paradigm revisited. *Public Administration Review*, *66*(4), 505–514.

Perry, J. L., & Thomson, A. M. (2004). *Civic service: What difference does it make?* Armonk, NY: M. E. Sharp.

Perry, J. L., & Wise, L. (1990). The motivational basis of public service. *Public Administration Review*, *50*, 367–373.

Peters, J. B., & Masaoka, J. (2000). A house divided: How nonprofits experience union drives. *Nonprofit Management and Leadership, 10*(3), 305–317.

Phillips, P. P., & Phillips, J. J. (2002). The public sector challenge: Developing a credible ROI process. In P. P. Phillips (Ed.), *Measuring ROI in the public sector* (pp. 1–32). Alexandria, VA: ASTD.

Phillips, J. J., & Stone, R. D. (2002). *How to measure training results*. New York: McGraw-Hill.

Pickering v. *Board of Education*. (1968). 391 U.S. 563, 568.

Pierson, J., & Mintz, J. (1995). *Assessment of the chief executive: A tool for governing boards and chief executives of nonprofit organizations*. Washington, DC: National Center for Nonprofit Boards.

Pincus, F. L. (2003). *Reverse discrimination: Dismantling the myth*. Boulder, CO: Lynne Rienner.

Pincus, W. (2007, August 23). Foreign aid groups face terror screens. *Washington Post*, A1.

Pitts, D. W. (2006). Modeling the impact of diversity management. *Review of Public Personnel Administration, 26*(3), 245–268.

Podolsky, J. (2003). *Wired for good*. San Francisco: Jossey-Bass.

Podsakoff, P. M., Mackenzie, S. B., Paine, J. B., & Bachrach, D. G. (2000). Organizational citizenship behaviors: A critical review of the theoretical and empirical literature and suggestions for future research. *Journal of Management, 26*, 513–563.

Points of Light Foundation. (2000). *A matter of survival: Volunteering by, in, and with low-income communities*. Washington, DC: Author.

Prah, P. M. (2007, December 18). Price tag for retiree benefits: $2.73 trillion. http://www.stateline.org/live/printable/story?contentId=265697.

Preston, A. E. (1990). Women in the white collar nonprofit sector: The best option or the only option? *Review of Economics and Statistics, 72*, 560–568.

Primoff, E. S. (1975, June). *How to prepare and conduct job-element examinations*. Washington, DC: U.S. Civil Service Commission, Personnel Research and Development Center.

Primoff, E. S., & Eyde, L. D. (1988). *Job element analysis*. In S. Gael (Ed.), *The job analysis handbook for business, industry, and government* (Vol. 2, pp. 807–825). Hoboken, NJ: Wiley.

Pulakos, E. D., Arad, S., Donovan, M. A., & Plamondon, K. E. (2000). Adaptability in the workplace: Development of a taxonomy of adaptive performance. *Journal of Applied Psychology, 85*, 612–624.

Rainey, G. W., Jr. (2005). Human resources consultants and outsourcing: Focusing on local government. In S. E. Condrey (Ed.), *Handbook of human resources management in government* (2nd ed., pp. 701–724). San Francisco: Jossey-Bass.

Rainey, H. G. (2003). *Understanding and managing public organizations* (3rd ed.). San Francisco: Jossey-Bass.

Rangarajan, N., & Black, T. (2007). Exploring organizational barriers to diversity: A case study of the New York state education department. *Review of Public Personnel Administration, 27*(3), 249–263.

Raymark, P. H., Schmidt, M. J., & Guion, R. M. (1997). Identifying potentially useful personality constructs for employee selection. *Personnel Psychology, 50*, 723–736.

Reddick, C. G., & Coggburn, J. D. (2007). State government employee health benefits in the United States: Choices and effectiveness. *Review of Public Personnel Administration, 27*(5), 5–20.

Reddick, C. G., & Coggburn, J. D. (2008). (Eds.). *Handbook of employee benefits and administration.* Boca Raton, FL: CRC Press.

Reester, K., & Braaten, M. (2006, May). Succession planning now, say Colorado municipal executives. *PA Times*, pp. 3–4.

Regents of the University of California v. *Bakke.* (1978). 483 U.S. 265.

Rehfuss, J. A. (1986). A representative bureaucracy? Women and minority executives in California career service. *Public Administration Review, 46*, 454–460.

Rehnborg, S. J. (2005). Government volunteerism in the new millennium. In J. L. Brudney (Ed.), *Emerging areas of volunteering* (pp. 93–112). Indianapolis: ARNOVA.

Riccucci, N. M. (2002). *Managing diversity in public sector workforces.* Boulder, CO: Westview Press.

Risher, H. (1998). Can gainsharing help to reinvent government? *Public Management, 80*(5), 17–21.

Risher, H. (1999a). Merit pay can be a hard sell. *Public Management, 81*(7), 8–13.

Risher, H. (1999b). Are public employers ready for a "new pay" program? *Public Personnel Management, 28*(3), 323–343.

Risher, H. (2002). Pay-for-performance: The keys to making it work. *Public Personnel Management, 31*(3), 317–332.

Risher, H. (2005). How much should federal employees be paid? The problems with using a market philosophy in a broadband system. *Public Personnel Management, 34*(2), 121–139.

Risher, H. (2008). The pay for performance alternative: A primer on cash incentives. *HRNews, 74*(3), 8–14.

Risher, H., & Fay, C. H. (2007). *Managing for better performance: Enhancing federal performance management practices.* Washington, DC: IBM Center for the Business of Government.

Risher, H., Fay, C. H., & Perry, J. L. (1997). Merit pay: Motivating and rewarding individual performance. In H. Risher & C. H. Fay (Eds.), *New strategies for public pay: Rethinking government compensation programs* (pp. 253–271). San Francisco: Jossey-Bass.

Risher, H., & Schay, B. W. (1994). Grade banding: The model for the future salary programs? *Public Personnel Management, 32*(3), 187–199.

Robbins, S. P. (1994). *Essentials of organizational behavior* (4th ed.). Upper Saddle River, NJ: Prentice-Hall.

Roberson, L., & Kulik, C. T. (2007). Stereotype threat at work. *Academy of Management Perspectives, 21*(2), 24–39.

Roberts, G. E. (2000). An inventory of family-friendly benefit practices in small New Jersey state local governments. *Review of Public Personnel Administration, 20*(2), 50–62.

Roberts, G. E. (2002). Municipal government part-time employee benefit practices. *Public Personnel Management, 33*(1), 1–22.

Roberts, G. E. (2004). Mental health benefits in New Jersey state and local government. *Public Personnel Management, 31*(2), 211–224.

Roberts, S. (2007, January 16). 51% of women are now living without spouse. *New York Times*. http://www.nytimes.com/2007/01/16/us/16census.html?th=&emc=th&pagewanted=print.

Rubaii-Barrett, N., & Wise, L. R. (2007). From want ads to Web sites. *Review of Pubic Personnel Administration, 27*(1), 21–38.

Ruderman, M. N., Ohlott, P. J., Panzer, K., & King, S. N. (2002). Benefits of multiple roles for managerial women. *Academy of Management Journal, 45*(2), 369–386.

Rutan v. *Republic Party of Illinois*. (1990). 497 U.S. 62.

St. Mary's Honor Center v. *Hicks*. (1993). 509 U.S. 502.

Salamon, L. M. (1995). *Partners in the public service*. Baltimore, MD: Johns Hopkins University Press.

Salamon, L. M. (1999). *America's nonprofit sector: A primer* (2nd ed.). New York: Foundation Center.

Salamon, L. M., & Sokolowski, S. W. (2006, December). *Employment in America's charities: A profile*. Baltimore, MD: Johns Hopkins Center for Civil Society Studies.

Sanchez, J. I., & Levine, E. L. (1999). Is job analysis dead, misunderstood, or both? New forms of work analysis and design. In A. I. Kraut & A. K. Korman (Eds.), *Evolving practices in human resource management* (pp. 43–68). San Francisco: Jossey-Bass.

Sanecki, K. (2000, January–February). Hands and hearts in government services. *Quality Cities*, pp. 53–54.

Savas, E. S. (2000). *Privatization and public private partnerships*. New York: Chatham House.

Savas, E. S. (2002). Competition and choice in New York City social services. *Public Administration Review, 62*(1), 82–91.

Schmidt, F. L. (1988). The problem of group differences in ability test scores in employment selection. *Journal of Vocational Behavior, 33*, 272–292.

Schmidt, F. L., & Hunter, J. E. (1998). The validity and utility of selection methods in personnel psychology: Practical and theoretical implications of 85 years of research findings. *Psychological Bulletin, 124*, 262–274.

Sclar, E. D. (2001). *You don't always get what you pay for*. Ithaca, NY: Cornell University Press.

Scott, M. (2003, April 29). Like a good neighbor, Oldsmar is there. *St. Petersburg Times*, p. 4B.

Scott, P. G., & Pandey, S. K. (2005). Red tape and public service motivation: Findings from a national survey of managers in state health and human services agencies. *Review of Public Personnel Administration, 25*(2), 155–180.

Search and Electronically Discover. (2007, Fall). Search and electronically discover: What ediscovery regulations mean for schools. *Converge, 4*(2), 52–54.

Selby, C. C. (1978). Better performance from nonprofits. *Harvard Business Review, 56*, 92–98.

Selden, S. C., & Moynihan, D. P. (2000). A model of voluntary turnover in state government. *Review of Public Personnel Administration, 20*(2), 63–74.

Shareef, R. (1994). Skill-based pay in the public sector. *Review of Public Personnel Administration, 14*(3), 60–74.

Shareef, R. (1998). A midterm case study of skill-based pay in the Virginia Department of Transportation. *Review of Public Personnel Administration, 18*(1), 5–22.

Shareef, R. (2002). The sad demise of skill-based pay in the Virginia Department of Transportation. *Review of Public Personnel Administration, 22*(3), 233–240.

Shellenbarger, S. (2007, October 12). "No e-mail Friday" edicts aim to tame excesses. *Wall Street Journal.*

Sherer, J. L. (1994, March). Can hospitals and organized labor be partners in redesign? *Hospitals and Health Networks, 68*, 56, 58.

Sims, R. R. (1998). *Reinventing training and development.* Westport, CT: Quorum Books.

Siska, D. M. (2007, March 8). Raising expectations. *Chronicle of Philanthropy, 19*(10), 31–33.

Sisneros, A. (1992). Hispanics in the Senior Executive Service: Continuity and change in the decade 1980–1990. *Review of Public Personnel Administration, 12*, 5–25.

Skinner v. *Railway Labor Executives Association.* (1989). 489 U.S. 602.

Slack, J. D. (1987). Affirmative action and city managers: Attitudes toward recruitment of women. *Public Administration Review, 47*, 199–206.

Slobodzian, J. A. (2007, December 4). Scouts ignore gay-policy deadlines: They held off on lifting a ban also barring atheists. The city said it would look for a new tenant for their Logan headquarters. *Philadelphia Inquirer.* http://www.philly.com/inquirer/local/philadelphia/20071204_Scouts_ignore_gay-policy_deadline.html.

Slobodzian, J. A. (2008, May 28). Boy Scouts sue city in building dispute. *Philadelphia Inquirer.* http://www.philly.com/philly/news/local/20080528_Boy_Scouts_sue_city_in_building_dispute.html?adString=ph.news/local;!category=local;&randomOrd=081208115829.

Smith, C. A., Organ, D. W., & Near, J. P. (1983). Organizational citizenship behavior: Its nature and antecedents. *Journal of Applied Psychology, 68*, 655–663.

Smith, K. C., & McDaniel, M. A. (1997, April). *Criterion and construct evidence for a measure of practical intelligence.* Paper presented at the 12th Annual Conference of the Society for Industrial Organizational Psychology, St. Louis, MO.

Smith, S. R., & Lipsky, M. (1993). *Nonprofits for hire: The welfare state in the age of contracting.* Cambridge, MA: Harvard University Press.

Smith v. *Arkansas State Highway Employees, Local 1315.* (1979). 441 U.S. 463.

Smith v. *City of Jackson.* (2005). 125 S.Ct. 1536.

Snelling, B. W., & Kuhnle, J. H. (1986). *When should a nonprofit organization use an executive search firm and when not?* In INDEPENDENT SECTOR (Ed.), *Aiming high on a small budget: Executive searches and the nonprofit sector* (pp. 1–8). Washington, DC: INDEPENDENT SECTOR.

Starling, G. (1986). *Managing the public sector* (3rd ed.). Chicago: Dorsey Press.

Starr, P. (1987). The limits of privatization. *Proceedings of the Academy of Political Science, 36*(3), 124–137.

State of Alaska. (2008). *Division of parks and outdoor recreation: Alaska State volunteer parks program.* http://www.dnr.state.ak.us/parks/vip/.

State of Illinois, Central Management Services. (2008, February 8). Upward Mobility Program. http://www.cms.illinois.gov/cms/2_servicese_edu/umprgm.htm.

State to monitor workers' Web habits. (2007, September 24). *Times Argus*. http://www.timesargus.com/apps/pbcs.dll/article?AID=/20070924/NEWS01/709240346.

Steinberg, R. J., & Jacobs, J. A. (1994). *Pay equity in nonprofit organizations: Making women's work visible*. In T. Odendahl & M. O'Neill (Eds.), *Women and power in the nonprofit sector* (pp. 79–120). San Francisco: Jossey-Bass.

Steinhauer, J. (2008, February 26). California creates cabinet post to manage volunteers. *New York Times*. www.nytimes.com/2008/02/26/us/26calif.html?ei=5070&en+e.

Stene, E. O. (1980). *Selecting a professional administrator: A guide to municipal councils* (2nd ed.). Washington, DC: International City Managers Association.

Stephens, J. (2007, October 5). Nature conservancy says spyware compromised employee data. *Washington Post*, p. D4.

Sternberg, R. J. (1985). *Beyond I.Q.* Cambridge: Cambridge University Press.

Stone, A. (2008, January 14). California attacks staff shortage by creating database of retirees willing to work. *Government Technology*. http://www.govtech.com/gt/print_article.pho?id=157293.

Stowers, G.N.L., & Melitski, J. (2003). Introduction to symposium. *Public Performance and Management Review*, *26*(4), 321–324.

Substance Abuse and Mental Health Services Administration. (2007, October 11). *Depression among adults employed full-time, by occupational category*. http://www.oas.samhsa.gov/2k7/depression/occupation.htm.

Sundeen, R. A., Raskoff, S. A., & Garcia, M. C. (2007). Differences in perceived barriers to volunteering to formal organizations: Lack of time versus lack of interest. *Nonprofit Management and Leadership*, *17*(3), 279–300.

Susswein, G. (2006, March 23). Tattooed troopers ordered to cover up: Long sleeves or skin patches required for DPA patrol officers. *Austin American-Statesman*. http://www.statesman.com/news/content/news/stories/local/03/23tattos.html.

Swift, E. W. (1992–1993). Glass ceilings and equity. *Public Manager*, *21*, 34–36.

Szerlag, J. (2005, July). It's (gulp) evaluation time. *Public Management*, pp. 11–17.

Tambor, M. (1973). Unions and voluntary agencies. *Social Work*, *18*, pp. 41–47.

Tambor, M. (1988a). Collective bargaining in the social services. In P. R. Keys & L. H. Ginsberg (Eds.), *New management in human services* (pp. 81–101). Silver Springs, MD: National Association of Social Workers.

Tambor, M. (1988b). Social service unions in the workplace. In H. J. Karger (Ed.), *Social workers and labor unions*. Westport, CT: Greenwood Press.

Taniguchi, H. (2006). Men's and women's volunteering: Gender differences in the effects of employment and family characteristics. *Nonprofit and Voluntary Sector Quarterly*, *35*(1), 83–101.

Taylor, S. (1989). The case for comparable worth. *Journal of Social Issues*, *45*, 23–37.

Tedesco, J. (2004, February 1). Head Start wage gap debate rages. *San Antonio Express News*. http://findarticles.com/p/articles/mi_hb5553/is_200402/ai_n22109548.

Teegarden, P. H. (2004). *Nonprofit executive leaders and transition survey 2004*. Baltimore, MD: Annie E. Casey Foundation.

Thompson, J. R. (2007). *Designing and implementing performance-oriented payband systems*. Washington, DC: IBM Center of the Business of Government. www.businessofgovernment.org.

Thompson, J. R., & Lehew, C. W. (2000). Skill-based pay as an organizational innovation. *Review of Public Personnel Administration*, *20*(1), 20–40.

Thompson, J. R., & Mastracci, S. (2005). Nonstandard work arrangements in the public sector. *Review of Public Personnel Administration*, *25*(4), 299–324.

Toohey, M. (2008, January 2). As boomers near retirement, a brain drain is feared in government: City, county, state all face uncertainties as those born 1946–64 leave their jobs in less experienced, younger hands. *Austin American Statesman*. http://statesman.com/news/content/news/stories/local/01/02/0102braindrain.html.

Towers Perrin. (1992). *Why did we adopt skill-based pay?* New York: Towers Perrin.

Toyota Motor Manufacturing Inc. v. *Williams*. (2002). 534 U.S. 184.

Trans World Airlines, Inc. v. *Hardison*. (1977). 432 U.S. 63.

Treiman, D. J., & Hartman, H. (1981). *Women, work, and wages*. Washington, DC: National Academy of Sciences.

Turque, B. (2006, February 26). Graying of workforce troubles county governments. *Washington Post*, p. C6.

U.S. Census Bureau. (2003, March 13). Census bureau releases census 2000 report on married and unmarried couples. *Department of Commerce News*. http://www.census.gov/Press-Release/www/2003/cb03cn05.html.

U.S. Census Bureau. (2006a). *Annual Survey of Government Employment*. http://www.Census.Gov/Govs/Www/Apes.HTML.

U.S. Census Bureau. (2006b). 2006 American community survey. Race total population. http://factfinder.census.gov/servlet/DTTable?bm=y&-geo_id=01000US&-ds_name=ACS_2006.

U.S. Census Bureau. (2007a, May 17). Minority population tops 100 million. http://www.census.gov/Press-Release/www/releases/archives/population/010048.html.

U.S. Census Bureau (2007b, May 29). American with Disabilities Act: July 26. CB07-FF.10. Retrieved 5/29/2007. http://www.census.gov/Press-Release/www/releases/archives/facts_for_features_special_editions.

U.S. Census Bureau. (2007c, July 9). Grandparents Day 2007: Sept. 9. http://www.census.gov/Press-Release/www/releases/archives/facts_for_features_special_editions.

U.S. Census Bureau. (2007d, December 3). Black History Month: February 2008. http://www.census.gov/Prcss-Release/www/releases/archives/facts_for_features_special_editions/010969.html_editions.

U.S. Census Bureau, Hispanic Americans by the number 12/19/07; 2006 American Community Survey.

U.S. Department of Labor. (2008a). *Internet applicant record keeping rule*. http://www.dol.gov/esa/regs/compliance/ofccp/faqs/iappfaqs.

U.S. Department of Labor. (2008b). The Uniformed Services Employment and Reemployment Rights Act of 1994 (USERRA 38 U.S.C. 4301– 4334). http://www.dol.gov/vets/programs/userra/userra_fs.htm.

U.S. Equal Employment Opportunity Commission. (1989). Guidelines on sexual harassment. http://www.eeoc.gov/types/sexual_harassment.html.

U.S. General Accounting Office. (2001a). *Federal employee retirements: Expected increase over the next 5 years illustrates need for workforce planning*. Washington, DC: U.S. Government Printing Office.

U.S. General Accounting Office. (2001b, September). *Securities and Exchange Commission: Human capital challenges require management attention*. Washington, DC: U.S. Government Printing Office.

U.S. General Accounting Office. (2002, March). *A model of strategic human capital management*. Washington, DC: U.S. Government Printing Office.

U.S. General Accounting Office. (2003). *Senior Executive Service: Enhanced agency efforts needed to improve diversity as the senior corps turns over*. Washington, DC: U.S. Government Printing Office.

U.S. General Accounting Office. (2004a). *Human capital: Selected agencies' use of alternative service delivery options for human capital activities*. Washington, DC: Author.

U.S. General Accounting Office. (2004b). *Human capital: A guide for assessing strategic training and development efforts in the federal government*. Washington, DC: Author.

U.S. Government Accountability Office. (2007a). *Human capital: Efforts to enhance diversity and ensure a fair and inclusive workplace at GAO*. Washington, DC: Author.

U.S. Government Accountability Office. (2007b). *Human capital: Federal workforce challenges in the 21st century*. GAO-07–556T. Washington, DC: Author.

U.S. Merit Systems Protection Board. (1992). *A question of equity: Women and the glass ceiling in the federal government*. Washington, DC: U.S. Government Printing Office.

U.S. Merit Systems Protection Board. (1993). *The changing face of the federal workforce: A symposium on diversity*. Washington, DC: U.S. Government Printing Office.

U.S. Merit Systems Protection Board. (2003a). *The federal selection interview: Unrealized potential*. Washington, DC: U.S. Government Printing Office.

U.S. Merit Systems Protection Board. (2003b). *Help wanted: A review of federal vacancy*. Washington, DC: U.S. Government Printing Office.

U.S. Merit Systems Protection Board. (2006). *Designing an effective pay for performance compensation system*. Washington, DC: U.S. Government Printing Office.

U.S. Merit Systems Protection Board. (2008). *Attracting the next generation: A look at federal entry-level new hires*. Washington, DC: U.S. Government Printing Office.

U.S. Office of Personnel Management. (1999a). *Looking to the future: Human resources competencies: An occupation in transition*. Washington, DC: Author:

U.S. Office of Personnel Management. (1999b). *Looking to the future: Human resources competencies, Part 2*. Washington, DC: Author:

U.S. Office of Personnel Management. (2000). *The HR workforce: Meeting the challenge of change: An occupation in transition Part 3*. Washington, DC: Author:

U.S. Office of Personnel Management. (2005). *OPM's workforce planning model*. http://www.opm.gov/hcaaf_resource_center/assets/Sa_tool4.pdf.

U.S. Office of Personnel Management. (2006). *Career patterns: A 21st century approach to attracting talent*. Washington, DC: Author.

U.S. Office of Personnel Management. (2008). *Senior executive service*. http://www.opm.gov/ses/define.asp.

United Autoworkers v. *Johnson Controls*. (1991). 111 S.Ct. 1196.

United States v. *Paradise*. (1986). 480 U.S. 149.

United Steelworkers of America v. *Weber*. (1979). 443 U.S. 193.

Updating a program to help nonprofit organizers save. (2007). *Chronicle of Philanthropy*. http://philanthrophy.com/jobs/2007/03/22/20070322–983512.htm.

Urbina, I. (2007, December 6). Boy Scouts lose Philadelphia lease in gay-rights fight. *New York Times*. http://www.nytimes.com/2007/12/06/us/06scouts.html.

Vogel, H. (2007, December 18). United Way chief's retirement package raises questions. *Atlanta Journal Constitution*. http://www.ajc.com/metro/content/atlanta/stories/2007/12/18/unitedway_1219.html.

Vroom, V. H. (1964). *Work and motivation*. Hoboken, NJ: John Wiley.

Waldron, T., Roberts, B., Reamer, A., Rab, S., & Ressler, S. (2004, October). *Working hard, falling short: America's working families and the pursuit of economic security*. Annie E. Casey, Ford and Rockefeller Foundations. http://www.aecf.org/KnowledgeCenter/Publications.aspx?pubguid=%7B09FAC2FF-1BC4–496F-9AB3–8BF6E0BA26C9%7D.

Wallace, M. J., Jr., & Fay, C. H. (1988). *Compensation theory and practice* (2nd ed.). Boston: PWS-Kent.

Wallace, N. (2001, February). A virtual army of volunteers: Charities find new ways to let people do good work online. *Chronicle of Philanthropy*, pp. 37–39.

Washington counties create training video on pandemic flu preparation. (2008, February 6). http://www.govtech.com/gt/print_article.php?id=261382.

Watkins, B. (1992, April 15). Reassessing comparable worth: The Minnesota experience. *P.A. Times*, p. 8.

Watson v. *Fort Worth Bank and Trust*. (1988). 487 U.S. 977.

Watts, A. D., & Edwards, P. K. (1983). Recruiting and retaining human services volunteers: An empirical analysis. *Journal of Voluntary Action Research*, *12*, 9–22.

Webb v. *City of Philadelphia*. (2007). U.S. Dist. LEXIS 46872 (E.D. Pa.).

Weisbrod, B. A. (1997). The future of the nonprofit sector: It's entwining with private enterprise and government. *Journal of Policy Analysis and Management*, *16*(4), 541–555.

Wetizman, M. S., Jalandoni, N. T., Lampkin, L. M., & Pollak, T. H. (2002). *The new nonprofit almanac and desk reference: The essential facts and figures for managers, researchers, and volunteers*. San Francisco: Jossey-Bass.

Wexley, K. N., & Latham, G. P. (1991). *Developing and training human resources in organizations* (2nd ed.). Upper Saddle River, NJ: Prentice Hall.

Wheeland, C. M. (1994). Evaluating city manager performance: Pennsylvania managers report on methods their councils use. *State and Local Government Review, 26*, 153–160.

White, G. (2007, July 22). Resuscitating Grady: Buyouts leave hospital with large talent drain. *Atlanta Journal Constitution*, pp. D1, D10–D11.

Whitmer, M. G. (2007). *IT security awareness and training: Changing the culture of state government.* Lexington, KY: NASCIO.

Widmer, C. (1985). Why board members participate. *Journal of Voluntary Action Research, 14*, 8–23.

Wiens, J. (2007, November 19). Strategic security: Take a stand against data loss. *InformationWeek*, pp. SS4, SS6.

Wilson, J. Q. (1989). *Bureaucracy: What government agencies do and why they do it.* New York: Basic Books.

Wise, L. R. (2005). *The public service culture.* In R. J. Stillman II (Ed.), *Public administration: Concepts and cases* (8th ed., pp. 342–352). Boston: Houghton Mifflin.

Wise, L. R., & Tschirhart, M. (2000). Examining empirical evidence on diversity effects: How useful is diversity research for public sector managers? *Public Administration Review, 60*(5), 386–395.

Wittig, M. A., & Lowe, R. H. (1989). Comparable worth theory and policy. *Journal of Social Issues, 45*, 1–21.

Woodlee, Y., & Haynes, V. D. (2008, May 4). D.C. conference chief submits resignation. *Washington Post*, p. C3.

Wright, R. (2007, April 16). At State, a friendlier workplace. *Washington Post*, p. A15.

Wurf, J. (1974). Merit: A union view. *Public Administration Review, 34*, 431–434.

Wyatt, K. (2000, October 22). Girl Scouts' recruiting drive tells old image to take a hike. *Tampa Tribune-Times*, p. 23.

Wygant v. *Jackson Board of Education.* (1986). 476 U.S. 267.

Yang, S. B., & Guy, M. E. (2006). GenXers versus boomers: Work motivators and management implications. *Public Performance and Management Review, 29*(3), 267–284.

Zedeck, S. (1996). Foreword. In K. R. Murphy (Ed.), *Individual differences in organizations* (p. 12). San Francisco: Jossey-Bass.

Zedlewski, S. R. (2007, December). *Will retiring boomers form a new army of volunteers?* Washington, DC: Urban Institute.

Zedlewski, S. R., & Butrica, B. A. (2007, December). *Are we taking full advantage of older adults' potential?* Washington, DC: Urban Institute.

Zernike, K. (2000, August 29). "Policy on gays costing Scouts allies, money." *The New York Times*, pp. 1, 3.

NAME INDEX

SUBJECT INDEX

D

E

F

G

J

M

Q

R

T

U

X

Y